HOWARD STERN

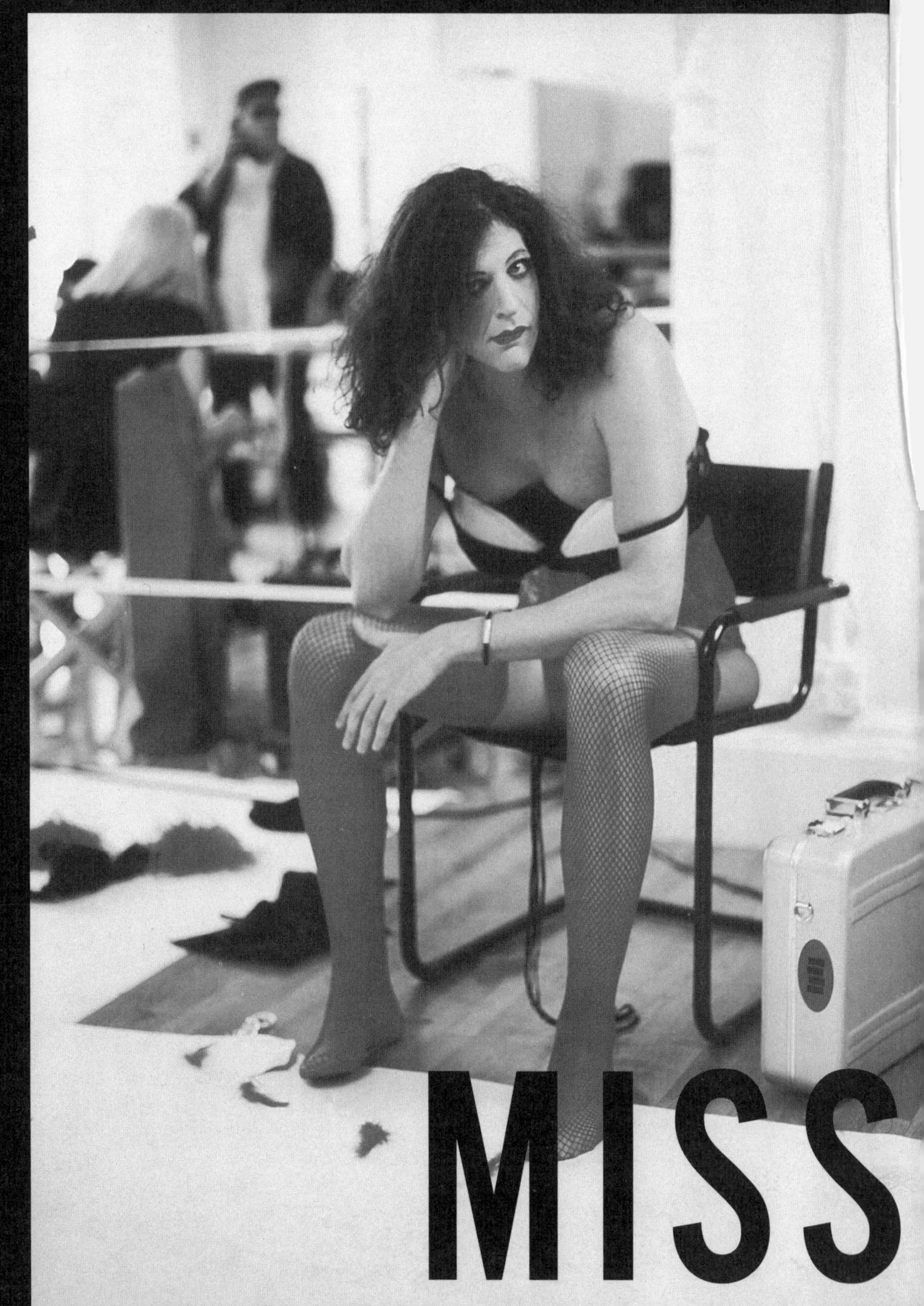

MISS

H S

M i s s
America

M A

I DEDICATE THIS BOOK TO MY INTERNS, all of them, the college students who work for free. They bring an infusion of energy, creativity, and excitement to my radio family and do a lot of the dirty work that isn't too glamorous. They deserve a lot of credit and seldom get it. A special debt of gratitude to Steve Grillo. For the last four years he has been my intern doing every lousy, menial task for me for free, including getting my meals and opening the door to the building every morning at five A.M. He's never late, he never complains, and he always has a smile on his face.

contents

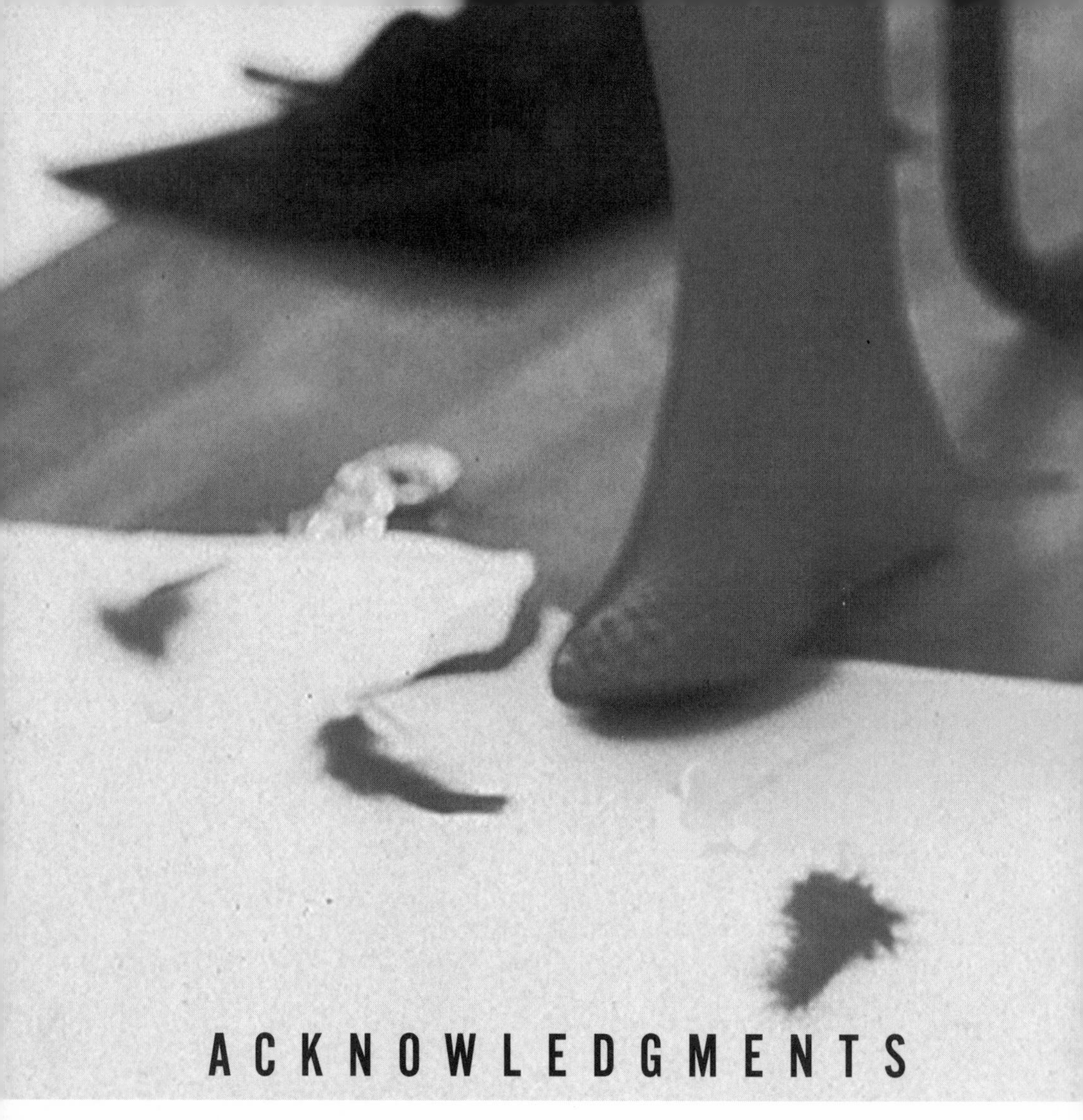

ACKNOWLEDGMENTS

FIRST OF ALL, I would like to thank the Miss America Pageant for naming me Miss America 1996. There were many times over the last few months that I doubted myself. So many of the other girls are so talented and poised that I thought I didn't stand a chance. I was devastated that I was voted least popular by the other contestants, but I stayed in the race. Now I know how Vanessa Williams felt when everyone turned on her. A special thank-you to Ms. Williams, who encouraged me to "stick with it" even after I was disqualified during the talent competition for trying to lift quarters off the floor with my vagina. I figured I had blown it, but Vanessa said to

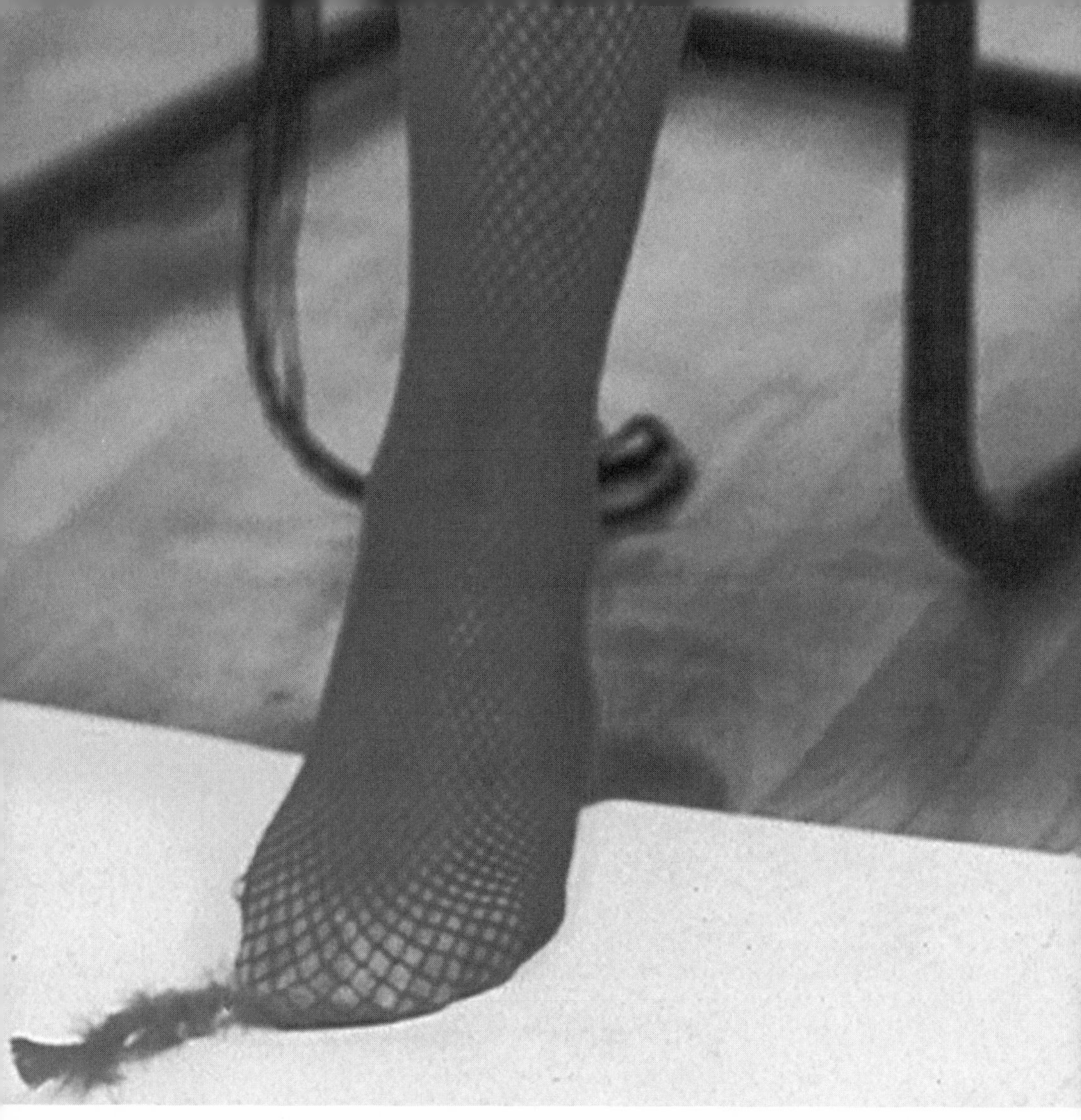

keep going. Thank you, thank you, thank you.

I want to thank Regis and Kathie Lee most of all. They treated me with respect and dignity. Regis, I will never forget your words of encouragement when we were alone in the elevator and you kissed me and told me I was "so cute." And yes, Regis, you are right. Bert Parks was a load! Joy Philbin, if you are not happy in life, then you can kiss my tits, because you are so lucky to be married to Rege.

And Kathie Lee, I love you so much. I won't hold anything against you, even though you resigned from the pageant and said this would be your last year because I won. Kathie Lee, you are such a cunt. Just kidding.

I OWE LOTS OF PRAISE TO THIS MAN, BEN STERN, who started training me to be Miss America at an early age. ***Every day he would dress up like this and teach me what it meant to be a woman.***

A gigantic thank-you, of course, to God. Without the Lord Jesus Christ in my life I don't think I would want to hang around this filthy piss hole we call Mother Earth. God gave me the strength to continue even when that deaf-as-a-doorknob Miss America 1995 kept droning on with all that unintelligible gobbledygook. As soon as I was crowned, she was hanging all over me trying to steal my moment. "I WANT TO BE YOUR FRIEND, I WANT TO BE YOUR FRIEND," she kept saying, while wetting my ear with saliva. "I WANT TO BE YOUR FRIEND." At least that's what I think she said. "Hey, honey," I said, "say it, don't spray it." I can't believe she ever won any pageant. I think the judges just felt bad for her because she was handicapped. Some handicap. All I know is, she can hear good enough to do that klutzy ballet routine. Sorry if I sound cruel, but **I vow that this Miss America will always tell it like it is, baby.**

So many people put in endless hours in improving my physical beauty and conditioning me for the pageant. My plastic surgeon, Dr. Heywood Jablowme. My wonderful dentist, Matthew Kaufman, who made my teeth shiny so these other bitches looked like the wicked witches they truly are. I'd like to thank Jon Basile, my physical trainer, who taught me that you can have an attractive bust without implants. It's true, girls! And, last but not least, my Man Friday, Ralph Cirella, deserves special kudos for blowing my hair and waxing my chest hair. OUCH!

Anyway, I'm looking forward to all of my duties as the reigning Miss America, and I hope to see all of you at a mall appearance real soon.

Howard Stern

Miss America

CYBERSURFING

CHAPTER 1

FOR VAGINA

I'M SUCH A SEX MACHINE I could take a piece of wood and turn it into something erotic, something sensual, something perverse. Take puppeteering, for example. When I was seven years old my mother gave me puppets and within weeks I had puppet orgies in my basement for all my friends to see. And not just people puppets. There were horses, caterpillars, and clown puppets fucking and giving head.

The puppeteer from hell and his straw hat from John's bargain basement

I've never changed. No matter what activity I'm engaged in, if there's a way to work sex into it, *that's where you'll find me.* For example, I've always loved using technology to create opportunities to have **orgasms.**

Take the phones: I started abusing those in high school. My first experience was with my friend Bill, who was the second biggest loser in my high school next to me—especially with women.

On the weekends we couldn't get dates, so all we did was play cards, eat pizza, smoke cigars, and talk about how fucked up all girls were because they wouldn't go out with great guys like us.

Our rap was that if girls could only look beyond the fact that we didn't have good looks and see that we had great personalities, they would fall in love with us. **THE TRUTH OF THE MATTER WAS WE HAD REALLY *BAD* PERSONALITIES IN ADDITION TO OUR UGLY FACES.** Even the losers called us losers. And we were.

I tried everything to get girls. I even tried growing my hair long so girls would think I was a drug dealer so they'd want to have sex with me. Nothing worked.

One Friday night during our pathetic card game we learned that the phone company had a problem with one of their lines. Through some mechanical error it was possible to dial one number where hundreds of people were on a party line.

What a great way to pick up chicks! Now they wouldn't see us—they would only be tuned into our great personalities. We quickly ditched our other loser friends at the card game and ran over to Bill's house to be alone with all the girls on the party line.

Now that we were about to make contact with females, we weren't sharing them. The other guys at the card game were cow-faced losers who were convinced we were never going to get girls. We showed them.

We got to Bill's house and, sure enough, the phone line worked. There were hundreds of girls and guys—all talking at once—gibberish, all yelling at each other. It was the Tower of Babel.

Bill and I started screaming our names out.

"Howard!"

"Bill!"

"Howard!"

"Bill!"

"HOWARD! BILL! HOWARD! BILL! HOWARD! BILL!"

Two nubile female voices responded, screaming out over the hundreds of yapping voices. We could barely hear them saying, "Give us your number, Howard Bill."

It was hard to make out their voices. Were they girls? Were they effeminate boys? Who could tell? Who cared?

We were two desperate men on a mission and they were breathing. Who could tell that they were even talking to us, but we screamed out Bill's number.

Sure enough, miracles never cease, the two girls actually called us. God had answered my prayers.

Now I'd have a chance to prove to some girls that I had a really good personality.

I wasted no time.

"Hey, girls! Want to meet me and Bill?"

"Yeah!" they replied.

See, I was right. It was absolutely true. Without my ***hideous*** face in the way, these girls were really getting charmed by my wit—and *joie da viver* or whatever. (I hate the French.)

We made a plan to meet at midnight at Southside High School. At the witching hour I'd have a girlfriend. Plus it would be dark so they could hardly see me. *In the moonlight my nose looks much smaller. Moonlight is my friend.*

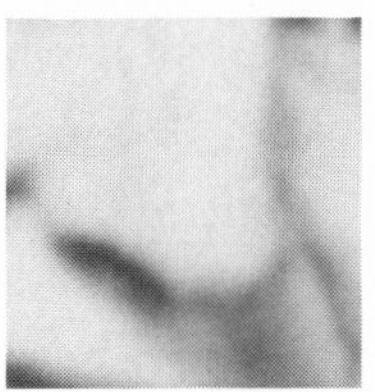

On our way over, Bill and I started fighting. I told him we should play it cool. We agreed we shouldn't whip out our rubbers right away, even if they wanted to fuck our brains out.

Gotta be cool about sex. Can't rush. Maybe we'd finger them a little bit. Then let them blow us. That was the plan. Let them hunger for our sperm.

So we get to the high school. It's 11:00 P.M.—an hour early. It's pitch black. We're waiting. The clock strikes midnight. No girls yet.

"That's okay. They're probably getting ready."

12:30 A.M. No girls.

"They're probably douching, so they won't be smelly for their dates," we decide.

1:00 A.M.

1:30 A.M.

Things aren't going too well. Bill and I are getting a little nervous but we figure it's okay, because the girls are probably busy shaving their hair so as not to interfere with our manly touch when we pull down their panties and explore their ***precious juicy caverns.***

I suggested to Bill that we work out elaborate hand signals so that we could speak a silent language that would say "You take the one on the right—I get the one on the left."

1:45 A.M.

God, the high school looks different at night.

2:00 A.M.

NO GIRLS.

2:30 A.M.

What were we thinking? You've got to be out of your mind standing around a high school like this. There could be a bunch of guys coming to get us, who'll beat us up and take our money. We're going to get our asses kicked. Now we were scared. Finally it dawned on us what assholes we were: Of course these girls weren't going to show up. We were two ugly guys with bad personalities.

WE'D BEEN SCAMMED.

PRERECORDED NYMPHOS

You can understand my elation, then, when the day came that there existed on this planet a way for me to ejaculate without ever having to meet anyone.

It happened around the time I was at NBC radio.

Being on the radio, you learn about things ahead of everyone. I learned of these 570 numbers, the three original lines with a recorded sex message on each one. As soon as I heard about it I couldn't wait to go home and jerk off. But there was one problem: ALISON HAD JUST HAD A BABY, AND SHE WAS ALWAYS IN THE FUCKING HOUSE.

She'd become a shut-in. (My sperm will do that to a woman.) I waited for days for her to go for a walk, go to a store, anything. My dick was about to explode. I needed to make that phone call.

Now!

The day finally came. It was unexpected. I had given up hope.

Alison announced she was leaving to take the baby for a walk. The park or some shit. Just leave. Take the baby to Mars. Get the FUCK OUT.

The second Alison was out the door, I ran downstairs and bolted the front door. I was alone! At last! ORGY! I already had a boner.

I ran upstairs and took off almost all my clothes. I needed to feel naked, but at the same time I needed quick access to lift up my pants the second Alison opened the door. I grabbed my tissues from the bathroom and grabbed a phone with a really long cord. I needed the cord to stretch into the hallway so I could lie down on the floor and keep an eye on the front door at the same time.

If the door started to open, my pants would be up in a flash. I might be in the middle of jerking off and my wife could come back because she forgot something. It would be like being a little kid getting caught with a boner.

To this day my wife still doesn't know that I masturbate almost constantly. I've said it on the air, I've said it in my book, and I'm about to act it out in a motion picture, but Alison Stern doesn't need to see the ugly truth. She's an ***honest, decent*** woman with a ***clean mind*** who doesn't know that she's married to a sexual incubus.

But when you think about it, how could she *not* know? I'm down to getting laid every three weeks, two and a half weeks tops. She never fucks me. She's always too busy.

And when she innocently and sweetly asks, "Howard, why do you always say you jerk off and stuff?" I look at her, sweep her into my arms, and say, "Frankly, my dear, it's just an act. You know my audience needs to be entertained and this way they feel like I'm one of them. **I'M FORTY-ONE YEARS OLD. I HAVEN'T JERKED OFF SINCE HIGH SCHOOL.**"

And she buys it, because, silly fool, she loves me.

So I'm in the hallway and I dial the first sex line. But I'm not comfy. It's hard to stand up, hold the phone, jerk off, and have my tissues ready. It's very important that you have tissues ready to go. GOD FORBID I SHOULD COME ON THE CARPET! EVIDENCE!

So I get down on my naked ass, one eye on the door, the other on the phone, and I dial. God, is this great! No credit cards. No complications. The house is empty. And in my book, *this ain't cheating*. In my mind, *unless there's actual intercourse, it ain't cheating.*

A woman's voice comes on the line.

Front door clear.

"Hi," the prerecorded voice says, "I want your dick up my horny wet hot asshole. Ah, yeh. Stick it in. Stick it in my shit box."

Now, this is good. I've got a really nice boner going.

Then the call is over. The calls are really short. They're like a minute. And I didn't want to hear the same one over again. That's really important to me.

So I dial the second line.

Front door clear.

No Alison.

No baby carriage. I'm in the mood for love.

"Hi. I'm Tina," the prerecorded nympho said. "I'm here with my friend. Oh yeah, she's got really great tits. Do you want me to suck them now?"

"Oh, yeah," I moan. "Suck her tits!" I yell. "Suck them now!" My hand pumps away on my massive shaft—all three inches—I told you I had a big boner going.

Time to take inventory.

Tissues by my side.

Front door clear.

Pants at arm's reach.

I'm so good at jerking off!!

And I'm holding the phone with my left hand.

Oh, I think I'm about to come.

SHIT, SECOND PRERECORDED MESSAGE OVER. That's all right. There's one left.

"Hi, I'm Geena. I love a big thick cock. Do you have a big cock? Mmmm! I bet you do, junior. I love to suck big thick hot cock! Mmmm. Do you mind if I play with my clit while I suck your throbbing meat?"

Okay. Here I come! OOH-OO! AH! Two tissues full.

And I clocked in under two and a half minutes. A record for me. Hey, I really held out. And no Alison. The perfect session.

Tissues in the toilet.

Extra tissues wrapped around my cock so I don't drip into my underpants.

No evidence.

Phone back.

Pants up. It's Miller Time.

The Bondage Farm

With the invention of the VCR I was one step closer to total sexual liberation and freedom. Especially when it comes to bondage.

I'm really into bondage tapes. For me, that's the greatest turn-on. I don't know why, but watching two chicks tied up, hanging from the fucking ceiling, with their legs spread, getting whipped with one of those little horse whips by a female dominatrix drives me crazy.

Listeners started sending me bondage tapes like crazy. And as soon as Alison left the house I would watch them. I watched them five minutes at a time—that's all it takes. One tape can last months. After I come, I get totally disgusted with myself and vow never to watch one again—until the next erection. I want to be above all this. I want to rise above the common man—like Gandhi. Wait a second, ***fuck Gandhi***. He was busy sleeping with thirteen-year-olds and doing high colonics. Some higher thinking *that* is.

My favorite tape of all takes place on a bondage farm. I don't even know if this film has a name. It's so sick, it looks like the real deal.

The storyline is simple: A female reporter with huge tits shows up at this bondage farm. The farm is run by this obese old guy with a ripped sweater. He's a real mess. She asks him if she could do a story on his bondage farm, but he tells her the only way that would be possible is if she will submit. She doesn't want to, but she really needs to get this story, so she begs him for the story. He refuses to give her an interview unless she submits. Meanwhile, she looks around, and there's a chick on all fours, tied up like a fucking calf with an antenna sticking up out of her ass.

Finally, the reporter agrees. He ties her up, shaves her pussy, and she's crying hysterically. It's the most realistic thing you've ever seen. And she's real cute, that's what kills me. I CAN'T

EVEN GET *UGLY* GIRLS TO DO THIS STUFF. Then he puts forty fucking clothespins on each tit, takes them off, ties her tits up with a rope, unties them, then takes two wooden clapboards, squeezes her tits together, and screws them tight.

I LOVE THIS TAPE. I pop it in and go to work on my cock like a jackrabbit and in two seconds, I explode. As soon as I come, I'm totally disgusted. I could have sworn by the time I was forty I'd be over this stuff. But I never get over it. I just get deeper into it.

So when personal computers were introduced to the marketplace, I knew it was only a matter of time before I found a way to achieve orgasm through them.

CYBERSEX: AT LEAST IT'S NOT CHEATING ... *or is it?*

This was the ideal setup for me. I could order all the computer equipment I'd ever need and Alison never even thinks to question it. Then I could lock myself in my basement and pretend to be working on a screenplay or a pay-per-view special or television ideas, whatever. This was important stuff. I was not to be disturbed. Genius at work.

But who was I kidding? I was no genius, just a lonely pervert trying to fuck his computer.

I'm a pathetic jackass. The brightest star in radio, a best-selling author, a TV personality, a fucking dickwad who could screw any hot stripper he wants—and I'm trying to figure out how to log on to a computer so I can talk dirty to a bunch of frustrated housewives ***who probably look like Brunhilde.*** Well, at least it's not cheating . . . *or is it*?

The Prodigy chat rooms are the equivalent of the old telephone party lines. Up to twenty-five people can sit at their computers in the privacy of their own homes and congregate and talk to each other in a single room. They divide the rooms up by topics like Entertainment, Religion, Business, and they even have a

Howard Stern room. That's where I go to pick up my girls.

I began going into the Howard Stern room using an alias. Everybody uses an alias or a nickname on chat. I wasn't going to log on and announce I was Howard Stern. After all, who wants the whole world to know that I'm a loser who calls computer lines? Anyone with a real life doesn't have time for computer hijinks. A person with friends and a social life doesn't live in the cyberworld. A dynamic man lives among real people, walking, talking, moving freely among the masses and breathing fresh air.

I'm sure there are those in my audience who think I'm busy going to parties and socializing with celebrity friends, but **THE PATHETIC FACT IS, I SIT IN MY BASEMENT WATCHING TELEVISION AND WORKING AND SELDOM EMERGE, EXCEPT FOR MEALS.** I am uncomfortable venturing into the outside world and find the idea of a computer chat room a safe haven.

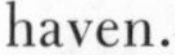

But don't be mistaken, the chat room is the bottom of the barrel, where no human goes unless he's desperate and has failed at interacting with normal human beings. The place where losers, assorted geeks, and social incompetents congregate. If you're **ugly**, if you're **deformed**, or if you're like me, ugly, deformed, and married for twenty years, this is the place for you. Here is where the misfit can be a giant. If you are not gifted with good looks it doesn't matter because personality rules in the chat room. Quick wit and typing skills are the requirements to enter a world where you are judged on mental prowess alone. No discrimination based on age, race, or nose size. HERE ON PRODIGY CHAT I'M A SINGLE, BRAD PITT LOOK-ALIKE, WITH A DICK THE SIZE OF A WATERMELON. Actually, on Prodigy chat I'm back in high school, on the party line without Bill at my side.

For the facially impaired, heaven is Prodigy chat and the rules are simple. Meet girls in the Prodigy chat room and then lure them into something called a private room where you can write back and forth to one another and talk dirty. I want dirty talk. I want nasty pee-pee talk so I can jack off next to my computer. I want new experiences where Alison can't accuse me of cheating. *Somebody shoot me! I'm hopeless!*

People told me that some girls will go into the private chat room and talk so nasty and sexy that you'll jerk off and spray into your keyboard. Well, hell, that's what I'm looking for and I ain't ashamed to admit it.

Actually, I am ashamed to admit it but I have to write about something and I can't think of anything else. I like this Prodigy chat concept because here's a way to be with new women and not have a guilty conscience afterward. I'll have complete anonymity. This is better than a phone line because they can't recognize my voice. I can't get caught. In my mind this ain't cheatin! Jerking off to a computer screen is just all-American wholesome fun.

Alison heard me talking about Prodigy chat on the radio. When she got me home, she told me, "That Prodigy thing is cheating." It *is* cheating, but I put her right in her place—I did what I always do when she becomes a pain in the ass: I lied and told her I never call in to those computer lines.

"First of all I have a beautiful family and a busy career," I said to my dear sweet, naive, and trusting Alison. "Do you think I have time to be dialing for computer sex?"

The woman was now stonefaced and wondering why she had wasted the last twenty years of her life with a sex maniac.

"Alison, get real. Why would I do something like computer sex when I have you? Get a life!"

She wasn't buying it. Better think fast.

"I'm just bullshitting about having computer sex when I'm on the radio. I lie." She looked at me, wanting to believe.

"You mean you *never* called into Prodigy?" Alison asked, starting to come around.

"I dialed it *once* so I could do research for my book. I swear!

How could you believe I would jerk off to such a thing? I'm not a loser, for Christ sake!" Yeah, right.

Well, it seemed to calm her down. I love that woman . . . she buys it hook, line, and sinker. Man, if she ever really thought I was jerking off to my computer, it would kill her.

It was confusing for a dope like me when I first entered the Howard Stern chat room. I had to give myself a nickname. Hmmm, what name would I use? How about "Mr. Big Dick"? **NO, PRODIGY WON'T LET YOU USE A NAME THAT CONTAINS FOUL LANGUAGE.**

Maybe I'll name myself after my best feature. Who am I kidding, **my best feature is my foot**. What kind of cruel joke did God play on me? It always upset me when women came on the show and said, "You have beautiful feet." What an insult! Look how far they had to search to find something decent looking on me. I'd like to fuck all of them with my feet and give them

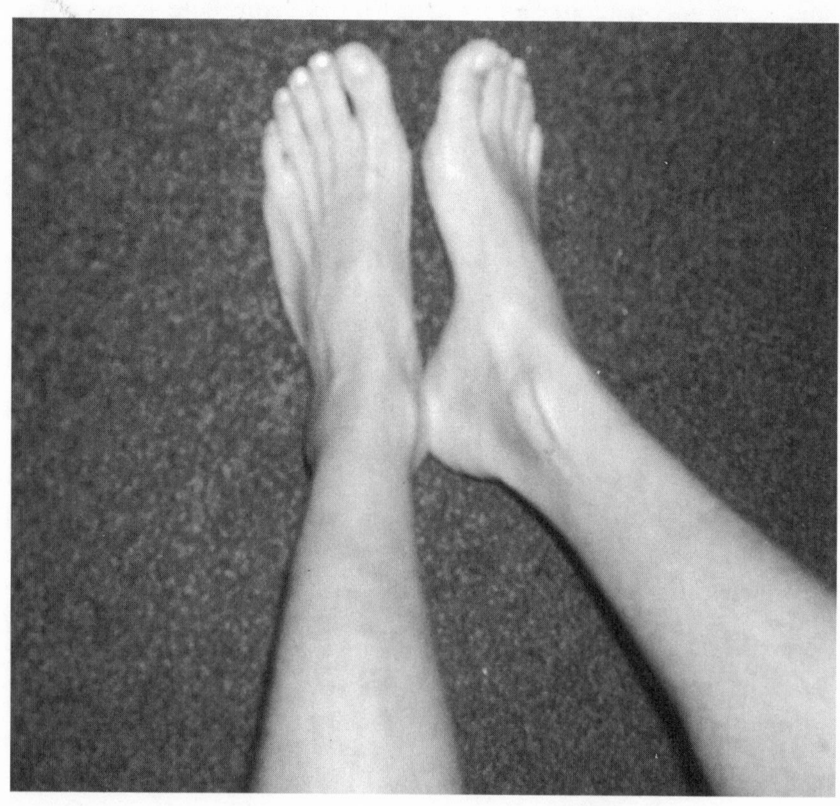

athlete's crotch. I'd do anything to look like Brad Pitt and have ugly feet. I don't want to nickname myself after my foot! Fuck this shit—I'm gonna give myself a cool name and see how many girls will pick my ass up.

I named myself "Casanova" and went in the Howard Stern Room and told all the girls I had a cock that would make them salivate. Check out this actual transcript of my first visit to Prodigy:

CASANOVA: Hey girls, who needs some cockmeat from a real man?

I couldn't wait for some hot little minky to respond. Not one but three babes—Betty, Joan, and Sweetypie—all wanted to let me know how badly they needed ol' Casanova's tubesteak.

BETTY: Get lost.

JOAN: Scram, you moron.

SWEETYPIE: What a jerk.

I couldn't believe I was being rejected. Why I'd show them. Take a look at my witty reply.

CASANOVA: Fuck off, you whores!

Within one minute a message came on the screen suspending me from Prodigy for two days. I wasn't on this thing more than five minutes and now I was in trouble. The cyberpolice on Prodigy had busted me. ***Evidently, you can call the authorities from a button on your computer and complain when profanity is being used.*** Someone must have hit the button and ratted me out. *Little babies! Bunch of girls!* Those three bitches were worse than Hitler youth turning in their parents to the Nazis.

Turns out you can't curse unless you're in a private one-on-one room. Now they tell me. Who knew there were private cursing rooms? I don't know anything about computers. I'm not Bill Fucking Gates. I'd have to wait two damn days to go trolling for babes again.

My first experience hadn't gone well, but I still liked the

whole idea of Prodigy chat. I could meet people and no one would know it was me. Having been famous for several years now, I'd not been able to communicate with strangers and make new acquaintances without them kissing my ass and laughing at my every word. Normal conversation with people had become impossible because they wanted to get close to a "celebrity."

Now that I was in cyberspace I could travel unnoticed among the masses. *Ahhhh! To be a nobody. Ahhhh! To be one of the faceless crowd. Ahhhh! Not to be stared at. Not to be the tall, gawky freak who has to make everyone laugh.* I wouldn't have to be onstage all the time. **THIS WAS THE FUTURE AND I LIKED IT!**

Two days later I was ready. I logged on with a new plan. My suspension was over and I gave myself a new mysterious and religious-sounding name. It was "HolyGhost." I would become a man of mystery who could charm the pants off any girl in the room. My HolyGhost persona was pretty smooth, and I soon had a few babes believing that I was a Calvin Klein underwear model who built a fifteen-thousand-square-foot house deep in the woods, complete with indoor waterfall. I bullshitted them and told them I was tired of modeling and wanted to settle down with one girl, that I looked like Brad Pitt except with darker hair. A girl named Partychick picked up on me. Read my actual encounter.

HOLYGHOST: I work out a lot ladies. I'm 29 and I've been modeling since I'm 21 and I'm going back to dental school. Modeling is not that lucrative.

PARTYCHICK: Oh yeah?

Partychick told me she was a stripper. Wow, she must be hot. Well, I would be a stripper too, who modeled on the side. I was on my way to cyber jerk-off heaven. I was now a great-looking model/stripper with brains who was soon to be a rich dentist—every girl's dream.

PARTYCHICK: Where do you go to dental school?

Hmmm, she was probably testing me to see if I was the real deal. I'd better think fast. Don't want to get caught in a lie. What's a good school? I know, I'll go Ivy League.

HOLYGHOST: I attend Columbia Dental School.

Does Columbia have a dental school? Who cares, she ain't with the FBI.

PARTYCHICK: You must have a good body if you're a stripper.

Yeah, this one is ripe, I'll lay a little more bullshit on her 'cause she sounds like she's ready to give me cybersex. I'll complain about how I hate shallow women. **Chicks love that crap.**

HOLYGHOST: I couldn't take stripping anymore. Women love my hard flat stomach, and they are always ripping at my clothes and rubbing their hands across my nipples and chest. It gets to be a drag. I'm looking for a satisfying relationship.

The screen was dead for a minute. I'm a rich, good-looking dental student who needs a faithful relationship. I'm so dreamy she can barely type. She must be falling in love and ready to give me *dirty-nasty-cum-in-buckets computer sex.* HOO-HAH!

PARTYCHICK: Why are you telling me this? Do you hope to turn me on?

What kind of fucking response was this?

HOLYGHOST: Yes. I'm telling this to turn you on. Should I stop?

PARTYCHICK: Probably.

HOLYGHOST: You mean I'm not turning you on?

PARTYCHICK: Just not in the mood. Sorry. I have a headache.

HOLYGHOST: OK.

And she was gone. In a flash.

Holy shit. What the . . . ? No sex? That's it? Rejected by a stripper? In real life I have strippers falling at my feet. That fucking bitch. I just wasted an hour seducing this hosebag and she has a fucking headache?

Well, a major theory of mine had just been shot down. For forty-one years I had always believed that I was one of those guys who had a great personality but women never noticed me because of my ugly face. Turns out, not only am I ugly, but I have a dipshit personality. I suck. I am nothing. I struck out on a geeky computer service. The great HolyGhost was a total, one hundred percent douchebag!

I was pissed. I was on fire. I was ready to take my wrath out on any prick who got in my way. I roamed the halls of cyberspace. I had been rejected and I needed to vent. I needed revenge on this cold, hard cyberworld filled with women who don't love me. So I went into a Prodigy chat area called Fantasy Room. The room was packed with guys into Bondage and Discipline. Just to fuck these losers up I told them I was a girl, a hot dominatrix. I had long, tanned legs and gigantic breasts. Every guy was begging me to let them be my slave.

SEVER: I want you. I'll do anything, Mistress.

I told you these guys were desperate. I knew I would feel better after I barked out a few orders.

HOLYGHOST: I want you to eat my fucking pussy.

SEVER: I would love to eat your pussy, Mistress.

This guy was a real asshole.

HOLYGHOST: But since you're such a worthless slave, I'll have to take a big shit on you.

SEVER: Whatever you desire, Mistress.

Now here was some poor slob in worse shape than me. I'm trying to get out all my aggression on this asswipe, ruin his night, and spew all my venom—and I'm failing! Well, I ain't failing for a second time in one night.

HOLYGHOST: I want to take your nuts and tie them to a tree and chop your fucking balls off and piss up your ass.

SEVER: Mistress, I adore you! I must meet you.

Damn, here I am trying to cheer myself up about being rejected and I'm being a nasty-assed woman who rejects men and he's falling in love. Men are such jerks. I'm embarrassed to be one.

HOLYGHOST: LISTEN, YOU FUCKING ASSHOLE, I'M A GUY!

The prick logged off—in a fucking hurry. GOOD! DIE! Now your night has been ruined. But I was still angry, so I went into the Rush Limbaugh Room. Good. Two people are in the room. I'll take out my pent-up sexual aggression on Pumpkinhead's fans, all two of them!

MR. COLLAR: Welcome, Rush Fan. Don't you think Rush rules?

HOLYGHOST: You fuckin' dope! Rush rips off everything from Howard Stern. He couldn't have a career without Howard.

JACK: Why the negative talk about Rush?

HOLYGHOST: You follow a man who shills for Pizza Hut–pizza that has cheese that tastes like rubber coming out of the back. Rush is a friggin' moron!

JACK: I assume you have views that differ with the conservative line?

I determined that Rush's fans must be on acid. One last good insult, and I would quickly exit before these dittoheaded dildoes called the cyberpolice and reported me. I was hitting everyone with insults and running.

HOLYGHOST: Rush is dirt. His wife must look at him and his blubber and smell his stink and then vomit.

I told them off! Punks! But I was *still* angry. Hurt. Rejected. I went into a place called the Friends of Bill W Room. Turns out, it was a room for AA members to discuss their battles with alcoholism. A sensitive room, a caring nurturing room, a room . . . filled with assholes.

BOB: Hello, HolyGhost. Hello friend, don't be embarrassed. We're all recovering alcoholics in here.

HOLYGHOST: Ah, you're all a bunch of loser drunks in here and you're all full of shit.

TOM: You're very defensive and you need support.

HOLYGHOST: Listen jerk, I'm no drunk and you're a fucking asshole. All you scumbags are doing is hiding behind your fucking illness.

BOB: Easy, Holy.

HOLYGHOST: Easy my ass, why don't you dweebs go out and get a drink and lighten up.

And with that lovely conversation, my angry rampage ended as the Prodigy Police Department hunted me down and suspended me for a week. A big box appeared on my screen handing me my second violation and it came with a stern warning. If there was one more violation, I would receive a life sentence—I'd be kicked off Prodigy forever. I think this time several people turned me in, and I became the target of the biggest manhunt the cyberpolice had ever conducted. Between the masochists in the bondage room, the Rush fans, and the drunken friends of Bill W, **I WAS PRODIGY PUBLIC ENEMY NUMBER ONE.** There was no jury or court of appeals in this situation, and I had been pronounced guilty by the on-duty computercops.

I couldn't type back to the cyberpolice and explain that I was a lonely desperate man who had just been scorned by some computer bitch.

"There were extenuating circumstances, officers," I wanted to say. "I grew up in a poor black community, my father constantly called me a moron and . . ." Well, fuck it, maybe I deserved this punishment. My profanity and nastiness had broken all of the Prodigy laws. I knew I had done wrong. I'd do my time like a man. I'd wait out the week. But when I got out of Prodigy prison, I was gonna get me a girl, even if it meant having to admit I was Howard Stern. In the meantime I'll just go upstairs and have sex with my wife . . . again.

The sad truth is, I need fame to get girls. I couldn't hide behind an alias anymore. Truth be told, I needed to be Howard

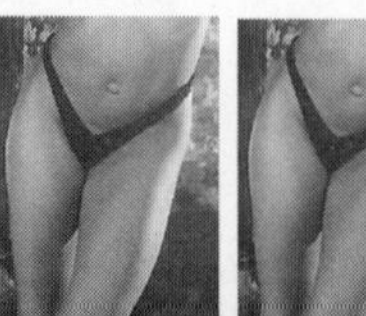
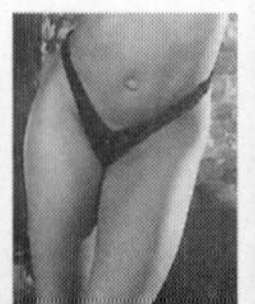

Stern. Screw being faceless in the crowd—being a nobody sucks. I was a high school nobody again when I used the Casanova and HolyGhost names and I couldn't score. I was a zero with girls and if I wanted to see any action, I'd better tell these ladies I was Howard Stern himself. This Prodigy shit was starting to teach me some painful lessons. What happened to the fun?

I wanted to have cybersex. I had served my time in Prodigy jail and my week was up. I needed a woman, *now.* It was Saturday night, and Alison and the kids had gone to the movies. The house was mine, for once. I could roll down my pants and enjoy my first encounter. I grabbed some tissues and left 'em next to the computer. I put the house alarm on so if my family returned early I'd be alerted.

With all that taken care of, I entered the Howard Stern Room and announced myself under my new nickname: Captain Japan. I took the name Captain Japan because that's what I call Judge Ito when I'm on the air.

CAPTAINJAPAN: I AM HOWARD! I AM HOWARD STERN!

Surely the excitement would be electrifying. These were all fans of my show in the Howard Stern Room, and they would welcome me with open arms.

JERRY: Hey, stupid. You ain't Howard. Everyone says they're Howard. And don't write in all caps. You're annoying.

They didn't believe me at first and it took me over an hour to convince them I was Howard. A girl named Cyberqueen asked me a million questions about the show and I had to answer them correctly.

CYBERQUEEN: How tall are you? If you're Howard you'll know exactly the right height.

CAPTAINJAPAN: Six-five.

CYBERQUEEN: Good. What's the radio station address?

CAPTAINJAPAN: 600 Madison Avenue.

CYBERQUEEN: What floor do you work on?

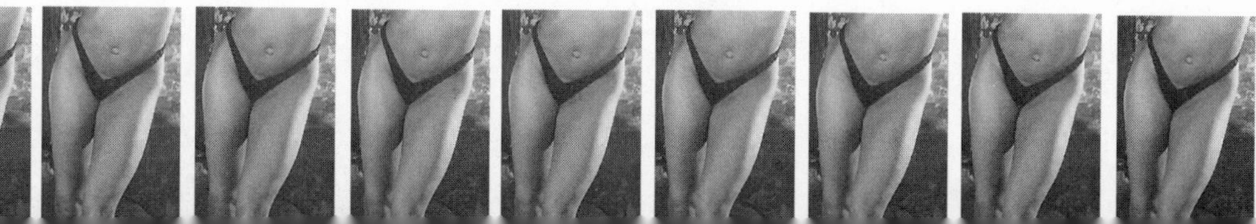

The Spanish Inquisition went on into the night. But I finally convinced her, and she finally said the magic words.

CYBERQUEEN: Howard, I love you. I've got a 36C chest—no fake implants, real breasts. I guess you could say I look like Sharon Stone. Blonde hair, brown eyes, 115 lbs. Tight body made for love and sex! I'm horny constantly. Especially for you.

Oh yeahhhhh! Bingo! Jackpot! I'm about to lose my cyber virginity methinks. I'm ready for love, but wait a second, how do I know this is a woman? I could be getting scammed. What if she's a guy?

CAPTAINJAPAN: How do I know you're not some guy?

CYBERQUEEN: I'm no guy. I'll let you in on a little secret. I'm getting very wet.

Whoa, that's no guy.

CYBERQUEEN: Are you turned on?

You know what? I *was* turned on, damn it. I had a little lump going in my jeans. I must be the horniest motherfucker this side of an IBM computer terminal. But, hey, let's have a reality check here for a minute. What if this girl takes this transcript and sells it to *Hard Copy* and tells them it's me?

Hold it, Junior, don't get paranoid. Let's think this through. I'm using an alias and no one can really prove it's me. But wait: Those *Hard Copy* assholes are pretty vicious. They could break into the Prodigy offices and look up all the nicknames and . . .

Whoa, hold on! Oh fuck! Here I finally have a girl, she's ready, willing, and able, and now I'm having second thoughts.

I am truly cursed. I must have done something bad in a previous life. I can't have a little jerk-off session without getting paranoid. I once saw a TV show where this lady had a computer encounter with Rush Limbaugh, and they were reading the transcripts on the show. He sounded like a horny loser.

CYBERQUEEN: Howard, my love, are you still there?

Oh fuck. For the record I better say I'm not Howard. But if I say I'm not Howard, she'll dump me.

CAPTAINJAPAN: I have to go.

Ahhhhhhh, I was chickening out. I finally had a partner and I was chickening out.

CYBERQUEEN: Please don't go.

Oh man, she's begging me for it.

CAPTAINJAPAN: I have to go, really.

CYBERQUEEN: Why?

CAPTAINJAPAN: I have someone waiting for me.

CYBERQUEEN: You've got me waiting too. HOWARD DON'T LEAVE ME! I'M ALL WET AND EXCITED!

C'mon, you spineless dickwad. This is what you wanted. The house is empty. You're so guilt-ridden and self-analytical that you can't have a little fun? Like the Nike ad says, "Just do it." (Oh great. Now I'm receiving advice from TV commercials.)

CYBERQUEEN: I'm too wet. Don't go. Let's fool around. Take my

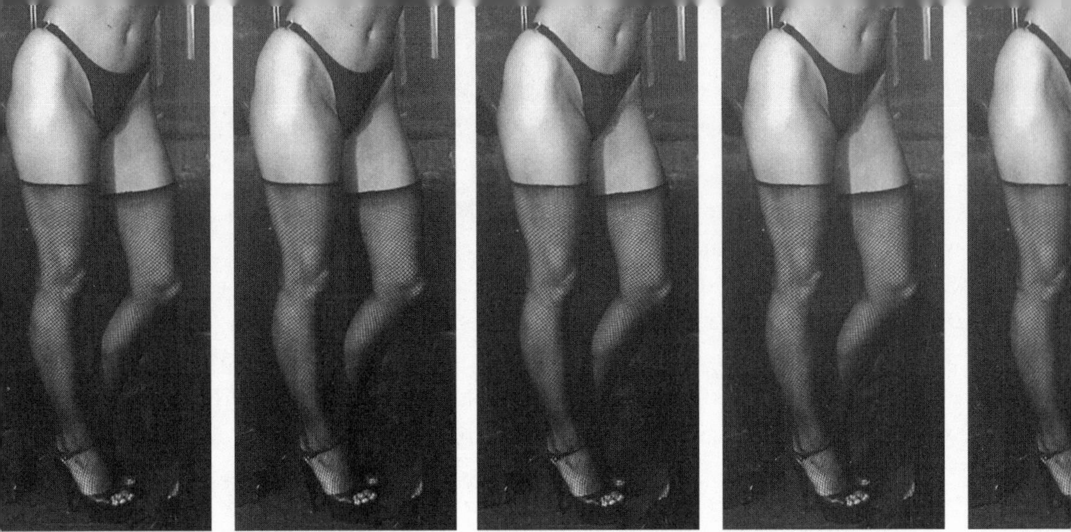

clothes off. Spank me. Hog tie me with silk ties.

Man, this babe had me going. She was doing all the work, instigating everything. Even though I was still paranoid about *Hard*-on *Copy,* I must admit I had a good-sized boner going and I was rubbing my crotch. I typed out the next sentence with one hand.

CAPTAINJAPAN: Are you at my total mercy?

CYBERQUEEN: Yes, oh yes. My nipples are so erect. And I'm dripping wet. Do you want me to take off my clothes?

CAPTAINJAPAN: Yes, what are you wearing?

CYBERQUEEN: Black silk pj's.

CYBERQUEEN: I'm taking off my panties.

There was a sixty-second delay. Maybe she really was taking off her panties.

CYBERQUEEN: I am naked now. I am so slippery wet. I am getting wet as we type.

CAPTAINJAPAN: Where are your hands?

CYBERQUEEN: In my crotch and on the keyboard. That's why it's taking some time.

CAPTAINJAPAN: Are you shaved?

CYBERQUEEN: I am shaved. My legs are spread. They are open and wet. Getting harder to type. Are you playing with yourself?

Shit yeah! This girl was mine. The truth was I had already slid my pants off the second she said "black silk pj's." I was rubbing my cock through my underwear and I was barely holding back my full load. But I sure as hell wasn't going to admit that on-screen. Playing with myself? What did she think I was, a loser?

CYBERQUEEN: Howard, are you playing with yourself yet?

CAPTAINJAPAN: No, not really.

I wished she'd stop calling me Howard. My name was Captain Japan.

CYBERQUEEN: I've had so many fantasies about you.

CAPTAINJAPAN: Tell me.

CYBERQUEEN: You were coming out of the shower and you caught me playing with myself. THE ROOM WAS SO HOT!

CAPTAINJAPAN: And were you aching for me?

CYBERQUEEN: Yes. You took your robe off and knelt between my legs. You started to kiss my calves working your way upwards.

Holy shit, I was really hot. I was stroking away at my shaft like John Wayne Gacy at a Cub Scout meeting. Is there something wrong with me? I could cum any second. Better get my tissues ready. I've got to make an effort to type back. I'll just stop stroking for a second.

CAPTAINJAPAN: Did I tongue your clit when I had you on your bed?

I guess I won't be getting any erotic writing awards with a comeback like that.

CYBERQUEEN: My darling, you gave my pussy sweet, soft butterfly kisses.

That's it. *I'm coming. Holy shit.* How fucking embarrassing. I have hit an all-time low. I'm going to hell. Not even two minutes into this cybersex and I blow my load. *I prematurely ejaculate even with computer sex.* I look like a total asshole, alone in my house, in a dark room, with a wet wad of tissues in my hand and my pants wrapped around my ankles. Thank God there are no mirrors in this room. *What the fuck is wrong with me?* I am biologically forty-one years old with the libido of a fifteen-year-old and the maturity of a seven-year-old. I'm getting out of here.

CAPTAINJAPAN: I have to go, bye.

CYBERQUEEN: No, Howard, don't go. We just started. Don't make me wait. There is more to my story. Don't leave me!

And I logged off. Good. The bitch probably thinks I'm a real man. I just left her hanging. It's about time a Sharon Stone look-alike didn't get her ass kissed by a man. I did the smart thing not saying too much because if *Hard Copy* ever gets a hold of this transcript, it will show that I wasn't even interested in sex. Phew, I'm glad that's over. I'm never calling in to this again. I'm going upstairs because Alison and the kids are coming home and I want to be a good dad and a model husband. I'm turning over a new leaf. . . .

Well, I turned over a new leaf all right. **I WAS CALLING INTO PRODIGY EVERY DAY.** This shit was *hot*!

Who was I kidding? I was a sex addict and my Prodigy bill was going through the roof.

I'm logging on twice a day now. The word's getting out that Captain Japan is Howard Stern, and I'm cyberfucking every broad in the Howard Stern Room. Now, don't give me any shit about this because at least I ain't running around like every other married guy cheating on my wife with real women. This is just fantasy play.

See, I told you I could rationalize anything. *I love my wife and kids, I love my wife and kids, I love my wife and kids, I love my wife and kids.*

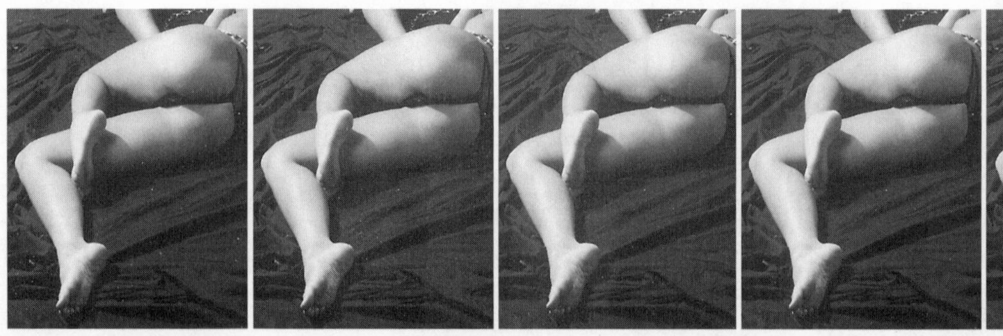

Sorry, just trying a little hypnotherapy. Hey, fuck the wife and kids. I love the fifty percent of my money that ain't going out the window 'cause I keep it in my pants.

Whenever I can slip into my office and log on, I'm doing a quick jack-off session. I always believed that as you got older the need to jack off would dissipate. Well, you can throw that theory out the window. My next session with Cyberqueen got steamier, even though it only lasted two or three minutes. I was still afraid to type back anything too sexy because of *Hard Copy*, those pricks. I let her do most of the work.

CYBERQUEEN: I'm wearing a short nightshirt and French-cut bikinis.

CAPTAINJAPAN: Good.

CYBERQUEEN: I wish your hands were rubbing up and down my thighs. I want you to fuck me on a gym bench.

This was real good.

CYBERQUEEN: Mirrors all around in the gym. The view is incredible. Want to lie down on the bench with me, honey?

CAPTAINJAPAN: Yes!

CYBERQUEEN: I would love to straddle you. Me on top of you. You could watch me sliding down on your cock.

I started getting a big arousal in my fucking pants. I quickly pulled my shorts and underpants down and I started jerking off real quick—even quicker than usual. Alison was home and asleep upstairs. It was late Friday night and I'd better be quick about it or else I'd get discovered. I needed to unload fast—or, as they say in the computer world, *download* fast—because if I didn't download fast and Alison caught me, she was gonna reboot my ass out

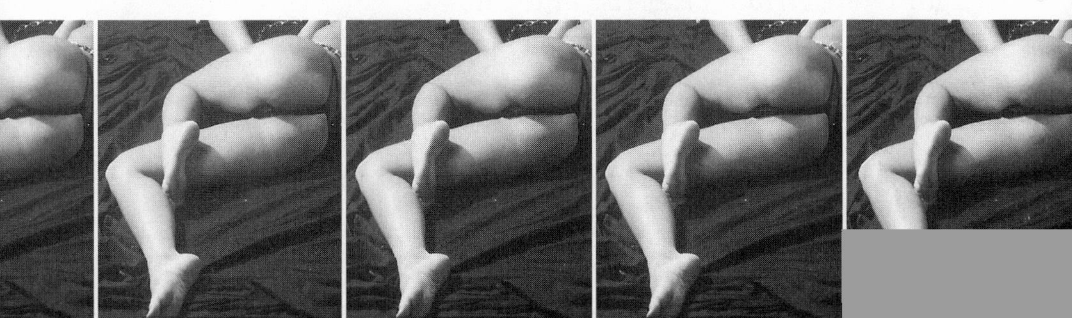

of the house. Better get some tissues and pray to God that Alison doesn't walk in on me. Good thing I have good hearing. I'll be able to hear her footsteps coming downstairs because the house is still and quiet at this late hour.

CYBERQUEEN: Let the head of your cock rub up against my wet clit.

CAPTAINJAPAN: Uh, huh.

Not a bad comeback for a guy with a four-year degree from Boston University. I'd jerk off a few seconds, then type something in, then go back to jerking off.

CYBERQUEEN: I'd put your pretty penis in me slowly. Just the head. And then take it out. And then back in again and take just a little bit more each time.

CAPTAINJAPAN: Right.

Oh, was I a lummox. But I was just playing it safe. What could *Hard Copy* say about a guy who says "uh-huh" and "right"?

CYBERQUEEN: My warm juices are flowing on your hard cock.

I was ready to shoot my load all over my lap.

CYBERQUEEN: I love how it feels inside me. So I take the entire length of you inside. Right to your balls.

CAPTAINJAPAN: You have that much control that you can stay just on the head?

What was I babbling about? I was trying to sound clinical so she wouldn't know I was really jerking off.

CYBERQUEEN: I'm so wet. I love rocking back and forth on the entire shaft.

That was it! I erupted like Mount Vesuvius. **Okay, all done.** Whoa! I should be real proud of this. Hey, I'm not letting my kids ever read this book—and don't fuck me up by giving it to them. Just as I was wiping up, Cyberqueen logged on with a request.

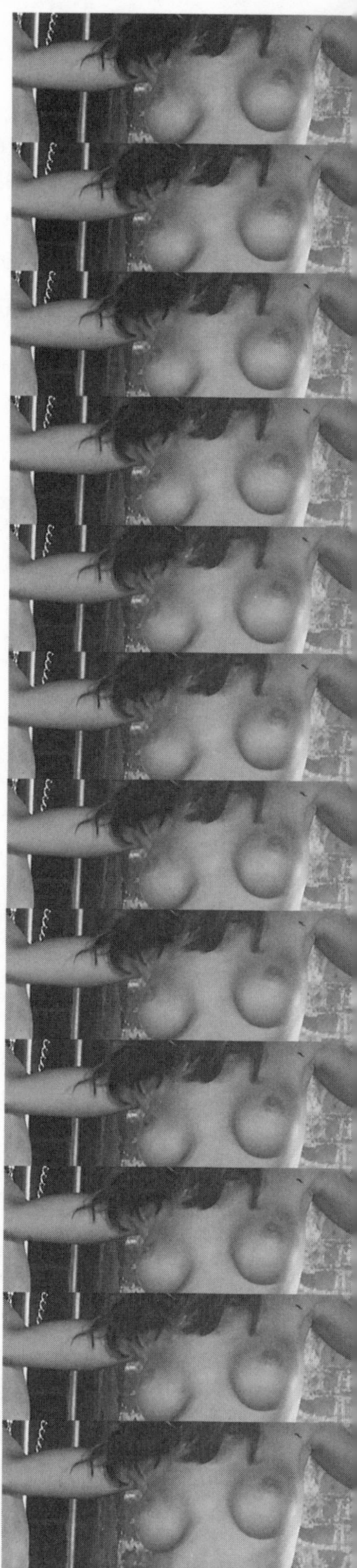

CYBERQUEEN: Can you tell me what you could do for me? I love a hot probing tongue, licking my lips, my clit . . .

Oh fuck, now she wanted me to get *her* off. She thinks we're just getting started—she has no idea she's with Quick Draw McGraw, or whatever that fucking cartoon horse's name was. (That was a horse, wasn't it? Whoever drew that thing ought to go back to fucking art school.)

CYBERQUEEN: Do something for me . . . my love.

Man, this is getting like a marriage. I came way too fast, and now I have a nagging, whining woman looking to be pleased. I tried to be nonchalant. I better cool this bitch in heat down.

CAPTAINJAPAN: Are you married?

CYBERQUEEN: Yes.

CAPTAINJAPAN: I think you should go have sex with your husband. I really have to go to sleep.

Now, that was nice. Here sweet Cyberqueen had given herself to me and I'm telling her to buzz off. Just like every other fucked-up guy, I was ready to roll over and go to sleep.

CYBERQUEEN: I probably will jump on my husband later, but I'd like to play with you for a while.

CAPTAINJAPAN: Sorry, forgive my exhaustion, but I'm really not that into this tonight. But I am absolutely convinced you have a career writing porn.

Well, gee. Wasn't I the great lover? What a lovely compliment: "I'm not that into this." I was so not into it that I shot through eighteen tissues. How'd you like my line, "You have a great career in pornography"? Some piece of shit I am. I'd fuck 'em, file 'em on a floppy, and forget 'em. I hadn't changed since high school. I *still* didn't know how to handle women.

CYBERQUEEN: Goodnight, I guess.

I wanted to be above all this computer sex, but damn it, I admit I was hooked. I started having sex with all different girls. I dumped Cyberqueen 'cause I didn't want to get tied down.

Next I was with **Puppetgirl**, who told me she looked like Teri Hatcher from *Lois and Clark.* She sounded like one hot babe. She said she had long, thin legs, huge tits, and liked to give massages with hot oil. And then while I'm computer-fucking the Puppet, I score with another honey named Rubberbaby. I was juggling babes like Warren Beatty in *Shampoo.* **Rubberbaby** was the sex queen of Prodigy. She said she was five foot three, weighed 110, and was *34-23-33* with a C cup. She claimed she looked like Janine Turner from *Northern Exposure,* whoever that is. I don't watch that show 'cause it takes place in Alaska and I only watch shows about hot climates with female lifeguards in thongs.

But even the name Janine Turner sounded good to me. Rubberbaby was married but her husband didn't mind that she was cyberfucking half the guys in the Howard Stern Room. She would even electronically fuck four or five guys at once. Oh man, I was gonna explore this girl in places her doctor had never seen.

RUBBERBABY: Do you like oral sex?

CAPTAINJAPAN: I'd like your lips wrapped around my cock.

Hey, I was even getting bolder. After all, no one had turned me into *Hard Copy* yet. Fuck *Hard Copy*!

RUBBERBABY: I'm kissing your forehead. Your cheek. Rubbing my soft cheek against yours.

CAPTAINJAPAN: Where are we doing this?

I like details. I want my fantasies to have an air of reality.

RUBBERBABY: We are in the parking lot of a club I go to.

CAPTAINJAPAN: In a car?

RUBBERBABY: Outside the car. It's dark. Some light from nearby.

Good! I don't want anybody seeing me outside a club.

CAPTAINJAPAN: What are you wearing?

This detail is really important to me for some reason. I need my girls wearing hot clothes.

RUBBERBABY: Short jean skirt and a white T-shirt.

CAPTAINJAPAN: Panties?

RUBBERBABY: No panties. Easy access.

CAPTAINJAPAN: Are you shaved?

Another important detail.

RUBBERBABY: Shaved some and then closely trimmed.

Right answer.

CAPTAINJAPAN: What kind of shoes?

Another important detail. I like big spiky heels on my woman. The kind that breaks ankles.

RUBBERBABY: Keds.

CAPTAINJAPAN: No heels?

RUBBERBABY: No, not tonight very casual. I wear heels with my leather.

She couldn't have worn her leather? Hey, you can't have everything.

CAPTAINJAPAN: So we're making out in a parking lot?

RUBBERBABY: It's more than just making out... it's tender kisses, and you're getting me wet. I find my way to your mouth.

RUBBERBABY: Letting my tongue trace around your lips.

RUBBERBABY: Slowly.

RUBBERBABY: Wanting to taste you. Pressing my lips against yours. Tasting you. Mmmmmm-mmmmmmmmm...

Whoa! I liked this action! And what's with the mmmmmmm? Well, shit, I'll mmmmmmm back. This babe knows how to talk dirty.

CAPTAINJAPAN: Mmmmmmmmmmmmmm...

RUBBERBABY: Getting wetter.

RUBBERBABY: And more excited.

CAPTAINJAPAN: Are you rubbing your clikt?

Damn, I was so excited I couldn't even type right.

CAPTAINJAPAN: Clit.

RUBBERBABY: Yes, I'm rubbing my clit. Oh, I wish you were here. I have been reaching down and touching myself since we started, baby. . .

CAPTAINJAPAN: Take off your shirt.

What a stupid comment. I never know what to write. But it didn't matter because she was turbocharged and all juiced up, and me, I'm about to shoot my load.

RUBBERBABY: I'm sliding my hands down to your shorts now.

RUBBERBABY: Are they elastic waist or zipper?

CAPTAINJAPAN: Zipper.

RUBBERBABY: Unzipping your shorts. Sliding my hand inside. Pulling you free.

CAPTAINJAPAN: My cock is so hard.

That's right, I'm telling my woman that my cock is hard. I'm throwing caution into the . . . into . . . into the something. Can't think straight. Who gives a fuck if *Hard Copy* gets a hold of this? They can't prove I'm CaptainJapan.

RUBBERBABY: I'm kissing right below your belly button now. Running my tongue across your belly.

CAPTAINJAPAN: I bet you're good at that.

I wanted to explode all over my monitor screen. But how would I explain that to my IBM service rep?

RUBBERBABY: Rubbing my soft cheek against your cock. Looking at your cock. Coming close. Tongue out. Closer, but . . . not touching.

CAPTAINJAPAN: You are driving me crazy.

Why not give my girl a little encouragement? This was a four-star performance. Boy, this sex was easy once I admitted I was Howard Stern. Hey, why fight fame? It has its perks. I would have never gotten her on my own.

RUBBERBABY: I want to taste the salty sweetness on your penis.

Well said.

RUBBERBABY: My mouth coming closer.

CAPTAINJAPAN: Kiss it. Kiss my penis.

Look at me barking out orders.

RUBBERBABY: Flicking my tongue on your head.

RUBBERBABY: Letting my lips rest on the front of your cock.

RUBBERBABY: Little hard licks. Up and down. Tiny movement.

CAPTAINJAPAN: I need that.

I know that's an asinine comment, but I just wanted her to know I was still breathing.

RUBBERBABY: You can feel my warm breath.

CAPTAINJAPAN: The head of my cock is so swollen.

And it was. I wasn't afraid to type it. Fuck *Hard Copy*. This was *gggggoooooooooood*.

RUBBERBABY: Kissing your balls. Taking your balls gently in my mouth.

CAPTAINJAPAN: And. . .

RUBBERBABY: Sucking you gently. . .

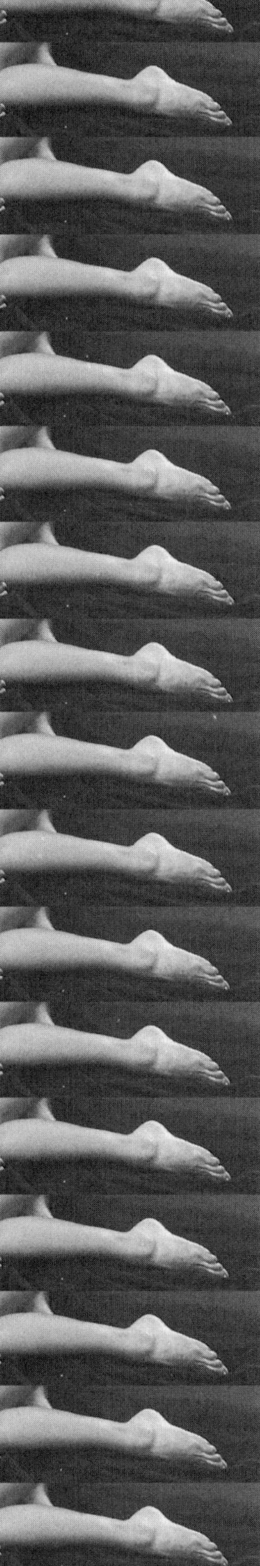

CAPTAINJAPAN: Ohhhhhhh!

Did I just type "ohhhhhhh"? I should be shot. Now look at what a jackass I'm making out of myself. I'm typing "ohhhhhhh" with one hand and jacking off with the other. I know this chick is gonna print this out and show it to all her friends.

RUBBERBABY: Bringing my tongue to the base of your cock

CAPTAINJAPAN: Yes

RUBBERBABY: Licking

RUBBERBABY: To the tip

RUBBERBABY: Taking you in my mouth

RUBBERBABY: And sucking hard

RUBBERBABY: Backing off

RUBBERBABY: Letting you go

CAPTAINJAPAN: FUCK!

RUBBERBABY: Blowing lightly on your wet cock

CAPTAINJAPAN: Driving me crazy

RUBBERBABY: Feels cool to you

RUBBERBABY: You want my hot mouth back

RUBBERBABY: I come closer to you

RUBBERBABY: My mouth hot and ready for you

CAPTAINJAPAN: SO HOT!

RUBBERBABY: I slide my hand under your balls

RUBBERBABY: And between your legs

SHIT, I HOPE THERE'S NO CHEESE UNDER THERE.

RUBBERBABY: Come closer to you. . .

CAPTAINJAPAN: And

RUBBERBABY: Take you in my mouth again

RUBBERBABY: Suck you

RUBBERBABY: Hard

Bingo! I'm just about done. Uh-oh! Footsteps. It's Alison. Pull the pants up. *Whoa! Coitus interruptus computerus.* If Alison notices my hard-on, I'm a dead man.

CAPTAINJAPAN: I'll be back in an hour. I have to go. My trainer is here. I have to work out.

RUBBERBABY: Wait . . .

Bam! Turn this fucker off. Get rid of the tissues. Destroy the evidence. *Whoa.* Close call.

I was back on in an hour. Rubberbaby was back in the room waiting for me. Man, am I depraved! I couldn't wait to log back on. Sure, there are little children starving in Europe. Yes, there are people dying in Africa that could use my help, but damn it, I'm such a superficial piece of garbage that I build my day around a computer girl named Rubberbaby. I needed her to make me come. My balls were bluer than the tip of Walt Disney's frozen nose.

I have to say Rubberbaby was the best at pleasing a man, but it occurred to me that I had been a selfish lover. I'd let her get back to my blue balls in a minute. But for the first time in my short, stupid, miserable cybersex life I wanted to please my computer partner. That's right, selfish, insensitive Howard wanted to give her pleasure and make her come. This hot little slut with the C cups and the Keds deserved it.

RUBBERBABY: Hold on . . . you want me to get the vibrator?

CAPTAINJAPAN: Yes.

RUBBERBABY: Great. Okay hang on a sec.

CAPTAINJAPAN: Okay.

RUBBERBABY: Okay . . . one more sec.

CAPTAINJAPAN: What's going on?

RUBBERBABY: . . . Extension cord . . . lol.

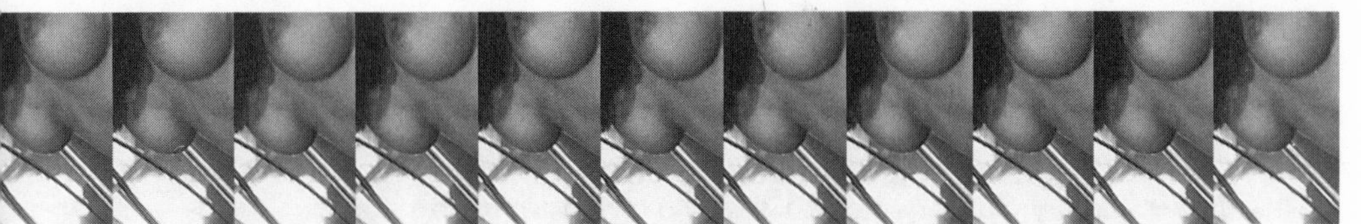

Lol meant "laughing out loud." I had transformed into such a complete technonerd douchebag that I actually knew the secret little abbreviations.

CAPTAINJAPAN: Are your shorts off?

RUBBERBABY: Going to take them off.

RUBBERBABY: Hold on.

CAPTAINJAPAN: Are you naked?

RUBBERBABY: Got my T-shirt on and that is all.

CAPTAINJAPAN: Good.

CAPTAINJAPAN: Does your chair have arms?

RUBBERBABY: Yes.

CAPTAINJAPAN: Can you spread your legs far apart?

RUBBERBABY: Yes . . . the arms are like U-shaped . . . can really spread my legs

CAPTAINJAPAN: Spread them

RUBBERBABY: Spread for you

CAPTAINJAPAN: And where is your vibrator?

RUBBERBABY: On the chair between my legs

CAPTAINJAPAN: Are you wet?

RUBBERBABY: Very

CAPTAINJAPAN: And are you touching your clit?

RUBBERBABY: Could slip you right in

RUBBERBABY: Yes

RUBBERBABY: Slow

CAPTAINJAPAN: Are you touching your clit with the vibrator?

RUBBERBABY: Yes

RUBBERBABY: Mmmmmm

CAPTAINJAPAN: Mmmmmmmm

There I go again typing "Mmmmmmmm" without shame. What a dipshit.

CAPTAINJAPAN: If I was there I would slowly go down on you . . . kiss your nipples

RUBBERBABY: Mmmmm

CAPTAINJAPAN: Move my head down and kiss your belly

RUBBERBABY: My nipples are sooo sensitive

CAPTAINJAPAN: And get closer to your pussy

CAPTAINJAPAN: And then skip to your feet

CAPTAINJAPAN: Kiss them

CAPTAINJAPAN: And move my lips and tongue up your legs

RUBBERBABY: Oh so hot. . .

CAPTAINJAPAN: Kissing your thighs

RUBBERBABY: My legs are soft and silky and tan

CAPTAINJAPAN: I bet

CAPTAINJAPAN: Then I would kiss your pussy for the first time

CAPTAINJAPAN: Just the outside lips

RUBBERBABY: Make me shiver

Huh? Not too shabby for my first time turning a woman on? How'd you like how just when I was at her pussy, I went to her feet? Now, that's technique, boys and girls. See, it builds anticipation. God, am I pathetic?

Now, I don't know about you, but I'm buying that she's buzzing away with the vibrator. I've got one of the hottest little honeys with her legs spread apart jerking herself off. I'm enjoying giving her pleasure. I'm really very proud of myself. This shows a sign of maturity on my part, delaying my own gratification in order to please others.

Holy shit! Have I gone off the deep end or what? Somebody send over Dr. Kevorkian. I think it's time for me to quietly hook up to the suicide machine. Anyway, my girl was getting into it, and now I was gonna eat her smelly pussy and give her a real thrill.

CAPTAINJAPAN: I'm gently teasing you with my tongue.

RUBBERBABY: Oooohhh

CAPTAINJAPAN: And then

CAPTAINJAPAN: On your pussy lips

CAPTAINJAPAN: Your clit would

CAPTAINJAPAN: Ache

RUBBERBABY: Pushing out to meet your face...

CAPTAINJAPAN: And then I would spread your lips

RUBBERBABY: Want you in my pussy...

CAPTAINJAPAN: And run my tongue along the outside

CAPTAINJAPAN: And up to your aching clit

CAPTAINJAPAN: Does your clit ache?

RUBBERBABY: Wriggling under your touch

CAPTAINJAPAN: Tell me what you're doing

RUBBERBABY: Squirming

CAPTAINJAPAN: Do you want more

RUBBERBABY: Pushing against the vibrator

RUBBERBABY: Imagining you

CAPTAINJAPAN: Are you very wet?

RUBBERBABY: I am soaked

CAPTAINJAPAN: Do you want me inside of you?

RUBBERBABY: I would love that

CAPTAINJAPAN: Ask me

RUBBERBABY: Oh god

CAPTAINJAPAN: Me

Hey, it's not easy to type with one hand and beat your meat with the other.

CAPTAINJAPAN: Ask me

RUBBERBABY: Fuck me please

CAPTAINJAPAN: Good

RUBBERBABY: Fuck me

CAPTAINJAPAN: But not so fast

CAPTAINJAPAN: First I take my cock and run it along your breast

I read this one in one of my wife's women's magazines. Cock along the breast, good one. I'm pulling out all the ammunition. The babes like a lot of teasing. What the fuck, I had a few extra minutes to spare. I'd tease her some more before I fucked her.

CAPTAINJAPAN: And then I run my cock down your stomach

RUBBERBABY: Mmmmm god that drives me crazy

CAPTAINJAPAN: And just outside your pussy lips

RUBBERBABY: Getting close to cuming

CAPTAINJAPAN: And the tip of my cock slowly inside

CAPTAINJAPAN: Just the tip

RUBBERBABY: Taking vibrator away

CAPTAINJAPAN: I'm so hard and swollen

RUBBERBABY: Or I will cum now

I could tell she was busy manipulating herself because her replies would take longer and longer to come back on my screen.

RUBBERBABY: Mmmmm

See what I mean?

CAPTAINJAPAN: Are you using your fingers on yourself?

RUBBERBABY: Yes I'm finger fucking myself.

CAPTAINJAPAN: Take your shirt off.

RUBBERBABY: Thinking of you. . .

CAPTAINJAPAN: Is your shirt off?

RUBBERBABY: No

CAPTAINJAPAN: Take it off.

Damn I'm forceful. Women like that, I guess.

RUBBERBABY: Off

CAPTAINJAPAN: Good

CAPTAINJAPAN: Rub your nipple with one hand and finger yourself with the other

CAPTAINJAPAN: Are you doing that?

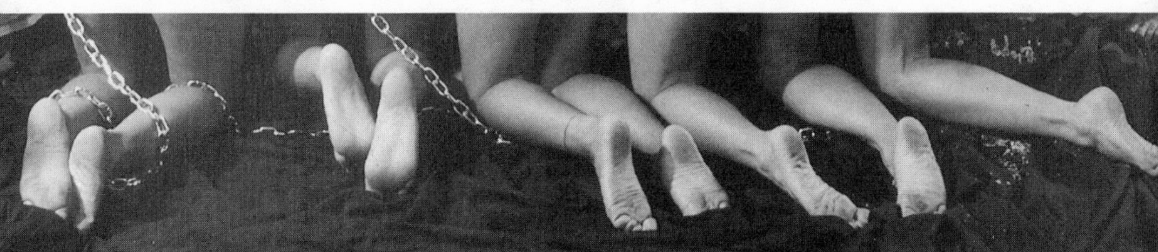

RUBBERBABY: Can't type then

CAPTAINJAPAN: Just briefly

RUBBERBABY: Okay

CAPTAINJAPAN: The head of my cock is in you

CAPTAINJAPAN: And I tease you with it

CAPTAINJAPAN: I rub your clit with my cock

RUBBERBABY: That is sooo hot

CAPTAINJAPAN: And I just rock back and forth on your clit

CAPTAINJAPAN: And then slide down your lips

CAPTAINJAPAN: And the head is inserted again

CAPTAINJAPAN: Slow

CAPTAINJAPAN: Slowly

CAPTAINJAPAN: Very slow

CAPTAINJAPAN: In

CAPTAINJAPAN: And out

You have to admit I'm not too bad at this. Well, shit, I've spent the last twenty years watching porno videos, reading dirty magazines, and jerking off—I had to learn *something* from all that.

RUBBERBABY: Mmm

Even her Mmms were getting smaller. She was hot. Way to go, Howie baby . . . I mean, Captain Japan.

CAPTAINJAPAN: Do you want more cock?

RUBBERBABY: Yes

RUBBERBABY: YES

CAPTAINJAPAN: Put on the vibrator

RUBBERBABY: FUCK ME

RUBBERBABY: Gonna come . . . not gonna take much. . .

CAPTAINJAPAN: I slowly

CAPTAINJAPAN: Go in

CAPTAINJAPAN: A little past the head

CAPTAINJAPAN: And then back out

CAPTAINJAPAN: I give you a little bit of shaft at a time

CAPTAINJAPAN: In and out

CAPTAINJAPAN: Deeper and then a little more

CAPTAINJAPAN: It's so slow

RUBBERBABY: Oh baby . . . yes. . .

CAPTAINJAPAN: Painful

CAPTAINJAPAN: Because you are ready for more

CAPTAINJAPAN: Now I go deeper

CAPTAINJAPAN: My shaft hard

CAPTAINJAPAN: All the way in

CAPTAINJAPAN: Slowly

RUBBERBABY: Oh

CAPTAINJAPAN: My balls against your ass

CAPTAINJAPAN: Deep inside your pussy

CAPTAINJAPAN: Are you coming?

RUBBERBABY: Squeezing you with my pussy

CAPTAINJAPAN: You are so tight

CAPTAINJAPAN: And warm

RUBBERBABY: Can't hold out . . .

CAPTAINJAPAN: My cock is swelling

RUBBERBABY: Here

CAPTAINJAPAN: Come

RUBBERBABY: It cums

CAPTAINJAPAN: Cum

RUBBERBABY: OH

RUBBERBABY: ;lds

And then the screen went silent for a good two minutes. I think I fuckin' killed her.

CAPTAINJAPAN: Are you still with me?

RUBBERBABY: Oh baby. . .

RUBBERBABY: Yeah . . . here

CAPTAINJAPAN: Are you in your chair naked?

RUBBERBABY: Yes

RUBBERBABY: I think so. . . . lol

CAPTAINJAPAN: Legs apart

RUBBERBABY: God . . . yes

CAPTAINJAPAN: I need verification

RUBBERBABY: Still coming down to earth

CAPTAINJAPAN: Fuck, I would love to know if you are really coming?

RUBBERBABY: I am, love, why do this if you're not gonna come?

CAPTAINJAPAN: Good question

Now that we got her off, it was time to get back to my very blue balls. That's the nice thing about girls, after they come they still want to hang around and help their man out. I told her to just concentrate on blowing me so I could come quick. And she did:

RUBBERBABY: Up

RUBBERBABY: And

RUBBERBABY: Down

RUBBERBABY: Fast

RUBBERBABY: Wanting to taste your cum

RUBBERBABY: Tongue working you

CAPTAINJAPAN: Suck harder

CAPTAINJAPAN: I'm coming

RUBBERBABY: Sucking you hard baby

RUBBERBABY: Pulling

RUBBERBABY: Everything out of you

RUBBERBABY: Mmmmmmmm

CAPTAINJAPAN: Swallow my cum

RUBBERBABY: Delicious

RUBBERBABY: Swallowing you

RUBBERBABY: All of it

Awesome! This girl was a pro. What a blow job! I couldn't wait to make arrangements to see her again.

CAPTAINJAPAN: Do you like to get fucked in your ass?

RUBBERBABY: Yes

RUBBERBABY: Gently

CAPTAINJAPAN: No problem

CAPTAINJAPAN: Next time

CAPTAINJAPAN: Until we meet again

RUBBERBABY: Next time, baby

That Monday I went on the air to tell Robin about my new Prodigy girl. I told her everything we did.

"That's called cheating," Robin said.

"No, cheating is when you take your penis and have it contact a woman," I decided. I was so excited that right then and there I needed to see my cyberwomen, all of them. I asked all my girls to call in—Rubber, Puppet, and Cyber. I told them I had to meet them. In my mind if they were willing to come in that meant they had to be hot because no slob would have the balls to show her face in public. I had to see them as soon as possible, these mystery women of the night. My beautiful wildflowers of love, and that, my friends, was the beginning of the end. The cardinal Prodigy rule is:

THOU SHALL NOT MEET THY CYBERSEX GIRLFRIEND IN PERSON.

CYBERPRINCESSES: HOT OR NOT?

Puppet was the first to call in. You remember her, **THE TERI HATCHER LOOK-ALIKE WITH THE LONG THIN LEGS.** I asked her to come on the show, and she accepted. This was fantastic. She must be hot if she's willing to come down and meet me. She sounded so sexy on the phone.

Rubberbaby was next. Ahhh, sweet, sweet Rubber. What a girl! What an imagination and **SHE LOOKED LIKE JANINE TURNER,** whoever that was. When I heard her voice for the first time on the phone she sounded, well, beautiful. My little peach.

"You sound so hot, my little punkin," I said to her, boasting proudly for the whole world to hear. I was excited to confess my lust for my new girlfriend. I had to meet her. Surely if she was telling the truth about her good looks she would not be embarrassed to show her face in public. But, what if, in reality, she looked like Roseanne's eating teacher? ***What if she was a shut-in with no legs*** hopelessly typing into her computer looking for a little warmth? No way!

"They call her Rubberbaby for a reason," Robin cracked.

"Listen, Rubberbaby, I'm not having any more computer sex with you until you come down here." I was anxious to see what this wild vixen looked like and prove Robin wrong. I mean, I knew on some level it didn't make sense that beautiful women were sitting at home typing away, sending horny words over hot modems, but I had thrown all caution to the, uh . . . thrown all caution to the . . . you know.

"Howard, I broke my ankle Rollerblading," Rubberbaby said, pleading for a delay in our meeting. Rollerblading accident? *Hmmmm,* that's encouraging. No fatso would be Rollerblading. She must be fit.

"I don't care. Get down here," I commanded my cyberslut. I kept the pressure on her and she finally agreed to come in.

I never should have bothered. Rubberbaby shattered my illusions. After great fanfare, she came into the studio, and I nearly shit. My dear sweet vixen was . . . well, she was a housewife—on fucking crutches. She wasn't ugly, but she wasn't exactly a fantasy woman. WHOEVER JANINE TURNER WAS, SHE'D BETTER FILE FOR DEFAMATION OF CHARACTER. The broad had a bit of a belly on her, plus ***her granny dress was not exactly a major turn-on.*** And the way she was hopping around the studio on one leg to give me a hug wasn't exactly filling me with fantasies.

Should I lie to Rubberbaby and tell her she resembles Janine Turner? She had been so good to me. She had blown me in the parking lot and had fucked me so tenderly, easing my cock in so slow, and now there was no magic. I tried to be sensitive but the words came out all wrong.

"Wait a second!! Come on!! You're a *housewife!*" I moaned. "I knew I should have followed my first instincts. IF YOU SIT AROUND ALL DAY ON A COMPUTER, YOUR ASS HAS GOT TO SPREAD."

Robin, Jackie, and Fred were all having a field day with me. The truth of the matter is, she wasn't a bad-looking woman at all. Compared to most of the housewives you see running around, she was doing pretty good. But she certainly wasn't jerk-off material for a guy who meets strippers and *Penthouse* Pets daily.

"Would you have sex with her again?" Robin asked, knowing full well that my answer was no.

"Don't pressure me, Robin" was all I could come up with for the moment.

RICKI LAKE

PUPPET

And what about Puppet, the Teri Hatcher look-alike? I was convinced she was going to be a knockout because she had practically begged to come down to the studio. When the big day arrived we called her into the studio. My heart sank. She wasn't a double for Teri Hatcher. **SHE LOOKED LIKE RICKI LAKE.**

To make matters worse, my first girlfriend, Cyberqueen, the woman who had taken my electronic virginity, couldn't make it down to the studio so she sent me a picture of herself. She was my last hope that good-looking girls surfed the Prodigy hallways but the photo looked like she was standing in New Jersey and the photographer was in New York. It was all fogged out and blurry and if you looked close enough, you could kind of see a woman. Something told me she was lying about looking like Sharon Stone when the best picture she could send was an aerial photograph.

Rising Above My Primal Sexual Urges

Was I done with computer sex? You bet I was. Sure, I tried it once more—but just because I'm a hopeless romantic, and guess what?

I started getting it on with some hot little cutie with a D cup named AllOverTan. I'd let you read the transcript but I burned it. You see, I found out the next day that AllOverTan was a guy. A big fan of the show who knew it was me the whole time. I was stroking my cock with a fucking guy at the other end! What a loser!! I was finished with computer sex.

I actually use my computer to do real work now. I wrote this book on my IBM computer using an OS/2 word processing program called *Describe.* I stare at the Prodigy chat room icon on my screen, but it's out of my system for good. That fucking guy AllOverTan made me swear off it. I'd actually learned my lesson. I realized that there was no substitute for the real thing. That as a man of the world, a role model, I must rise above those primal sexual urges. I must behave better than an animal.

I, Howard Stern, swear to you, my reader, that I have turned over a new leaf and will not use the computer for sexual purposes, ever again.

Unless, of course, they ever develop those 3-D goggles with virtual-sex capabilities. Then I'd have to give it a whirl. The way I envision it I'll have a special sex chair to sit in, and I'll strap on some goggles and choose between Heather Locklear, Cindy Crawford, or Three Hot Lesbians. I'll slap on some latex gloves and my schweenie will be hooked right into a rubber tube that goes directly into the computer. And I'll have hot monkey love with all my new girlfriends and there won't be any guilt and *Hard Copy* will never know.

I'LL NEVER HAVE TO TALK TO ANOTHER LIVE HUMAN BEING, EVER AGAIN.

Please, dear God, let this happen. I'd never leave the computer. They'd have to put a tube in to feed me. When they invent 3-D virtual-reality girls I'm buying all the gear and I'm locking my basement door and making sure I've got plenty of tissues.

Hold it! I hear Alison coming.

In the meantime, I'll go have sex with her.

"I'll be right there, honey."

STERN

MICHAEL JACKSON:

IF YOU LOVE CHILDREN SO MUCH,

WHERE ARE

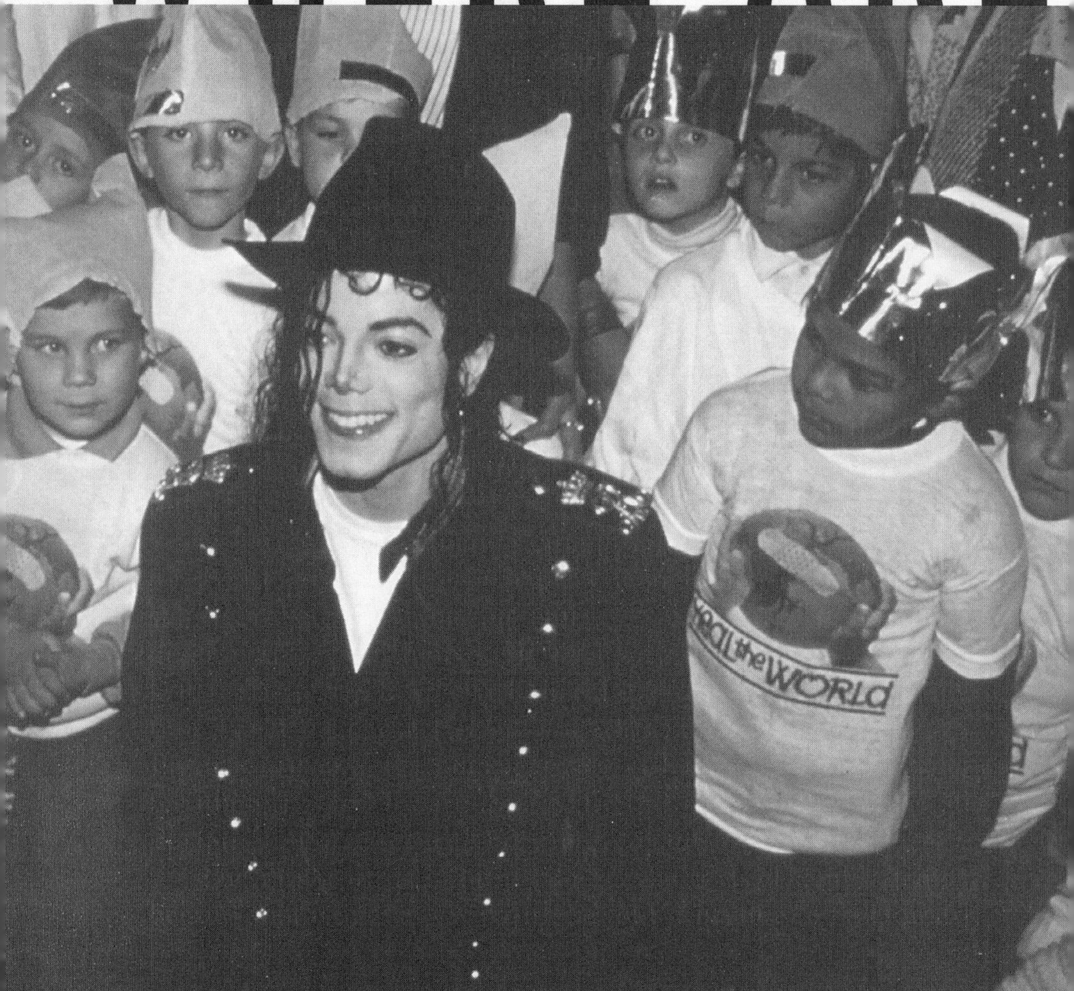

CHAPTER 2

THE GIRLS?

And now the story I refused to talk about on the air: my meeting with Michael Jackson.

Why did I keep my lips sealed about this top secret tête-à-tête?

Did I remain in silence because I will never betray the confidences of high-level executives who swear me to secrecy?

Do I have a set of ethics that forbids me from opening my mouth when someone asks me to please keep things confidential?

Hell no, I knew this story was so good that for once I'd keep my big mouth shut and not talk about it on the radio so I'd have something totally fresh to put in my new book. I'm always admitting everything about my life for free. Even though Robin begged me to tell her this story on the air, I played it smart and now I'm getting paid for my secrets.

So here it is, the exciting story of how the King of All Media met the King of Pop—or the King of Schween or whatever Michael Jackson calls himself. How did I end up in Dolly Parton's apartment overlooking Central Park having a business meeting with one of the biggest celebrities in the world? Why would a superstar come to Howard Stern seeking help and guidance? The plain and simple truth is . . . **desperation.**

You would have to have sunk to an all-time low to start crawling underneath my rock, and Michael had pretty much hit rock bottom. Child molestation charges! The only thing worse is finding out the *National Enquirer* just got tapes of you fucking your brother and not only did you make him bleed but you broke his crib. Let's face it, when all else fails why not go to the miracle-maker, Howard Stern. Of course, it's always risky because Howard Stern can help you but he can also sting you and write about your meeting in his book.

My entire career has consisted of toilet-bowl radio stations at the bottom of the barrel that have come to me when their ratings have disappeared and they needed a nuclear bomb in mornings to jumpstart their pathetic operations. So Michael Jackson, the disgraced superstar was ready to talk . . . and so was I. I mean, what else did I have to do?

LIVE FROM THE CHEVY CHASE THEATRE, IT'S THE HOWARD STERN SHOW

The whole story began about a year ago when I was at a particular high point in my career. Three television networks were actively courting me for various programs. About twice a year they call me to save late-night television, especially after I do something spectacular. When my first book became the fastest selling book in the history of Simon & Schuster, I began getting calls from every film executive and television type. Suddenly, I was a mainstream performer who had real clout in the marketplace—I was bankable. Immediately they would all forget about my most controversial material and the fact that I could be real dangerous as a broadcaster. Hey, let's face it, I've sold a lot of product. If you totaled all the revenue I've generated in radio, books, video, and audiotapes, it would be a bigger gross than *ET*, *Jaws*, or *Indiana Jones*. Of course, Hollywood usually forgets this fact except when it's glaring them right in their stupid faces.

So, here I had written a bestseller and my old friends at Fox Television immediately needed me. Fox was always doing a dance with me. The first time they approached me was years ago when they wanted me to take over Joan Rivers's show and go head-to-head with Johnny. They were a new network and the whole proposition seemed like a disaster with all of the confusion a startup operation brings. Several years later, when Fox didn't have the rights to NFL Football, they approached me again about doing a halftime show so they could steal viewers away from CBS during the Super Bowl. One of the ideas they suggested was a live interview with Sylvester Stallone, Arnold Schwarzenegger, and Bruce Willis. The four of us would sit around, and I could ask them whatever the fuck I wanted. It sounded interesting to me because in a live situation we could really go wherever we wanted without any second-guessing from the edit room. I liked the idea, but it never got off the ground because Fox is always interested in me working for them as long as there is no big price tag involved.

Now I was hearing from Fox again with frantic daily phone calls. Chevy Chase had just finished his stint in the *Guinness Book of World Records* for the "chump with the shortest late-night television show in history." You remember *The Chevy Chase Show*, the one with all the innovations—like a fish tank behind Chevy's head, a piano keyboard built right into the desk, a theater named after him. Well, like the Nostrildamus that I am, I had predicted in my book that the show would last only six weeks, and I was off by only seven days—Chevy only lasted five.

So here I was, bestselling author and sage, and Fox wanted to talk. They wanted me to step into Chevy's shoes. I knew that if I took the job, I would immediately kick ass in the ratings and be the new darling of late night. The show would be cutting-edge and I would do it from the Chevy Chase Theatre. How great would that be? Live from the Chevy Chase Theatre, it's *The Howard Stern Show!*

The Chevy slot intrigued me because I didn't want to end up competing with pushovers like Conan or Tom Snyder. My name was always being kicked around for a late-night slot to compete with Conan, and I considered it an insult. I'm a little too good to be stuck in a twelve-

thirty rut. Conan and Tom Snyder battling for a 1.2 rating wasn't my idea of a competition. I wanted a

shot at Letterman and Leno, because it was clear that they were not filling the needs of the audience. It's pitiful and shocking that *Nightline* beats the both of them. When fun entertainment can't beat serious topics at eleven-thirty at night, something is wrong.

Because of time limitations, it's very hard for me to create original television programming on a nightly basis. Take a look at guys like Letterman and Leno—Letterman, particularly, is behaving like a psychotic. These guys are ready to crack from the pressure. I read that Jay is hiding in closets eavesdropping on NBC executives, and Letterman's beating up walls whenever he thinks he did a particularly bad show.

I firmly believe they are both so beatable that it's ridiculous. For example, when Salman Rushdie was on, Letterman had him read a top-ten list. I mean, that's absurd. A top-ten list? Fuck that. Here's a guy who has been in hiding from Iranian hit men—I want to know what his life is like. Can he get laid? Are there chicks who find it cool when you're in hiding? What's his day like? I want to know. I don't want to see him read a top-ten list. I want him telling me about life on the run. Letterman should be trounced.

Unfortunately, Jay Leno is not a broadcaster and doesn't understand how to do it. He's doing okay, but late-night audiences want something more dynamic. He's doing an imitation of Letterman's show. I truly like both Jay and Dave, but I know I am a better performer and could fill the late-night void, no sweat. Did you know that a Jenny Jones rerun on Channel 9 in New York City beats both of them? Her stupid show is working because she's giving the audience something real, something to get worked up about. No monologue, no jokes, no bits, and she wins consistently.

Anyway, I loved being courted by Fox and was extremely flattered. In my convoluted logic, if they were willing to pay Chevy nine million a year, I was worth at least three times that—I'm a proven winner on TV and radio. Still, I was in no particular rush to sign up with a late-night show because there were two years left on my radio contracts. The idea of doing two of these projects a day seemed mind-numbing, but a good buck can always turn this girl's head.

Fox was coming fast and furious, but when it came to money they were being ridiculously cheap, as usual. For an unproven commodity like Chase they were paying nine million and now they were looking at me as cheap goods. Besides, while I have no love for Chevy, I was shocked at how Fox treated Chevy when they dumped him. As soon as the critics began ravaging his show with bad reviews, Fox executives were ripping Chevy a new asshole in the press. Now that ain't right but it's typical of broadcasting executives. None of them wanted Chevy's fresh blood on them so they distanced themselves and blasted him in the newspaper.

Years from now everyone will remember that Chevy bombed, but they won't remember that Lucie Salhany was the executive in charge of the network.

So I kept turning down the Fox offers. If I was going to go into a long and arduous schedule, I wanted to be compensated. The Fox execs were shocked that a lowlife like me wouldn't come begging to them for this opportunity, but I'm no fool. Who else could pull off this kind of late-night miracle for them: **Greg Kinnear? Rosie O'Donnell? Whoopi Goldberg?** Wrong. I

guess word got to Rupert Murdoch that I wasn't jumping at the late-night offer and he summoned me and my agent, Don Buchwald, up to his beautiful offices to convince us to take over the eleven P.M. slot.

I found Murdoch to be a real down-to-earth guy who was anxious to win. I liked that. After a great pitch by his closest broadcast associates—I call them the Australian mafia—I leaned in and asked Mr. Murdoch one question: If I did something on the air that was outrageous or I got in trouble with the FCC because some listener complained, would he stick by me or would he feel compelled to fire me? I was honest with Murdoch and explained that when you truly innovate, the public and critics often react to an irreverent new show negatively. In essence, I said, you're sending me in to detonate a nuclear bomb in late night: Will you hang in there when the going gets tough? With the look of a priest about to offer absolution he said, "Of course."

Bingo, that was the right answer.

But it didn't matter—deep down, I didn't believe him. I don't believe anyone.

I was hot and everyone was coming at me. NBC was anxious to get involved in prime time, day time, night time, anytime. Warren Littlefield and I got chummy and we danced for quite a few months with intense negotiations and discussions. Once again, the deal wasn't lucrative because for some reason everyone wants to get me cheaply. I know why they find it hard to pay me: they're thinking that if I am too controversial they can ditch me and pay off a small contract. So I told Warren that I needed some autonomy. I said, "When I start to do things that don't look like typical boring television and the critics ravage me, will you stick by me and not panic?" He, of course, also said "Yes."

I didn't believe him, either.

Next it was CBS and Howard Stringer's turn. I guess I always thought Letterman and CBS would come to me and offer me the slot after Letterman. First of all, CBS is desperate for ratings and Dave is a big fan of mine. Any broadcaster with half a brain would recognize that if you have a program on after Letterman that is truly original and worth staying up for, it would be an asset to

Dave's ratings. A buzz would start happening. CBS would look hip.

When Letterman hired Tom Snyder as his follow up, I knew he was doomed to fail. In fact, Snyder can't even beat Conan O'Brien. I think Letterman was too insecure to choose someone like me because I might steal some of his thunder. The fact of the matter is, I would have added to the excitement and helped to make a late-night dynasty. Stringer and Letterman were aware that Fox and NBC were after me and that I could do serious damage to them on another network.

In order to keep me away from late night, Stringer offered me any other kind of show I wanted: I could do specials several times a year or a sitcom. Most of all, Stringer wanted me to develop a show to go up against *Saturday Night Live.* He said if I didn't do it he would have to just run a movie on Saturday nights.

Well, my head was so swollen I could have been mistaken for Rush Limbaugh. I was dizzy with the power at my fingertips, and it kept on snowballing. Fox called again because word got out about CBS's Saturday night offer and they too wanted me for Saturday nights.

Actually, CBS was really starting to interest me. I had just set up the Howard Stern production company. I truly believe that with films, books, and TV I could develop a comedy franchise, much like National Lampoon did in the seventies and eighties. I had already begun developing scripts and had been talking to many people about a bunch of ideas. With CBS, I could start to create specials. I discussed this with Stringer and he loved my ideas. I wanted my first CBS special to be a blockbuster, something that would blow the minds of the industry.

THE NEVERLAND VALLEY FAIRY TALE RANCH

I had always considered doing a Barbara Walters–type special because **BARBARA WALTERS IS SUCH A KISS-ASS.** I could really shake up that world of the celebrity prime-time interview. I would profile four celebrities, but in no way would it resemble those lightweight, suck-ass interviews that everyone does. ***I want to know how Bruce Willis* fucks *Demi Moore—in what position and how many times a week.*** I could give a shit about his next movie.

Anyway, God must truly be on my side because while I was putting together this production company and coming up with ideas, my agent, Don Buchwald, calls me and says that Michael Jackson's manager, Sandy Gallin, called him. Michael Jackson wanted to come on my radio show, but Sandy needed to talk to me first because certain issues needed to be discussed.

"**DON,**" I said, "**THERE MUST BE SOME SHIT IN MY EARS**—I thought you just said that the reclusive bizarro I've been goofing on for the past year wants to come on my radio show."

Don said I had heard him correctly. I was shocked. What did Michael Jackson want from me? If he wanted to talk he must really want to kill me, because I hadn't exactly been kind to him over the years. In fact, I never really got the whole Michael Jackson thing anyway. His music never seemed particularly interesting or innovative to me. I was a fan of some of his videos, and I recognized that he was instrumental in elevating the look of rock videos. But mostly I considered him to be **PATHETIC AND FREAKISH**.

I first started goofing on Michael Jackson when he started showing up in the tabloids and doing wacky stuff like living in a hyperbolic chamber. Once it was reported that he had been trying to buy the remains of the Elephant Man from a London hospital for $1 million. I was so incensed at Michael's crass behavior that I called up the hospital on the air and bid $2 million.

"He's not for sale," a stodgy representative of the hospital told me. "It's for research in the medical college. It's not up for bids."

"Haven't you guys done enough work on him? All I really want is an arm or a leg. Or his hump," I pleaded.

I kept this woman on the line for a good ten minutes. Those English are so polite they can't even hang up on a jerk like me.

"We wouldn't sell him no matter how much we need the money. He's not for sale!"

"We can take care of the remains better than Michael Jackson. He's quirky, he's wacked out," I said.

"We're not selling it," she stood firm.

"All right, do you have any other remains that are ugly that I can buy?" I asked her.

"That is sick," she huffed.

"But I have a museum," I explained.

"That is really sick. I'm awfully sorry, I haven't got the time." Even she had reached her limit.

"No weird remains? Sheep boy? Chicken girl?"

She hung up on me. Those British—no sense of humor.

So I really wasn't surprised when Robin announced that Michael Jackson had been accused of child molestation and that the L.A. police department was investigating the charges. My first reaction was that this guy was incredibly ripe for a blackmail situation. After all, we never heard Webster or Macaulay Culkin say anything about being molested. But if you're so concerned about helping sick kids, donate money to a hospital. Build a freaking hospital, don't build a zoo in your backyard.

Robin then reported that the full name of Michael Jackson's ranch was the Neverland Valley Fairy Tale Ranch.

"Guilty," I announced.

"I like to bring the boys there and we watch movies," I said, imitating Michael's voice.

"Where do you watch the movies?" I said, taking the part of the D.A. "In seats?"

"No, I built a special bedroom for little boys to watch the movies in case they're sick."

"Mr. Jackson, the jury is back."

"But they never left."

"They don't need any more time to decide. Count their hands. Twenty-four guilty votes."

"But there's only twelve members of the jury."

"They all raised both hands."

I suggested the LAPD set up a sting operation to determine Michael's guilt. They should parade a bunch of nude children around him and see what happens.

"You think Michael Jackson wears a white glove so he won't leave fingerprints on anybody?" I wondered. "But I don't believe the accusations. I think they'll find it's a blackmail attempt."

When it came out the next day that the parents of the allegedly abused kid were wealthy, I began to change my tune. After all, it was extremely weird for a grown man like Jackson to traipse around the world lavishing attention and presents on prepubescent boys. If any other adult started hanging around a neighborhood and calling a kid up four, five times a day and buying him expensive gifts, the parents would flip out.

Take a woman to the Bahamas. Don't take a ten-year-old boy there.

Then Robin read an article by syndicated columnist Lisa Robinson. She defended Michael because she had known him for years and when her mother was dying he sent her flowers. Lisa said that Michael's so innocent and childlike, his favorite TV show is *Sesame Street.* SESAME STREET?! That's the Playboy Channel for child molesters.

By the third day of the scandal, as details of the allegations surfaced, I had a new theory: Michael had had his face continually changed so each young boy wouldn't recognize him in a lineup.

It seems to me that Michael Jackson would fit the textbook description of a child molester: All of the neighborhood kids love him. Michael Jackson raises money for kids with pediatric AIDS and stuff like that. These guys always have really cool kid gear set up in their houses—like video game arcades or toys or movies to show the kids.

With Michael's wealth he doesn't just have movies—he has a theater. He doesn't have a pet dog—he has a zoo. He doesn't have a video game—he has an arcade.

Now I ask you: ***Has everyone out there lost their minds? What the hell is he doing with these boys?***

Then Ryan White's mom comes on TV and says, "Michael Jackson was a lovely man and he didn't touch Ryan." What do you expect? Ryan had AIDS!

I had child star Corey Feldman on my show to defend Michael. Under intense cross-examination he wound up admitting that Michael and he had spent a night together in the same hotel room after a day trip to Disneyland, but nothing sexual had happened. Then Michael's sister LaToya disclosed that she had observed over fifty boys who had

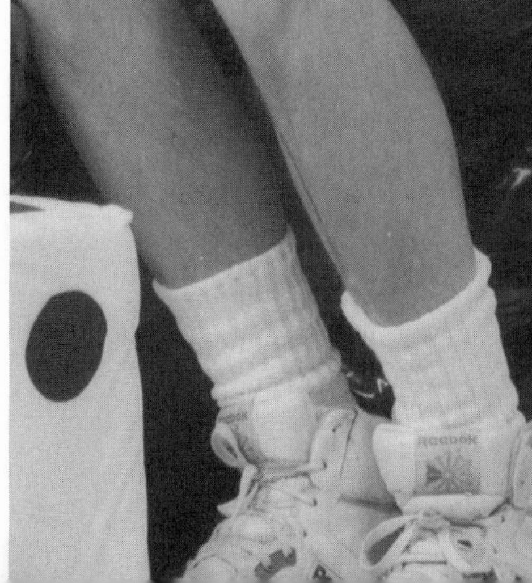

spent the night in Michael's bedroom when she and her brother were living under the same roof as their parents.

Everybody started getting into the act: former cooks, housekeepers, and security guards all surfaced to report that Michael had a fondness for sleepovers. **LaToya** got into the act again, revealing on my show that her mother hated the fact that Michael kept these young boys around. She had told LaToya in disgust that Michael was a "fag."

By the middle of September 1993, the kid had filed a civil suit against Michael, alleging activities that included oral sex and masturbation.

"Throw him in jail," I thundered. "This is turning into the evil clown story. The guy who's a friend to all children. It all fits together. I wouldn't spend five minutes with kids. He rents entire amusement parks just to be with them."

Even Paul McCartney, who hasn't written a hit song in decades, opened his yap. (Well, at least it wasn't that hag wife of his, Linda, the veggie. Can you believe their marriage has lasted? She must tie him up every night and fuck him up the ass real

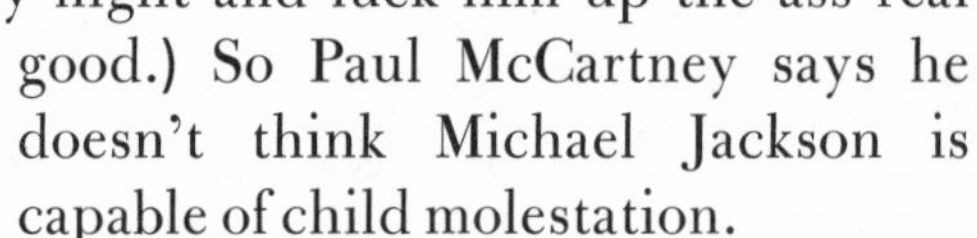

good.) So Paul McCartney says he doesn't think Michael Jackson is capable of child molestation.

"Why doesn't he leave his grandchildren with him?" I asked the wall, which I often talk to.

After police raids on Neverland and his parents' home, Michael remained in seclusion in Mexico. Then that other pillar of mental stability, Elizabeth Taylor, flew to meet with him.

THAT'S ME AS MICHAEL JACKSON AND MY PAL AL ROSENBERG AS LIZ TAYLOR.

"Liz, could you come here," I said in my best wimpy Michael voice, "AND BRING A CUB SCOUT."

Over the weekend, Michael made a taped statement that he was addicted to painkillers and he would seek treatment abroad.

I read my own version of that statement, again, in my best Michael Jackson voice: "I need painkillers. I need some young sphincter. You would be on painkillers too if every time you got horny someone accused you of greasing up a first grader. That's painful. I do miss my animals in California. At least Liz is here—*she's* a pig. I love boy children. That's not wrong. I guess sliding into a Jell-O tub with some Cub Scouts is probably against the law, right?"

On the thirteenth of December, 1993, Michael returned to the States, with two young New Jersey boys in tow—what balls! And a few days later, it was announced that Michael would make a live two-minute statement to the press. And he would not entertain questions.

Of course, we beat him to the punch.

"MANY PEOPLE HAVE ACCUSED ME OF SEXUAL MOLESTATION WITH THEIR CHILDREN. I HAVE BEEN ADVISED—NOT ONLY BY ELIZABETH TAYLOR'S PEOPLE BUT I'VE ALSO BEEN IN TOUCH WITH CAPTAIN KANGAROO AND MR. ROGERS. SHARI LEWIS WAS NOT AVAILABLE FOR CONSULTATION—SHE WAS ON THE ROAD WITH THAT SMELLY SOCK SHE CALLS A PUPPET. ARE THE TWO MINUTES UP YET? THIS STATEMENT WILL CLEAR MY NAME SO WE CAN GET ON WITH THE BUSINESS OF MAKING MUSIC AND MONEY. AS SURE AS MY PENIS IS SPECKLED, I TELL

YOU I AM TELLING THE TRUTH. NUMBER ONE, I'D LIKE TO SAY TO MY SISTER LATOYA, 'SHUT YOUR BIG BLACK MOUTH WITH THAT JEW HUSBAND OF YOURS.' NUMBER ONE, I AM INNOCENT. NUMBER TWO, I AM A GENTLE MAN-BOY. NUMBER THREE, I'M NOT GUILTY. NUMBER FOUR, I NEED A SIX-YEAR-OLD TO FRENCH KISS—JUST KIDDING. NUMBER FOUR, GREASE UP MY GIRAFFE. A LOT OF CHILDREN DO COME TO MY HOUSE FOR CANDY, PEZ, CHOCOLATE, AND CHECKS. I STILL PLAN TO ADOPT MANY OF MY LITTLE FRIENDS. I WANT TO GO BACK TO TYING BALLOONS TO MY GENITALS. I WILL NOW START THE ENGINE OF MY CAMOUFLAGE PLANE SO THAT I CAN LEAVE THE COUNTRY WITHOUT BEING DETECTED. DO I HAVE ANY TIME LEFT?

LaToya, shut your big

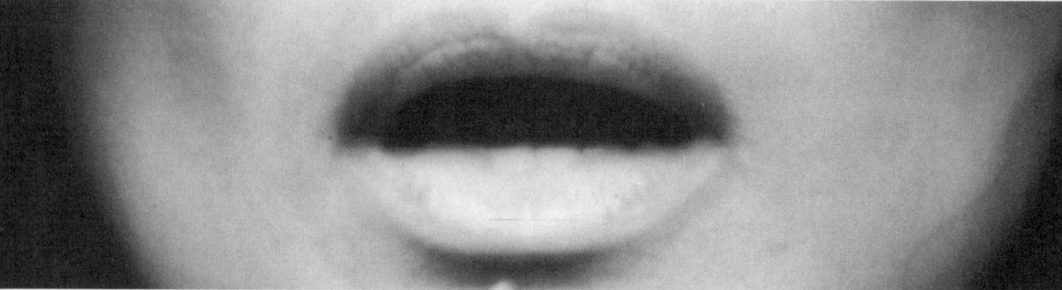

black mouth."

When Michael himself met the press, it was an anticlimax, compared to my statement.

After his statement, Michael laid low, but we didn't. We opened our New Year's Eve Pay-Per-View Pageant with a skit featuring Michael Jackson and one of his little friends, played by a midget.

We had an announcer do a disclaimer:

"We don't know what's going on with Michael Jackson, but the stories that people are coming up with are getting wilder and wilder. What's next? Something like this?"

I was dressed and made up like Michael. I was playing with a young boy. I waved goodbye to his parents.

"Goodnight, Mr. and Mrs. Stupid."

Then I closed the door, did a 360-degree spin move, and threw my stupid Indiana Jones hat off. I grabbed the kid and we both moonwalked.

"Ooh, we're having fun on New Year's Eve."

I hugged him.

"Look at you, you little pecker. Roseanne Barr takes bigger shits than you. What shall we play? I want this New Year's Eve to be the best of your life, little Dexter. You know what little children like to play? They like to play chain-the-white-boy-to-the-bed-and-shock-his-balls."

I picked up the midget and threw him onto a bare mattress frame.

"Come on, little boy, there you go."

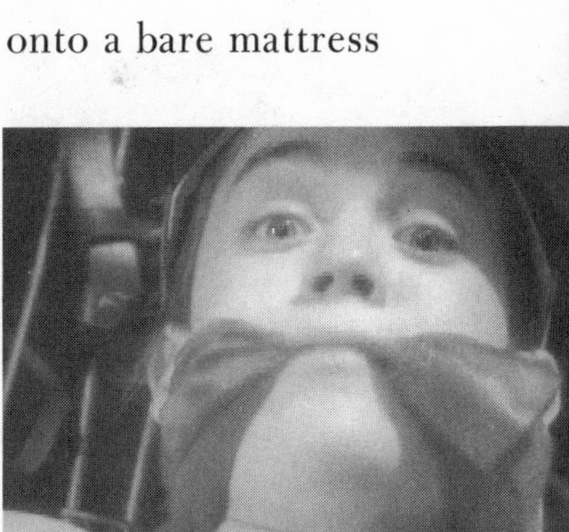

I tied him down, gagged his mouth, pulled his pants off, and ripped his shirt off. He was left with only his underpants on.

"Oh, look at all this hair." I ran my fingers lovingly across his legs. "Ooh, you got more male hormone than I do."

I got up and went over to the wall. I hit a secret panel, and the wall turned around.

On the other side, there was a huge assortment of S&M paraphernalia.

"Look at this wall, we have everything. Hey, Dexter, do you like Barney?"

The midget nodded. I pulled a Barney

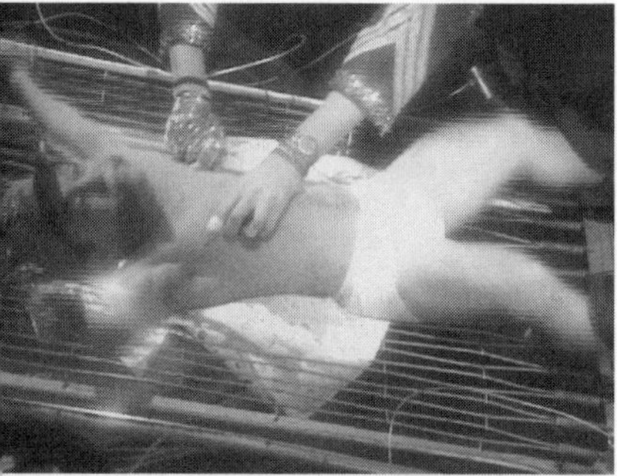

doll off the wall. I walked back and began stroking his body with the doll.

"You like him, right? He's going to feel real good when I SHOVE HIM UP YOUR ASS!"

I rammed the doll into his rear. Then I held up two battery booster cables.

"How would you like to make friends with Mr. Negative and Mr. Positive?"

The midget's eyes widened and he shook his head no. I touched the two cable ends and they sparked.

"Mr. Wizard can kiss my ass," I said as I clamped the cables onto his nipples. His whole body began jerking. Suddenly, his parents walked in.

"What is going on here?" his mother screamed.

"Ooh, ooh, uh, well I was just writing you a check for . . ."

I did some Kung Fu special effects moves with my hands and suddenly a check magically materialized.

". . . fifty thousand dollars." I handed them the check. His mother stuck it down her dress.

"Well, you boys have fun," she said. They waved goodbye and left again.

"Ooh, where were we? It's about time for me to plug my TV set right into your ass."

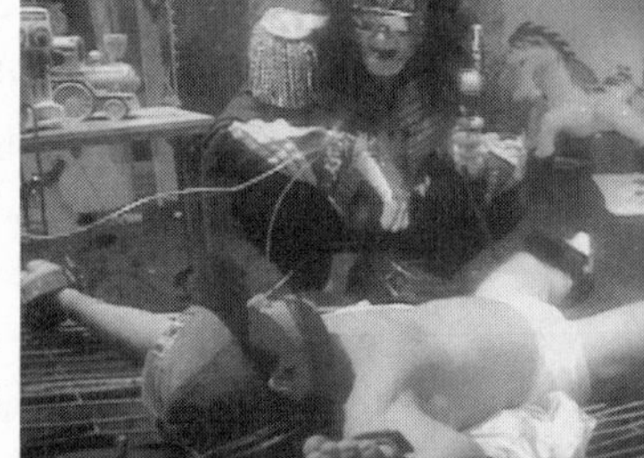

I plugged it into his butt and he started screaming and shaking.

"Now stop being such a baby, little Dexter. I'll get better reception this way. Look!" I pointed to the screen. "It's that sick, perverted show I ordered for New Year's Eve. I've been waiting all year for this. It's *Howard Stern's New Year's Rotten Eve!*"

PIMP-ASS PARENTS

Except for me, everyone seemed to forget about Michael and his troubles. Until a month later, when lawyers for Jackson and the boy settled the civil suit out of court. There were rumors of a $20 million settlement.

"I wish I had a son," I announced on the air. "I'd say, 'Boy, here's the deal. I introduce you to Michael Jackson. You spend a weekend with him. First night, you play hard to get. Jump in the tub naked but don't let him get in with you. By Sunday night, he'll want something off you. Probably digital manipulation. Some fondling and petting. Sleep in the same bed with him. Then we sue him for twenty million."

"Okay, Dad, you're the boss."

Quite frankly, I don't blame Michael Jackson that much. I blame the star-fucking pimp-ass parents of these kids who, let's face it, wouldn't be sending their precious prepubescent to spend a weekend in Harlem with just any guy. And, believe me, Macaulay Culkin's parents only let their cash cow out for the weekend because of Michael Jackson's superstar status. Why do you think more boys haven't stepped forward? Because the parents would be prosecuted.

With the settlement, Michael's troubles seemed to have faded away. Under California law, the boy could not be compelled to testify. Without the boy's testimony there was no way to prosecute. Now it was time to rehabilitate Michael's tarnished image. And believe it or not, after all of my Michael-bashing, after months of my unbelievable tirades against him, what did this space cadet do? He turned to me, proving, by the way, that he lived on another planet.

HALFTIME, WITH MICHAEL AND ME

So Michael Jackson wanted to come on my radio show. Frankly, I was shocked. Forget that I had been hammering him on the air for the last year—the pay-per-view skit alone should have been a huge embarrassment to him.

So, with all the ballbusting and crap I had been dishing out about Michael Jackson, I was truly shocked when Sandy Gallin, Michael Jackson's manager, made a pitch for a meeting. I got the impression that Sandy and Michael were completely out of it, so caught up in their Hollywood ivory towers that they only had a vague notion of what I was about. The only thing they knew about me was that I attracted large crowds when I signed books.

I don't think either one of them had actually bothered to listen to a broadcast of mine. Sandy had seen the footage of me outside of a New York bookstore and believed that I was someone who could attract the same massive crowds for Michael. Sandy's vibe was that I was a man of the people, and he wanted me to tell my radio audience Michael was okay, that he wasn't a child molester. He wanted me to urge everyone to come out onto the street, leave their homes, and show support for Michael Jackson *by staging massive demonstrations across the country.*

We would begin spontaneous mass demonstrations that would show public support for Michael. For three days they would need me to scream on the air about poor Michael Jackson and how the press and the public had abused him with these false molestation charges.

"Okay, people! Let's take to the street, and demonstrate for Michael Jackson." Those words sounded like they could come out of my mouth . . . if there was a gun up my ass.

There was more to the plan: After days of massive demonstrations, Michael would come on the radio show unannounced and thank me and my audience for standing by him while the media continued to try to frame him. I guess their thinking was that because I'm sort of a counterculture type, they would be able to reach out to that white earth-dog audience of mine and receive mass acceptance of Michael from the white middle class that worshipped me.

They were missing the point: the reason I had credibility with my audience was that I was the kind of guy who would *never* sell out and go along with a moronic notion like this. But from their point of view I was the one that could say, "Hey, man, Michael Jackson's no child molester. He's the real deal. He's a good man." ***They actually wanted me to do this!***

Of course it was a great plan except for one problem: There was no way in hell I would go along with this insanity.

I was dumbfounded. What a fucking plan this was. First of all, it was absolutely absurd. Who in their right mind felt Jackson had been cleared of all charges? Number two, who in this cynical world would take to the streets for three days over *anything*, especially accusations about Michael Jackson? In Bosnia, there's a holocaust and people don't take to the streets. And number three . . . why would you approach a sarcastic, honest-to-a-fault asshole like me with such a cockamamie idea? Maybe Rick Dees is asshole enough to go along with this—he makes Dick Clark look hardcore.

Well, when Don finished this story, I started rambling like a mental patient about how absurd all of this was. Could these guys really think I was going to go along with this? Did they know anything about my show? How jive would I sound to my audience as I took to the mean streets of New York and demanded respect for an all-American looney like Michael Jackson? In the past I had often thought Michael Jackson's ability to use the media and hype any project was well thought out. When he was thinking clearly, he constructed a mysterious aura and leaked out information slowly. His interview with Oprah was released at just the right moment to create a publicity bonanza.

It was now apparent that all of his previous publicity plans had happened quite by accident.

Don and I decided to present a better idea, an idea that could capitalize on our new relationships with the networks, especially CBS. I didn't want Michael for a radio show. I had bigger plans. Howard Stern and Michael Jackson meeting together was more important than just radio. Michael Jackson coming in unannounced was not grand enough for the great King of All Pop.

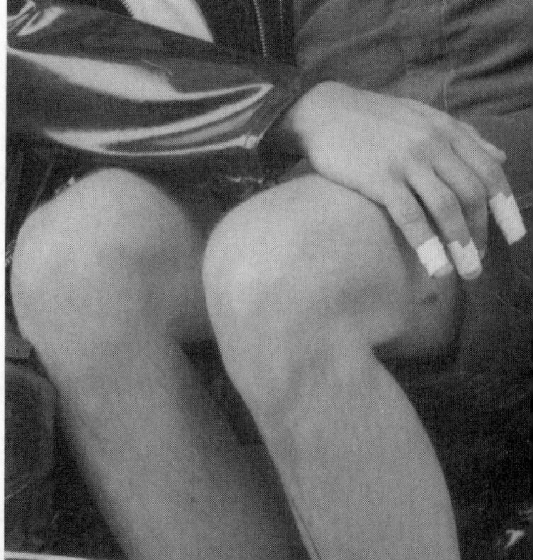

WHAT WAS REQUIRED WAS A FACE-TO-FACE MEETING, LIVE ON WORLD-WIDE TELEVISION. LIVE! NO DELAY.

Think of the danger, the anticipation, as meek little Michael got in the ring with raving lunatic Howard Stern. No rules and no question off limits. Since CBS was waiting for a list of specials, what better kickoff than a live Howard Stern—Michael Jackson broadcast? I never would have believed that I had a shot to deliver such a show, but now I had Michael's and Sandy's ears and I was gonna chew on them till something happened. I knew all of this was a long shot. Even if Michael agreed to do this, eventually he would listen to my show and get the shit scared out of him. But I was willing to try.

I knew CBS would jump at the chance, especially when Don and I laid out our master plan for the special. CBS had recently received a crushing blow when Fox stole the rights to NFL broadcasts. Imagine how Howard Stringer and CBS would salivate as we announced a special of this magnitude to go on halftime against Fox TV's first broadcast of the Super Bowl. Do you love it? What a pitch! What a special! The King of All Media does it again!!

Don waited a few days to hear back from Sandy. We didn't want to seem too pushy. Finally, Sandy called and was all jazzed up about the radio-taking-to-the-streets-totally-out-of-touch-bullshit interview idea. Don told him that we were not interested in the radio concept under any circumstances, because it wasn't special enough. If we were going to help Michael with his credibility problem, we were looking for something special, something exciting, and, of course, a big payday. We needed to do a TV special. This was probably very frustrating to Gallin because he was used to getting his own way when it came to representing these high-profile performers. But it was incredibly arrogant that he thought I would ruin my entire reputation and career by kissing the ass of Michael Jackson with a parade in the streets just for a stupid interview.

Sandy said he would think about it and if there was any interest in the TV interview, he would call.

AFTER A WEEK OR SO I FIGURED THE IDEA WAS AS DEAD AS THE DICK IN MY DAD'S PANTS. But then Sandy called Don and requested a meeting to be attended by Sandy, Michael, Don, and me. The meeting would take place after my radio show at Sandy's incredible New York apartment that he shares with one of his other clients, Dolly Parton. Sandy was coming there to talk about the radio and we were there to push for the live TV interview.

The day of the meeting I rushed off the air to be there on time. I said nothing on the air about it, which is amazing because I'm always looking for shit to talk about. But I knew that talking about it would kill the whole deal. I was so good about keeping my mouth shut that I told no one. Thoughts raced through my head about how weird Jackson is. *Fucking Never Neverland!* If I had his money and I was single, I'd have Pussy Pussyland. No time for children's rides.

Anyway, Don and I go to the meeting. On the way over I'm plotting and planning my pitch and going over it with Don. I've got to get through to this wack job to get him on live television. Motherfucker has to go along with it. The fucking scumbag is real quiet so I'll probably have to schmooze him and make him trust me. Oh, fuck!

With Ronnie driving the limo, we pull up to this really nice building, and the doorman is expecting us. Don is talking in the elevator but damn if I know what he's talking about. I'm lost in my own world. I'm getting one shot at this and I better be good. Would Jackson be there or will we arrive first? Will he be a quiet little mouse? Will it be like pulling teeth? Oh fuck, am I gonna have to kiss his ass?

Gallin greets us at the door and explains Michael isn't here yet. Good! Gives me time to feel out the situation. Gallin gives us the tour of the apartment. It's a really classy place with lots of dough poured into the decorating. There is some guy in the kitchen who is an assistant and he's washing some dishes in the sink and looks like he's doing the shit work. We sit down and we're bullshitting, and Sandy's telling us all about how he shares the apartment with Dolly, and all his clients and *blah, blah, blah.* Sandy drops Barbra Streisand's name a couple of hundred times and how she wants to buy Sandy's house but she won't pay the price.

You get the idea.

Meanwhile, no Michael Jackson. I knew it. The fucker won't show up. We're waiting fifteen, twenty minutes. That fucking mousse-haired, white-skinned, needlenose scumbag better show up, 'cause I'm getting bummed. About twenty-five minutes into this, there's a knock at the door. I've got to admit, my heart is pounding, because it's probably Mr. Wonderful, and no matter how sophisticated and blasé you think you are, you're about to meet the biggest star in the world. This guy's huge and he is so fucking famous and so bizarre—what the hell is this gonna be like? He will probably be wheeled in, in an oxygen tank.

It suddenly occurs to me when Sandy gets up from this couch that costs more than Guam, that Jackson will probably be wearing that stupid glove. I've always felt he was obsessive-compulsive and that's why he wore the glove, so he wouldn't get germs on his hands. He'd probably appreciate it if we didn't shake hands, and I'm sensitive to that. Fuck 'im. I'm gonna shake his hand anyway. That's the way *I* do business.

HE'S MELTING! HE'S MELTING!

So in walks Jackson and he's dressed up in that big fucking hat he wears—the Indiana Jones hat—and he's wearing military garb. Damn, he even dresses up on days off. He's living the Michael Jackson character twenty-four hours a day, seven days a week. The great star. He looks like he's in the gay militia.

There's a lot to take in: the pants, the penny loafers. Sheesh, what a mess! I'm sizing him up and I am surprised by how tall he is. We stretch our arms out and I give him a strong, manly handshake. Hmmm, no glove. Just some . . . surgical tape rolled perfectly around each finger tip. I say, "Pleasure to meet you," and he is silent. I hate that: Ooohhh! Wait till I get him on TV . . . live, in front of the world! I'll tell him he should speak up when spoken to. Damn, I'm having weird thoughts. I better clear my mind and stop staring at the dude or I'll get lost in the wacky clothes and blow the whole deal.

After we shake hands, Michael plops down on a chair, kind of falls backward, and sinks in. Sandy starts to talk about how Michael is in a bad situation because he's still being persecuted by the media even though he's been cleared. Fuck, is that an absurd statement. No one has been cleared, just paid off, that's all. Some kid's parents were paid off, but I'm not really listening to Sandy anyway. I'm focusing in on Michael's face. I get a close look. He's sitting no more than two feet from me, directly across, schlumped up in the chair and he's looking strange. So strange that I want to stand up, glue Sandy's mouth shut, and scream, "Let's be quiet for at least five minutes so I can stare at the mess on Michael's face!" I don't want to be caught staring so I try to catch him in my peripheral vision.

First of all, he has thick white makeup on, like Bozo the motherfucking clown. It's so thick you feel like you could take a hunk of it off and stucco a wall. And there, in the center, is this perfectly square nose, like a scarecrow wrapped in surgical tape. And his nose is wrapped like a mummy's except at the tip. At the end of his nose the tape is unraveling, so it just sort of hangs. Screw the peripheral vision. I'm looking at this weirdo, 'cause nobody does this to himself unless he wants to put on a show.

It's a hot summer day and this guy has makeup and heavy clothes, and damn, I'm getting lost in my thoughts. Better concentrate on what Sandy is saying 'cause I'm here to convince these guys that they should do a TV show with me. I'm also here to convince them that I'm a sane guy to do business with, so I better hold it together and stop staring.

Sandy's going on: "You know,

Michael's had some terrible allegations made against him in the press, but he's clearly innocent." I'm thinking to myself, ***He paid off some kid!*** It doesn't mean he's clearly innocent, but just nod your head and quit looking at the fucking surgical tape on the fingers and the nose. Stay focused on the target, Howie baby, get ready to razzle-dazzle these mothers with the pitch of the century.

Listen to Sandy . . . don't stare at Michael. They are going to want to hear from me and not Don. Don ain't the guy on the air and they want to be assured that I'm rational.

While I am staring at Michael I start to become very self-conscious. It dawns on me that Michael Jackson most likely has no idea who I am. He was probably expecting a guy who looked like Morley Safer or some disc jockey type like Rick Dees, and here I am with the schnozz and the hair stringing into my face. He is probably unnerved by my look—just as much as I am by his. He is most likely shocked that I look more like a praying mantis than a journalist. When I get my chance to speak I'll have to be real clear and show them I'm not some drug-addicted-rock-star-wannabe but a guy who's pretty levelheaded.

"And what we're thinking here is"—Sandy continues his absurd scenario—"because your radio show is so powerful, and your listeners and your fans love you, that starting tomorrow, start to talk about how Michael has been wronged and how horrible it is."

Okay, Howie, now would be a good time to nod and agree even though you don't agree at all. These guys must think I'm the world's biggest asshole if they think I'm buying this shit. Like, why don't they just bend me over the couch and stick their cocks in my ass. They're crazy, but you don't want to blow the whole fucking deal right out of the water. Just look interested and don't interrupt just yet. *For once, just listen!*

Sandy drones on with more horseshit in his very serious voice, "And we should all take to the streets and Michael won't come in at first. No one will know that Michael is coming in. We'll all take to the streets."

Sandy must be putting me on. No guy could orchestrate major careers and be serious about this idea. I know I'm supposed to be listening to this, but I find my thoughts and eyes drifting back to Michael's face. It is getting hot in Sandy's apartment and every few minutes Michael is wiping his face. The tape on his fingertips is filthy and all blackened as if he's been reading a newspaper or something. Michael keeps rubbing his face, and now there are big black smudge marks running all over it.

Now, this was weird. Michael has yet to say a word. The tape on his nose is now black because he's been rubbing his nose. *The fucker is melting!* Does Don notice? He's got to. The guy notices everything. When I'm on Letterman, Don criticizes the way I cross my legs and reminds me that I look awkward in leather pants. How could he *not* notice this? I know Don is taking in this whole scene and can't believe it. Don is not a reader of the tabloids, and he has no idea that Jackson wears the masking tape, so he must be really unprepared. How the hell is he keeping himself from laughing? How the hell am *I* keeping myself from laughing?

Shit, and look at Sandy, he keeps on talking like Michael is normal. Fuck, **I want to stand up and call 911: Come quick, we've got a melting Michael Jackson on Dolly Parton's chair. Over!**

My thoughts are racing and Sandy keeps interrupting the process with the same pitch in the same monotone: "Your audience will take to the streets, and then Michael will show up and join you in thanking the audience, and we'll talk about *blah, blah, blah.*"

How long would he go on with this drivel? Meanwhile, over in Michael's corner, the oils from his hair are now dripping onto his face. These two are a tag team from hell.

THE EMPEROR: NO CLOTHES, NO NOSE

I swear to you, I have never seen anything like this in my life. I want Sandy to discreetly whisper in Michael's ear that maybe he should excuse himself and go pull himself together in the bathroom, but obviously this is a case of the emperor having no clothes. It's tragic that when you get to be that big a star everyone is so concerned with kissing your ass that no one tells you the truth. (And by the way, when you read this, you better tell me this is funny or you're fired.)

Sandy sounds as if he is winding down on the radio pitch, and I am just about on. My mind is still racing with nose-tape questions. I read in the tabloids that the guy has had so many nose jobs that his nose caved in. I've seen pictures of it. And he threatened to sue anyone who says his nose is crushed. Looks like one too many nose jobs to me. The cartilage doesn't support the nose, so I guess he wears the tape over it. It's all wrapped perfect. I wonder if he wraps his own nose? Good question, I'll ask him that on the TV special.

"Tell me about your day, Michael. At what point do you wrap your nose? Michael, the thing is in a perfect triangle—how'd you learn to do that? How come you can't get the last piece of tape to stick?" Only a rich guy could get away with looking like a mummy. Who the fuck would leave the house with tape all over his nose?

I mean, the guy has no fucking qualms just sitting there . . .

"Howard, what do you think?" Don says.

Oh shit, I'm on.

Don is sitting next to me, and Michael and Sandy are across from me, and I focus my attention right in their eyes. I alternately look at Sandy and Michael.

Sandy has finally come to a halt. Now it is my turn and I had better get my shit together even though my brain is still locked on Michael morphing into Freddy Krueger over in the corner. My point is going to be simple and clear: Their plan is not believable and quite frankly there isn't another personality on earth who can take Michael and turn him around with the public, but they will have to trust my instincts. In order for this to be accomplished, it has to be done in a credible way.

For sure, there is one thing that is true about me, I don't take people for a ride or try to dupe them. And I wasn't gonna try and hose them by telling them an idea was good when it wasn't. In fact, if I don't believe in something, I don't take part in it.

So with the sincerity of Mother Teresa I say, "Look, guys. No one in their right mind is going to take to the street for Michael Jackson."

Oh, fuck . . . great opening line. Sandy looks disturbed and Michael looks, uh . . . as melted as an ice cream cone.

"That's not true," Sandy protests. "Did you see Michael's fans in England and Japan?"

"Yes, that's true, Sandy. But those are Michael's hardcore fans. I assume by coming on my radio show, you are trying to reach people who are skeptical about Michael Jackson. I don't have twelve-year-olds listening to my show who are going to storm-troop through America. If my audience was at a book signing, they

were there because they wanted to have a book signed. Yes, it turned into a big crowd, but storming the streets over Michael Jackson's innocence is *not going to happen.* Three people are going to take to the streets: the guy from the insane asylum and two other people following with a net."

I go on.

"If I were to interview Michael, it would send out a signal to the cynics in my audience that Michael was brave enough to face an honest and tough inquisitor. My audience knows one thing about me, my critics know one thing about me, even the people who hate me know one thing about me: I'm honest. I will ask Michael all the questions in a forthright and simple manner. If you do an interview with an Oprah Winfrey or a Barbara Walters everyone will just say 'Candy-cane journalism. Fluff piece.' This interview must be more important than that. It should be done on television—different from the Oprah interview. It has to be live and dangerous—no editing, no falsification of the record. Michael can't be accused of avoiding the issues. And that's your only hope of convincing America."

THE WOODEN DUMMY

What a pitch. I have won them over. The room is silent. Sandy looks at me and whines in a monotone, "No, that's not what we had in mind. We don't want to do that. We don't *want* to do that. We want to come on the *radio.* That's not going to fly. That's not going to work."

And Michael? He just stares off into space. Still hasn't spoken. He's a fuckin' wooden dummy, and we're putting on a show for him. I've got to learn how to do that. I've got to learn to sit in a room like a zombie and have everyone talk around me.

This is going badly. Sandy says they want the radio idea. It will work. They aren't really even interested in the radio interview. They are interested in this demonstration stuff. They wanted me to build hype. It is all so artificial—everything I'm against.

"Look," I say, "I know what I'm talking about. Consider this:

Everything that Michael Jackson does is done in a big way. He's a superstar. If you come on a local radio show, it's not important enough. What is big is the Super Bowl. Opposite the Super Bowl . . . LIVE! . . . Michael Jackson and Howard Stern. The anticipation will be great. There will be a sense of danger. The critics will be guessing and the audience won't know what to expect. Someone once said that sports is the only really good television because no one knows the ending, not even the players. A live interview will have the same effect.

"The credibility you will get from that, Michael, will turn everything around for you. Because, Michael, if you've got something to say, you're saying it to me, a broadcaster people trust. It says you're sincere and not afraid of any question or any interviewer, no matter how tough he might be. Michael, you say you've been wronged, and if you've been wronged, it's a horrible thing. Now's your chance to speak out in a humorous but very honest forum."

All of a sudden Michael stands up. Wow, I really got to him. For the first time all afternoon the wooden Indian looks excited. He's ready to take the challenge. God, I'm good.

"WHO IS THAT? WHO IS THAT?" Michael says in his high, squeaky, effeminate voice.

Oh shit, I drove the guy over the edge. Now he's hearing voices. Who is he talking to? The son of a bitch has a voice higher than my wife's.

What kind of comment is "Who is that? Who is that?"

"Who is that?"

It's the men in the white coats ready to fucking lock you up and throw away the key, you mental case. What are you talking about?

Michael continues ranting, "WHO IS THAT? YOU TOLD ME THAT THERE WAS GOING TO BE NOBODY IN THIS APARTMENT, SANDY, BESIDES MYSELF AND THESE TWO GENTLEMEN AND YOU."

Sandy jumps to attention. "Michael, that's just my assistant," he

says, way too apologetically. "He's in the other room. He's here all the time. He's harmless. He won't do anything. I'll get rid of him."

So Sandy now runs out of the room, and it's me, Don, and Michael. *Alone.* Great! This is going real well. The only time **PUPPETHEAD** has anything to say is if his superhearing picks up noise from another room. Who the hell can get a read on Sarah Bernhardt, the brooding artist over here? Oh shit, now I have to force conversation. I think Jackson would have just sat there in that trance and waited for Sandy to come back and said nothing. But maybe I can use this opportunity to build some trust here. Let me engage the dude in a little light conversation, 'cause otherwise we won't know if he is still breathing. As Jesse Jerkson would say, "Let's build a little common ground."

I remember that Michael has gotten involved with an ancient Indian form of medicine called Ayurveda through his association with Dr. Deepak Chopra. Chopra was big in the Transcendental Meditation program, so I know something about him (I've been doing TM for over twenty years), enough to bullshit my way through a conversation with Michael Jackson. I have tried Ayurvedic medicine and was even pulse-diagnosed, which is a form of detecting illness through the pulse.

I figure the key to getting Michael comfortable is to give him the feeling that I am spiritual. I'm sure he and Liz Taylor must sit around and talk about their swamis, so I figure I'll razzle-dazzle him with a little of my own spirituality.

I'm not giving up on this meeting. I want this TV show. I am tasting this TV show. I can smell it. P.U. That's a strong smell. It is going to be big!

Let him trust me. Who knows what the hell he knows about me at this point. Does he know me? Is he familiar with my work? Shit, on New Year's Eve I was fantasizing that Michael was molesting a midget. I didn't know what this guy knew, but clearly he was in the ozone. He was busy taping his nose. He wasn't listening to my show. So I break the silence.

"You know, Michael, I understand that you're a follower of Deepak Chopra," I say in my most sincere and charming voice, like the one I use to get a girl in bed.

"Oh yes, Deepak Chopra," **Mr. Bubblehead** says.

And all of a sudden, he kind of lights up—as much as one can with fifty pounds of clown makeup caked onto his face. But Michael has managed four words. Wow, I want to throw him a dog bone for this incredible feat.

My agent doesn't know what the fuck we are talking about, but you can tell he is glad somebody is saying something.

"Yeah, Michael, I'm a big fan of Deepak and Ayurvedic medicine, and I've been doing TM and I just started the Sidhis program."

Michael's mouth starts to move. The makeup is cracking around the lips. "Yes, Deepak told me how to do TM and the flying technique in the Sidhis."

I am getting some conversation going. We are rapping about various Indian foods with healing powers. I throw in a quick story about my mother, how she changed through spiritualism and TM, how I brought her back from a deep depression. I figure if I sounded like a wussy momma's boy, he will trust me. Maybe, if he thinks I helped a depressed person he will think I am gentle. *I want that fucking TV special!* This is all going down in a brief sixty seconds. **I HAVE TO MAKE HIM THINK THAT I AM A HARMLESS PUSSY, AND IT LOOKS LIKE IT IS WORKING.**

"Michael, I took care of it," Sandy interrupts, after locking his assistant in the bedroom or something.

Michael seems satisfied that Sandy has taken care of things.

I tell Sandy that Michael and I have had a great conversation while he's been out of the room, and I turn to Michael and tell him that these are the type of things we can talk about on TV. Shit, I certainly wasn't gonna tell him that once I got him on live TV he'd get a better grilling than Perry Mason could ever give. I assure them that our conversation will be as comfortable as the TM discussion.

Whoa, am I a bullshitter? But Sandy and Michael seem to be buying it. Hell, if they could buy a scenario where everyone is going to parade in

the streets, then they could certainly buy this. I am convinced Michael had been won over.

LISA MARIE: A PIECE OF ASS

Sandy wrapped up the meeting by saying that what I had to say made a lot of sense but he had to talk to Michael about it. He was very excited about my honesty and was certainly more intrigued with the TV notion. With that, Don and I got up to leave and I shook Michael's hand goodbye.

At that point I was feeling good. I knew I'd turned things around because Jackson was almost smiling. He told me that he hoped we could do this and I said, "So do I."

Don and I left the apartment. The hallway was lined with about five huge black guys who bodyguard Michael. Suits, bow ties, shaved heads, the works. Real stonefaced.

But Don and I got into my car feeling good about the meeting. The point had been made that I WAS THE ONLY ONE WHO COULD HELP MICHAEL JACKSON. Even though I had made this point and Sandy seemed to buy it, I knew the real truth: By the end of the interview he'd be dizzy from my questions. At the end of the hour, I'd probably have gotten some sort of confession. Maybe not enough for him to spend the rest of his life in jail, but with good behavior he'd be back on the street in three years. **But seriously, by sitting through my intense interrogation, he would have achieved Sandy's goal, which was to humanize him.**

Don agreed that we had given it our best shot and that a live television special was now looking like a reasonable idea to Sandy.

Business wasn't the only thing on our minds, though. That face kept haunting us. We could not believe the mess that lived on Michael Jackson's head. We were swapping stories on how we kept ourselves from laughing during this meeting. We also admitted it was pretty sad. Who was the pathetic plastic surgeon who performed that operation? DR. MENGELE?

And then we waited for our big deal to come through. We waited. We waited some two weeks and still there was no word from Sandy. Something had obviously gone wrong. I decided to take a last shot by sending a letter to Michael and Sandy. I was sure they had blown off the idea, but I badly wanted that live TV special so I wrote a quick note.

July 8, 1994

Dear Michael and Sandy,

It was great meeting with you and I enjoyed our discussion. I had a thought I'd like to share with you. I believe one of the coolest moves Michael made was his approach to the *Thriller* album when he decided to use Eddie Van Halen on guitar. Up until that point Michael was thought of as an r&b artist, and by using Eddie on the album it gave Michael instant acceptance with the MTV generation. The attitude of that constituency was that if Eddie thinks Michael's happening, we had better give Michael a chance. The result of that endorsement spoke loudly for itself.

We know that by sitting down with me, Michael will get a positive response and the same kind of acceptance. Let's do it!

Regards,
Howard Stern

Maybe Michael could see that Eddie Van Halen and various rock stars had given him acceptance in the music world and maybe Howard Stern had the ability to get him acceptance in the world of public opinion.

The letter didn't work.

We heard back from Sandy a few weeks later that it was a no go. I figured that those huge bodyguards of Michael's had told him that I was an asshole and I'd been fucking him over for years. Who knows? All I do know is that they decided that they weren't going to restore Michael's image by having him sit down with me and let me ask him tough questions. **BOY, WERE THEY RIGHT!**

What they did do was to take my live unedited interview idea and hand it to Diane Sawyer. It was hyped as a big deal because Michael had married Lisa Marie since my meeting with him and the sexuality questions still needed to be addressed. The interview was supposed to be different because there would be no editing and no question would be off limits. Sound familiar?

But of course, Diane Sawyer blew it. Candy-cane journalism. She sold out and obviously bought into Michael's and Sandy's bullshit. The interview was pathetic. She did everything but beg the audience to take to the streets for MJ. It was one long infomercial and the public saw through it. I had tried to make Michael and Sandy realize that an interview like this was as good

as no interview at all. It accomplished nothing. Fluff! Diane Sawyer, who's just Sally Jessy Raphael with better skin and hair, was as bad and gushy as Oprah.

"I don't like young boys. I swear. It's true. Children love me. They follow me everywhere," the high-voiced wonder told the blonde-bimbo Sawyer.

"Hey, Michael," I would have said, "why are children sleeping in bed with you?"

Lisa Marie, who, by the way, turned out to be a piece of ass that I'd like to fuck, chimes in with, "They follow him into the bathroom and kick me out of my own bed." Boy, with all that money the Presley estate has, you'd think they could have sent her to a Swiss finishing school to teach her how to speak properly.

Hey, Diane, where were your friggin' follow-up questions?

"Why are these kids running around unsupervised in the house?"

"Where are their parents?"

"Why are kids along on the fucking honeymoon?"

"What about the kid who sued?"

"Why weren't his allegations aired?"

"Why don't these friendships last?"

"Why are these boys dumped as soon as they hit puberty?"

"If he loves children so much, where are the little girls?"

HEY, DIANE, I DON'T HAVE A FANCY JOURNALIST'S BACKGROUND, BUT ANY MORON ON THE STREET WOULD HAVE ASKED THESE QUESTIONS. YOU SELLOUT!

And what's with the nose?

Diane blew it. She was embarrassed to do the interview and it showed.

"Michael," I would have said, "let's go through your day at home. When do you tape the schnozz? Where do the parents stay when the kids are sleeping over?"

I watched the Diane Sawyer interview and laughed when the end credits came up. You could see the lights go down and Michael jumping up and down. I could just picture Sandy Gallin and the other salaried spin doctors standing behind Diane Sawyer going, "Bravo, Michael. Home run. Home run." And Michael's doing these weird poses and dancing around thrilled that he's off the hook.

And then I realized that the son of a bitch even got the masses into the street for him. Of course, he had to pay them, but take a look at that stupid movie trailer that Diane Sawyer ran during the show. The streets are lined with weeping fans. They're holding up signs saying KING OF POP. And here comes Michael, like a conquering monarch. He's got the gay militia outfit on, with the hockey shinguards, and he marches into town, surrounded by troops, waving, blowing kisses. The camera is pulled back so you can't see the melting face. It's a perfect world. There's confetti and tickertape falling and fans are fainting. And then they unveil a giant statue of Michael. It's interesting that the only line of dialogue in that whole video is spoken by an eight-year-old crewcut white boy who looks at the statue and says, "Michael, I love you." Up there on the screen is the bizarre scenario I was supposed to create. Sure. Only in the movies. My fans would have booted me in the ass.

And everybody falls into line. VH—1 does the MJ weekends and MTV premieres the video and ABC gives free ads and NBC premieres the second video. They're all sellouts. Not me. I'm pure. I'm the man. I'm the only asshole who didn't get anything going with Michael Jackson. I'm real proud of myself. My father was right: I'm a moron. Maybe I'll write another letter to Michael Jackson. I'm a pitiful *schmuck!* (But I did get a chapter in this book out of it, didn't I?)

Meanwhile, Michael's record sales go in the toilet. Why? Well, partly it's just that the music sucks, and partly it's the nasty smell of those charges, charges that linger in the public's mind because there are questions that were never answered, like "Hey, Michael? Why are you afraid to deal with the Howard Stern inquisition?"

We'll never know.

CHAPTER 3

THE KING OF ALL MENTAL ILLNESS

Every celebrity book should have revelations. Oprah Winfrey has a great story. She's been molested by half her family tree. Lucky fatso. Richard Pryor grew up in a brothel. Classic. Look at Roseanne and her great revelations about molestation and broken marriages. Tim Allen's served time for dealing coke, and Jerry Seinfeld revealed, well, that he didn't like airplane food. So Jerry's a little shallow. Take a look at Robin Quivers—she's been through the mill. She was lucky. Her father fingered her, so her first chapter was dynamic. But, me, my big revelation was . . . my Dad called me a moron. Who the fuck is going to get excited about that? God, how I prayed when I wrote my first book that my father had fucked me in the ass instead of just yelling at me. If only my mother had punished me with ENEMAS.

"Good evening, Ladies and Gentlemen, I'm Dan Rather, CBS news. We interrupt tonight's *Murder She Wrote* to bring you this special announcement. According to unnamed sources who have seen advance copies of Howard Stern's new book, he was strapped down to the kitchen table while his mother, the Butcher of Roosevelt, administered ***chocolate milk enemas.*** Filling his huge asshole with liquid was punishment for not cleaning his room and not paying attention during piano recitals. Many experts say that this is the worst case of child-rearing, pardon the expression, in history. We apologize for the graphic language, but shit, this is big news. Good night and be brave."

Okay, maybe it wouldn't be on CBS Evening News, but I'd bet Fox would have been all over this.

When I wrote *Private Parts*, even my editor was looking for a little juice. "C'mon, you have to reveal something big."

I said to her, "LISTEN, JIZZ PIE"—that's my nickname for Judith—"I have a secret I've never told anyone but I don't know if I want to reveal all." She told me to write it up and let her look at it. So, I wrote it up and threw it in my drawer. Fuck her, I didn't feel like sharing my mental illness with the world. I knew it was best to save this for a second book. The first book sells on curiosity alone, but you have to have real juicy garbage for your follow-up or you're gonna get your ass kicked. So here's the revelation. Tim Allen better shoot six people if he wants to top this. **Ellen DeGeneres better go lesbo and eat out sixteen women in Macy's window** because I've got a good story here. Sit back, relax, and feel good about your own miserable existence because your pal Howie's life is a nightmare.

For twenty years, I'd been in the grips of a devastating mental illness, OCD—**obsessive compulsive disorder.** Unknown to anyone around me, even to my lovely wife, Alison, **I WAS A SLAVE TO A SERIES OF RITUALISTIC BEHAVIORS THAT MADE ME A PRISONER OF MY OWN PSYCHE.** I suffered alone, too embarrassed to talk to anyone about it. Even though I could be locked in rituals for hours at a time, I hid it from the world.

Now, for the first time ever, I will reveal the depths of my psychic hell and relate how my redemption came at the hands of a little old man in a long white coat, Dr. John Sarno. Saint Sarno, to me.

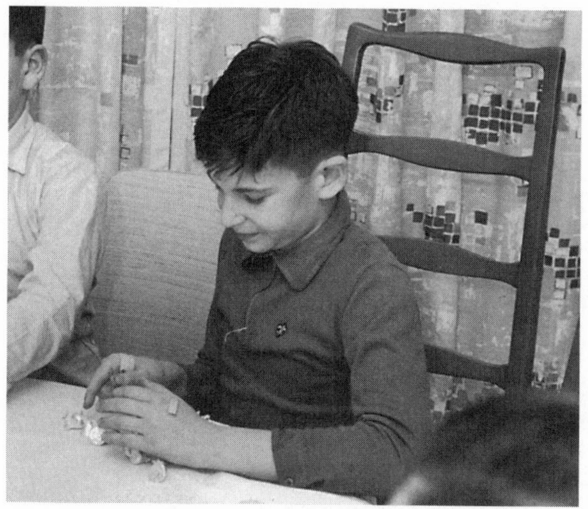

I never had any symptoms of OCD as a kid. I never worried about black cats crossing my path, or stepping on cracks, or any of that bullshit. It wasn't until I was in college that I began to experience some weird obsessional behavior. And I was convinced that it happened because of my experimentation with drugs.

When I was in ninth grade in Roosevelt, a police officer came to visit our class. He brought a huge wooden display case, the kind you might collect bugs in. But this one was filled with all sorts of different drugs. He'd point to each drug and do a little lecture on it. "This terrible drug makes you sleepy and horny. This pill makes you lose all sense of reality . . ." I was like, "Wow!" THIS WAS THE GREATEST ADVERTISEMENT EVER FOR TAKING DRUGS. I was the kind of kid that once I learned something, I couldn't wait to do it. ***I wanted to take every drug in that frigging display.***

I began by smoking pot and hash in high school, but I never really dug it. Pot made me completely paranoid. I would sit in a room full of people and I would think they were all talking about me. But I would use grass as a way to get laid. To the girls I hung around with then, a nickel bag was like being with a major dealer. I'd turn them on and, if I was lucky, I'd score.

When I started at Boston University, my drug taking accelerated. I tried amphetamines, but I hated them. My eyes would be wide open on speed and I would have this perpetual haze in front of me. I was totally wired. I hated that feeling.

I liked 'ludes. Quaaludes were the greatest drug ever invented as far as I was concerned. 'Ludes were a combination muscle relaxant, tranquilizer, and sedative, all packed into one white pill that cost twenty-five cents. It was like being drunk without any of the side effects of drinking. **A 'LUDE COULD TRANSFORM AN UGLY, SKANKY CHICK INTO A *PENTHOUSE* PET.** On 'ludes, I fucked girls you wouldn't even look at. Then I'd drop another 'lude and fuck them again.

My freshman year at B.U., I started hanging out with the druggies. I remember one time this dealer named Bob offered to turn me onto cocaine. He handed me a straw and I did the classic Woody Allen move: I blew out and half his stash went flying off the table. He was ready to kill me but then he laid out some more lines. This time, I inhaled.

Right away, I started feeling weird. I thought coke was supposed to be like a rush, but my body started feeling like I'd done about a hundred 'ludes. **Then my nose started bleeding.**

"Are you sure this is coke?" I asked him.

"I'm not sure what it is. Some guy sold this to me," he said.

Turns out it was HEROIN, but I didn't know that then. I just remember I roamed the halls of my dormitory propostioning girls because I had the euphoric notion they would like me.

I didn't really want to experiment with heavy drugs that you could get addicted to, but I did want to hallucinate. To my immature mind that would be the ultimate. This guy Bob knew that, so one day in a science class, he handed me a big capsule.

"It's peyote," he said.

I looked down at it. There was all sorts of weird stuff crammed into this clear gel capsule the size of a horse pill. Actual twigs were coming out of the sides of this thing. And the whole pill was being held together with Scotch tape! Who cared? Like a moron, I popped it right there. I didn't hallucinate, but I did get sick.

I decided that the only way to really hallucinate was to take LSD. That was the big kahuna. It turned out that one of the guys I copped 'ludes from had just scored some acid. This guy was the greatest salesman for acid, too. He was a blond jock. Totally unassuming.

"Acid is great," he told me, and he gave me a tiny piece of paper divided into four squares. This was blotter acid, he explained. Each square had a hit on it. In the middle of the square, you could see the little outline of the acid. It looked almost like the circle on caps, the things you bought for your cap gun when you were a kid.

"These are four four-way hits. You put it under your tongue and just suck on it for a while," he said.

I had no idea what he was talking about. What's a four-way hit? I just saw four squares.

"Do I swallow it?" I asked.

"You can, but you don't have to. Just stick the piece of paper under your tongue. It'll go right into your system almost instantly. You're gonna hallucinate your brains out."

I ran back to my room. My roommate, Lew, was there. I was all excited and wanted Lew to trip with me but he was too level-headed. He was going to be a doctor and he didn't want to fuck up his career by taking drugs. So I just threw the acid in my drawer.

MY FUTURE COLLEGE ROOMMATE LEW AND I AT THIRTEEN YEARS OLD

A few weeks later, I met this cute girl named Lisa. She came up to my dorm room and we went to one of the lounges. We were just talking when, all of a sudden, I leaned over and we started making out. I was shocked. I thought that I could really nail her. What was great was that I wouldn't even have to take a 'lude to think she was cute.

So we're making out and then she says she has to go.

"I'd like to see you again," I said. How suave.

"Why don't you come by my room tomorrow morning?" she said.

That night, I could hardly sleep. The next morning, I knock on her door and she opens it. And I'm in shock. There's this guy named John sitting on one of the beds. Lisa goes over and sits next to him. I'm forced to sit on the bed opposite them.

Now I don't know what to do. **Why is this guy John here?** Is he gonna split soon? Am I gonna get laid?

"Want to smoke some hash?" John asked.

He pulled out a pipe and we started smoking hash. And smoking. And smoking. I'm totally stoned. I'm sitting there like a lump and all these paranoid thoughts are racing through my mind. Why isn't he leaving? Am I supposed to leave? Why did she invite me? Last night she was making out with me like crazy, so why's this guy here?

Meanwhile, this guy's rapping away like crazy. And I'm convinced that she panicked overnight and she thought that I would want sex, so she called her friend to sit there with her so I couldn't make a move on her. This whole thing becomes like a stoned Mexican stand-off. Nobody's blinking. Finally, around eight P.M., I got up to leave. In my paranoid mind, I think I saw a sign of relief on her face, like *finally this jerk's leaving*.

I'm so stoned that I barely made it back to my room. Then, for some ***insane*** reason, I decide to drop the acid. What was I thinking? Lew will not trip with me, no matter how much I beg him. Also, **IT'S PROBABLY NOT THE BEST IDEA IN THE WORLD TO DROP ACID AFTER YOU'VE JUST SMOKED HASH SPIKED WITH GOD-KNOWS-WHAT AFTER YOU'VE BEEN REJECTED BY A GIRL WHO WAS SUCKING**

YOUR TONGUE LIKE THERE WAS NO TOMORROW THE NIGHT BEFORE.

But I was a moron. I took one of the four-way hits and popped it under my tongue. Then I lay down and started talking to Lew. What I didn't know, and what that asshole acid salesman didn't explain to me, was that each four-way hit was supposed to be divided into four separate pieces. I had just dropped enough acid to get *four people* stoned out of their gourd.

A few seconds later, I looked over at the wall at a poster of a waterfall and the picture had come to life. Water is rolling off the wall, leaves are blowing, the clouds are moving. I'm going, "This is fantastic!" I'm having a great time.

For about thirty seconds. Then it dawned on me that ***my mind was totally out of control.*** A horrible sense of panic seized me. All of a sudden, I'm smelling burnt flesh. I look over at Lew and he's turned purple. It turned out that the blotter acid was laced with speed, so now not only am I stoned on hash and tripping on a quadruple hit of acid, but I'm also speeding like crazy. I'm convinced that I'm never coming down from this.

Then Lew does a ***terrible*** thing. He goes, "I know what'll get you off." So he puts on a Grateful Dead album, BUT

I HATE THE FUCKING DEAD. Now I'm bumming out even more.

I can't even get off the bed now. Lew runs out of the room and he returns with this guy named Steve. Steve walks in and starts staring at me like I was a fucking animal in the zoo. That's making me feel much better. Then they both run out and come back with this other guy named Mike. This guy Mike is a senior and he's the King of the Druggies.

He takes one look at me.

"You got to get him some oranges," he says. Apparently, Vitamin C is supposed to help you come down off the acid. But I had done so much acid on top of the hash that I could have eaten **TWENTY THOUSAND ORANGE GROVES** and it wouldn't have helped. But Lew starts trying to force-feed me oranges.

"Lew, get all these people away. Get the fucking oranges away from me," I screamed.

The other guys split. Then I slowly got up and I looked into the mirror. I saw my face turn purple, then black. ***Then the flesh ripped off my face and I saw the bones of my skull. My veins turned into worms and the worms started crawling out of my eye sockets.*** On top of this, I'm experiencing the worst thoughts and smells imaginable.

So I decided to light up a cigarette. I sucked in some smoke and I blew it out and it came out black. I looked down at my arms and all the hairs on my arms started growing—then they turned into bugs, running up and down my arms. But I tried not to panic. I looked up at the clock to see what time it was and I couldn't read the fucking clock—the numbers had each folded into themselves and it was all a blob. Now I'm convinced I'll never get my sight back. I was permanently brain damaged. I rushed over to the wall and tried to read the posters. Each letter was dancing on the page.

That's when I heard that horribly familiar voice. It was shrill and it pierced my consciousness. It was my mother. "HOWARRRDD! LOOK WHAT YOU'VE DONE! YOU

DID ACID, AND THIS IS WHAT HAPPENS. YOU'VE LOST YOUR MIND!"

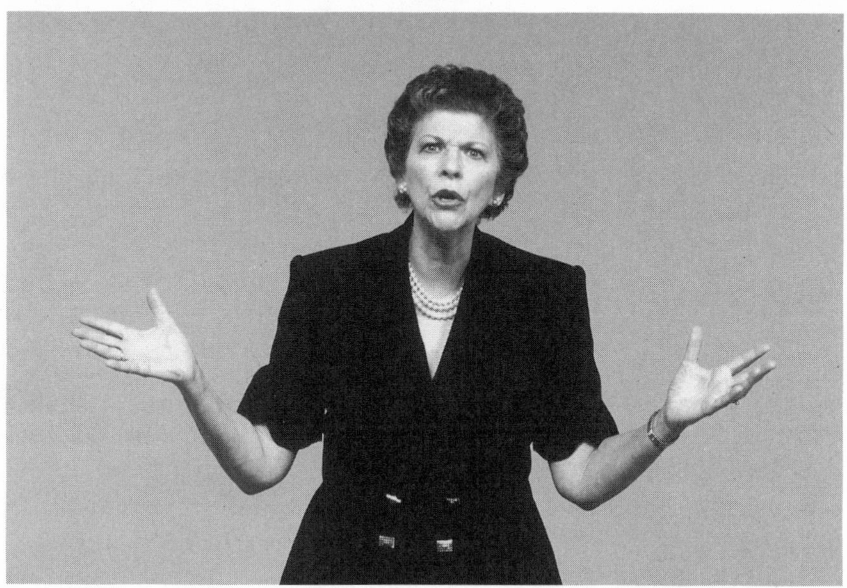

It made sense. When I was a kid, if I went out of the house without a coat, she thoroughly convinced me that I would get a cold. Cause and effect. Now look what I'd done. Instead of just flowing with this weird new experience, my mother's fears were exploding in my head. I couldn't relax and get off on this alteration of my perception. I was convinced that I had fucked myself up, maybe permanently.

I decided to try to sleep. I wanted to take a piss before I went to bed. Lew assists me into the bathroom and I go to pee and I can't feel my cock. My cock is minuscule to begin with, but now I can't **find it**, I can't **feel it**, it's **totally numb**. It feels like a tiny piece of wood. That freaked me out. With pot I could turn off the paranoia by shutting my eyes and going to sleep. So Lew helped me back to bed, we shut out the lights, and I closed my eyes. Now the hallucinations are completely out of control. Now, even with my eyes closed, the hallucinations won't go away. I was totally fucked.

"Lew, I gotta get out of this room," I said.

Lew helped me to the elevator, but I refused to go on. I didn't want anyone to see me like this—so Lew grabbed me by the hand and helped me down twenty flights of stairs. I remember taking the first few steps and I was totally exhausted and out of breath. To this day, I don't know how I made it down all twenty flights.

We got outside and Lew wanted to go visit our friend Rita. But that idea freaked me out. I didn't want to see anybody. I couldn't talk, I couldn't walk, I couldn't read, I couldn't think

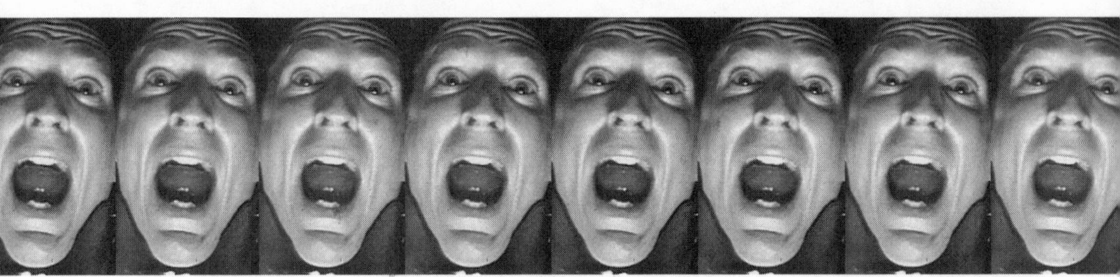

straight. I figured this was it for me. I had made the classic blunder, like the kid who dives into the swimming pool and there's no water and he breaks his neck and he's in a wheelchair for the rest of his life.

I was fucked.

Lew took me down to the Charles River and we sat there. I looked up in the sky and I saw the moon and I went, "Oh, look, the sun, the sun." I WAS A TOTAL VEGETABLE. Every few minutes, Lew checked in with me. It felt like we were sitting there for five minutes, but it turned out that we were there till four in the morning. It was the longest period of quiet I've ever had in my nonstop motor-mouth life. Finally, Lew got tired and he dragged me back to the room. He wanted to get some sleep because his parents were visiting us in the morning.

Lew went to sleep but I just sat up in my bed. I think I dozed off for an hour or two but then at around ten in the morning, all these sirens went off. It's a fucking fire drill. I'm jarred out of bed, and my glands are completely swollen, I can't swallow, and I'm still tripping! Again Lew has to help me down the twenty fucking flights of stairs and we're standing in front of the dorm when Lew's parents show up. I just told them I was sick and I was going back to bed and Lew took off to go to breakfast with his parents.

I was VIOLENTLY ILL FOR THE NEXT TWO WEEKS. My glands were swollen and my throat was a razor.

But at least I came down off the acid. I had a few mild flashbacks, but I felt that my sanity was restored.

You'd think after a horrible experience like this a sane person would have no desire to ever touch another drug again. But **there's nothing sane about me.**

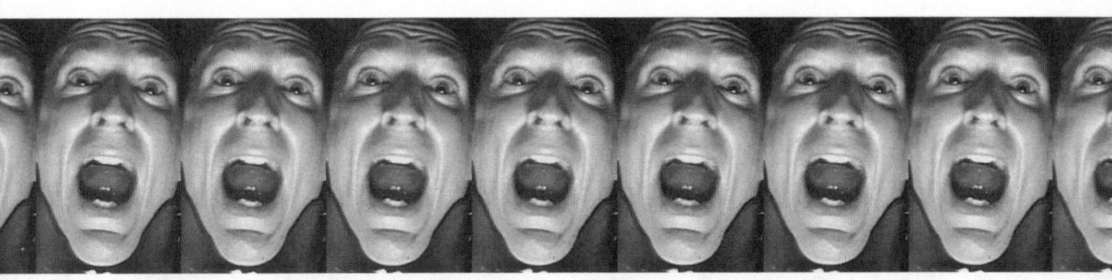

My Space Odyssey

Naturally when a few of my friends decided to go and see *2001: A Space Odyssey*, I had to go. I'd seen the film already and hated it. Everyone told me the reason I hated it was because the director, Stanley Kubrick, designed it for people to see on acid. "Oh, my God!" my mother's voice yelled in the back of my head, "I CAN'T BELIEVE YOU'D BE SO STUPID TO TAKE THAT GARBAGE ACID AGAIN! FEH!"

I split two tabs of acid with my friends Dave and Barry. I figured I'd be fine because now I knew the proper amount of acid to take.

We get to the theater and I'm flying pretty high. I was convinced everyone in the theater was staring at me. Of course they were staring at me. I'm a six-foot-five gork.

I turned to my friends and said, "Everyone in this whole theater is looking at me."

"Shut up, asshole. No one's looking at you," my friends said. "The whole damn theater is on acid. No one gives a shit about you. Stop thinking you're so important. Just stare at the fucking screen and shut up."

The movie started, but I was totally distracted by the design on the ceiling.

"Guys!" I whispered. "Guys. Dave. Barry. Moe. Larry. The ceiling. It has holes. They're opening up. *They're dripping on me!*"

"Sh-sh-sh. Quiet, asshole. I'm trying to watch the movie," Dave said.

Things were getting really bad.

People were staring at me.

The ceiling was dripping on me.

The movie was boring.

STANLEY KUBRICK CAN SUCK MY COCK. THE CEILING HAD A BETTER PLOT THAN THE MOVIE.

"Guys. Guys. Look at the ceiling!" I started getting really loud. I was panicking! The ceiling was filled with holes that were getting bigger, as big as the holes in my head.

"GUYS! LOOK! THE HOLES! THE HOLES!"

Now everyone *was* looking at me. My friends were really pissed. I was ruining their trip. They were "sh-sh-shushing" me. Everyone was sh-sh-shushing me. Strangers were sh-sh-shushing me. The holes in the ceiling were sh-sh-shushing me.

I was no Tim Leary. I was a total fucking embarrassment to my two friends who were just sitting there watching the movie . . . until . . . HAL, the computer and star of this dumb movie, spoke to Keir Dullea's character, who just happened to be named "Dave."

"DAVE," HAL the computer said in a flat, frightening monotone. "DAVE . . . I THINK WE BOTH KNOW WHAT'S GOING ON HERE. DAVE . . . DON'T TRY ANYTHING FUNNY. I THINK WE BOTH KNOW WHAT YOU'RE UP TO."

I looked over and my friend Dave was under the chair. He was turning colors. Dave thought the movie was talking to him.

"DAVE! What's wrong with you? Are you crazy?" I said.

"The movie's talking to me," Dave protested, from under his chair.

"*DAVE*," HAL continued. "DAVE . . . What are you doing, DAVE?"

Dave started screaming, "THE MOVIE IS TALKING TO ME!"

I tried to calm him down. "Dave, get with the program. The movie is NOT talking to you."

He started to relax.

"Dave, you want to get upset? Look up at the ceiling! The fucking ceiling has almost completely melted! We've got five minutes to live!"

By now everyone in the theater was asking us to leave.

Barry and I pulled Dave out from under his chair and ran out of the theater.

MY BRAIN HICCUPS

I never took another drug again. But that was also the beginning of my battles with OCD. Years later, when I started reading up about OCD, it was characterized as a brain hiccup. My brain first started hiccuping after that disastrous acid trip. I can recall sitting at my desk at B.U., studying for exams, and having the strange feeling that ***if my pencil wasn't in a certain position, then things wouldn't work out right with my test.***

From that, I graduated into other obsessions. Somehow, I decided **I would have to read certain sentences three times** if I was going to do well in class. Then I had to open my books a certain way or I wouldn't do well. There was no real logic to these decisions, there was only a dull feeling of anxiety that if I didn't go through these rituals, I wouldn't do well in my classes, or I'd never find a job after graduation. It got so bad that if I was studying in the library and I had finished and wanted to take a break, I would look up at the clock. If the clock read 3:06, I would have to sit in my chair and wait until it turned to 3:07 because **I HAD SOMEHOW CONVINCED MYSELF THAT ODD NUMBERS WERE LUCKIER THAN EVEN ONES.** Whatever I was doing, I must have been doing it right, because I wound up acing most of my courses and graduating B.U. magna cum laude.

Now I had a degree in broadcasting, and I had to try to crack one of the hardest occupations. Since I was a little kid, one of my biggest fears had been that I wouldn't be able to earn a living. MY FATHER USED TO YELL AT ME ALL THE TIME, TELLING ME I WAS WORTHLESS, I wasn't good at anything. Plus, I never had a job because my mother felt that since I was having such a hard time at high school, a job would be further distraction from my studies.

I was so hung up on this fear of earning a living that **I was even frightened to marry Alison.** I was just starting out in radio, making less than a hundred a week in Westchester. Alison was getting her master's degree in social work. We weren't into having a kid right away. Yet with all that, I was still worried about supporting a family that we weren't even planning yet. It got so bad that I even gave up my radio job and took a bullshit job in advertising. Thankfully, my mother and Alison persuaded me to quit and get back into radio, even if it meant initially sacrificing the salary.

I got my job back at the Westchester station and then I took a job in Hartford. And although it didn't affect my on-air performance, my OCD rituals were beginning to become a real pain in the ass. It took me forever to close down after my on-air stint. If I had a tortured way of reading a book, imagine the machinations I had to go through to put my records away. ***I had to put the record back into the sleeve a certain way***, then it had to be filed just right. That was one of the reasons I hated having to play music. During my show I would just throw all the records on the floor because I didn't have time for the elaborate ritual it took to file each one away.

Of course, I couldn't tell anyone about these stupid games I was playing in my head. I had to be a tower of strength. My parents thought psychiatrists were a big waste of money. You just couldn't think you needed psychiatric help if you were Ben Stern's son. In a way, I'm glad because I think it would have made my problem even worse if I had sought help from conventional medical sources. I probably would have gone on medication and had all sorts of side-effects. I was still operating under the assumption that I had somehow **FUCKED MY BRAIN** during the acid trip so I decided that if I ate a lot and built my body up, somehow that would help my brain chemistry.

I was also trying to combat a chronic history of minor medical ailments. Every time I started at a new station, I would lose my voice. Then almost every weekend, I'd come down with colds, sore throats, and swollen glands. This started when I left Hartford for Detroit. Everything revolved around the four hours a day that I'd be on the air. It was like I'd hear my mother's voice again: "YOU'D BETTER NOT GO OUT WITHOUT A JACKET OR YOU'LL CATCH A COLD." I was deathly afraid of doing anything that would jeopardize those four hours a day.

So while I was in Detroit, I started eating to build myself up. You have to understand that I knew **absolutely zilch** about nutrition.

THIS IS THE BOY WHO ATE PORK CHOPS AND MASHED POTATOES WITH CHICKEN FAT AND A SALAD DRENCHED IN THICK DRESSING HIS WHOLE LIFE.

My idea of dieting was to cut back to two pieces of fried chicken instead of six. I would eat muffins and gravy and fried egg sandwiches for breakfast, then McDonald's for lunch. Dinner was just as bad. On top of this, I was always taking antibiotics for fear of coming down with sore throats.

FAT AND FRIGHTENED

By the time I got to Washington, I had built myself up all right. ***I was up to 240 pounds.*** The first time Robin met me she was shocked because she was expecting the guy from my press photo. I show up in Washington in person and I've got a bad moustache, 87 chins, and I'm this huge beast. It's amazing that Robin didn't run away and go back into nursing.

Meanwhile, my eat-to-get-fit strategy wasn't exactly working. Robin and I would order a huge breakfast and **EAT IT ON THE AIR FOR TWENTY MINUTES** at a time. Then when our shift was over, we'd race over to Roy Rogers and get a double bacon cheeseburger, fries, and a chocolate shake. Robin said she used to watch me walk down the street in front of her and I would waddle like a duck. Of course, by matching me meal for meal, she was no lightweight herself.

Instead of getting hardier, I was getting sicker and sicker. My throat, which was constantly tickling me in Detroit, flared up. One doctor wound up putting me on heavy steroids. But still I ate. And Alison was an enabler. Not only was she cooking these gigantic dinners, she was going to the Big Men's store and continually upgrading my pants. It wasn't until we visited my parents that I was shocked back to reality. We got in late on a Friday night and went to sleep shortly after arriving. The next morning, my parents barged into our room at six A.M.

"Howaaarrd, come into our bedroom immediately! YOUR FATHER AND I NEED TO HAVE A LITTLE TALK WITH YOU," my mother pronounced. I was still

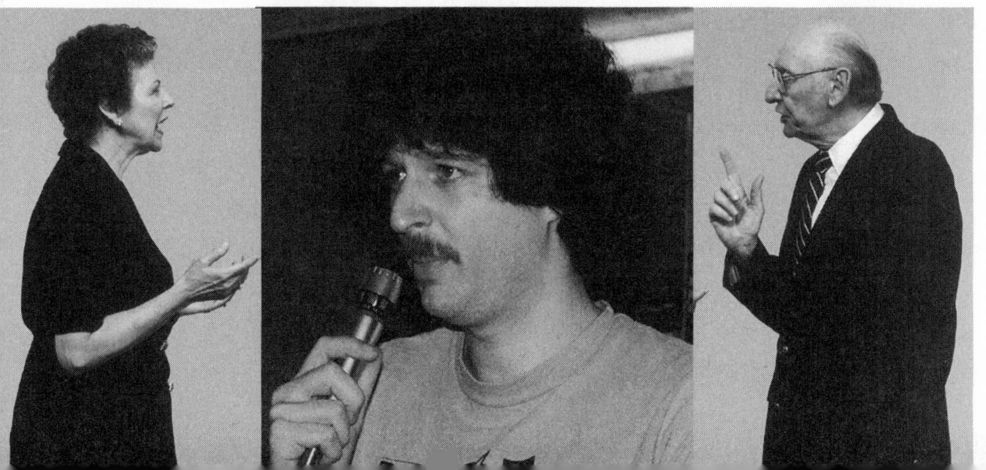

groggy, but I got out of bed. I'm sure Alison had no idea what was going on. She must have thought they wanted to talk about her. But she was off the hook. I was the one that they were intent on berating.

"You look disgusting. So fat. Look what you've done to yourself." Today they would call what they did an intervention. Back then, I just thought it was an interrogation. But I needed it. **I was bloated, out-of-shape, and sickly.** Plus, I was about to leave Washington and come back to New York at WNBC. This was my dream job, my return to my home town, and I didn't want to do anything that would fuck up my big chance.

HOWARD, YOU ARE GOING TO DIE

Of course, it took me a while to heed my parents' advice. I started at NBC and had to leave during my first day on the air because I lost my voice. After Robin joined us at WNBC we continued our wonderful eating habits. I would order in Chinese food and pizza during every show. Then I would go home a few hours later to my lovely enabler, Alison, and she would make over two pounds of spaghetti with about a pound of meat sauce.

My nutritional habits just about ruined the joy of seeing Alison give birth to our first child. During Alison's labor, I snuck downstairs and bought a hamburger out of a vending machine. It looked like a **dehydrated hockey puck**, but I popped it in the microwave and scarfed it down. I made it back upstairs to see Alison pop Emily out, but the hamburger made me nauseous. I went home, **THREW UP**, and came down with food poisoning. I couldn't even go back to the hospital to see Emily and Alison for two days. By eating that way, I wasn't exactly helping combat the colds and sore throats.

It was another doctor who sent me on the path to my eventual physical and mental health, a Dr. Jacobs, who had an office in Queens. **"You keep on going the way you're going and you're going to die very soon,"** he told me.

I was scared shitless. "How can I die? I'm not that sick. I just get these chronic sore throats and colds."

"You have a case of ongoing pneumonia," he said. "You've been on antibiotics for years. **YOU HAVE NO IMMUNE SYSTEM LEFT.** Plus, you're overweight. If the pneumonia doesn't kill you, a heart attack will."

"So what do I do?" I asked.

"If I were you, I'd join a gym and start exercising."

That was all he said. I don't think he even knew what to do, I was so fucked up. But I took his advice. I joined the North Shore Health Club. The gym totally intimidated me. I was so embarrassed about the way I looked that I jogged on an outdoor track before I even started at the gym.

I needed someone to teach me the secrets of the gym, which was filled with all these big guys who were in unbelievable shape. I saw this one huge, muscular guy who was working out there and I went up to him and asked him if he'd like to train me. His name was Steve Basile and it just so happened he had always wanted to make his living running a gym and teaching fitness. So I hired him.

Steve and I hit it off right from the beginning. He showed me how to do weights. He taught me about aerobic activity. He put me on a workout schedule that wasn't mindbogglingly intense but would reap great dividends if I followed the proper form. Most important, Steve taught me proper nutrition. I'd been to hundreds of doctors, but none of them helped. He taught me about carbohydrates, both simple and complex. He showed me I could eat in stages throughout the day—I didn't have to binge and have three huge meals.

I immediately cut out all sugars. I began to take nutritional supplements, vitamins, and minerals. It got to the point where a plain baked potato started tasting like a hot fudge sundae to me. I astounded Steve with my discipline. The weight dropped right off me. I got into decent shape. My colds and sore throats disappeared. I was psyched. Now I was convinced I was on the right track to a sound body.

I figured that since I was finally feeding my brain properly, between my nutritional gains and my meditation, I would be free from my OCD rituals once and for all. Little did I know that NOT ONLY WOULD THE OCD WORSEN, but within a short number of months, I would begin battling far more serious physical ailments than a little laryngitis.

My Right Side Domination Scheme

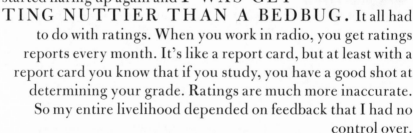

Getting fired by NBC didn't help my mental stability. Alison and I had finally started a family, we had moved into a nice house, and now the rug was pulled out from under us. Even though I was the most popular personality on the station, it was a stunning blow to my self-esteem. I had been publicly humiliated. All my recurring nightmares of earning a living to support a family were resurrected. Although **my agent** was suggesting I sit home and collect on my NBC contract while he sorted out offers, I urged him to negotiate a deal so I could get back on the radio.

At K-Rock, the pressures of reestablishing myself at the top of the radio heap were wreaking havoc on my delicate psyche. My OCD started flaring up again and I WAS GETTING NUTTIER THAN A BEDBUG. It all had to do with ratings. When you work in radio, you get ratings reports every month. It's like a report card, but at least with a report card you know that if you study, you have a good shot at determining your grade. Ratings are much more inaccurate. So my entire livelihood depended on feedback that I had no control over.

Since I'm pretty much a control freak to begin with, I found myself doing ritualistic things that I thought would assure me that my ratings would dominate my competitors'. I still believed that my brain was hiccuping these messages thanks to that four-way hit. **THEN I BEGAN TO BELIEVE THAT THE RIGHT SIDE OF MY BODY DOMINATED THE**

LEFT SIDE. Therefore, I would have to do certain things with my right side to insure my success.

Let's take ratings sheets, for instance. When I'd get the monthly reports, I had to read them a certain way. The right side of my face had to be above the page. Then, in order to turn the page, I had to grasp the tip of the top right corner of the page with my thumb and my pinky. Who in the world turns a page that way? I did. I had to because my pinky was the farthest right finger on my right hand, so by turning the page over that way, I would dominate the page and therefore dominate the ratings.

It gets even nuttier. If I wanted to watch TV, say, Letterman's show on Channel 4, first I had to tune past Channel 4 to Channel 5 because five dominated four. Therefore, I was greater than four and I dominated David Letterman and anything I would do would be better. ***This drove Alison nuts*** when we watched TV together. When we were ready to turn off the set and go to sleep, I would click through all the channels up to the end, which was 37, and then turn the set off to static. Of course, by doing that I could go to sleep knowing I would dominate every one of those channels. Thank God I lived in Long Island where we get Cablevision. Imagine if I had a good cable company and could get 125 channels!

Suddenly, I found that everything I was doing was tied into this right side domination scheme. I couldn't just walk through a doorway—I had to make sure that my right side went in first. If I wasn't thinking and I entered a room with my left foot first, I would have to leave the room and reenter the right way. **When I brushed my teeth, washed my hands, tied my shoelaces, my right hand had to dominate.**

Forget about going to bed at night. I needed Alison to come up and say goodnight to me, not only because she provided me with emotional support, but also because just turning off the lights and closing the door and positioning the alarm clock and turning off the phones might take me over twenty minutes to accomplish. I had to turn the clock a certain way, touch the top of the door three times (because ***odd numbers were better than evens***), turn the TV to static, and on and on. With Alison it got done in two seconds, lights off, clock set, goodnight, boom, the door's slammed.

I have to laugh when I hear that my radio competition thought I might be stealing material from them, because I was so caught up in these OCD patterns that I couldn't even listen to their shows or read about them in the newspapers. If I was driving in my car, I couldn't tune into another radio show unless my head was positioned just right over the speaker, the station had been tuned in properly (going one past the station and then back to properly dominate), and I had tapped the correct number of times with my right hand on the radio. Rather than go through all these nine hundred machinations, I just wouldn't turn on the fucking radio.

I couldn't even bear to read about my competition. It might take me ten hours to get through one copy of *Billboard* magazine. So I asked Alison to read all the trades and report the relevant news to me. She just figured that would save me time and she was happy to do it. She had no idea that she saved me from straining my neck and twisting my pinky and tapping my fingers nine million times.

The tragic part of this was that sometimes I couldn't even kiss my kids. We'd had another daughter, Debra, which meant more pressure to make a living and support the ever-growing Stern family, which meant MORE OF THESE INSANE RITUALS. But even when I'd be with my kids, I had to make sure I held them the right way so that I could be greater than them and therefore be able to provide for them.

And it wasn't just my kids. Whenever I would leave anyone's presence, I would have to be positioned over them a certain way and then I'd turn my head and walk away, because the last impression I had of them had to be one where the right side of my face was over them, which meant I was greater than them and then I would do well in the ratings. Thank God I was six foot five. And thank God I never had Shaquille O'Neal as a guest on my show.

PEOPLE WHO LIVE IN GLASS HOUSES
SHOULDN'T THROW STONES

These crazy rituals dominated my life for the next few years. Meanwhile, my success was astounding. We went to number one in New York, we went to number one in Philadelphia. We expanded to L.A. and trounced the competition there. Deep in my heart, I knew that my silly little rituals had nothing to do with my triumphs, that this was all irrational behavior. I just couldn't stop.

It was ironic because we started getting calls from a kid in New Jersey named **Mark Brown** who suffered from OCD. He had a horrible case. He had aversions to numbers like three and six and especially thirteen. For him, his rituals would ensure that his mother and sister would be protected from horrible accidents. Any time something would happen that threatened his little universe, he would rapidly count out loud to four, four times.

While I thought he was pretty brave to come out of the closet with this embarrassing disorder, ***compassion never enters into my world when I'm doing the radio show.*** This guy was humorous and he was pathetic so we had to make fun of him. We brought him to our WOR TV show and put him on with a motley crew of assorted freaks. I berated him and told him he was a seriously disturbed man suffering from a wacky disorder. Then, in an attempt to cure him, **we handcuffed his hands behind his back and I pulled shredded paper out of a bag and threw it in front of him.**

He had such a compulsion to pick up the paper that he actually started trying to put the paper back into the bag with his feet.

Every time he called the radio show, we were merciless. One time he was telling us that he had to eat four additional pieces of cake because he forgot to chew the last piece of the original slice of cake on the right side of his mouth.

"Look, **THIS GUY'S LIFE IS MISERABLE.** He doesn't even have a woman in his life. He's got a crummy job that he's worried about losing so he's eating nine pieces of cake," I told my audience.

"You ought to say to yourself, 'I got such a crummy life anyway that this whole thing isn't working.' It isn't like you got an empire to protect, like Donald Trump. 'Oh, I better eat four pieces of cake or I'll lose Marla and I'll lose the Taj Mahal.'"

Meanwhile, nobody in my studio, or for that matter the entire audience, knew that I was going around touching things three times to protect my own empire. Many times I had to take extra bites of food just to hit the right numbers as well.

Mark called us again a few months later and I was as relentless as ever with him.

"This guy's really mentally ill. If anybody should be locked up, it's him," I said.

"I was. I was in for two weeks in April," he said. "That's why I've been trying to get through to you because the last time I talked to you, just as I hung up, you announced it was 7:13 and it's been driving me crazy. I wonder if you could say 7:14. Thirteen's a bad number."

"I will say it's not 7:13 now. Goodbye," I said.

"OH NO! NO! NO!" he screamed.

"You mean if I hang up and say the word 'thirteen' again, it's more bad luck for you? What happened that's so bad to you? You're still alive," I told him.

"I lost my job," he said.

I had him describe all his stupid rituals for the audience.

"How many times do you wipe your ass?"

"Four."

"What if you have extra stuff hanging around like dingleberries?"

"I can go to five, but then if I hit six I have to make sure to go to eight."

"Why'd you lose your job?" I asked. He had been working at a casino in Atlantic City as a card dealer. Just the thing for a guy who has to count every second of his life.

"I was hiding it good but then they evaluated me and I wasn't dealing fast enough."

"Couldn't you put that stupid compulsion of yours out of your mind for a couple of hours and do your job and then go home and be into it?"

Sound familiar? I was able to hide it at work. Sometimes I would wonder why I could control it while I was on the air. But I wouldn't spend too much time analyzing my problem. I'd rather not deal with the whole embarrassing mess. I was in denial.

"You're hopeless. Go back to counting," I said.

"Don't forget to say it's 7:01 when you hang up on me," he pleaded.

"Hey, it's seven THIRTEEN," I screamed and slammed the phone down. "There you go, you son of a bitch. He's gonna sit there and sweat all day. He needs something to keep him busy. Put him in a concentration camp for a few weeks and he'll forget about all that. Where else but in this country could you find a guy with that problem who completely indulges himself, loses his job, goes on public assistance."

We went to commercial and **I FELT TERRIBLE.** There was a thin line that divided him and me. One number. I was hitting threes and he was chanting fours.

Maybe I felt bad because he had gone public with his problem and he was being treated by these know-nothing doctors who gave him all sorts of medications that made him gain weight, and urinate more, and constipated him. I knew I could never go that route. I would just have to live with this ridiculous, embarrassing disease. I was resigned to my private prison of rituals. I heard the commercial coming to an end and I knew it was time to get up and get back in my chair. You see, I was thinking about all this while I was laying flat on my back on the studio floor—***because I was also suffering from the most excruciating back pain imaginable.***

MORE PAIN, NO GAIN

My severe back pain was the culmination of a series of physical ailments that began back at the end of my NBC days. Thanks to Steve Basile and my new nutritional regimen, I had broken the cycle of colds and sore throats that had plagued me since Hartford. But as soon as I began working out in earnest, a whole new set of medical problems emerged. It began with neck pain.

I'd suffer an occasional backache or shoulder strain that I felt were due to my workouts—either my weight lifting or karate lessons. In fact, it was a karate injury that led to the entire chain of events that would culminate in the agonizing back pain that brought me to Dr. Sarno.

In the fall of 1991, I started doing karate with my daughter Emily until a groin pull incapacitated me around February of 1992. I stopped karate and went back to working out with weights.

By the spring, I was a mess. First, my shoulder started bothering me. Then the pain shifted to my back. I figured that I had pulled something doing the weights. By the summer of 1992, I was almost immobile. My shoulder was fucked up, I couldn't lift my arm, and my back was literally killing me. I couldn't bear the ride into the city, I couldn't sit in any of my chairs, I couldn't think of doing any exercise. In fact, I couldn't even bear to be with Alison and the kids. The only way I could get any kind of relief was to lie down on the floor and watch TV. IF I LAID ON THE FLOOR WITH MY HEAD PROPPED UP A CERTAIN WAY, IT ALLEVIATED PRESSURE ON MY BACK. Of course, it took a lot of manipulations to get into the proper position and to tune in the channel just to satisfy my OCD, let alone my back. But once that was done, I could lie there and watch TV for hours without pain. ***Unfortunately, doing anything else was pretty much out of the question.***

The pain was intense enough to drive me to a sports medicine doctor. He X-rayed me and examined my shoulder and told me I have a structural condition that only 10 percent of the population has and eventually I would need an operation. I got home and Alison decided that I should see a chiropractor. So I go. But going to a chiropractor is about the same as visiting an astrologer. You have to study for four years to be a chiropractor, but I think that **THREE AND A HALF OF THOSE YEARS ARE SPENT LEARNING HOW TO GET MEDICAL INSURANCE COMPANIES TO PAY FOR THESE WACKY TREATMENTS.**

So the first thing this chiropractor does is have me hold my arm straight out. She presses down on my arm. "See, you have no resistance." Okay, now she has me hold a bottle of vitamins in my hand and then hold my arm straight out. She presses down on

my arm again but miraculously this time my arm doesn't go down as much. Of course. You're putting out more resistance the second time because you know what's going to happen, but she says it's because I have a vitamin deficiency. And, of course, **she just happens to sell these special vitamins** that are so superstrong that they build up my resistance when I just hold a bottle of them.

Next, I lie down on the table. She tells me she doesn't believe in manipulations so this is going to be very gentle. My shoulder and upper back are aching so bad that I'll go along with anything at this point. So she starts moving her hands over my body and she finds these spots where the energy is blocked and she actually starts snapping her fingers over the spots. Why didn't she just say "Abracadabra"? ***I'm paying sixty dollars a visit for someone to snap their fingers over me?*** I could've gone to a doo wop concert for half the price and gotten twice the finger snapping.

The pain got so bad that I spent most of my summer vacation in a physical therapist's office. After two weeks I got back a little of my motion in the shoulder. But the back pain was driving me crazy. This dragged on for months. Alison was pregnant with Ashley. I was already thinking that I'd hook up a closed-circuit TV set to the delivery room and watch the birth while laying flat on my back in my bedroom. In fact, there seemed to be no hope at all until the late fall when Alison and I were having dinner with Fran Shea, the executive producer of my E! show. I was complaining, as usual, about my back pain and she stopped me short.

"You know, it's all in your head. I had it too and I'm totally cured."

I thought she was **A TOTAL KOOK.** I explained how my problem was caused by the karate and the weight lifting and she just smiled and told me it was all psychological.

Coincidentally, a month or so later, Alison and I were out, and we ran into some friends of ours. This guy Bruce had the worst back pain in the world. He used to bring pillows to the movie theater so he could last through the picture. Yet we see him and his wife now and they're all bubbly. His wife tells Alison he's a whole new man—he's skiing, they're playing tennis, the works. I look at Bruce. He's happy-go-lucky. This guy was miserable for years. He tells me he went to see this guy Dr. Sarno, who told him that the back pain was all in his head. Now, Bruce is no kook.

By now it's January and I'd been suffering for almost six months. And what's worse, my ailments were beginning to spill into my radio show for the first time. By now, I was routinely

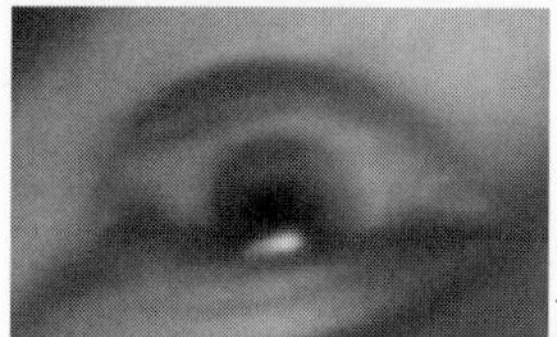

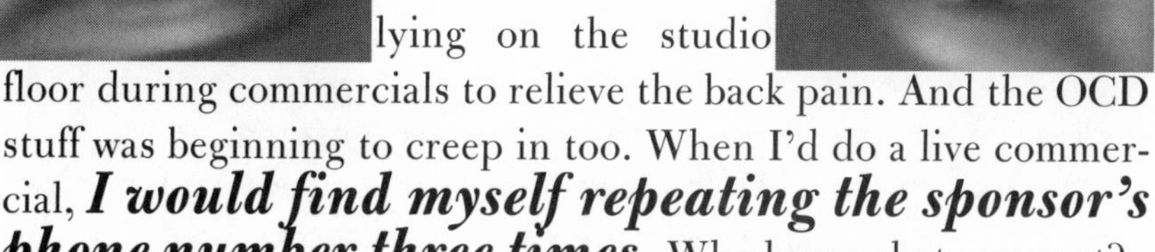

lying on the studio floor during commercials to relieve the back pain. And the OCD stuff was beginning to creep in too. When I'd do a live commercial, ***I would find myself repeating the sponsor's phone number three times.*** Who knew what was next?

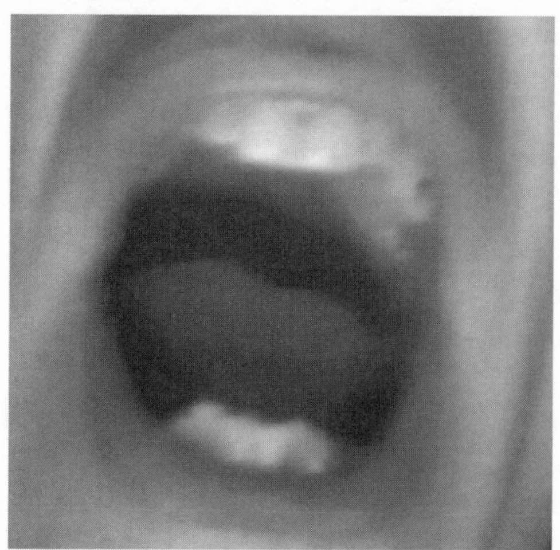

It's all in my head

So I call and make an appointment with Sarno. Sarno is affiliated with the Rusk Institute of Rehabilitation Medicine at New York University Medical Center. Rusk is probably the greatest rehab place in the world. THIS GUY AIN'T NO FINGER SNAPPER.

I go to his office. Sarno is a tiny guy, maybe five foot two. He sits me down and goes, "What's the problem?" So I start in with my litany of neck pain and then the shoulder and the physical therapy, and then it went into the back. After about ten seconds of this, he cuts me off because it's obvious he's a no-bullshit guy. It's time for an examination.

Now I know that the examination was probably unnecessary because Sarno has already got me sized up. But he does it and it's good because it sets up his credibility as a medical guy. I think you need to see this guy in a white coat in the Rusk Institute who's going to tell you that the whole thing is in your head. I don't think the message would be as effective if the guy's got a gray beard and he's in the lotus position and there's incense burning.

So I sit in the chair and he pokes me a little bit. Did absolutely nothing. Then he tells me I'm the prime candidate for this syndrome he's discovered—**TENSION MYOSITIS SYNDROME.** So, in effect, he's telling me that all the pain is coming from my head. I start to argue with him, "No, you don't understand, the shoulder thing is because I'm in the ten percent of the population with this structural abnormality and the back was wrenched weight lifting—"

He cuts me off again.

"There's nothing wrong with your shoulder and there's nothing wrong with your back. Read my book and come to the two lectures."

Then he dismissed me.

So I went home and read his book. Since I've still got my OCD going full blast, it takes me forever just to turn the fucking pages and the book's real thin. Basically, what he says in the book is that this whole TM syndrome is a condition caused by the mind to distract you from psychological issues. We repress anger and anxiety and the brain sends messages to constrict the blood flow to parts of our body and the pain comes from the loss of oxygen to those muscles. ***IT'S NOT STRUCTURAL.*** It has nothing to do with the back. In fact, the back is one of the most durable parts of the body. If you break your leg and do nothing for it, the bones'll heal in a few weeks. So why do we believe the back doesn't heal?

Sarno maintains that we believe that because the brain tricks us. He notes that back pain has become a culturally validated affliction only since World War II. Before that, we did the same physical activities, **BUT WE DIDN'T HAVE PROBLEMS WITH OUR BACKS.** In fact, the vast majority of people who have back pain are people who are between the ages of thirty and sixty, the years of responsibility. For these people, especially men, it isn't socially acceptable to react to stress by crying or having a nervous breakdown. But **it's totally acceptable to**

sequester yourself from your wife and children and lie down on the floor and watch TV to gain relief from the agonizing pain of a bad back.

So if this is true, Sarno is saying that with all the pressure in my life, my back pain keeps me occupied so I can't worry about work? Hmmmm . . .

Okay, let's give Sarno the benefit of the doubt. Let's say that the pain is a distraction the brain uses to get the person to focus attention on his body and not on his emotional state. It's a defense mechanism. So how do you cure this syndrome? It sounds like years and years of psychoanalysis before you can get to the root of the repressed emotional problems.

Amazingly, Sarno says that's not the case. In fact, he maintains that the pain will disappear as soon as the patient accepts the diagnosis that the pain is actually stemming from a psychological, not a physical, condition. **ONCE THE PATIENT TRULY ACCEPTS THAT TO BE THE CASE, THE MIND'S TRICK HAS BEEN EXPOSED AND THE PAIN VANISHES.**

After I finished reading the book, I was still confused. Intellectually, I got what he was saying, but I didn't believe it. It seemed like a big leap of faith to take. But I decided it was worth trying so I went to the first lecture. It was amazing. ***The whole room was filled with people who were squirming around in their chairs, all victims of this incredible back pain.*** Everyone looked miserable except for the guy next to me, who seemed totally carefree.

"Sarno is a genius," he told me. "This is the second time I'm coming to the lecture. I just want to hear it again. I'm completely free of my back pain."

"You're kidding," I said.

"Not at all. It was all in my head. I figured out that my wife was bringing me down, **so we got a divorce and the pain left."**

Now I'm totally confused. Does that mean I have to divorce Alison to get rid of this fucking pain? I don't think I'm suffering with this because of her. If it's my job that's producing all this pain, does that mean I have to quit? Now my back is killing me, I'm totally dejected, I feel I'm never gonna get rid of this thing but I listen to the first lecture and I understand all about the biology of the back. And from what Sarno says, it's pretty hard for the back to be aching for physical reasons. Still, on the way home, my back is killing me.

That night, I'm sitting in my chair alone in my bedroom and I'm thinking about all this stuff. In fact, I'm talking out loud to myself. That's one technique that Sarno recommends, that you actually talk to yourself about your problem. I'm thinking and I'm talking and I've never really been this introspective before. I usually just took for granted what was happening and worked and ate. But now I'm engaging in the most critical self-examination I've ever done in my life. I'm thinking about my back pain and I'm also thinking about my OCD.

And for the first time in twenty years, I actually confronted the OCD. I stepped outside of it for a few moments. I talked to myself about it. And I had a startling insight. It was almost similar to what the Buddhists refer to as *satori*, ***THAT SUDDEN FLASH OF ENLIGHTENMENT.*** Now I'm not saying I'm like that fat Buddha, but I did have an experience of enlightenment. And what I discovered was that the obsessive-compulsive behavior was directly linked to my back pain. It was all part of the same defense mechanism.

The OCD rituals were my distraction. When I was in college and nervous about entering the world of broadcasting and earning a living, the pressure was enormous. MOST PEOPLE WOULD HAVE HAD A NERVOUS BREAKDOWN. Women are allowed to cry at least, but a man, especially Howard Stern, Ben Stern's son, had to be strong. No crying. No nervous breakdown. **As a defense mechanism, my brain had set up an elaborate maze of rituals that kept me from confronting my fear.**

Now this might sound like a bunch of psychobabble to you, but it all made sense to me. I started talking out loud, arguing with myself. "DON'T YOU SEE, STUPID? YOU'VE BEEN GOING THROUGH THESE RITUALS AS A DISTRACTION. AND THE BACK PAIN IS A DISTRACTION TO KEEP YOU FROM THINKING ABOUT THE OCD. YOU DIDN'T HAVE A PROBLEM WITH ACID. YOUR MIND WAS DISTRACTING YOU—KEEPING YOU FROM THINKING ABOUT YOUR CAREER, YOUR FEARS, YOUR FUTURE."

As soon as these thoughts entered my head, in that split second, the OCD just went. It was gone. Flew right out the window to who the fuck knows where.

FLYING OUT OF THE OCD CLOSET

I couldn't believe it. I had no desire to do any of those stupid rituals. I got up and walked out of the door and I made sure to put my left foot through first. Didn't matter. I rushed into the bathroom and turned on the sink with my left hand. Didn't matter. Meanwhile, my back was killing me. My whole body was starting to shake from the pain but I was ecstatic. I was running around the house like a madman doing things. I went down to my office, turned on the computer, and was typing in two seconds, record-breaking time for me. I turned on the TV and switched channels like a normal person. I couldn't wait to get up in the morning and get dressed. I was cured of these sick obsessions.

I ran upstairs and found Alison.

"I've just had the most incredibly freeing experience."

"Oh, your back pain's gone?" she said, hopefully.

"No, the back pain's still there but I'm a new man. I feel revitalized. I'm totally energized. I owe it all to Sarno." It was funny, I still couldn't tell her about the OCD. But I knew it was gone forever.

I had to tell Sarno. The man had just changed my life. A few days later, I attended the second lecture. Sarno went through the entire psychological mechanism of TMS. When the lecture was over, one of his assistants told me that Sarno wanted to see me. I rushed into his office.

"So how's it going?" he asked me.

For the first time in my life I told someone about my OCD. I was talking a mile a minute.

"Look, Dr. Sarno, I have to tell you something. My back isn't any better. I understand everything you've been saying but forget about the back. I've had obsessive compulsive disorders for over twenty years and now they're all gone." Sarno stopped me.

"HOLD ON. YOU HAD OCD?"

"Yeah," I said.

"Gee, I never heard of anyone saying that they've been cured of OCD from this," he marveled. "By having that kind of distraction in your life, that shows this is very deep-rooted in you. You really should see a psychiatrist."

He wrote down the name of a psychiatrist who was versed in Sarno's theories and then he told me to keep working on my back pain. If I accepted his diagnosis the back pain would also lift.

For the entire ride back home, my back was killing me, but I didn't care. I had conquered OCD! I was thinking about it and everything just fell into place. It made total sense that I would choose OCD as a distraction in my life. ***I had been raised like a veal in a box by my parents.*** With the OCD, I was just substituting another box that kept me from the dangers of the outside world.

MOM-DAD, *HURT-SICK*, *Cause and Effect*

Both my parents are very compulsive people. Not obsessive compulsive, just compulsive. My mother is a complete worrier, even though she's got an image of herself that she's carefree and loose. She's not. She's the most rigid person I've ever met in my life. If I say I'm going to go bike riding, it's "Don't bicycle ride, something'll happen." Okay, so I take up roller-skating. "What do you need to roller-skate for? You'll hurt yourself. And put on that jacket or you'll catch cold." That was her mantra to me. Hurt, hurt, sick, sick. Cause and effect.

Plus, she had all these zany rules in the house. I was afraid to keep the milk out when I was having milk and cookies because the milk had to be rushed back and rerefrigerated right away or it would go bad. Everything had to be spic-and-span. If a piece of junk mail accidentally made it into the house, boom, it was thrown out in two seconds. No clutter. My room had to be immaculate. My mother once left me a note—in plain sight, so all my friends could see—chastising me because I had left a T-shirt on my bed.

And my father was just as bad. I couldn't just plop down and sit on the couch. I can hear my father now:

"I DON'T WANT YOU PLOPPING. You'll hurt the back of the couch. This is the way you do it: You PLACE yourself onto the couch, like this. You gotta use the upper thigh to make contact." I never saw anything like that in my life. I'M CRITIQUED ON HOW TO SIT ON A FUCKING PIECE OF FURNITURE. GOD FORBID, I PUT MY FEET ON THE COUCH. I'D BE EXECUTED.

Now, maybe being raised like this wouldn't affect everyone. It certainly didn't affect my sister. She just told my parents to fuck off and went into her room. But I was younger and I guess there was more pressure on my mother to get me in line, since Ellen was ignoring her. And I liked being dependent on my mother. I was no rebel. Hell, I would have my mother take me shopping for clothes when I came home on breaks from college. **My mother actually went shopping with me** for the first gift I ever bought Alison—a set of sexy baby doll pajamas.

On top of all this compulsiveness, my father was drumming into me that ***I'm a totally useless schmuck.*** How do you combat that sense of worthlessness? You need an outside force to intervene here. **YOU NEED TO TAP THINGS THREE TIMES AND TWIST YOUR NECK SO YOUR RIGHT EYE**

CAN BE AT JUST THE RIGHT ANGLE OVER THE PAGE SO YOU CAN READ IT.

I don't want my parents to read this and think it was their fault. That's Sarno's point. You can't sit and analyze your problems away. You can't blame your upbringing. You just have to accept the diagnosis.

It made total sense to me. The OCD was distracting me from the anger and anxiety I had been repressing from this zany childhood. That also explained why I was able to function so well on the radio. In real life, I couldn't express the anger and the hurt. But once I got behind that mike, it was full steam ahead. Nothing was sacred or held back.

And then I remembered something else from my childhood. My father used to get tremendous back pain. It was so intense that he had to be in traction in a hospital for weeks at a time. That scared me shitless. I was just a little kid and my father was laying in some hospital bed, wrapped up like a mummy, connected to levers and pulleys. And here I was years later, lying on the floor, trying to cope with my own back. But now Sarno was telling me to sit any way I wanted—sit like a monkey—it has no effect on the back.

So I'm pondering all this stuff until I have to go to bed. I'm alone that night because Alison is sleeping downstairs with our newborn, Ashley. Suddenly, about midnight, I'm rocked out of bed. ***INTENSE, INTENSE PAIN.*** Never before had the back pain actually woken me up. In fact, I'd never had pain in my sleep before. And now the pain starts shooting all over my body, from the back to the shoulder to my neck, back to the back—the most excruciating pain I'd ever felt.

I start pacing the room, talking to myself out loud: "I've always believed the back pain is from an injury. But Sarno says that the back would have healed a long time ago if it was a physical trauma."

All of a sudden, I had this unbelievable revelation: the OCD was a distraction. Back pain was there because it kept me from thinking about OCD.

"There is absolutely nothing wrong with my back. I don't

care about this back pain anymore," I said out loud. **"You know what, I like it."**

The back pain started to feel almost erotic to me. And I thanked the back pain for alerting me to the OCD. I embraced the pain as a great barometer of what's troubling me, something that tells me when I'm upset and when I should slow down and relax.

By now I had been pacing for a few hours. I went back to bed and I woke up the next morning, still with horrible back pain, but I had a big smile on my face 'cause I knew it was gonna go away. I knew that the back pain was just testing me right now, so I decided to enjoy it.

On the way into work that morning, my back really began acting up. I had excruciating shooting pains running up and down my back. So I started laughing. I was laughing hysterically at the pain. And in one split second, it vanished. Totally. It was gone.

Then I sat there trying to get it back. I said, "NO, NO, I WANT IT BACK." I was laughing hysterically and squirming around to all different positions trying to get the pain back. But it was gone.

We got to work and Ronnie opened the door of the car. I jumped out.

"Ronnie, Sarno's right. It's all in my head. My back doesn't bother me anymore."

"It just went away like that?" Ronnie asked.

"Ronnie, it's gone. The pain is all in your mind."

"Sure, whatever you say . . ."

But I knew it was true. Sarno was a fucking genius. And to this day, over three years later, I have never had another attack of back pain.

the miraculous HEALING

"You who suffer out there with back pain, neck pain, shoulder pain, foot pain, thumb pain, listen up."

I got on the air that morning like a man possessed. I had been cured!

"Some of you have gone the surgical route only to have the pain return after a couple of months. Some of you have gone to chiropractors and the next day the pain returns. You may have been diagnosed with a herniated disc, a slipped disc, ailments way too long to be discussed here. I am here to tell you that there is a cure and it absolutely works. I am living proof of it. This is not a paid commercial, this is just one pain sufferer to another.

"TO SAY HOWARD STERN IS PSYCHOLOGICALLY DISTURBED IS AN UNDERSTATEMENT. To say I am stressed out and full of anxiety is true, you hear it every day. I had tremendous back pain. I had been diagnosed with a rotator cuff shoulder problem that was causing upper back pain. I had gotten lower back pain from doing squats in a gym, I thought. I had excruciating pain to the point where you can't even sit in a chair and today my pain left me completely.

"It was done through one man's work and I am here to compliment this man. This guy saved my life. I should wash this guy's feet. You should write down the name of this man and buy his book."

Not only was I cured, but I was now a man with a mission.

IT'S ALL IN *YOUR* HEAD, TOO

I believe that Dr. Sarno is on to a much bigger thing than he himself acknowledges. The framework of his TMS cure can be used to combat a whole host of aberrations and deviant behavior. My cure frightened me in some sense. It made me ask what other tricks my mind might be playing on me. What else was it holding me back from? I now firmly believe that my inability to lose the last few pounds of fat around my stomach, no matter how insanely I diet, is all psychosomatic. Until I envision myself with that flat, hard stomach and rippled muscle, it will not happen.

What other behaviors that we attribute to chemical imbalance or genetic makeup can be altered using Sarno's TMS methods? I'm convinced that homosexuality can be cured the same way my OCD was cured. Now, before ***gay people go crazy and try to burn me in effigy***, let me explain. Everyone acknowledges that homosexuality is, by definition, a deviation from the norm. The current thinking is that it's a result of an unusual genetic formation. But, to me, that's like saying it's due to a chemical imbalance. A genetic hiccup.

I think homosexuality is just another distraction, albeit a much stronger distraction than even OCD or back pain. Homosexuality seems to be a way for men in our society to avoid the responsibilities of being an adult male. It's not genetic. It's all psychosomatic. Why? I maintain it's because those are the guys most likely to attract women and attract this responsibility, and this is their way of escaping. It's a fear of making a living and supporting a family to the nth degree. If you're gay, it's almost as if you're perpetually caught in boyhood. You hang out with the guys. You don't have the wife and kids and the house and the mortgage. Hey, it sounds really good. **Maybe I should try it.**

I know that people will read this and say, "Aww, he's full of shit," because they're not going to understand that obsessive compulsive behavior, back pain, homosexuality, PMS, and a host of other problems are all tied in with psychosomatic illness. I'm sure that homosexuals don't want to think of themselves as ill. And I don't blame them. **I'M NOT ANTIHOMOSEXUAL. IF YOU'RE HAPPY BEING GAY, THEN BY ALL MEANS, BE GAY.** Besides, that means there's more pussy for me.

IF YOU'RE GAY, AND YOU'RE HAPPY, GOD BLESS YOU. But when you find that being gay is hurtful to your life, when deep down inside you're depressed about your sexual orientation, you can do something about it. If you're the stereotype of the old queen walking around lonely and depressed for having lived in the closet his whole life, you can change. If a gay person could accept that his homosexuality is a psychosomatic illness, truly accept it, understand it, and think of it in the same way I thought of my obsessive compulsive behavior, it would disappear.

You may not know it but you are holding in your hand the most powerful self-help book ever written. Millions of people who are suffering silently from diseases could be cured by accepting Sarno's diagnosis. Just substitute homosexuality, PMS, OCD, or pyromania for back pain and you're on the road to recovery.

There are plenty of people out there who don't want you to. Dr. Sarno's methods are considered controversial by the medical establishment. For good reason. HE'S SHOWN THAT A $20-BILLION-A-YEAR INDUSTRY, THE BAD BACK INDUSTRY, IS BUILT ON A FOUNDATION OF SAND. X-rays show that all of us have slipped discs and herniated discs—they're a part of aging. Believe it or not, in 99 percent of the cases there is nothing wrong with your back.

And while his approach lends itself to a psychological cure, his amazing innovation—prescribing that you talk to yourself—obviates the need for overpriced charletan psychologists or psychiatrists except in less than 5 percent of the cases of TMS. So take it from me, a former prisoner of ritual and now a fully self-actualized human being: Accept the diagnosis and you will be free!!

PLEASE SEND DONATIONS TO:

THE HOWARD STERN INSTITUTE FOR MENTAL HEALTH

c/o *SCORES*, a strip club

I've *Changed*

One of the benefits of surmounting these sick obsessional thoughts and overcoming compulsive behavior is that you don't have to feel that need to kowtow to the people whose pressures provoked some of your sick behaviors. In other words, you can become totally and completely selfish and self-absorbed without one whit of shame or remorse or GUILT eating away at you.

When I was mired in those OCD thoughts, I always thought Alison was my lucky charm and that if I ever cheated on her, my life would be destroyed. CAUSE AND EFFECT. Now, I feel that some chick could blow me and I won't lose my job. Now, I'm faithful out of respect, not obsession (actually, I'm faithful because I'm still germ-phobic, but it sounds better the other way).

The truth is, I am a selfish pig and I *have* changed. My mother knows best.

HOWARD: I understand, Mom, that you've noticed a change in me the last couple of years?

RAY(MOM): I've seen a merging of how you act on the air and how you act personally lately. And I don't like it.

HOWARD: So I've changed in my attitude to you?

RAY: Right.

HOWARD: Even off the air?

RAY: Right.

HOWARD: You've seen a personality change in me the past two years? A definite, dramatic change?

RAY: I think so. More self-absorbed. Into more of the male-bonding type personality. There's a certain macho insensitivity to others, because, "Hey, I'M busy, I'M blah blah," Look, this is too painful. I can't tell you everything. I like when people come to their own conclusions, too.

HOWARD: Dad, do you sense this as well?

BEN(Dad): I tell you, I'm not as sensitive as your mother is to people's feelings.

HOWARD: Maybe now I'm doing what makes me happy, but maybe Mom feels it's insensitivity when I'm happy, when I'm not kowtowing to others.

RAY: Thinking of others, not kowtowing.

HOWARD: Part of living life is to please others?

RAY: Well, that's my life.

BEN: Your mother's always lived her life to please others.

HOWARD: Are you reacting to what's on the radio or in real life?

RAY: What's happening with my relationship with you, Howard, is I'm hearing more about it from the radio than I am from you. Just this week I had a very traumatic experience. We went to see *The Bridges of Madison County* and in that movie they showed Clint Eastwood as the most sensitive, wonderful, loving, glistening kind of a man. And I came home and I said to your father, "There isn't a man walking this earth that can fit into that role." It's very traumatic for me to admit this because **I always thought that man had a possibility of existing in my son.** And I thought,

"You know what? He ain't got it, either."

THE HISTORY OF

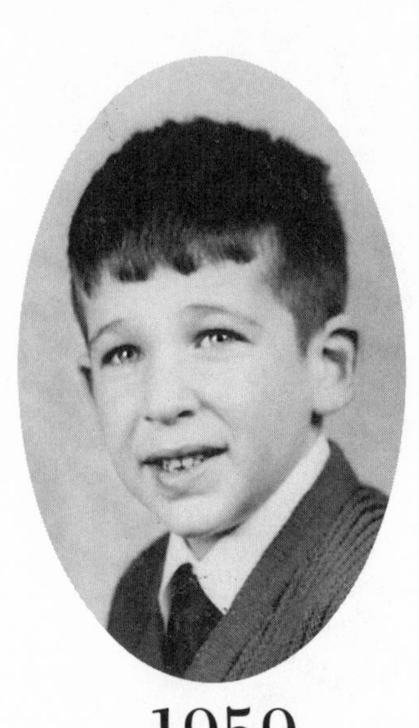

1959

1968

1972

1987

1989

1990

HOWARD'S HAIR

1980

1984

1986

1991

1993

1995

Howard Stern's
MISS AMERICA
Chapter One
DF

CHAPTER 4

THE STERN *PONDEROSA*

ROMEO STERN, PAMELA ANDERSON, AND THE YENTAS

"Can't you spend time with us? You're the life of the party at work and you come home and you lock yourself up downstairs."

—Alison Stern, September 5, 1995

Alison starts our daily argument the same way each time. She's right, I *am* the life of the party at work. Of course I'm the life of the party at work—I'm the life of the party because I get ***paid*** to be the life of the party. Pretty much the only reason I'm even motivated to breathe anymore is to get paid.

When someone pays me I really turn on the charm. I give 110 percent of radio's finest programming to my employer.

On any given day I'll start with a few finely crafted doody jokes. Then a little pee-pee humor with a few **real farts**—right into the microphone—thrown in for good measure. Then I might make fun of the deaf Miss America for ten to fifteen minutes. Hey, what the fuck, I can't offend her because SHE CAN'T HEAR MY JOKES ANYWAY.

Continuing my dazzling romp in prime-time, morning-drive radio, I'll segue into a raucous essay on why I don't eat pussy, then I'll seamlessly glide into the final hour with a little ethnic humor.

The ethnic joke *du jour* is O.J. Simpson. I'll do a dead-on Kingfish voice as O.J., then top it off with a little *Chinee* impression of Judge Ito. That's called a hard day's work on the Stern Ponderosa.

When work's done, it's time to pack up the briefcase and **get the fuck out of there**. *Lights out. Good night.*

CIRCUS MONKEY

When I get home, the last thing I want to do is entertain Alison. I'm burnt out after being on the radio. It takes a lot of energy to be a circus monkey for millions of people all morning. BEING AN ASSHOLE IS HARD WORK. My wife thinks I'm out having fun all morning. If I'm doing my job well it should sound like I'm having a blast, but there's ***nothing fun*** about crafting the perfect penis joke. Turning pussy farts into mainstream humor requires intense effort. It takes *discipline*. It takes *craftsmanship*. It takes a lot out of me.

That's why when I get home, I wish, just once, my woman would greet me at the door in a sexy outfit, with her lips pursed, ready to accept my greedy member.

"Howie, baby," she would say. "Come here. You did an incredible show today and now it's time for your reward. Pull down your pants and **GIVE ME THAT NEEDLE DICK OF YOURS, ALL TWO INCHES OF IT.**"

Instead, the King of All Media opens the door and hears:

"CAN YOU WATCH THE BABY WHILE I TAKE A SHOWER?"

Gee, just the words I wanted to hear. I, of course, know enough to put my foot down and nip that crap in the bud. If I watch the baby while Alison showers *just once*, it will become an expected event.

"No, I can't watch the baby," I say forcefully—you have to say it forcefully or you'll never get away with it. Then you indicate how important everything else in your life is.

"I have work to do and I need to call my agent. Alison, I told you to hire help to watch the baby."

"The housekeeper is sick," she whines back to me.

"Hire a fucking army!" I tell her. "I don't care if the housekeeper is sick. Hire a backup person! Hire fifteen fucking people! Hire a damn ass-army of people to assist you. You told me when I agreed to have a third kid that I wouldn't be bothered with this horseshit!"

One more sentence with the word "fuck" and she'll know I'm serious. "I'm FUCKING exhausted when I get home from work," I say.

"You *must* be exhausted from spanking lesbians all morning," Alison replies, shutting me up once and for all.

Well, fuck her. I march downstairs and tell her to "fucking get a life." Then I put on my TV, start to make my phone calls, and spiral into a seemingly endless guilt trip. *Why am I such a prick to the woman who traveled the country with a ninety-six-dollar-a-week disc jockey?*

I march right back upstairs and . . . watch the baby while she showers.

Ahhh, romance. Nothing like twenty years of togetherness.

ME, *EVERY WOMAN'S WORST NIGHTMARE*

Believe it or not, it *is* hard work spanking lesbians. All right, maybe the spanking part is fun, but putting the whole show together and keeping it moving is tiring. Preparation is key to being on top of the radio game, and when I prepare I need time to think, to ponder, to soak in the day's events, like a sponge, yeah, I need to soak in everything like a sponge—you think I'm full of shit? You think I don't prepare?

Well, I *do* prepare. *Yes,* I prepare. WELL, I PRETEND TO PREPARE.

I go downstairs and watch TV. Most husbands who try to veg out on a couch can't get away with it. Me, I've figured it out. When Alison complains, I tell her, "I'm not watching TV. I'm looking for hot topics for my show."

Look, I need time just to watch TV, read newspapers, and generally research pop culture.

Yeah, research! I'm not downstairs listening to music for enjoyment, I'm downstairs absorbing today's music to integrate it into my vast musical awareness. *Get the idea?*

Alison's other big gripe is that she wants me to go to parties and social events with her. I've explained a million times that I can't go anywhere cause I'm a big star and people will stare at me. Of course, I wouldn't go anywhere anyway. It has nothing to do with fame. I just feel awkward. I'm six foot five with a strange face and PEOPLE HAVE BEEN STARING AT ME SINCE HIGH SCHOOL.

I hate leaving my house. I'm lucky I'm famous because I have an excuse to stay home. The bottom line is I'm a hermit and I'm totally in love with myself. **I'm a self-centered, selfish prick who's impossible to live with.** In truth, I'm every woman's worst nightmare.

ALISON, *I DON'T NEED TO IMPRESS YOU ANYMORE*

I know you are supposed to support and nurture your wife in the nineties. And as far as I'm concerned, I have. I *hired* someone to do the laundry. I *hired* people to cook and clean. I even found a store that delivers the food to the house so Alison doesn't have to go shopping. In fact, I've made it so easy for my wife that she should **kiss my feet every day** when I walk through that door.

Hey, look, I'd like to be more fun when I get home, but every available charming cell in my body is used up. Yes, it's true I'm Mr. Excitement at work and I'm a dull, boring, tired mess when I get home, but at some point I need to turn off my internal computer and reboot. I need to turn off the pilot light and recharge the engine. I need to . . . I need to . . .

"You know what, Alison? ***Think of me as a circus clown.*** Once the makeup comes off, I'm a regular guy."

"When I first met you I fell in love because you were always funny." Alison delivers this line like an actress who has been trapped in the same play for twenty years.

"Well, yeah, that's what guys do when they first meet girls. They act funny and witty—**THEY WANT TO GET LAID**," I say to her, giving her the benefit of all my wisdom. "But we've been together twenty years—I don't need to impress you anymore."

In my sick mind, I'm a great fucking husband and provider. I get up every morning at four A.M., do legendary radio broadcasts, come home, write books, work on movie scripts, jump in the shower with my bar of Dove soap, ***scrub any fecal matter out of my ass*** that remains buried due to inadequate wiping, go to sleep, and then wake up and do it all over again. That's my job and I do it well. I don't bitch about it. (Okay. I bitch about it constantly, but I certainly don't ask her for help.)

She wants me to work and then come home and be some pussy whipped, Long Island house husband who takes the kids to birthday parties and arts and crafts classes. Why not just jam your finger down your throat and vomit in my mouth? Because I'd prefer that to making clay ashtrays.

I can't tell you how many husbands on Long Island work full-time, then come home and suddenly turn into POOFSTERS like Mrs. Doubtfire, doing all kinds of domestic chores. Well, I'm not doing that. I know one guy who has to strap on one of those baby papooses every time he wants to go jogging. **I'd rather take a dick in my ass** than do that. I love my kids, but I play with the kids ten, maybe fifteen minutes and I get nuts.

WHAT IF . . .

I sometimes wonder what it would be like to be single. Not that I would ever leave Alison. No, I'm way too guilt-ridden to dump the woman who stood by me when no one else would even talk to me. Actually, **I'M WAY TOO IN LOVE WITH FIFTY PERCENT OF MY MONEY** to do something that stupid. But what if Alison were to die? If, say, her heart gave out or she was in a car crash, or she choked on her own vomit while eating a ham sandwich?

What if I was suddenly free to date?

"Would you remarry?" Alison always asks me.

"Alison, after you, I would never want to marry another woman. It wouldn't be right." That calms her down. And I am telling the truth. I would *never* marry again.

I wouldn't marry again because **I'D BE TOO BUSY FUCKING MY BRAINS OUT** with strippers and assorted babes. Man, oh, man-oh-schewitz, would I be dating up a storm!! How long would I wait to date after the funeral? Alison wants to know. Would I wait a month, six months, a year? Fuck that, I'd be dating the day of the funeral. I'd bring Amy Lynn, the *Penthouse* pet, to the funeral and fuck her right on Alison's coffin.

Who would I date? I would start with a list of eligible females I've met through the radio show. Who to call first? Who to fuck first? The choices, the opportunities are endless. For the first time in ***my miserable horny life*** I would have women available who would never look at me under normal circumstances. But with the success of the radio show the opportunities would be staggering. I know models, strippers—and some of the women

I know from work are pretty incredible. *Oooohhhhh*, interns. College girls who worship me.

Maybe I'll just pick up the request lines and get a babe off there. No, wait. I'm not thinking clearly. I have a new plan. I need to think this through intelligently. Don't want to just end up screwing wildly without giving thought to what I'm doing. I'd use some brains for a change and not just think with my penis. I'd do what any newly single disc jockey should do: I'd call my book editor, Judith Regan.

Judith is really smart *and* good looking. She has hot pouty lips and she looks like she's a great lover. She's the type who probably doesn't want marriage or a relationship, just some hot monkey sex every once in a blue moon. Unfortunately, Judith is one of those Catholic prudes who would never do anything. But I'd call her, and ask her to **do me a favor and blow me** just to get that big load out of my balls so I could sit down and make an intelligent decision about who to fuck next. Good plan. Once Judith blows me, I'll be able to run down the list that I've been storing in my head for years and make a prudent decision. A clear mind is an organized mind.

MY FANTASY FUCK LIST

CAROL ALT

OCCUPATION: Ex-supermodel and B-movie star

AVAILABILITY: Forget it. Happily married

CHANCE OF SCORING RIGHT AFTER ALISON DIES: 0 percent

DESCRIPTION: A real goody-two-shoes, probably can't fuck that good, anyway—although her husband, the great Ron Greschner, might have taught her how to bang like an ape. She is so in love with her husband that it's not a reality anyway. Let's move on.

DIAN PARKINSON

OCCUPATION: Former *Price Is Right* girl, Playboy centerfold

NEGATIVE TRAITS: Tried to sue Bob Barker for sexual harassment

AVAILABILITY: Single, very available. Made it clear to me that she was interested

CHANCE OF SCORING: 97 percent. Really came on strong.

Description: Tall. I like that. Legs incredibly long and thin. Height really gets me because I'm such a big gork. I'd kiss her legs and then I'd eat her giant-sized hairless pussy for an hour, really turning her on. Getting on in years but still looks great. When she was younger, probably would've ignored me, but now she'd probably fall head-over-heels in love with me and be grateful that I'd be willing to eat her aging pussy. It's not about my pleasure—it's about making chicks who wouldn't look at me in high school fall in love with me, about wanting her to fall so fucking in love with me that she follows me around like a retarded puppy dog. Would tongue her so good, she'd be moaning. She'd scream that she never came like this before, with anyone. Then I'd dump her.

PHOEBE CATES

OCCUPATION: Actress who looked so fuckable in *Fast Times at Ridgemont High*

AVAILABILITY: Married to Kevin Kline

CHANCE OF SCORING: 0 percent. Wouldn't fuck me even if she was single. Wouldn't fuck me if I threatened to slice off her tits. Wouldn't fuck me. Period. End of statement.

PAMELA ANDERSON

OCCUPATION: *Baywatch* babe

AVAILABILITY: Married, not an option

CHANCE OF SCORING: 0 percent

DESCRIPTION: Real nice to me on the show, almost seemed interested in a date. I swear. Robin didn't think so, but she had that certain something in her eye. Maybe it was an eyelash. Think she needs Howie's love tool. Wouldn't call now because she's been with a couple of big-haired, big-dicked rock stars and if I ever pulled my pants down in front of her, she'd probably be disgusted. Seems like she would want a real fun guy who would take her out all the time. She would think I'm the world's biggest drip. I have no rap with women and my courtship would be over after I dribbled my premature ejaculate on her thigh.

MARILYN CHAMBERS

OCCUPATION: Aging porno star

AVAILABILITY: Who the fuck knows

CHANCE OF SCORING: Who the fuck cares

PATTI DAVIS REAGAN

OCCUPATION: Former president's daughter

AVAILABILITY: Single

CHANCE OF SCORING: 90 percent. Seems to really dig me. Comes from a fucked-up background. That's good. It's easy to nail chicks with fucked-up backgrounds. Hates her parents. Needs to rebel. Would definitely jump my bones to fuck up her parents' heads. I'm Ronald Reagan's worst nightmare and Patty knows it.

DESCRIPTION: Nice girl. I would fuck her just to say I screwed Ronald Reagan's daughter.

MELISSA RIVERS

OCCUPATION: Joan Rivers's daughter

AVAILABILITY: Single

CHANCE OF SCORING: 100 percent. Seemed to dig me. I'd definitely go for it. She's not too bad on the eyes and she's a celebrity's daughter.

DESCRIPTION: Joan ain't got that long to live and Melissa inherits the mother lode. Joan's got lots of dough-rey-me and bad QVC jewelry. Melissa is the only heir. Melissa's probably not that good in bed but whoever nails her can roll the Brinks truck right over Joan's corpse and into the back door of the luxury condo. A mighty fine investment.

BARBI TWINS

Occupation: ?

Availability: Single, I think

Chance of Scoring: 67 percent. Would have to put in some time before I got in their pants. Maybe it was an act, but I would swear to God that these two were really coming on to me. They invited me to their house. Maybe they were inviting me because they knew I couldn't go, but I think they might have wanted my hot beef injection.

Description: If single, I would definitely call them. Well, I wouldn't call—I'd have my producer call. That's the way you do it with those two. They are a man's dream come true. Would love to fuck them so bad. Would come on their plastic-looking titties. Anxious to please, my tongue would end up buried deep between their butt cheeks. Only under unusual circumstances would I place my tongue in a bunghole, but with them I aim to please. No germs to worry about. Their assholes are as clear and clean as a plastic Barbie doll's, fresh out of the box.

NICOLE EGGERT

Occupation: Ex-*Baywatch* girl, left to do movies

Availability: Single

Chance of Scoring: 3 percent. A real longshot.

Negative traits: Removed her breast implants

Description: Great looking but definitely has no sexual interest in me. Maybe if I drugged her.

TAWNY KITAEN

OCCUPATION: Sex kitten, actress

AVAILABILITY: Single

CHANCE OF SCORING: 75 percent. Seemed interested and gave me the vibe that she wouldn't be nauseated sleeping with me.

NEGATIVE TRAITS: Might have balled O.J.

DESCRIPTION: Hot little minky. Would definitely bang her if Alison were dead. Those big cow tits would wrap nicely around my minuscule schlong.

JAID BARRYMORE

OCCUPATION: Drew's mom and *Playboy* model

AVAILABILITY: Single

CHANCE OF SCORING: 100 percent, no questions asked. A sure thing. Made it very clear that she wants to fuck my brains out. In an interview said that next to her daughter I was the most important person in her life. Met this woman once and now I'm the most important person in her life? Definitely wacky. Like that in a woman. Admires me because I had her on the show even though she's no one. Am I her David Koresh or what? I could fuck her and then leave and come back whenever I wanted it again and I think she would be fine with the arrangement. Think I'm exaggerating? Read the letter she sent to me:

Dear sweet, sweet, sexy Howard,

I'm sure you know by now that I've told everyone I have an enormous crush on you (I hope you don't mind). And if anyone asks why, I simply tell them that you are so completely brilliant, sexy, handsome, talented, and sassy—so how could I possibly resist?

I also want you to know that I hold you in the highest regard and hope that my presence on your show did not create any problems with your beautiful wife. If it did I extend my sincere apology and promise I will do my best to keep my hands off you when next we meet. If, however, it did not cause any problem, I would love to sit in your lap again, look into your beautiful blue eyes, and plant a tiny baby kiss on your luscious mouth.

If there is anything I can ever say or do, anytime, anywhere, that could be of help to you in any way, please please don't hesitate to ask because it would truly be my pleasure.

Please know how much I look forward to seeing you again, because in addition to all of the above you are simply dreamy.

xxx

Jaid.

DESCRIPTION: Incredible body. I dig that Drew Barrymore came out of that little snatch. I could come in her hair and she'd thank me.

GRETCHEN BECKER

Occupation: Martin Landau's date to the Academy Awards

Availability: Single

Chance of scoring: 97 percent. She went out with an old coot like Martin Landau and actually made out with him during the Academy Awards. Why not me?

Description: Cute. Real tall. Lean. Athletic. I would fuck her hard. With her long legs wrapped around my back, she'd moan, "Oh Howard, it's so good to be with a young man instead of that old fart, Martin Landau." Would definitely fuck her a few times, then dump her body in the woods.

TEMPEST

Occupation: Stripper

Availability: Single

Chance of scoring: 100 percent. She's assured me that she will be there for me the day Alison dies.

Description: Hubba hubba, take a look at the picture.

SANDRA BERNHARD

Occupation: Comedian, actress

Availability: Single. Lesbo, but I think would fuck a guy occasionally

Chances of scoring: 13 percent, if she was real high

Description: Actually turns me on. Probably could suck a mean cock if she could stop eating pussy for five minutes.

TULA

OCCUPATION: Transsexual model

AVAILABILITY: Hey, she's a guy

CHANCE OF SCORING: 87 percent. Call me crazy, but the dude grabbed my balls in the studio and I popped a boner.

DESCRIPTION: Ten times better than most of the broads you'll ever get to fuck. Killer long, thin legs. A great ass. Tight, hard stomach. The nicest set of tits I've seen in a long time. Okay, so the vagina looks like it's made out of plastic—you can't have everything. I know I wouldn't fuck the guy but I'm almost 100 percent sure I'd accept a blow job. I would definitely take a hand job. Hey, call me a homo, but you'd do the same.

LINDA BLAIR

OCCUPATION: *Exorcist* chick

AVAILABILITY: Single

CHANCE OF SCORING: 79 percent

DESCRIPTION: Love her big tits and the fact that show business has not been kind to her. Desperate for my love and would show her appreciation by letting me fuck her in every orifice. If Alison is dead, Linda comes over for the weekend because my kids are on another planet. With the house empty, we go in the pool. Strips down, pulls off my trunks, blows me in the water. After, we fuck multiple times on every available piece of furniture. Many times I fuck her in the ass with my cum always ending up on her huge tits.

LIBBY PATAKI

Occupation: First Lady of New York

Availability: Married

Chance of Scoring: This chapter is getting a little sick! What the fuck is wrong with me? This is a decent, caring woman and I shouldn't be thinking about her that way.

AMY LYNN

Occupation: *Penthouse* pet, stripper

Availability: Single

Chance of scoring: 100 percent. Has made it clear she's ready to date me.

Description: A goddess. Would have me eating out of a dog bowl and doing dumb shit like sending her roses every day. Fuck roses, buying her cars every day.

ELAINE MARX

Occupation: Miss Howard Stern 1994

Availability: Middle of divorce

Chance of Scoring: 100 percent. Has made it clear that if she was ever single she would blow me, fuck me, and wash my sphincter with her tongue.

Description: I get her in bed. Jealous ex-husband blows my balls off with a shotgun. Better steer clear.

DANIELLE BRISBOIS

OCCUPATION: Archie's niece on *Archie Bunker's Place*
AVAILABILITY: Single
CHANCE OF SCORING: 67 percent
DESCRIPTION: That little, ugly, annoying ten-year-old grew up to be a real piece of ass. Multicolored hair, mostly blue. After Alison dies, would take her out to clubs and go dancing. She would wear next to nothing and would beg me to fuck her. Believing I could do something for her career, she would be ready to please my kielbasa, Howard Junior. Would love to kiss and lick my penis for hours. Would enjoy receiving my manhood in her ass many times. Wouldn't have to do much to impress her. Am bigger than she is on the Show Business Food Chain so she has to impress me. I like that.

SAVANNAH

OCCUPATION: Dead porno star
AVAILABILITY: Single
CHANCE OF SCORING: 100 percent. She can't run away.
DESCRIPTION: Great-looking corpse. You know what? I've hit the bottom of the barrel. I'm talking about a dead woman. Time to move on.

GOD, MEN ARE DISGUSTING

Look at the hell I'm in: I think about sex twenty-four hours a day and I jerk off constantly. Sometimes I jerk off so much the side of my dick gets all sore and irritated. I was sure that by forty-one my sexual needs would diminish. They haven't.

Right now, I have a hard-on. My cock is so hard that my balls ache. I jerked off twice today and I *still* have a hard-on. As I'm typing, I'm pushing **my swollen, baby-sized prick** against the plastic keyboard casing. I'm not even thinking about girls and I'm rubbing my dick against the stupid computer keyboard. If I just push the side of the head of my dick against the rim of my keyboard gently, I feel, wait, like I'm going to come! *Oh! Ohhhhh! Yes! Mmmmmmmm! That's good.*

I'm going to get some tissues and take a break and jerk off. I'm going into my bathroom across from my office and standing over the toilet bowl and beating my meat. I'm staring at the toilet and I'm about to come. God, men are disgusting.

Alison is banging on the door.

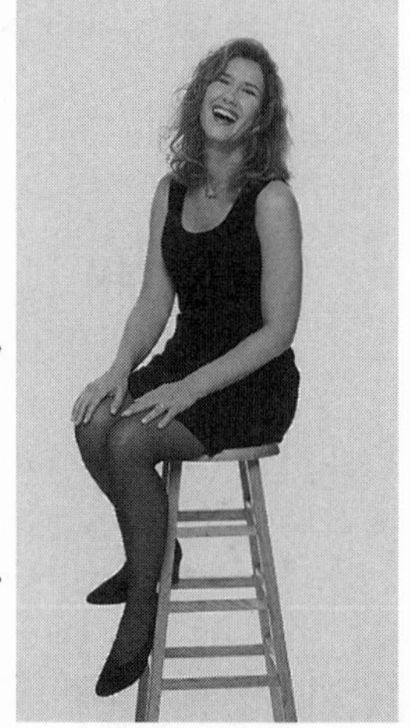

"Howard! Open up! I want to talk to you about the party!" She's screaming at the top of her lungs.

Can't a guy jerk off in peace?

"Hold on, I'm taking a shit," I lie. Oh fuck, better think quick. I know. I'll roll off some toilet paper and make it sound like I'm finishing and then I'll flush. I'll make the flush last at least thirty seconds. That'll give me enough time for my boner to diminish. If it decreases even thirty percent while the toilet's flushing, I'll be able to tuck it back into my underwear with minimal pain. I don't want to be discovered. Oh, good. My boner is evaporating. I'm tucking it into my pants. God, it hurts. I know why Alison wants to talk to me. She wants to talk about this **DUMB FORTIETH BIRTHDAY PARTY** that she wants me to throw for her. Doesn't she know

I'm too busy? "Parties are dumb," I say, as I open the door. "Why do you want to give a bunch of strangers our home address?

"I don't want to hang around a bunch of your friends and their dopey husbands who'll fuck up my head all night telling me about my show. ***Have the fucking party. Just don't bother me with it."***

"Okay," Alison acquiesces. "So I'll make it in the afternoon with just my girlfriends."

Damn, my penis aches. I wonder if she can tell that I've been jerking off? If I had any brains I would throw her on the bed and fuck her, but I don't want to waste time bullshitting around with all that foreplay and getting her wet with her vibrator for **HOURS.**

Alison is talking but I don't hear her. She'd better speak up if she wants to be heard over the voices in my head.

". . . At the party," Alison says.

"I'm sorry, what? I didn't follow you," I say. I'd better concentrate here.

"At the party, **I want you to give a *speech*** about me," Alison repeats.

I hear her that time. Better nip this shit in the bud.

"YOU MUST BE FUCKING NUTS!!" I yell. I'm unable to think clearly. My hard-on is still at three-quarters strength.

"You want me to get up in front of all your Long Island housewife yenta pals and confess my love? I'm *not doing it!"*

She leaves the room crying. Great. Hey, fuck that noise. I know what Alison wants and that's a non-negotiable item. She wants me, THE CIRCUS MONKEY, appearing at her party and making a public confession about my love for her, to all her shitstain friends that screw with her head all year and tell her I'm a ***lousy husband*** because I carry on with hot girls on my show.

Sure, I have girls on the program, but at least I'm not fucking any of them. Some of these yentas' husbands cheat but they keep it quiet. I don't need to humiliate myself and profess my love in front of these yentas. I'd rather get fucked by Mr. Ed while Wilbur watched. I don't give a rat fuck how much she cries! I'M NOT DOING IT!

You can suck my dick if you think I'm going to give these rat JAP bastards the satisfaction of seeing me make a public confession about my relationship with my wife. I know I love my wife and I'm not gonna be publicly humiliated by admitting it!! She should know I love her and that's final. Fuck her crying. I'm putting my foot down.

BACK TO MY PENIS

I'm going to go back and jerk off and not put a second thought into this crap. I'll close the door and get back in the mood. I'm not going to start chasing Alison all over the house. I'm not caving in. I'm fucking famous.

Now, where the hell is my penis? Shit! Look at this shriveled peanut. *Ahh, yeah,* where was I? I'm with Amy Lynn, *Penthouse* pet, in Hawaii and I've been a widower for two years now. Amy walks in the room wearing a little black thong. Her large, full breasts are taunting me. "Howard," she says softly, ***"your mother is on the phone."***

"Amy, what the fuck are you talking about?" *Whoa.* It's Alison banging on the door.

"Your mother is on the phone. Pick up."

Great. My dick is in my hand and now my mother is on the phone.

I'm lucky that when I redid my house I had phones put in the bathrooms.

"What is it, Ma?" I ask.

"You're going to say something nice about your wife at her party, aren't you?" she says.

Holy shit! Alison called my fucking mother and put her up to this? This is fighting dirty. This is **HUSBAND ABUSE!**

Well, I don't care if the Pope, President Clinton, and the Virgin Mary are on the phone. I am *not* giving any speech to Alison's friends. I'm a grown man and I don't have to listen to my mother. I'm my own person with my own set of rules.

"Look, Mom, this is none of your business. I have my reasons for not making a speech," I say.

"Listen!" she yells at me like I still live at home. "Your wife needs you to do this. I think it's a lovely thing to do for her. She's very good to you and you are a family man. You are no . . . "

My mother droned on for what seemed like hours. My penis was drained of all blood, reducing it to the size of a turtle's head. I am positive I suffer from a disease called **Microphallus.** If I don't have the disease, then I'm borderline.

". . . Are you going to make a speech for your wife? Howard? Howard?"

Damn, the old bag was getting to me. Maybe I was being a heel. Fine. I'll do it, but I won't give her the satisfaction of letting her think she had anything to do with it.

"Mom, look, I have every intention of making the speech. I don't need you to tell me what to do. I know the right thing to do. Okay?"

"Okay, Howard, that's my boy. I love you."

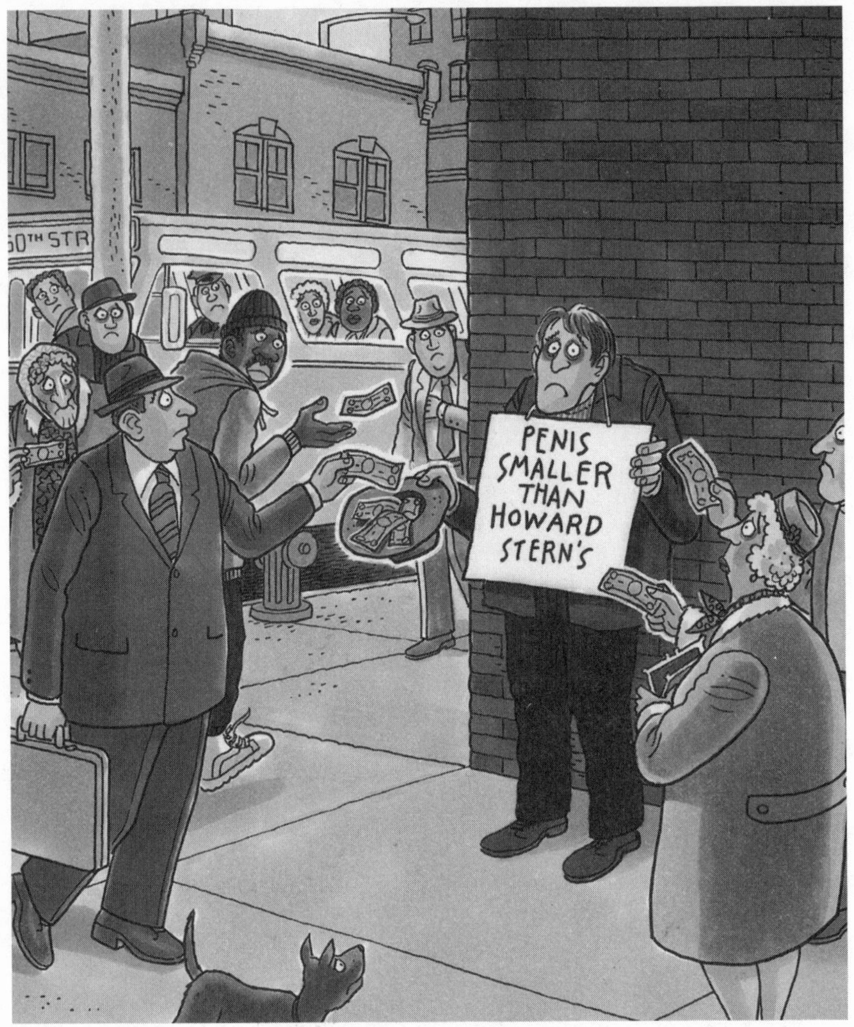

HUSBAND HELL

And that was that. I swear, I need a head transplant. Man, am I pussy whipped.

The birthday comes and I walk in the door to a posh, catered party that must be costing me a fortune. A whole house of Long Island yentas, looking over my possessions. Every move I make will be big news on the Long Island Gossip Network. I'm in *husband hell.* I walk around the room and schmooze the crowd. I eat and drink, but in the back of my mind the minutes are ticking away until speech-time. First, my mother-in-law gets up and makes a speech that she wrote in poem form. The woman is always making up poems. I don't know what the fuck she's talking about. They go on way too long and everyone snoozes after the first few seconds, but at least she comes prepared.

Me? I haven't given a moment's thought to what I'm going to say. I've been busy crafting penis jokes all week. I can't be writing speeches. Not to worry though, I'm a professional communicator. I should be able to razzledazzle this crowd like Johnny Cochran.

I grab the mike. A sea of big-haired, heavily perfumed, manicured and pedicured hausfraus are staring at me. Every one is front-row and ready to see the biggest spectacle since King Kong. Ladies and gentlemen, boys and girls, here he is, the Bad Boy of Radio, the Wild Man of the Airwaves, breaking down and making his first public love speech. It's *Romeo* Stern.

The man who spanked women and fondled lesbians was going to let his hair down and speak from the heart about his adoring wife. All the little backstabbers who tried to convince my wife that I was a bad man were in this room. I could hear what they were saying. I knew how they talked behind my back: *I was undeserving of Alison's love. I was an unfaithful boor who painted women's breasts green on St. Patrick's Day.* This was not an easy crowd. This was the speech of my life. I needed to convince this all-female jury that I was innocent of all charges. If my speech was tender and warm I would silence them. Shut them up once and for all.

WHEREFORE ART THOU, ROMEO?

I can't believe I didn't prepare. I should have made up a fucking boring poem. This shindig was catered and there were at least five people from the catering firm serving the food. I was going to profess my love in front of five fucking strangers. What a nightmare.

They were all staring at me. The caterers, the waiters, the bartender, my mother, my sister, my mother-in-law, and every woman who had ever carpooled, played tennis, or went to school-board meetings with my wife. I opened my mouth and waited to hear my own words. **I HAD NO CLUE** what I would say.

"Ladies," I began nervously. They were watching my mouth form the words. I was feeling very awkward. If I looked like Richard Gere instead of a deformed insect, it would be a lot easier to win this crowd over.

"Ladies, in honor of my wife, I would like to do a song."

My wife was in shock. The yentas were in shock. *I* was in shock. *Where was I going with this?* "I need to divide the room into three sections. I'm a big fan of 'row-row-row-your-boat' and I thought it might be fun to do it as a group."

What a jerk! I was leading Alison's party in a synchronized sing-along. What a romantic! I told you this speech was a bad idea. ***My mother-in-law was vomiting*** in the back of the room.

"Section one, you start. C'mon, everybody. *Row row row your boat gently down the stream.* Okay, section two, you start . . ."

The yentas were singing. I was on a roll. The room was bursting with the sound of music. They were laughing. I was winning the yentas over.

"*. . . life is but a dream.*"

I was proving I could tell a joke, but that wasn't what this crowd was here for.

After the song it was time to get serious. The ladies were here for *romance.* What pressure. I don't have enough shit to juggle in my life. The room was silent. I began my speech.

"First of all, I was not pleased with what went on at Jackie O's funeral. When Jackie Onassis died, her son and her daughter stood up there like a bunch of dummies and they read a bunch of stuff they got out of a book," I said.

The women and especially Alison were not bowled over with this but I continued anyway. *I had a point, I think.*

"Caroline and John John didn't really say anything from the heart

about their mother. I believe in speaking from the heart. In this case it happens to be about my wife. Although I do look young enough to be Alison's son." Lots of laughs. *I was doing good, I think.*

"I want to say a few nice things about my wife except I'm so heartless I don't really know what to say." Big laughs. *Way to go, Howie!* But they still wanted romance. I continued.

"What I wanted to say is that when Alison married me, I was a real mess." With that I picked up my wedding album from the coffee table and spoke eloquently.

"Now I'm going to walk around and prove to you what a mess I was. So take a good look at these pictures." I passed the book around. The women gasped.

"THAT IS WHAT I LOOKED LIKE WHEN ALISON MARRIED ME. ALISON? COME HERE, SWEETHEART. THANK YOU FOR MARRYING THIS MESS AND SAVING ME FROM A LIFE OF MISERY."

I sucked Alison into my gangly arms. The yentas let out a collective *ohhhhhhhhhhhh!*—the kind of sound yentas make when they see a newborn baby or a good romantic movie.

"Come here, darling." I was on a roll.

Then I made out with my wife in front of them. ***Take that, yentas.*** Let's see you give my wife shit now about what a fucked-up husband I am, you rat bastards. Now I was a hero. My wife was glowing. I was giving the yentas what they came for. Clutching my forty-year-old bride, I continued: "I want to thank Alison for taking the best years of my life."

A little joke. The yentas laughed. That's good! More laughs, good. This speech wasn't going too badly. I wondered what I was going to say next?

"I want to thank Alison for everything she ever did for me and, quite frankly, if you look at me, I'm not the type of person you want to do things for."

Self-effacing humor. Gets them on your side. More laughs. I was giving the speech of my life. Time to drive it home.

"Alison is so giving. And she gave of herself . . . "

Okay, so I'm not Shakespeare. I was ad-libbing.

". . . and we have three beautiful children together and we have a life together, and I love her very much for it and I want to profess my love in front of all of you." Laughter and spontaneous thunderous applause filled the room.

"I love you, Alison. Happy fortieth birthday."

And with that I swept her into my arms and made out with her again. Alison played it beautifully. She acted surprised by **THE SPEECH THAT SHE YELLED AT ME TO DO.** She had forgotten what a shit I was when I first refused to give the speech while I was jerking off over the toilet. All that mattered was . . . ***THE YENTAS.***

Everyone was in love with me. The room was mine. It was all too perfect. No, perfect wasn't the word I was looking for. It was all too . . . *disgusting*. Better get back to the jokes before these women put me in a dress and parade me around the house.

I turned to the crowd and said: "You know, Alison, now that you're forty, we'll take the marriage one year at a time. You're aging and I want to make sure you hold up. I don't want to get locked into anything long term."

The yentas even laughed at that. Nothing else mattered. The kissing and the love talk was what they needed to see and hear.

Joking was fine as long as they saw kissing and love talk.

"I want to thank everyone for coming. I love Alison. Wanna see one more kiss?" I asked the crowd.

The women screamed, "YEAHHHHHHHHHH!"

I swept her up in my arms and practically fucked her in front of them. My sister was choking back emotion, or maybe she was choking on the chicken-and-noodle dish I paid a fortune for. Those sun-dried tomatoes are expensive. **My mother was practically fingering herself.** My mother-in-law had to go change her panties she was so drenched. Best of all, my wife was thrilled. No longer would anyone complain to her that Howard Stern was a shitty animal and horrible husband. This would finally get everyone off her back. And her off my back. Now, I could get back to something important . . . MY PENIS.

FRED GARY STUTTERING JOHN MISS AMERICA 1996 ROBIN BILLY JACKIE SCOTT THE ENGINEER

CHAPTER 5

MY SECOND FAMILY

COOKIE PUSS, HITLER YOUTH, TIT JOBS, AND THE POTATO

Do you understand the constant pressure I'm under? I'm giving speeches, jerking off into toilets, and spending day and night thinking about my radio show. I'm responsible for a growing media empire that demands my constant attention, and I have to hold my home life together on top of that. How is it that a guy who got into radio because he wanted to be a kid the rest of his life ended up being responsible for so many people?

I'm a ***married guy***, with ***three kids***, ***a cat***, ***a hamster***, a radio career, books, an agent, a publicist, ***a small penis***, and a movie that starts shooting as soon as this book comes out. And on top of all of that, I have an even bigger responsibility: I have a *second family*. No, not like Johnny Cochran. I don't have a white broad doing me and a love child on the side. No, I have a **radio** family. A ragtag group of performers, each with an individual set of insecurities, problems, and troubles.

And what a group I've assembled. My closest associate was molested by her own father, suffered a nervous breakdown, and then went and **LOPPED HALF HER TITS OFF** in a breast-reduction operation. Another member of my crew was so sheltered he couldn't even open a bank account on his own, and, when he finally did, he bought his mommy a three-dollar Carvel Cookie Puss ice-cream cake for Mother's Day.

I could bring just about any talent I wanted into my radio family because I have the hottest show in the business. And what do I do? I adopt a joke writer who writes songs about beer and pot, then curses me out behind my back, calling me a **cheap Jew** when I don't buy him champagne. How the hell did this happen? How is it that I am so attracted to dysfunction? If I am so overloaded in my personal life, why don't I look for calm and tranquillity in my professional life? Why am I so attracted to weirdness? Why am I **FLYPAPER** for the walking wounded?

ROBIN QUIVERS, *QUEEN OF ALL MEDIA*

Actually, thank God I have a radio show, away from the madness that is my home life. Here at work I'm safely nestled in the cocoon I love. The silence of dead air waiting to be filled. The soft warm glow of the flashing lights from my radio equipment, the whirring sound of tape recorders, which are as soothing as Tibetan chanting. No one yelling at me about surprise fortieth birthday parties or how I ignore my responsibilities. No need to fantasize about women here because I can open that mike and request a girl and have her there within moments. If I want my next meal, there is a ***slavelike*** intern ready to fill my request. Ahhhh, I truly am the king of . . . of my castle. No, the King of All . . .

"HOWARD, HOWARD." Ahhhh, the sweet voice of my on-air partner for years, the beautiful Robin Quivers. I know that confident voice belongs to a true broadcast professional. No doubt she is ready to do the morning's *shtick.* She is totally in sync with me. Ready to perform. Ready to be Laurel to my Hardy, Abbott to my Costello, my Sacco to her Vanzetti.

"Yes, Robin," I answered cheerfully. Life was sweet.

"First of all," Robin said, her tone growing **angry**. "I have a bone to pick with you."

Yikes! This sounded real bad. I could tell she was getting ready for an on-air battle. I didn't want any battles. I shot Robin a "I didn't do anything wrong" glance.

"You really hurt my feelings. I think you're getting to be a very strange person," Robin said, turning up the volume.

OOOFAH. This is for real. Suddenly I wanted to go home and plan a surprise birthday party for my wife. Robin is building up a head of steam and I can hardly imagine what it is about. I could say to her, "Why don't we talk about this off the air and avoid all the embarrassment of an on-air fight?" But that wouldn't be right. The show is about honesty and Robin was being honest. I'm the one who encouraged her to be herself on the radio and throw off the chains of traditional newscasting, but ***who wants to get into a real argument on the air with Robin?***

"How did I hurt you, Robin?" I tried to say nonchalantly, while I catalogued what the hell I might have done. Don't forget this is the Robin Quivers who wrote the bestseller *Quivers: A Life,* the same woman who found it easy to take up jogging because **SHE ENVISIONED MY FACE BELOW HER FEET** as she pounded the ground with each stride. Ouch! This was my Robin, who had been molested by her father, the woman who lost touch with reality and for years had problems dealing with people and understanding the meaning behind their actions. Many times in the past Robin and I hadn't talked for days because Robin imagined that I was plotting against her. I'd rather be in

Beirut right now than preparing for this psychological warfare.

"Tell me, how did I hurt you?" I asked, not really wanting to know.

"Well," Robin said, "I've been discussing this in my own head."

Whoa! **She's discussing stuff in her head.** That sounds like a new ***mental illness***.

She had that tortured look on her face that I had seen before. The look from the past let me now flashback to the bad old times. I can do it cheerfully now because me and my best gal, outside my family, are together in sync and in love. I never brought up our problems in my first book because I felt that Robin and I should always present a united front on the air. But the truth is, we had some misunderstandings over the years, sometimes barely able to talk. I also felt that Robin's mental illness was her own business. But because she revealed it in her book, I feel confident in telling you that **SHE WAS ACTUALLY MUCH CRAZIER THAN SHE ADMITTED.**

NBC was a particularly stressful situation. They'd beat the shit out of me daily and scream about Robin as well. Every day I was in there fighting for her, for me, and our show. Then I'd come out of these meetings and sometimes I'd get some irrational behavior from Robin. She would have some beef with me, real or imagined, and she'd either rip me a new asshole or give me the silent treatment. When she calmed down, I'd sit her down and we'd talk. I would talk to her like a father—not the father that fingered her, but a rational parent. We'd hash it out slowly and she'd be pacified. Until the next outburst.

So here we were again, with Robin giving me the face that I had seen so many times before. "Free yourself," I bellowed with false bravado on the air. "Go ahead. Today it's your birthday and I want you liberated. Free yourself! At forty-three, you should be liberated to say what you want to say." Who was I kidding? Robin was always saying what she wanted to say. "All right," Robin began, ***"I really don't think that you have observed my birthday properly. I think it's irresponsible and not right for you to say that you have, when you haven't."***

My mind was on fire. WHAT'S WITH THESE WOMEN

> ROBIN QUIVERS
> "Howard's the only person who could figure out how to not make radio fun. He could be a goofy radio guy but he turned us into a business."

AND THEIR BIRTHDAYS? FIRST MY WIFE WITH THE BIRTHDAY AND NOW ROBIN. I DON'T WANT ANY MORE BIRTHDAYS! Robin was **ranting** and I was getting good and pissed. What the hell was this complaint about her birthday? I was *sure* I had gotten a great present. My wife and I had decided to give her theater tickets and dinner. Robin is very important to us and we have a long history together so we've always tried to come up with a special gift. Robin loves theater and sampling new restaurants. Then my wife thought it would be great to bring the kids in and to share the day with Robin. My kids love being with Robin and they hadn't seen her in a while.

"I got you a birthday gift, Robin," I said.

"What birthday gift?" she answered. "That's not a gift *from you.*"

"Of course it is. That was a *family* gift, Robin," I explained.

"That's not a gift from *you*!" Robin repeated.

I wasn't sure where any of this was going. **I JUST WANTED TO GO HOME AND JERK OFF TO *MELROSE PLACE*.**

"Robin"—I was exasperated—"I consider the theater tickets a gift from *me*. I sat down with my wife . . ."

"No," she interrupted, "you've ***forgotten*** my birthday. It's *not* a birthday gift from you!"

"No," I screamed,

"my wife and I planned it *together.*"

"No, *we* didn't," Robin volleyed.

Oh brother, what the fuck was she talking about?

"YOU HAD NOTHING TO DO WITH IT!" Robin said.

"*Yes, I did,*" I blasted back.

Here we were again. I didn't want the audience to think Robin and I were not the inseparable powerhouse we let on to be. This was much too real.

In the Beginning

I was thrilled when I was first matched up with Robin in Washington. I knew I hit paydirt the first time I ever talked to her on the phone. Within seconds, it sounded like a radio show. She was interesting, she had opinions, and she could carry a conversation. I wanted to work with the best person in the business, and I knew I had found her in that first conversation.

I still had about five months left on my contract in Washington when I signed with WNBC. I knew I could work on them and get them to hire Robin. My plans for the future always included Robin. But she was understandably upset. Then **IT ESCALATED TO WAR.**

Off the air, Robin stopped talking to me. Even on the air, she'd do a news report and then turn off her mike and lapse into silence. Shortly before I left for New York, she gave me a two-page letter that was one long, vicious, hate diatribe. "YOU FUCKING RACIST MOTHERFUCKING HONKY ASSHOLE . . ." I wish I had that letter, but I ripped it up and threw it out. I was furious, but in the back of my mind, I knew that we'd be reunited. I ignored her letter because she was great for the show and my best friend. The show comes first in my life, and I was willing to put all else aside. I also loved Robin and felt the bond between us was so strong it would endure all obstacles.

Sure enough, I finally wore the executives at NBC down and they hired Robin. Before she came, I called her in Baltimore and we had a conversation that cleared the air. I'm sure we both hoped it would be great again between us. But when we were reunited at WNBC, things got even worse. Robin was ***not easy*** to be around. I had no clue that Robin was going through severe problems, and I couldn't understand her reactions. Her mood swings were unbelievable. She would lash out at you one moment and five minutes later act like nothing had happened.

Robin had the ability to put up a great front. She'd be wonderful with my parents and Alison. She'd hold it together when she was on the air. Then two days later, we'd get off the air and it was war again. I had to devise elaborate psychological tactics to deal with her. I found, for instance, that the worse Robin thought I was feeling, the more nurturing and calm she'd be. So I'd go to her and complain about things in my life. I'd fake spraining my ankle or having a fight with my wife just so she'd know I was in a bad mood. That was the only way to keep Robin off my back.

I thought things might get better when we started at K-Rock. The management was really enlightened. They were willing to let us do the kind of show we wanted. Professionally, we had never had it better. But Robin would still get into funks. And sometimes even her funk had funks. She had started therapy when we were still back at NBC, but now and then her irrational behavior would spill over onto the air.

One day, Robin was out sick and I needed to fill four hours. I brought in **BO THE LESBIAN**—a wild, wacky, and sexy listener. She was a hot blonde and she stripped down to everything but her panty hose. Naturally, we kept her on for a long time. Hey, I had to do something to fill in with Robin gone. At one point, we even let Bo read some of the news.

The next day Robin went **ballistic**. She came in and was so **furious** with me that she barely talked to me the whole show. I thought some of her **anger** was generated by the good response we got from Bo. In no way would Bo be an appropriate choice to be my on-air partner. Robin was my cohost. How ridiculous that Bo could replace her.

After two days of the silent treatment on the air, I knew I had to go in and have a talk with Robin. It wasn't just me who was bearing the brunt of her outbursts. She was **an equal opportunity abuser**. For example, Gary was walking around like a beaten man. He had no idea how to deal with Robin. Things came to a head one morning when Robin came into my office **screaming**. It was quarter to six in the morning—minutes away from the start of the show. I had reached the breaking point. Our relationship had gotten so strained that I didn't enjoy coming to work. The last thing I wanted to be was a boss. I would have been thrilled if Gary or somebody else was the boss of the show. I didn't want to be a daddy at work. I didn't want to be a guidance counselor. I just wanted to be a goofy radio guy.

I turned to Robin. "Look, Robin, I gotta be honest with you. This is not fun anymore. Maybe this is my fault, I don't know, but I don't think we can work together anymore."

There was a stillness for about a second. Robin was startled. We were getting a divorce. Then the dams burst. She started crying. I started crying. After all these years, the whole thing was going down the drain.

"Well, maybe you're right," Robin said, "maybe we can't work together anymore. But I don't want that to happen." And suddenly Robin became like a labor mediator. She got logical and rational and she outlined all the reasons why we should try to work these difficulties out, and she did. From that day on, she really held it together with me. Until this new thing about the birthday, we had a lovefest going.

The Untold Story: Robin's Secret True Love

"I SHOULDN'T BE A BOTHER! IF IT'S A BOTHER, DON'T DO IT!" It was like old times. Robin was still ***carrying on*** about the birthday gift.

"Thanks for *not* getting me a gift. It's okay, though. I am not offended. **I AM NOT OFFENDED THAT YOU DIDN'T GET ME ANYTHING FOR MY BIRTHDAY!"**

She sure sounded offended to me. So I explained it one more time, slowly, like when you talk to a foreigner who barely comprehends English.

"YOU . . . ARE . . . GETTING . . . TICKETS, FOR . . . YOUR . . . BIRTHDAY . . . FROM MY FAMILY—A NIGHT ON THE TOWN." I SAID TO DEAF EARS. SHE WASN'T EVEN LISTENING. "I . . . GOT . . . YOU . . . A . . . GIFT."

"No," Robin said matter-of-factly. "Your *wife* called me, and *she* arranged to celebrate my birthday."

"Robin," I fired back, hoping to snap her out of this fixation, "you're insane. A gift can be from *both* me and Alison. I had *plenty* to do with it. ***Who do you think paid for it***?"

"Alison!" She fumed.

"No!" I smiled. "Alison hasn't figured out how to make money in her entire life. She's useless." Great—now I was attacking my wife.

"Alison," Robin continued, "figured out how to make money: *She married you!*"

"That's it! I'm going to jog on *your* face tonight!" I joked.

I wanted to go home. I wanted to leave the radio business and retire to Arizona immediately. I wanted to wake up and go hiking every day, get prickly cactus spurs caught on my arms and legs—anything—just get me out of this!

"I know how you got my gift," Robin bellowed. "You said, 'Oh, God! Alison, *you* take care of it.'"

Gary interrupted. Alison was on the phone. Thank God for Alison. She had always been good with Robin. Finally, my wife's master's in social work from Columbia University could be put to good use.

"Robin, I am so insulted," Alison said.

"Don't be insulted!" Robin said. "I didn't say anything about *you*."

"You're missing the whole point," Alison explained calmly. "We're a family unit. We decided that this is what we would get you. Howard's paying for it and he thought of it."

"Of course, she comes to your defense," Robin said. "Who's going to be there?" she asked. "You and the girls. *That's* the 'we'?"

"I *did* do something for your birthday, Robin," I protested, for what had to be the millionth time. "Why can't you understand that?"

"I don't see it," Robin said, regally.

"It's because she's not married, she's not in a relationship, she doesn't have a family," Alison said. "She doesn't understand that couples do things together, like buying gifts."

Bingo! That was it. Robin wanted a special gift from me—not us. I had been right all these years. Robin *is* in love with me. **I am the love of her life—her one and only! It's me! Yes, I'm her man!**

Oh, if only I had the balls to act on it. **I WOULDN'T MIND GETTING MY HANDS ON HER LUSCIOUS MELONS.** I was in the middle of a lovers' spat. Robin wanted something special. From *me.* She wanted *me* on that date with her. Like a good husband. I'm not even a good husband to my wife. I don't take my *wife* out.

I've accused Robin of harboring a secret love for me for so long that she recently allowed herself to submit to a lie-detector test. We asked her about everything. According to the results, she didn't lie about the molestation charges in her book. She also was truthful when she said ***she had never had sex with her cats*** and that she never cupped her hand over

her butt, farted, and smelled the noxious fumes. But amazingly, she also tested truthful when she said that she didn't have sexual thoughts about me.

That had to be a mechanical error. **HOW COULD SHE NOT LOVE ME?**

Then again maybe it isn't physical love that Robin feels for me. Maybe Robin doesn't want me sexually, but she's still in love with me. Maybe she sees me as a father—or a brother—or the family that she never had. I'm Robin's family—the guy who just wanted to be a disc jockey and have some fun for four hours. **What happened?**

Sanity

"I think," Gary said, "that sometimes Robin gets herself into these positions and she knows in the back of her mind, she should just say, 'I'm wrong,' but she can't back down and she fights her way out." Who knew FaFa Flooley was FaFa Freud?

And with that Robin started to laugh. Gary had hit home. Her anger was starting to subside. In the old days she never backed off a position. A simple little discussion like this might have put Robin into one of her spiraling funks.

"All I know is I'm the only one around here who talks about what they're feeling," Robin reflected.

Maybe Robin was right. Of course Robin was right. What did she expect? I'm a guy. And guys aren't sensitive. They don't have emotions. They have penises. **WOMEN CARE ABOUT HUMAN FEELINGS. MEN CARE ABOUT PENIS FEELINGS.** It's that simple. Men are penocentric and I am the King of Penocentric People.

Truthfully, **I love Robin.** There is absolutely no better partner/friend in the world. It's a mindmeld. We don't need to look at each other or plan—it just happens. It's a perfect relationship. I always laughed when I read stories about teams like Martin and Lewis and Abbott and Costello—how they couldn't get along. All those idiots had to do was get along, but they fucked it up.

Look at the fucking Beatles. ***Just go to work.*** Make music. Have fun, you dumb bastards. Who gives a shit that Yoko has to wheel a bed in during recording sessions? Let the fucker sit there. Just keep the group together and rake in the bucks. For a while it looked like Robin and I were going to end up being idiots like them.

Keep the act together was my mantra during the tough times. I never wanted a different partner.

Robin is one of my closest friends and one of the few people in the entire universe who understands me. Remarkably, there has never been anyone in my entire life more supportive of me or more loyal to the show. If anyone tries to attack me, Robin reacts like a rabid dog. She hops on them and bites their fucking ear off. When I've been depressed, she's magically lifted me out of it. Who's talking like a loved one now? **GOD, MAYBE I'M THE ONE WHO'S IN LOVE WITH HER?** Maybe I do have emotions.

Robin contributes to the show in ways people can't see. She's an integral part of our brainstorming sessions, and when we have a guest on, Robin, who has a feed that goes right into my headphones, might surreptitiously whisper, ***"Why don't you ask them if they ever fucked a donkey?"***

But there is a reason that Robin sits in a separate studio. **ROBIN REPRESENTS THE AUDIENCE**, so I want her response to be fresh—and I want it on the air. She's really the only person who's allowed to talk freely on the show. Jackie or Fred might say things if we call on them, but Robin talks whenever she feels like it. In fact, Robin's the only person I play to. If you ask me who the prototypical listener is, I might say a guy driving to work in his car. But when I'm on the air, I'm not talking to anyone but Robin. Robin *is* my audience.

THE LAUGH

Robin makes me feel funny. A lot of people don't like Robin's laugh, but I know it's truly genuine. If you heard Robin in a room alone with me, she'd laugh just as much. Her laugh is a great tonic for me. Sometimes she laughs at things I don't realize are funny. And that keeps me going on a topic. If she doesn't laugh, I might lose confidence and go on to something else. When I hear Robin's laugh, I feel that I'm on target.

Robin laughs at stuff that guys won't laugh at sometimes. I wouldn't do as much family humor or talk about my dynamic with Alison if it weren't for Robin sitting there, wiping her eyes because she's laughing so hard. In fact, the few times that I've done the show without Robin, my timing is way off.

And she's very courageous. For years I wanted to get a nose job and have a normal schnozz between my eyes. I never had the balls to do it. But when Robin decided to lop off some of her enormous tits, she went right ahead and did it. It didn't matter that thousands of fans and Jackie kept saying, "Don't touch those beauties." And it was an **extremely painful** procedure. THEY HAD TO REMOVE HER NIPPLES, SCOOP OUT THE TISSUE, AND THEN SEW 'EM BACK UP. HER TITS LOOKED LIKE THE FRANKENSTEIN MONSTER WITH ALL THOSE STITCHES.

Now all she needs is to allow someone to ***suckle on those babies.*** The issue of Robin's sexuality fascinates our listeners. For years, people have been speculating whether Robin is a lesbian. Not true! I know that Robin is honest. If she were a lesbian, she'd be a ***FLAMING*** lesbian. She'd be out and quite vocal about it.

I think that Robin's like a Vulcan when it comes to sex. Like Spock, every seven years, she gets this incredible urge to mate. And she becomes a dating machine. Her last steady boyfriend was a Jamaican guy named Warren. We met him and we all liked him. They dated for a few years. Then it was New Year's Eve. They went out and then went back to Robin's apartment. Robin put peaches on his stomach, poured syrup over them, and sensually ate every drop of this love confection. They had wild, ravenous love. The next morning she prepared a big breakfast. Warren asked her if she had any New Year's resolutions and she told him she did. She wanted him out. Warren got the heave-ho. ROBIN'S LIKE A BLACK WIDOW THAT DEVOURS HER MATE.

ROBIN CURED

"Let's just forget what just happened." I offered her a truce over the birthday gifts issue.

"Yes, please, it's an **ugly** moment," Robin agreed. "The jury should disregard that outburst," she said, actually acknowledging it. Robin has changed. The new Robin is a lot of fun and the greatest and most generous radio partner in the world. I breathed a sigh of relief. So much for another quiet day at the office. My cocoon was back in order. **NOW I COULD GO HOME AND JERK OFF.**

FRED NORRIS

Describing Fred isn't easy. Describing Fred's job isn't easy. He does a little of everything. He's a great impressionist, a quick-thinking joke-and-sketch writer, and an all-around utility guy. Fred can write, produce, and sing song parodies better than anyone in the world. Fred plays taped sound effects throughout my show, creating a daily soundtrack filled with farts and belches. These sounds are played at the precise right moment by maestro Fred. He is a radio Renaissance man. He is blessed with many talents. The **PROBLEM** with Fred is that he is reluctant to share these gifts with me or anyone else.

I've known Fred Norris for over fifteen years and I still can't say with any certainty that he is *not* from Mars. Fred is an enigma. Half the time when we look for Fred for our after-show meeting, we don't even know where he is. The station isn't that big and there really is no place to hide—***but Fred manages to disappear.*** It's one of those scary, inexplicable phenomena that keeps the Martian myth alive.

Sometimes when I talk to Fred his eyes gloss over and he looks up toward the sky and appears to have traveled to another planet. He doesn't really socialize with anyone from the show. He guards his privacy with the zeal usually exhibited by mass murderers. He used to wear two watches on one wrist and wouldn't tell me why.

Amazingly, my longest broadcast association has been with this man, Fred Norris. People ask me all the time, "Why Fred? Why does he get to be part of the greatest radio show on earth when he acts in such a peculiar way, in ways unknown to man? Why does this ***odd and quiet*** Fred get all of my loyalty? Why is it that out of all the radio professionals in the world do you make it a point to get Fred on your show wherever you go?"

Well, let me finally put your curiosity to rest and expose the embarrassing truth.

Fred He so angry He's not
you But Howard/Freds impressi
aren't Even as Good as your
You make Good impressions Fred
impressions stink Every Body
He trys to sound like you
Do Better plus Fred isen't
Hansome the only impression
Fred Does Good is when He
Try's and I mean Try's to
imatate Stturing
John who Fred seams to
Enjoy Doing and He cant
Even Do that Right

PEE-SHY

One day I was in the bathroom at the radio station where Fred and I first worked. I was at the urinal and I was pressed up against the cold porcelain so no one would see my miniature cock. Fred walked in and immediately I tensed up. I didn't want this new associate seeing that I was hung like a **PIMPLE**. I didn't want to be made fun of at my new radio station as word spread on the smallness of my member. Fred took his place at the urinal next to me, pulling out his ***massive, Latvian, uncircumcised, hillbilly cock.***

He began talking to me and looking over into my urinal. I became uncomfortable and pee-shy, unable to urinate because of his penetrating gaze. He was staring at my shriveled dick with great intensity. I couldn't hide my penis from his strong brown eyes. I was expecting him to laugh at my organ that was no bigger than a woman's clit, but Fred was different. He didn't laugh like so many others had. He just stared and remained expressionless. Then, with the swiftness of a jaguar, he pushed me back against the wall. I was trapped and sure he was about to kill me.

Surprisingly, like a butterfly, Fred delicately reached down and placed his thumb and forefinger around the rim of my glans penis. Gently rubbing and manipulating my cock and balls he brought me to full arousal. All one inch of me. I was shocked but it felt good and I let out a soft moan as FRED, MY DEAREST FREDDY, JACKED ME OFF TO HEIGHTS OF ECSTASY LIKE NO WOMAN HAD EVER DONE. THERE WAS NO SHAME, NO FEAR, ONLY PLEASURE.

Fuck you, you bastard! I can't believe you fell for that story. I resent that you would think for one minute that Fred and I are not 100 percent all man. For God's sake, that's not the reason I stick with Fred, ***you asshole,*** and I resent you falling for that cheap literary trick!

Back to the real reason I stay with Fred. I've never revealed it before because quite frankly no one paid me to. But now, because you bought my book, I can tell you Fred will always have a job with me for as long as he wants because of . . . ***records.*** Yes, records—albums, LPs, the things they don't make anymore because of CDs. Fred has my undying loyalty and friendship because of one simple act involving record albums. I know it sounds cryptic, but let me explain:

I met Fred back in Hartford, Connecticut, in 1979. I was the new morning man at WCCC radio, a legendary station in Connecticut that rocked like a motherfucker and covered all of southern New England. It was my first real morning job. No one was convinced that I could pull off this radio show, especially me. It was heavy-duty responsibility and my bosses were expecting real fireworks from their new morning star. Management paid me nothing and expected huge ratings six days a week. In addition,

> FRED NORRIS
> "We've all grown as individuals. I mean, Gary's a fucking father. But every day you walk into that studio you jump back ten years to where you started. I get in there and I feel like this fucking tongue-tied rube from fucking Bug Tussle again."

after my show each day I had to write and produce commercials for hours. I was also responsible for producing, hosting, and booking the guests for a public-affairs interview show that aired every Sunday. The only thing they forgot to assign to me **was putting a broom up my ass** so I could sweep up while I walked. I was a nervous wreck.

I felt completely alone on this powerful 50,000-watt radio station—and extremely vulnerable. I had never really been a morning man before. The other jocks at the station all seemed so secure, so established, and here ***I was, the new douchebag*** in town who was doing all this untested bizarre material that no one was quite sure was working. Especially me. I was going where no disc jockey had been before and I was scared.

They were expecting a high degree of professionalism and, let's face it, I wasn't too polished. In fact, I'm still not too polished. Not only did I have to be funny, but during the show I had to record phone calls while music played, prepare and read news, run the required FCC meter-reading tests that measured the station's transmitter output, and keep a log of the exact time the commercials ran, down to the second. But none of that was so bad that I couldn't handle it. The worst part of my job, the part I hated the most, was keeping the studio neat and clean by being a good clerk and filing my records into the proper slot in the wall. It drove me over the edge.

It might seem trivial to you, but I was trying to entertain Connecticut's commuters and my program director would come in and yell at me that my records were all over the floor. I couldn't get it together to put my records away after I played them, so the carpeted studios of WCCC became wall-to-wall vinyl. The entire floor was covered in albums and I was breaking all the LPs by rolling over them with my chair.

"Put your records away right after you play them or you'll be fired!" my boss finally yelled at me one day. This sent me into a panic. First of all, I was obsessive compulsive, so the records had to be put away in just the right order or else something tragic would happen. In the middle of a show, I didn't need to hear from that voice in the back of my **DISTURBED** head that put me through these lengthy rituals. With my **mental problems**, putting the ZZ Top album away could take hours as I put my fingers in just the right place to ensure my success in broadcasting. Forgetting the obsessive thoughts, on general principle, in the middle of the show I needed to concentrate on being funny, not on trying to make sure the Doors album found the right place in the wall. What was the big deal if I waited till after my show to put away the records? ***Why didn't anyone understand this?***

Enter Fred Norris, "Overnight Disc Jockey." He was going to college full-time and doing the graveyard shift at the station. It was the longest graveyard shift I had ever heard of in the business: midnight to six A.M. Fred was also a scary-looking individual. You wouldn't believe the way Fred would act and dress in those days. He wouldn't talk to anyone and wore a ***stupid floppy cab driver's cap*** that he would never take off.

I thought he was going bald or something, the way he'd wear that ugly thing. Then he wore really bad blue jeans, the kind that you'd buy if you were a farmer. Add a drab workshirt and off-brand, cheap-shit sneakers called Kangaroos that you'd get in the bargain bin at K-mart, and you have a portrait of Fred Norris, interplanetary radio geek and serial killer look-a-like.

Fred was mysterious. If he worked full-time at night and went to classes during the day it didn't take Angela Lansbury to figure out that Fred **didn't sleep**. Everything about Fred was strange. He **FRIGHTENED** almost everyone and carried a shovel with him wherever he went. Some speculated he did farmwork with his shovel. Others dared to say that maybe Fred was indeed a serial killer and it was used to dig the graves of all the people he killed.

Me, I never said anything. Maybe that's why he chose to make contact with me.

Although Fred rarely communicated with humans, I was selected as a liaison between Earth and Fred. Most people at the station had never really seen Fred because of his strange hours. I was one of the few who actually knew what Fred looked like. After Fred's incredibly long midnight-to-six radio shift he would hang around my show and do impressions for me—mostly stuff he had seen Dan Ackroyd do on *Saturday Night Live.* He would tell me he thought I was really funny and that I was on to something fresh and new in radio. Remarkably, one morning, with some vigorous prodding on my part, shy and bashful Fred got on a phone extension in another room and effortlessly did funny impressions of Nixon and Howard Cosell live on the air. He was one of the most talented people I ever met. From that day forward, if I asked Fred for help with a routine, he would do it.

Fred:

Never said no.

Never said, "Hey, you don't pay me for this."

Never said, "I'm dog-tired man and not only did I work all night but I have to go to school now. So go fuck yourself."

Never said, "Hey, you make more money than me—why don't *you* do it?"

Man's best Fred

Fred just did it. I was a nobody and he was a guy I hardly knew, ***but Fred did it.***

But don't get me wrong—that's not why I'm loyal to Fred. That shit was great and I appreciated it, but the thing that made him a friend for life, the one thing that endeared him to me, was that ***he helped me with my records.*** *Unsolicited, the son of a bitch would get on his hands and knees and put away the* ***mountain*** *of records I hadn't filed.*

It was the most unselfish act and the nicest thing anyone had ever done for me in my short broadcast career. In this awful broadcast world I lived in everyone was busy kicking one another in the teeth. All announcers were too busy and worried about their next announcing gig to help anyone. *Fred took time out of his busy schedule to help a nobody like me succeed.* There was nothing in it for him. No hidden agenda.

I once read that dogs were the only beasts in the animal kingdom who had chosen to align themselves with man. Out of every stinking animal on this planet only the dog wanted to be aligned with man. Like a dog, Fred had chosen to be aligned with me for no apparent reason. And like a dog, I chose to be aligned with Fred. Just as no one could explain why the dog chose man, no one could explain why Fred chose Howard, and why Howard chose Fred. Fred was an ally.

There isn't a disc jockey alive who likes putting his records away, and Fred certainly knew it was a chore (having just put away his own records for six hours), but FRED SAW MY PAIN AND ***cared***. However, if you think Fred isn't a tremendous **PAIN IN THE ASS,** here are just a few responsibilities that come along with Fred, and I am not exaggerating:

1. FRED NEEDED HELP OPENING A CHECKING ACCOUNT

Fred, at twenty-five, had never opened a checking account. He kept his money in mattresses. I couldn't take it anymore, so I drove him to a bank. He was nervous and didn't want to do it. Thinking quickly, I came up with a brilliant strategy: Fred idolized Dan Ackroyd. Fred would do not only impressions of Ackroyd but also impressions of Ackroyd doing impressions. Since Fred felt more comfortable doing characters, I told him to speak to the guy at the bank as Ackroyd doing Nixon and to make believe that he was a lawyer when he spoke to the bank officer. He went in there and put on a whole different voice and became Fred Norris, Esq. That was how Fred was able to speak to a bank exec and open his first checking account. It was exhausting dealing with this but don't forget, *Fred helped me with my records.*

2. FRED NEEDS HELP WITH EATING

Fred takes bites and chews food **without swallowing** and forms a **BIG POUCH** in his mouth. His pouch will just get bigger and bigger. He is like the main character in the remake of *The Fly*. Remember Brindle Fly, half man, half insect? He is Brindle Fred. It's a lot to suffer through, but remember, *Fred helped me with my records.*

3. ONCE FRED PLANTS HIMSELF SOMEWHERE, HE NEEDS HELP LEAVING

One Friday, when I first moved to New York to work at NBC, Alison and I invited Fred to stay over at our apartment because there had been a terrible blizzard and his car was snowed in. On Saturday it rained and the snow washed away, but that night Fred slept over again. Sunday morning Alison said to me, "I don't think Fred's going to leave." I told her not to worry. By Sunday afternoon, there was **NO SIGN** that Fred was going **ANYWHERE**. Alison asked me to talk to him.

"Fred, there's no more snow on the ground. The rain washed it all away," I noted.

"Really?" he said. He looked out the window. "Yeah, right."

"So maybe it's, uh, time to go?" I asked.

He was insulted. But he finally left.

4. FRED ATE ALL HIS MEALS STANDING UP IN A LITTLE 24-HOUR DELI

Gary became Fred's best friend. And according to Gary, Fred's second best friend was the Vietnamese woman at the deli across the street from his house. Fred had his choice of hundreds of restaurants, but he'd eat all his meals at this little twenty-four-hour deli. And there wasn't even anyplace to sit there; it was a takeout joint. Fred would eat while hanging out with this Vietnamese woman. Fred doesn't befriend many and when he does choose a human to communicate with, it's always an interesting choice. Fred's a lot to handle but . . . *he put away my records.*

5. FRED NEEDS HELP USING THE PHONE

"Howard, this is Fred Norris." I've known this guy forever and even to this very day, every time he calls he identifies himself by using his full name.

6. FRED NEEDS HELP WITH HIS MOTHER'S TITS

I once asked Fred if his mother had big tits. He told me he didn't know. He claimed he never looked.

"Fred," I said, "surely in all these years you've looked at her body in clothes, you've noticed if she has large breasts."

"It's **SICK** to look at your mother's body!" he yelled and stormed away.

7. FRED HIDES HIS LIFE IN A PLASTIC BAG

Whenever I ask Fred to write a routine, he claims it's in his bag. Fred carries a bag to work. Everybody on the show carries his or her material in something: I use an aluminum briefcase. Gary's got a shoulder bag. Robin's got seventeen purses. Jackie uses an L.L. Bean bag. But Fred carries his stuff in a plastic supermarket bag, just like a bag lady. I was always fascinated with what he keeps in that thing. If I'd want to do a Kurt Waldheim bit, Fred would dig into that bag and pull one out. But he's also got his food in there: nuts, berries, bananas, and yogurt. Fred eats yogurt without utensils. He just puts the cup up to his mouth and downs it in three swallows. Like the Fly.

I was determined to find out what else Fred had in that bag. I felt that since Fred did carry show-related material in the bag and I was paying him for his material, I had a right to see what was in the bag. I explained this to him on the air but he disagreed.

I knew that Fred always takes piss breaks while the show is on. So I waited for him to leave the studio and I asked Jackie to hand me Fred's bag. Jackie was too scared and he refused. So I ran around the console and started rummaging through the bag. He had a ton of shit in there. There were papers and food and a book entitled ***Coping with Alcoholic Parents.*** I read the title on the air. By the way, ***Fred's parents are*** NOT ***alcoholics,*** which makes this even stranger.

All of a sudden, I heard Fred's footsteps outside the studio. I quickly threw everything back into the bag and ran back to my chair. After a few minutes, I couldn't keep the secret and I told Fred that I had gone through his bag on the air. He went ballistic. I kept up my front and argued that I had every right to do that since I was paying for his creative material, but I was truly frightened. Fred told me he'd **KILL ME** if I ever went through his bag again. It was scary, but the records—*he helped with the records.*

8. FRED NEEDED HELP GETTING MARRIED

Even when Fred was ready to mate I set him up on my Dial-A-Date program, a warped version of *The Dating Game.* After a several-year mysterious courtship, Fred married Allison, his Dial-A-Date winner. I can't tell you about the wedding because I wasn't there. The one guy who has been with him for fifteen years and got him his wife was not invited. I was sitting at home during a vacation when the phone rang: *"Hello, Howard. This is Fred Norris. I just wanted to*

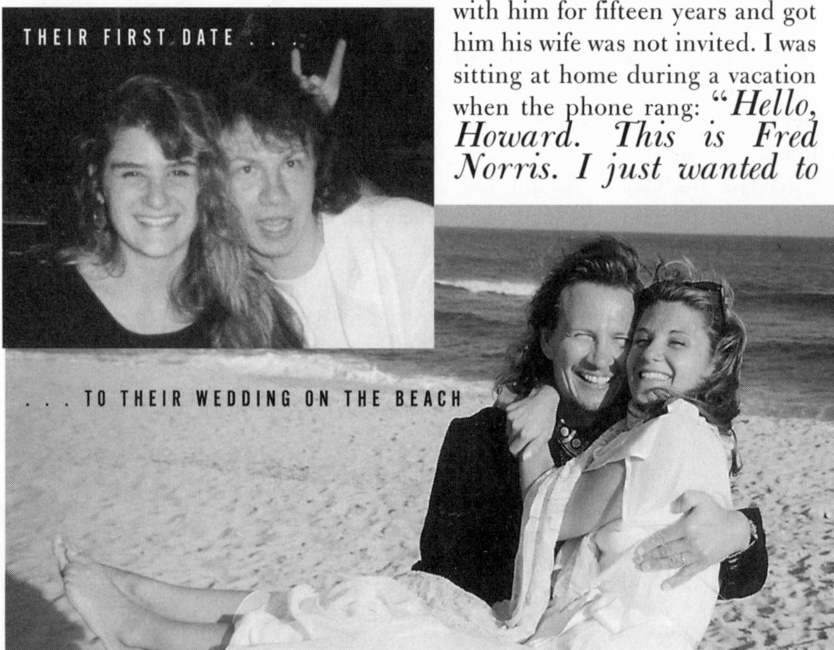

THEIR FIRST DATE . . .

. . . TO THEIR WEDDING ON THE BEACH

call and let you know that I'm now married." It was strange . . . but *the guy picked up my records,* on his hands and knees.

9. FRED NEEDED HELP AT HIS OWN BACHELOR PARTY

I was so happy about Fred getting married I decided to give him a bachelor party at Scores strip club to celebrate his nuptials. Fred reads a tremendous amount to learn about human behavior because he lives a sheltered life. He must have read that when a guy has a bachelor party, he gets drunk. Fred has no concept of moderation. So he's sitting at Scores and he's downing tequila shots and beer chasers. He must have had about sixteen of them. Then he wandered up to the couch area where I was sitting, enjoying some lap dances. Fred plopped down next to me and before I knew it, my leg is soaking wet. I figured that the drunken bastard spilt his drink on me. Then one of the dancers started **SCREAMING**. They jumped up and I saw that Fred was **RETCHING** all over my leg.

FRED'S FAVORITE LAP-DANCER GAY RICH

I went to the bathroom to clean up. When I got back, Fred was sitting on the couch. Instead of a topless dancer on his lap, our intern Gay Rich was perched there, wearing only a tiny leopard-skin thong. Gay Rich was kissing Fred on the cheek and Fred was stroking his back. I couldn't believe my eyes. ***The world's biggest homophobe was petting with the gayest guy alive.*** Everybody stopped watching the naked girls. We were all staring at Fred and cracking up.

Suddenly, Fred pushed Gay Rich off his lap and stood up. Like Frankenstein's monster, he lurched toward the steps leading to the downstairs area. My friends Neil and Ronnie the Limo Driver tried to steady him, but Fred stumbled and went **face-first** off the top step. He wound up facedown on the carpet. I don't think that it was an accident, though. I'm convinced that *Fred was so shocked to discover that he really was gay* that **HE TRIED TO KILL HIMSELF.** Actually, Fred is definitely not gay. He was so inebriated he had no idea it was Rich on his lap.

At first, we were alarmed that Fred might be seriously injured. Blood appeared to be running out of his mouth and we had him rushed to the hospital. He was unconscious for hours. The doctor had no way of telling if he was paralyzed or just drunk. The bleeding had been caused by a huge gash in his chin, which had to be repaired by a plastic surgeon. Fred was so drunk that they didn't even have to administer anesthesia. He just tried to **SWAT** the needle away as if it were an annoying fly.

By the time Fred finally came to, he had **THROWN UP** twice on the nurse. Then around seven that night, he opened his eyes and smiled, like Otis the drunk. His wife and his mother-in-law carried him home and he **PASSED OUT** again. It was an **UNBELIEVABLE** hassle, but ... *I owe him for putting away my records.*

FRED, THE SOPHISTICATED RUBE

I thank God that Fred got married. I love Fred's wife, Alison, for taking him off my hands. She's actually a real good influence on him. You have to understand that Fred is like a chameleon. He'll take on the traits of whoever he's with. Because of Alison's influence, Fred is getting more and more normal. He's dressing like a human being. He's grooming himself better. He only drinks Sapporo beer. He dines at fine restaurants instead of eating hot dogs from Papaya King. Since Alison's an actress, Fred is now taking acting lessons.

One day a few months back, Robin was in the office, telling us about *Lost in Yonkers*, a play she'd just seen. Fred came in on the conversation.

"Who played the lead?" Fred asked Robin.

Robin mentioned some obscure actress.

"I saw it when it opened with Mercedes Ruehl and it was much better then," Fred informed her. A few years ago Fred didn't know how to hail a cab. Now he's a theater critic. Hey, you've come a long way, pal. Thanks for all the good times and sticking by me.

Don't let this essay on Fred fool you. Fred's an important player in this mess I've created, and I couldn't have done it without him. He's responsible for some of my funniest moments on the air and sadly just might be the most normal out of my entire crew, myself included.... **AND HE HELPED ME PUT AWAY MY RECORDS.**

JACKIE MARTLING

Fuck Jackie! Fuckin' Jackie never has a nice word to say about me. Why should I write good stuff about Jackie, who for years has ripped me a new asshole behind my back?

Seriously, Jackie is four times as talented and as important to my show as any of you might think and . . . he is one-tenth as talented as *he* thinks. Let me tell you the good and the bad about my friend and cohort Jackie Martling.

Jackie started working with me back at NBC, and any

regular listener of the show knows Jackie is the head writer. He writes sketches and gags throughout the morning and also is a stand-up comedian. Jackie is super-talented at all these things, and I give him full credit for the wonderful material he comes up with on a daily basis. But writing is not his main job on the show. ***His main function is to talk behind my back and bad-mouth me to anyone within earshot.***

It is also Jackie's job to turn the rest of the staff against me when it comes to salary. Jackie has no influence over Fred and Robin but manages to rile up everyone else. This is strange, since I don't pay the salaries. We all work for someone else: Infinity Broadcasting. When Jackie gets crazed about his contract negotiations, there are:

Four universal truths about Jackie:

Universal truth number 1. Jackie always feels **abused.**
Universal truth number 2. Jackie always feels **downtrodden.**
Universal truth number 3. Jackie always feels **underappreciated.**
Universal truth number 4. ***You can't win with Jackie.***

ANNOYING HIGHLIGHTS ABOUT JACKIE

1. WHEN I FIRST HIRED HIM, HE WOULD GET DRUNK AND TELL EVERYONE THAT HE WAS THE BRAINS BEHIND THE SHOW.

But that never bothered me. I knew that wasn't Jack Martling talking. That was Jack Daniel's talking.

2. AT MY NEW YEAR'S EVE SHOW, "LIVE FROM THE FELT FORUM," JACKIE RAN AROUND BACKSTAGE YELLING TO ANYONE WHO WOULD LISTEN THAT I WAS A CHEAP JEW. JACKIE LIED. I'M NOT A CHEAP JEW. I'M A CHEAP HALF-JEW.

I hadn't done many live shows and I was totally preoccupied with getting through the performance. After the show there was an impromptu gathering in my dressing room. Someone from the promoter's office had brought down a case of champagne and put it out for us.

Howard,

You know Jackie is an Aye Hole. I met him at one of his crummy shows and aside from his blatant smell, he was drunk and rude. The guy could barely make any sense with his warbled speech and so-called jokes. He barreled on to the stage pissing and moaning about You and what a douche you are to work for, then proceeded to rank on Robin claiming that she was a no talent Token. I thought this guy was cool.

Finally he starts in with these ancient one-liners that my great grandmother could only relate to, then he starts hawking his junk like a Yenta at a Long Island garage sale. This lard is lucky to have you as an employer because he sucks as a comedian. There is no way that he could go national, unless maybe as a two bid drug dealer.

I tell ya, I'm so pissed that I couldn't get my money back after this comedy charade that I'll be waiting at Roy's to personally beat the "fried chicken" crap out of the load. Martling Beware ! Martling Beware ! Martling Beware !

Meanwhile, Jackie had somehow gotten wind of this fact. He went nuts and cursed me out, calling me a cheap fucking Jew, amazed that nobody—meaning me—had given him champagne. I would have given him the whole fucking case. I didn't even know the champagne was there. **I don't even drink.**

Instead of being happy that he'd just played the Felt Forum on New Year's Eve, rather than a strip club in North Carolina, Jackie was bitching to anyone within shouting distance that I was a ***scumbag*** *over a bottle of champagne.*

But you know what—and don't tell him this—Jackie deserved a bottle of champagne. He's the guy who stripped down on the Felt Forum stage and exposed his butt cheeks for the good of the show. He was the creator of that now-immortal Stuttering John question to Ted Williams: "Did you ever fart in the catcher's face?" Hell, he deserved a whole case of champagne.

3. JACKIE CLAIMS TO BE A GENTLE HIPPIE WHO DOESN'T CARE ABOUT POSSESSIONS, BUT HE IS CONSUMED BY MONEY.

Jackie thinks I'm cheap. This coming from a guy who sent me a twenty-nine-cent baby gift when my daughter Ashley was born. Ashley got a blue night-light from Jackie and his wife. Who gets a blue night-light for a baby girl? I'm sure it was something that he had lying around the house. My wife shrugged it off and gave the night-light to our maid. In all fairness, Jackie did send a polyester outfit along with the night-light that still had the price tag attached: It cost a whopping **$14.99.**

Jackie is the TIGHTWAD who runs around calling everyone else CHEAP.

But through thick and thin, through every one of my radio battles, Jackie's been a great warrior. It was JACKIE who thought up the idea to dangle succulent whole chickens from the ceiling in front of Richard Simmons and his fat friends on my TV show. So he's not a great shopper! Who cares?

4. JACKIE BLAMES ME FOR HOLDING BACK HIS CAREER.

Jackie feels he is underpaid despite the fact he now owns **three homes**, **new cars**, *and dines on* **lobster** *almost every night.* Rather than admitting that his exposure on the show has helped his comedy career, Jackie believes the show has limited his rise to the comedic heavens. "I'm being held back. If I wasn't waking up early and coming down here, who knows where I'd be by now? I could always go out to Hollywood and punch up scripts," he always tells me.

JACKIE MARTLING

"We don't have quality time off the air anymore. When you hang out, you find out things about each other, maybe mend things. The last thing this show needs is for anything to be mended. The more wounds, diseases, and scabs, the more there is to work with."

5. ONE TIME I TURNED TO JACKIE FOR HELP AND IT TURNED INTO ONE OF THE BIGGEST NIGHTMARES OF MY LIFE.

Alison was fed up with our social life. She wanted me to go out to dinner and movies with all her Long Island yentas and their husbands every Saturday night. I'd had it with that domestic shit. Most nights, the husband would corner me and start yapping about what he didn't like about the show. "Don't make fun of Jews," these garment-district experts on broadcasting would tell me.

While I was getting a lecture in the corner, Alison would be with the yenta. The yenta would get Alison all fired up about what a **piece of shit** I was because I had sexy girls on my show.

"If that was *my* husband I'd throw him out of the house," they'd say. "You're a saint, Alison, the way you put up with Howard fondling those girls."

Just what I need on a Saturday night: some little instigator coming between me and Alison. We'd get home miserable. "Alison," I'd say, "I don't like going out with couples on Long Island and talking about me all night and what I do for a living. I'm bored with all the bullshit conversation and would much rather stay home and stare at the wall."

Alison would get **UPSET** and **CRY** and say that she was fed up with my antisocial behavior and she wanted a husband she could do things with. Alison must have ***BITCHED*** to my mother again, because my mother called me up and told me it was a husband's responsibility to go out with his wife and her friends. What the fuck that was all about I don't know, but there was a big campaign to get me out of the house because my sister started working on me too.

In order to get everyone off my back, I came up with a solution: We would only go out with show-biz couples—famous people who would understand that what I did for a living wasn't fondling, it was acting. This was a great plan, a brilliant plan. The only problem with my plan was that I didn't have any famous friends.

"Oh *great*, now we'll never go out," Alison bitched at me.

"Exactly," I said. That was precisely my plan. Alison looked like she was going to **CUT MY NUTS OFF**, which motivated me to come up with an idea.

"Wait a minute, we'll go out with Jackie and his wife, Nancy. They're in show biz!"

So the four of us met at a Long Island restaurant. I was proud of my plan. This was a great decision to have a Saturday-night outing with Long Island's **show-biz power couple**, Jackie and Nancy Martling. We weren't ten minutes into dinner when I started to question that decision. Out of the blue, Nancy starts attacking me for being in bed with the two porno stars on my *Underwear and Negligee* pay-per-view special.

"I don't know how you take it, Alison. I wouldn't let *my Jackie* get in bed with two women like that," this troublemaker said.

I flipped out. I could see Jackie biting his lip.

"I don't know. I wouldn't let *my Jackie* do it. Alison is a very brave woman to put up with all that shit. Everyone I know says so," she said.

I looked over at Alison. She's got this weird look on her face. I knew what was going on in Alison's head.

"Let me ask you something," I said to Nancy. "If Steven Spielberg came to you tomorrow and said you had to be in a love scene in one of his movies, would you do it?"

Nancy said, "Uh, well, no."

We all looked at Nancy. Nobody believed her response.

Nancy Sirianni

Now we're in a full-blown argument. Jackie's downing the drinks and putting his head in his hands. Alison's freaked out. I'm ranting like a lunatic. We went home that night and I told Alison that was it, I'm never going to socialize again.

Meanwhile, about a month later, Jackie puts up some money, and Nancy is starring in a free play. She's playing a vampire who wears a see-through negligee. During her big scene she's kissing some guy, **TONGUE AND ALL.**

Nothing like a night out with my show-biz friend Jackie.

6. JACKIE'S HYGIENE IS DISGUSTING.

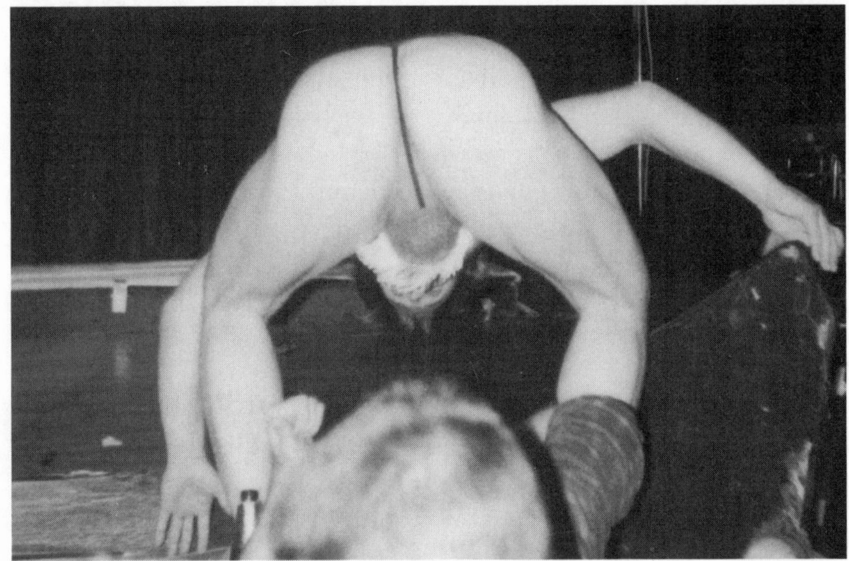

Jackie will go into the bathroom and take **A HEARTY, SLOPPY, SMELLY DUMP** complete with foul noises and splashing toilet water. Then he'll come out of the stall and just walk right back into the studio *without washing his hands.* "What's the big deal? I didn't shit on my hands," he'll shrug.

Jackie uses a filthy pen as a stirrer when he puts sugar in his coffee, *which he drinks out of the same* **foul encrusted** *cup that he uses every day without ever washing it.*

Jackie will sleep over at your house and use your toothbrush in the morning. *He has no idea that this is wrong.*

Worst of all, with all his foul hygienic habits, Jackie stays healthy as a horse. *It makes me crazy.* If Jackie is still alive, why am I so worried about germs? Jackie is in the best health of anyone on the show—except for his feet. On close examination, it looks like there is some kind of fungus brewing down there. They look all YELLOW and CRUSTY and ROTTED. Does Jackie worry about it? Of course not. He calls a podiatrist he finds in the local *Pennysaver*. Talk about being a cheapskate. Who goes to a doctor from the *Pennysaver*? He goes to this guy and has the doctor PULL OUT EVERY ONE OF HIS TOENAILS. *No second opinion!* End of problem.

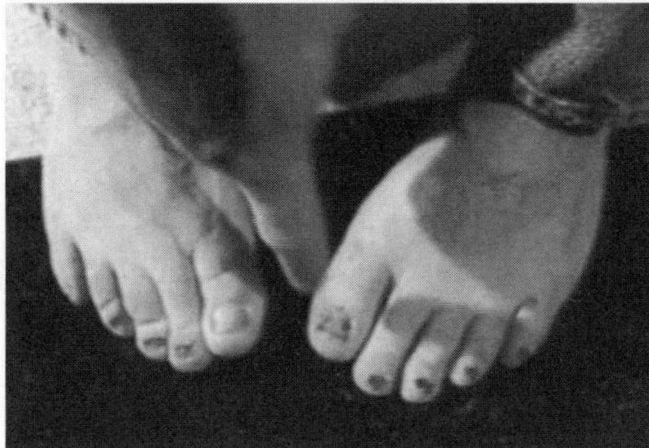

End of toenails.

HE'S SO HEAVY, HE'S MY BROTHER

As far as I can tell, I am the only motherfucker in the world who has been good to Jackie. I am Jackie's biggest fan and think he is one of the most talented comic minds in the country . . . and most important . . .

JACKIE IS GOOD FOR BUSINESS

Jackie is part of my family. Jackie is part of the reason I do radio. He makes my morning fun. It's hard to be the guy in the background who writes a great joke only to watch me deliver and get the credit for everything. But JACKIE DESERVES AS MUCH CREDIT. Jackie is also good for Robin's mental health. If Robin throws a tantrum, Jackie will just laugh and make fun of her. Robin, I know, will dispute this. You can't act angry in front of Jackie because he doesn't take anything seriously. He's a true comic. Jackie can razzle-dazzle you with his wit. He's the man

who walks through the door at six A.M. and says "Let's fuck with a Beatle today" and sends Stuttering John off to the Ringo Starr press conference to ask Ringo the funniest mean-spirited questions I've ever heard.

You know what, Jackie? You're worth the hassle.

GARY DELL'ABATE, *MY PRODUCER*

Believe it or not, Gary was the best-looking girl in the studio. In person he looked hot, but in the photograph he looks like a fat Italian chick. I admire that Gary shaved his moustache for the picture—that shows true dedication to his craft. (Who knew he had *a craft?)*

Last name: **Dell'Abate:** D-E-L-L-*apostrophe*-A-B-A-T-E. That's some name—and that apostrophe, how impressive. It took me years to figure out where that apostrophe went. Was it over the A, the first L, the second L? How many guys do you know with an apostrophe? Probably none. You know why you don't know anyone with an apostrophe? *Because most normal people would drop it because it makes no fucking sense and it's a big pain in the ass!*

In fact, it's all a big mistake to begin with. When Gary's grandfather got to Ellis Island from the A R M P I T of Italy, Naples, he picked his nose and wiped his dirty booger on his immigration papers, creating an apostrophe over the last "l" in Dell'Abate. Gary's smart relatives have all dropped the apostrophe and the "Abate" and just gone with "Dell," but Gary has to leave it there so he can confuse everyone.

I hear him on the phone all day spelling that fucking name for people. It takes an hour. He could probably get a lot of work done if he just dropped the goddamned apostrophe. He could do the work of two people if he dropped the "Abate." I walk by and hear this everyday:

"Hello . . . yes, that's D-E-L-L-apostrophe, yes . . . yes . . . the apostrophe goes after the L and . . . yes, apostrophe—that's A-P-O-S-T-R-O-P-H-E—yes, the apostrophe *before* the A but then you have to **capitalize** the **A**. Right. That's **CAPITAL** A . . . No, I'll start over. D-E-L-L, apostrophe over the L and then a capital A, then SMALL B, SMALL A, SMALL T, SMALL E. *Right.* Dell'Abate."

Then the pronunciation takes fifteen more fucking minutes. Most people say "dellabate"—like it rhymes with masturbate.

It's easier to construct an atom bomb then spell and say his fucking name. What a fucking name. Say it loud and it's music playing. Say it soft and it's almost like praying. *Dell'Abate.* I'll never stop saying Dell'Abate. That name drives me crazy. Only Gary and gay porno stars have an apostrophe.

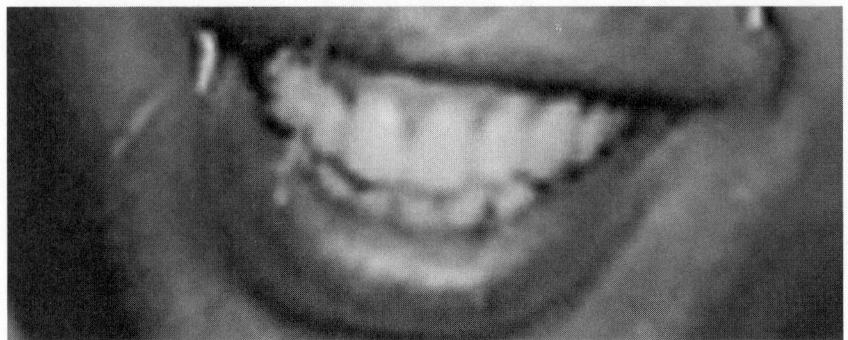

DISTINGUISHING CHARACTERISTIC: Big huge teeth
EXACT SIZE OF TEETH: Unknown
APPROXIMATE SIZE OF TEETH: Big, thick, white, Chiclet-sized caps

WHY I TREAT GARY SO BADLY: Gary was not broadcast savvy when I hired him right out of college. Gary is *still* not broadcast savvy. Quite frankly, *I'm* not broadcast savvy. I hired him for $150 a week. After much introspection—okay, after *some* introspection, truthfully, after five seconds of introspection—I finally figured out why I yell at Gary so much. Yes, I love working with him. Yes, we've been together since NBC and, yes, he does a great job.

Yet he gets yelled at on the air at least once a day, with vicious diatribes that usually end up with me calling him "STUPID" or "MORON" or "**STUPID SMELLY MORON**." I'm not proud of these outbursts, but it is my way of *teaching* Gary about ***my needs***.

In other words, I yell at Gary the way my father yelled at me. Gary is the son I never had. And if my relationship with Gary is any indication of how I would be with my own son, then there truly is a God who spared the world another Stern family father-son relationship.

They say that children who have been abused either grow up to be abusers or they rise above it. I always thought I had risen above it—but not in Gary's case. I am absolutely unrelenting in my quest to mold Gary in my own image. No matter how hard Gary works, I feel he is being lazy. I work twenty-four hours a day and because he doesn't, I find him imperfect.

Gary,

You Dumb stupid mother-fucker Monkey shit! Howard should fire your big-toothed neanderthal ass, you fuck! Why don't you brush your fuckin teeth you douche-bag Hey Bosthhh! Fa-Fa-Flunky Ra-Ra-Retard

You should be shot!

-MR X.

I rely on Gary to do all of the **shit** work I don't want to do: like opening mail and booking guests. Gary will actually develop show ideas and edit material, and I am convinced he does this better than anyone on the planet. But because we are such a ***low-budget*** show, Gary gets stuck with administrative tasks that end up being a real pain in the ass.

Although I am satisfied with Gary's producing work, I feel his administrative duties get all screwed up and that's when we conflict. I am convinced when Gary screws up ***he doesn't***

GARY DELL'ABATE
"Howard's amazing. Sometimes it's only seven o'clock in the morning and he's already screamed at me, Jackie, Fred, and John."

use common sense. My father was convinced *I* had no common sense. My father taught me common sense by humiliating and emasculating me. He taught me right from wrong by calling me a dummy every time I fucked up. He beat the snot out of me. Not with fists but with abusive language like "jerk," "dope," and the overused "stupid." Words were his whip. Words molded me into a warped workaholic whose only moments of comfort come from being successful at his job.

It's pathetic. *BUT IT WORKED.* And it will work on Gary, damnit. I'm gonna teach that boy some common sense and he'll thank me for it. I thank my dad for my writing this book. I'm driven to write this book just to show my father how fucking smart I am. My dear dad called me just the other night. I told him I was holed up in the basement writing.

"Boy, that's something," he said.

He was blown away that I could write a book. He thought I couldn't write my name. I needed him to tell me I was brilliant. How fucked up is it that a forty-one-year-old guy still needs his parents' approval?

I egged my father on. "Oh really, Dad? What do you mean?"

"To write another book—I never could imagine that you would have that ability," my father said with true amazement.

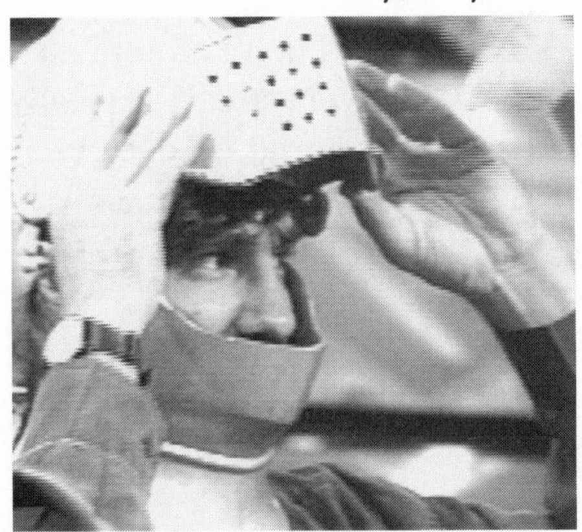

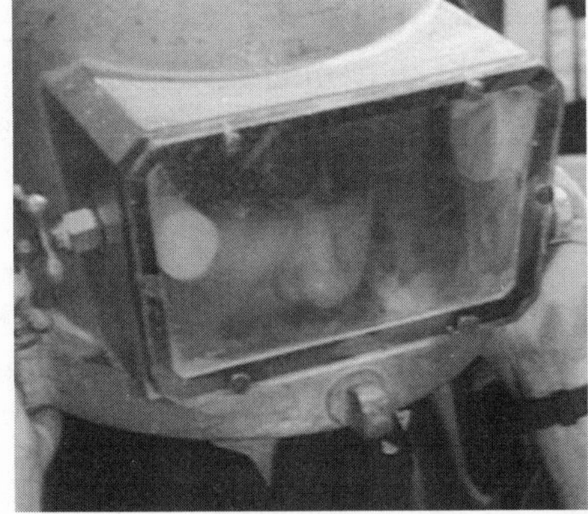

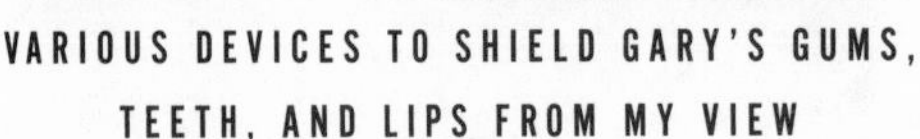

VARIOUS DEVICES TO SHIELD GARY'S GUMS, TEETH, AND LIPS FROM MY VIEW

"Yeah, Dad, lots of pressure. Barnes and Noble already preordered 450,000 copies," I crowed, the proud son.

"Wow, boy, you *are* a genius, Howard." Yeah, baby, give it to me. Those are the words I needed to hear. ***Unfortunately, I needed to hear them when I was five, not now.***

So I expect perfection from Gary, and **YELLING** does work. Gary says I treat him like a retard but you will see that Gary learns from my constant harassment. For example, Gary answers my phones. For years he did something with my calls that drove me crazy. Every time I was embroiled in a controversy, reporters would call looking for a comment. I didn't want comments coming out of my office. My attitude is that I'm not going to talk to reporters because they screw you every time by misquoting and putting their own spin on a story. I also figure any comments I make should be on my radio show and not in some newspaper. So the reporters got smart and figured they'd ask Gary for comment.

I told Gary a million times *not* to talk to reporters.

"Gary," I told him, "I don't want to see any quotes in the newspapers attributed to you." I told him, "Just say, 'Howard is not here and I'll take a message.'"

"But what do I say if they don't take no for an answer and keep asking me the question?" Gary asked.

"Just say, 'I don't know.'"

Gary would get a confused look on his face. "But I'm the producer of the show and what if the guy asks me a simple ques-

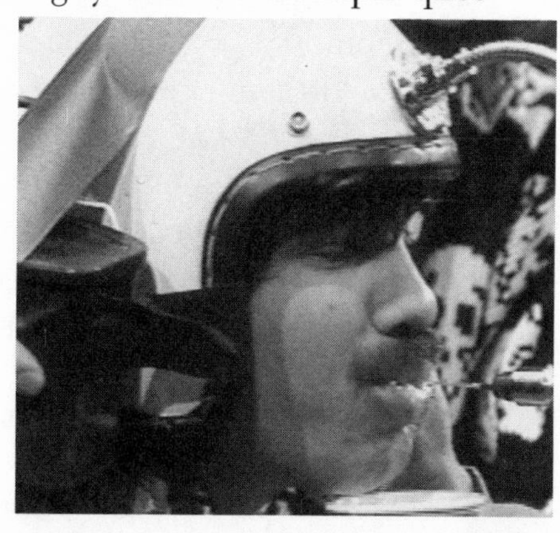

THE ULTIMATE: A HELMET THAT SPRAYED GARY'S DRY CAPS WITH LIFE-GIVING LIQUID

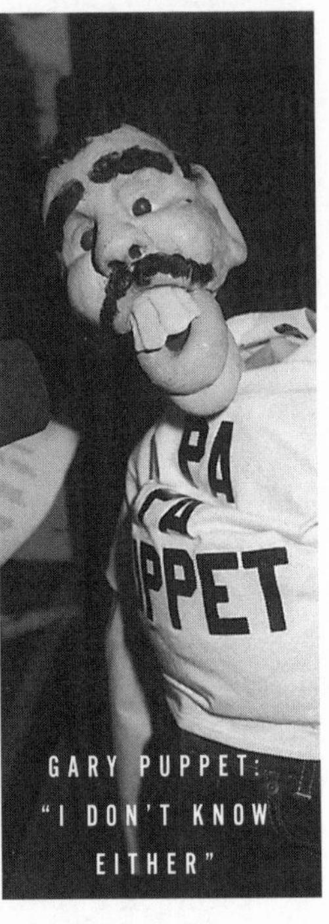

GARY PUPPET: "I DON'T KNOW EITHER"

tion?" Gary would try to understand, but it was hard.

"FORGET that you're the producer. Just don't answer. Just say, 'I don't know,'" I would tell him calmly. Starting off calm was just the way my old man started off with me. You always get one minute of calm before the storm.

"I can't say I don't know. I'll sound stupid," Gary said.

"You *are* stupid!" I replied. The humiliating words were beginning to flow. Hurricane Howie was brewing.

"Repeat after me," I said.

"I'm *not* going to repeat after you." Gary was defiant.

"YES YOU ARE, AND THIS WAY I'LL KNOW YOU LEARNED. REPEAT!" I barked my orders.

"I . . ."

"*I* . . ."

"DON'T . . ."

"*DON'T* . . ."

"KNOW!"

"*KNOW!*"

Surely Gary understood. So why did his face have that blank look? Gary opened his full lips and uttered words that startled me.

"Should I say, 'No comment'?" he asked.

"No, 'no comment' implies you are trying to hide something. Just say *I DON'T KNOW*," I said.

Days after I thought we straightened out the situation, Gary was in the newspaper again with comments. Gary always had an excuse. One time it was that he was trying to get Mayor Dinkins on the show. An article appeared in the *New York Post* about how Mayor Dinkins was doing every radio show but ours. The mayor's office said that Gary had called but the mayor refused to come on. The reporter called Gary for comment. Gary thought if he spoke nicely to the reporter about Dinkins, perhaps the mayor would read it and come on the show. We run into problems whenever Gary thinks on his own. **HE DEFIED MY ORDER!!**

With a sinking heart, I read the *Post* item out loud:

"Gary Dell'Abate, Stern's producer, acknowledged that he had invited Dinkins, but he said he had not yet heard from the mayor's office. 'I think he would have been a great guest. He would have had a great time and he would have been treated with the utmost respect,' Dell'Abate said."

I was furious!

"Who . . . where . . . what . . . I *never* said he'd be treated with the utmost respect," I sputtered. "What is Gary Dell'Abate doing talking to the press? Gary, get in here."

Gary rushed into the studio.

"I made an executive decision," he explained.

"What did I say to you the last time? If someone from the press calls up, what do you do?" I quizzed him.

"Say, 'I DON'T KNOW.' We went through this," Baba Booey said. "I know what to do and I chose not to. I'm trying to get a guest on the show, and I felt that this was a good opportunity to."

"To talk to the newspaper guy?" I said.

"I thought Mayor Dinkins's person would look at this piece today and it would help." Gary was giving us a peek at the fascinating mind that resides behind those giant caps.

"And what quote do you think would be a help?" I asked, sounding more and more like my father.

"The fact that we would treat him with the utmost respect," he said.

"I will *not* treat him with the utmost respect!" I insisted.

"Yeah, *we* know that, but we want to get him here," Gary said.

"But I don't want *that* in the paper, that I'm going to treat him with the utmost respect when I'm not. That's LYING!" I was almost screaming. Gary still didn't get it. I wasn't paying him to make executive decisions, **I was paying him to be a robot.**

"I *am forbidding you from talking to the press!*" I screamed.

"You're out of your mind if that hurts you," he said.

"We're going to have to ban you from answering the phone," I added.

"Great." Gary brightened. "I hate answering the phone.

"Look, I knew *exactly* what I was doing. I made a *conscientious* decision," Gary said, indignant.

"*Conscious*, not conscientious. I wish for once you made a conscious decision," I said. I could see it was time for another lesson.

"I . . ."

"*I . . .*"

"Will tell . . ."

"*Will tell . . .*"

"All important calls . . ."

"*All important calls . . .*"

"That they have the wrong number."

"*That they have the wrong number.*"

"In my spare time . . ." I continued.

"*In my spare time . . .*"

"I will concentrate . . ."

"*I will concentrate . . .*"

"On learning to . . ."

"*On learning to . . .*"

"Say 'I don't know.'"

"*Say 'I don't know.'*"

"I will do my best . . ."

"*I will do my best . . .*"

"Not to drool on the receiver."

"*Not to drool on the receiver.*"

You think that's **cruel?** You think that's **wrong?** Maybe. But I'll tell you this, it's **effective.**

Gary has answered the phone properly ever since.

ART THERAPY: MY RENDITION OF GARY TALKING TO THE PRESS

MY FAVORITE GARY'S TEETH STORY: Gary had the worst cap job I've ever seen. They look like giant tombstones. Each tooth is colored differently and has a **wooden** appearance. Every day at NBC, Robin, Fred, and various NBC staffers would pile into my office and make fun of Gary's humongous teeth, his big, full, innertube-sized lips, and

his purple-colored gums. Then one day, we had been talking on the air about nose jobs and other cosmetic surgeries and Gary actually came back to the office after the show and said, "I bet you guys didn't know that I have caps."

That opened the floodgates. We talked about his caps on the air. We talked about how stupid he was that he didn't think we knew he had caps. We talked about the way he'd lick his stupid caps constantly—because his lips couldn't make their way over the gargantuan caps, **HIS FAKE TEETH WOULD DRY OUT**. Gary constantly needs to run his tongue over the caps in order to irrigate his mouth. His lip would even catch on the teeth if the caps got too dry. Gary was a heavy smoker, so the combination of the smoke and the foods that he ate and the caps and the licking the teeth made for ***the worst breath you could imagine.*** Gary, though, was convinced that he didn't have bad breath.

BEST BAD BREATH STORY: I figured out ways to torture him on the air about his breath. I'd make him breathe into his cupped hand and smell it. One day, I brought his phone into the studio and had everyone smell it. We all wanted to retch. Gary charged in, took a whiff, and denied that it smelled. So I dragged an old Italian construction worker who was doing some work around the radio station into the studio. He smelled the phone.

"OH MY GOD!" He was repulsed.

Gary was **EMBARRASSED** and **HUMILIATED.** Most human beings would have taken pity and would have stopped right there with the abuse, but hey, this was good radio.

"Hey, it's gotten so bad that Gary's proctologist put his finger in Gary's mouth by mistake," I said.

IS GARY A HARD WORKER? It's not that Gary doesn't try hard. He has always given me his all and has always been supermotivated. One of the first tasks Gary performed when I hired him was to drag my drum-and-cymbal setup back to my office after every show. I'll never forget the sight of Gary, fresh out of college, carrying that drum and cymbal down the NBC halls that first day. He confessed to me recently, "Howard, I was so proud the day I walked down the halls carrying the drum and cymbal. I considered it an honor." He looked like he was carrying the American flag during assembly in sixth grade. He held his drums and cymbal and flashed a big toothy smile for all to see. What a dummy.

GARY'S AIR NAMES: Boy Gary, Baba Booey, FaFa Fooey, SaSa Smelly, GaGa Gooey, RaRa Retard, and MaMa Monkey.

HOW GARY GOT ALL HIS NICKNAMES:

BOY GARY: Gary's first name was Boy Gary. All of my producers were always called "boy." This demeaning name came about because of the abuse my college roommate and lifelong friend, Dr. Lewis Weinstein, and I used to heap on each other. Lew and I shared a small cubicle in college. We'd known each other since we were nine years old and we're used to fucking each other's heads up on a regular basis. We used to bust each other's balls over everything. The constant goofing got so bad that even a simple thing like turning the lights out at night became a battle of wills. We'd both be lying in bed with the overhead light on. When it was time to go to sleep, Lew would turn to me and instead of saying, "Can you turn the light off, please?" he'd say, "Boy, why don't you go turn off the light?" The room was the size of a closet and we slept on two military style cots side by side. It would have been easy to get up, take one step, and turn off the light, but nobody, and I mean nobody, was going to call me "boy." I was nobody's slave.

"Fuck you, boy. You get the light," I'd reply.

Now it was war. This battle would last into the night.

"I said, 'Boy, get the light.' Now be a good boy." Lew would taunt.

"I don't know who you think you're callin' boy but I'm your massa and you bess learn that. Understand, boy?" I replied in a deep southern drawl.

"All right," Lew would say, "I won't call you boy."

"That's better, I'm glad you learned your lesson," I said.

"Since you don't like 'boy,' your name is now **GUNGA DIN.** Gunga, why don't you be a good boy and get the light?" Lew would say.

We'd go back and forth like this for hours. Finally, we'd *pass out* with the lights on.

Because the word "boy" got me so crazy I decided that since I was hiring a new slave, every time I got a producer I would torture him with the name "boy."

BABA BOOEY: Gary got the special name Baba Booey because he has the dopiest hobby in the world, collecting cartoon art. Here's a guy who **doesn't have a pot to piss in** and he's busy collecting pictures of Yogi Bear and Yosemite Sam. One day he told me he agreed to make a personal appearance in exchange for cartoon art.

I questioned him on his idiotic new venture and he just got defensive.

"I don't have to tell you how I spend my money," Genius said to me.

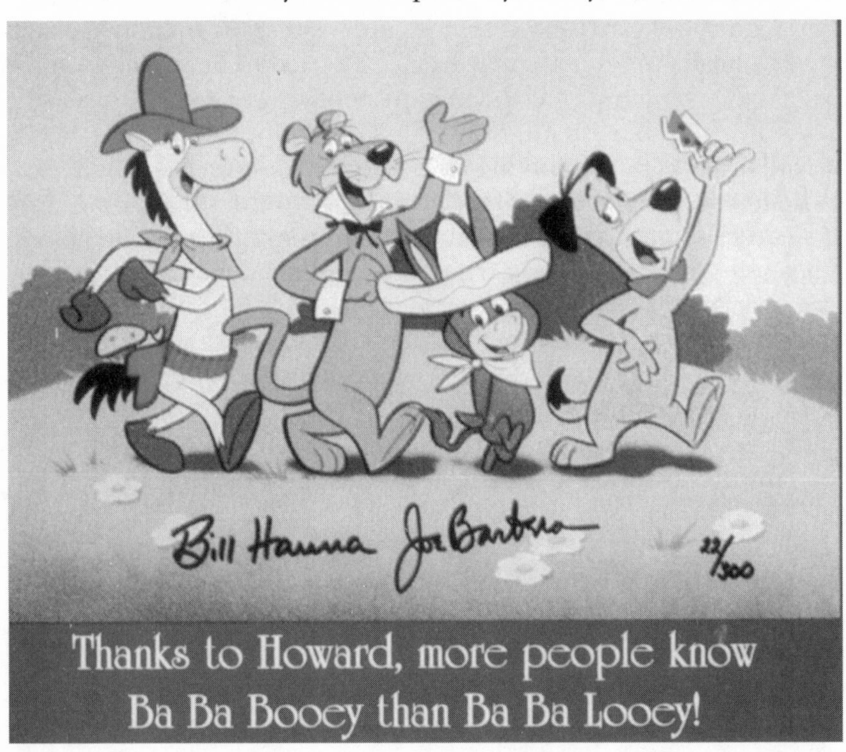

Bill Hanna Joe Barbera
22/300
Thanks to Howard, more people know
Ba Ba Booey than Ba Ba Looey!

"Take it easy, man, no one is putting you down here," I lied. "You're among friends. We're just trying to learn."

His prize possession was a Bugs Bunny picture ***badly painted*** on a ***piece of plastic shit.***

"You are such a loser. How could you buy Bugs Bunny pictures?"

"These aren't pictures—they are cartoon cells," he corrected me.

"What did that cell cost you?" I asked mockingly.

"I paid five hundred dollars for Bugs and I love it. And if you knew anything about cartoon art you would know that's a great price."

"You are such a loser. I hope you're not going to buy any more of this **crap**."

Sounding very much like Forrest Gump, he said, "I'm interested in one more piece."

Was he actually calling this shit "a piece," as in serious art collecting?

"My favorite character is Baba Booey and I just want one of those," Gary said.

"Baba Booey, huh?" I asked. I couldn't believe my ears. He was talking about Quick Draw's sidekick, Baba Looey. The fucking stupid horse's name was BABA ***LOOEY,*** NOT BABA ***BOOEY***. He didn't even know the name of his favorite stupid character.

"What's his name again?" I wanted him saying it a million times.

"Baba Booey, Baba Booey," he repeated, the soon-to-be-mantra of the retarded.

"Sure you don't mean Baba *L*ooey, genius?" I said. I was laughing so fucking hard I vomited on my shoe.

Gary turned red. Man, did that ever clash with his big green teeth. "It's Baba Looey? I always thought it was Baba Booey, I don't know, I'm confused, is it Baba Looey?"

Well, there was a unique situation. Boy Gary confused.

"Well, from now on, your name is Baba Booey!!" I announced.

"Have your fun now," he said to me. "I know you guys will forget about this name by tomorrow." Famous last words. Gary's been Baba Booey ever since.

FAFA FLOOLEY, FAFA FLUNKY, RARA RETARD, SASA SMELLY, ETC.: The list of names just kept growing. Billy West, who joined our show recently, would just sit in a corner and repeat "Booey." Over and over again, just . . . Booey . . . Then the name mutated to Fooey. Then FaFa Fooey, and now it's ***just about anything you can think of.*** Make up your own name. Our listeners have.

MAMA MONKEY: A listener wrote me a letter and said that if I would start calling Gary "monkey," Gary'd flip. It worked. We began calling him MaMa Monkey. Then one crazed fan started dressing up in an ape head and went to all of Gary's personal appearances. He then started sending Gary crude crayon drawings of Gary as a monkey on plastic to goof on Gary.

BEST CARTOON OF GARY BY THE STAFF: Inspired by the ape head painter, Jackie and Fred and I then got into drawing cartoons of Baba Booey. Whenever we'd get writer's block during our writing sessions, we'd start doodling stupid pictures of Gary. Every drawing would have to feature A MOLE, BIG TEETH, AND A HAIRY MOUSTACHE. Then Jackie decided that Gary was all teeth so he just began painting big white blocks. Whenever Gary would say anything to me it would end up in the cartoon.

My masterpiece

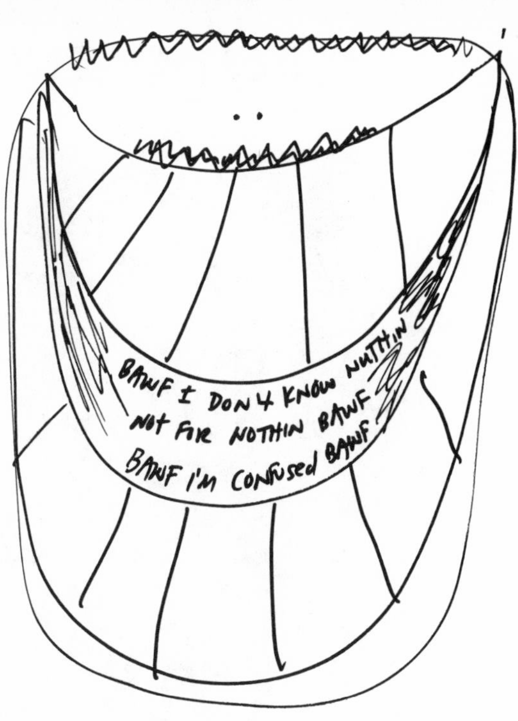

Jackie's minimalist approach

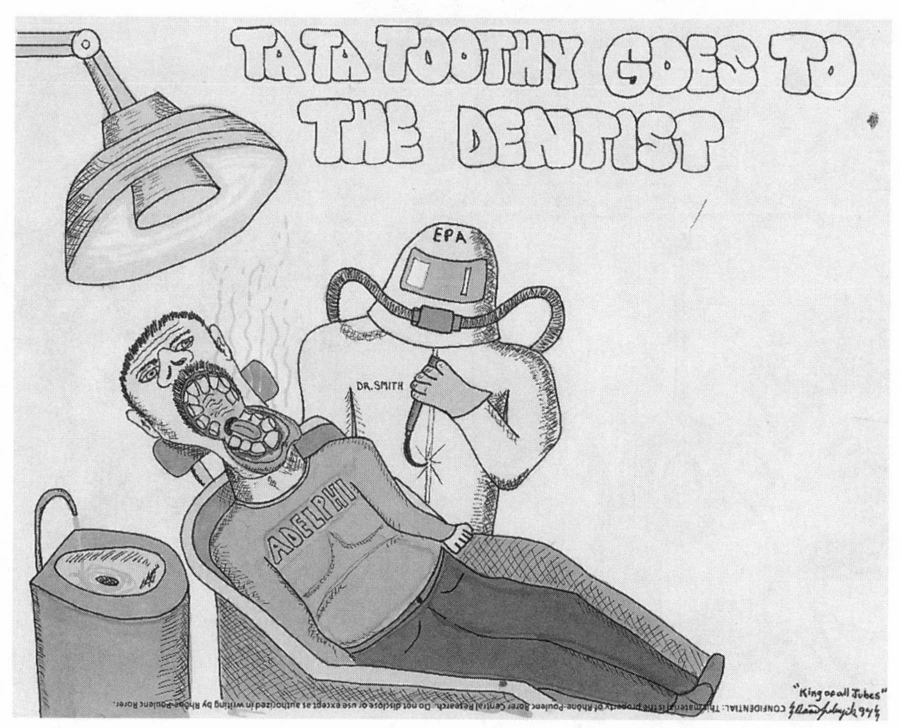

A listener gets in on the fun

BEST LISTENER CARTOONS

BEST GARY PAINTING:

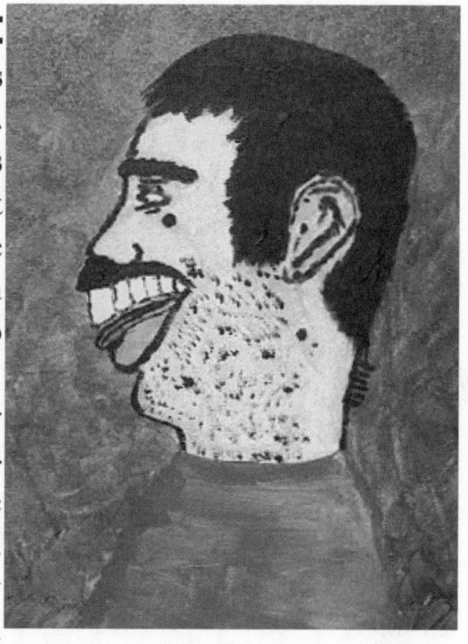

We would actually don berets and smocks and paint for hours. We had an entire set of oil paints and brushes. We heard that painting was relaxing and we would spend hours at the station painting Gary. Fred came up with the best painting of Gary.

Fred worked on this for months experimenting with different tones of red just to get the background right. I told you Fred was **nuts.** One of my best paintings of Gary hangs in the castle of Rolling Stone Ron Wood. I worked on one painting of Gary as Early Man crawling out of the sea that I never completed.

GARY'S PREDECESSORS:

PRODUCER STORY #1: I went through several producers before Gary. One of my producers at NBC was very dedicated, and rumor had it that he even went as far as **fucking one of the secretaries for paper supplies.** NBC was like a *concentration camp* and the supply closet was locked to us. It was locked to all DJs except Imus. We were desperate. We didn't have paper clips or stationery. My man/dog boy intern was so dedicated to me that he fucked for paper goods. He was a good kid, and I never would have unloaded him but NBC caught him turning in phony parking vouchers for extra money. He made $150 a week and couldn't afford an apartment and food.

PRODUCER STORY #2: BOY LEE: Lee got fed up with the small pay and humiliation. Each day at NBC I devised a new on-air **TORTURE** for Boy Lee. I sent him out with a hidden tape recorder and made him do stupid and humiliating things. One day I sent him to a Pakistani newsstand to buy gay magazines like *Blueboy*. There was nothing funnier than this macho man asking foreigners for gay magazines. Foreigners would never understand Lee's requests.

"What magazine? I no understand English. You want *Blueboy*? What kind of magazine is that?" the magazine man from another land would persist.

"It's for *homosexuals*," Lee whispered. God forbid someone should hear.

"What, *homo*? You want a *homo* magazine?"

Lee would literally turn blue from embarrassment.

Then he'd come back to the studio and we'd play the tapes back and humiliate him for hours. Eventually it escalated, and we were forcing Lee to buy adult diapers, hemorrhoid cream, suppositories, buttplugs for gay sex, and hundreds of boxes of Kotex. The druggist who sold Lee the Kotex was flabbergasted.

"But why do you need a *hundred* boxes?" the puzzled druggist would ask.

"Because my girl has a heavy, heavy flow," Lee was instructed to say.

MOST BRUTAL GARY HUMILIATION: One time I got so mad at Gary I called the Association for Retarded Citizens and tried to get him tested to see if he was a retard.

"I'll bet that if you test Gary, his I.Q. would not be over ninety," I told the spokeswoman for this association. "Gary's caps alone are the size of those ***potholders you guys make***." She got real upset that I kept calling Gary a retard.

"I hope you're not this snippy with people of lesser intelligence," I huffed.

"No, I'm not this snippy with people of lesser intelligence because they're not rude like you and go around calling each other retards."

SHE WAS RIGHT. I APOLOGIZED. IT WAS A CRUEL WORD.

"From now on, in honor of my retarded producer's last name we'll call the retarded the Dell'Abated," I promised her.

THE TIME I WAS MOST PROUD OF GARY: Discussions like the one about the retarded drove my mother crazy. She'd call up the show and demand that I stop insulting Gary. But I'd ignore her. It was too much fun. Then Gary's mother would get all upset after hearing my mother. One day Gary's mother couldn't take it anymore after we hammered Gary for over an hour so she called my mother at home.

That night, my mother called me at home. I felt bad and I called Gary up. I apologized for upsetting his family. But Gary just got angry that his mother had gotten involved.

"Don't change a thing," he told me. "You hammer me tomorrow as hard as you hammered me today if you want."

ALL-TIME WORST HUMILIATION OF GARY:

So hammer him I did. I made him PUT HIS FACE UP TO MY ASS AND BREATHE IN MY FARTS. It was during the NBA finals. It was going down to the seventh game. Gary was a big Knicks fan, so he bet on the Knicks. Gary kept bragging that I knew nothing about sports and that I would lose my bet. Just to be contrary, I took the Rockets, whoever the fuck they were. We made a two-part bet. The first part was straight money—five hundred to the winner. But the second part of the bet was the fun part. The loser of the bet had to place his face on the winner's buttocks and hold it there for one minute after the winner had ripped a fart.

Well, the Knicks choked and lost the game. The next day I came into the studio wearing the *sheerest* pants I could find. I wanted Gary to savor every last molecule of gas that wafted his way. Just to help induce a fart, I set up a microwave and cooked a concoction of **broccoli, onions, and tomatoes.** I added a nice hit of Paul Newman's medium-strength salsa. I ate all this and washed it down with a can of club soda. I brought Gary into the studio. He looked like a condemned man.

I had him repeat after me. "Boy, oh, boy, . . . do I love . . . the stench . . . of Howard's gas. I hope . . . I'll lose . . . my next bet with Howard . . . so I can once again . . . accept my boss's rancid poopy juice . . . This is the highlight . . . of my very low life."

But despite all the food and carbonated water, I couldn't deliver my methane cocktail. I tried to cut a rat the whole show but I didn't have any gas. Of course, Gary thought that I was just trying to torture him by prolonging his misery. That day, everywhere Gary went, people stopped him on the street, "HEY, GARY, DID HOWARD FART TODAY?" Gary's father even called him at home that night and told him he was an idiot for making the bet.

But I was finally able to deliver the goods the next day. I dragged Gary into the studio and made him assume the position. His nose was pressed up against my butt cheeks. I let a fart fly. Gary had been practicing for days to hold his breath for a whole minute. After a minute, his ordeal was over.

"I didn't smell anything, really I didn't," Gary lied.

"Liar. Believe me, it was on his face," I said.

"It's over! I can have a good weekend," Gary exulted.

But it wasn't over until I made him repeat after me once more: "My boss knows how to bet basketball . . . I, . . . Gary, . . . promise . . . to continue to amaze you . . . with how annoying . . . dumb . . . smelly . . . and incompetent . . . I remain."

But I had to give it to Gary. Even though he didn't really suck my noxious fumes in, he took his punishment like a man.

SUMMATION: I'm proud of my Boy Gary. He accepts being hammered for the good of the show. Gary, Baba Booey, is not a young man anymore. He is thirty-four and not that far off from my own age, yet I think of him as a college boy who is learning while earning credits. When he started working for me he was a gullible kid right out of Adelphi University. Now he's thirty-four, married to a lovely woman, and he's got a cute little boy.

OFF THE AIR: I always tell Gary I care about him and there is no other person I would rather have as a producer. The dude ***works his fucking ass off for me*** and deserves tons of credit.

THE REST OF THE GANG

BILLY WEST

Billy West is one of the ugliest women I've ever seen and is the latest addition to our radio family.

I don't know Billy long enough to go through a big psychoanalytical discussion about my relationship with him. To be quite honest I've just about run out of steam on this chapter. My editor called and she wants me to hand this thing in already. She thinks I've spent way too long on this chapter and wants this fucking book out by Christmas. She could give a shit about art, she wants results.

So, Billy, you get fucked.

You might know Billy as the voice of Ren and Stimpy. He's also some sort of insect on the "Honey Nut Cheerios" commercial. I think he's a fucking bee. He's also a McNugget.

HOW I FOUND HIM: I hadn't hired anyone new for the show in a long time. My boss at Infinity, Mel Karmazin, played a tape of him for me and I knew that Billy would be the next one to be part of our family. He was doing a Larry Fine from the Three Stooges impression. Who the fuck does Larry? Moe and Curly I understand but you have to be **insane** to do Larry. I immediately hired him for our show.

OTHER GREAT VOICES: A killer Jay Leno, a demented Grandpa Al Lewis from *The Munsters*, and female voices that really sound like women. He does a killer groove as Marge Schott, owner of the Cincinnati Reds who was accused of making racist statements. I don't know what the fuck Marge Schott sounds like, but Billy does a high-pitched, whining old bag with a Boston accent who starts ranting about "NIGGERS, KIKES, SPICS, WOPS, DAGOS, AND POLACKS." Anytime we do a bit about any woman who is a racist it's the same impression with the Boston accent. It makes no difference that Marge Schott is not from Boston.

SCOTT THE ENGINEER

Now if you think Billy got short shrift, wait till I blow by Scott the Engineer. Scott was voted the ugliest woman at the picture shoot.

LOVE NOTE: Just because we are always

so brutal to Scott, I must go on record to say **Scott is the best engineer I've ever worked with.**

HAVING SAID THAT, LET'S GET TO THE GOOD STUFF: Scott is always overlooked. If we are not picking on Scott it's because we forget he's around. Robin left him out of her book. At Christmastime, we always forget to get him a present. If we get tickets for screenings, we forget to give him one. Out of sight, out of mind.

Scott the Engineer is the ***Sad Sack*** of our show. He's Beetle Bailey. He looks downtrodden, he is downtrodden, **he's just a mess.** He's the easiest guy to pick on because he just stands there expressionless while you make fun of him.

He's got so many lousy things going for him. HE'S BALD, so we constantly rag on that. Then we'll pick up a hairpiece sponsor and Scott will get a free rug. He seems to be happy with his toupee, then one day, we come in and he's ripped it off. It turns out that the free visits were over, and they wanted Scott to start paying for his treatments. Next, I take Scott's hairpiece and put it on top of an O.J. Simpson mask and create artwork.

> SCOTT THE ENGINEER
> "Howard's a control freak. He has to have his hands everywhere. If he wants something done, then it'll be done. He doesn't have to worry, but he does."

We have the most fun with Scott when we rag on him for smoking like a chimney. Even though his father died of cancer when he was only sixty-two, Scott smokes like a fiend. He smells like a dirty ashtray. You can smell him when he walks into the studio—an odd mix of tobacco and breath mints. Once a year, I force him to take a lung test. He pisses and moans but finally he agrees. He has to blow into a tube and after a few seconds it looks like he's going to have a coronary on the spot. Then they analyze his lung strength and give him the results. The first year he took the test, they told him he had the lungs of an eighty-four-year-old man. That was about twice his real age. The next year, he scored a 105. The lungs of a 105-year-old man!

Right after we rag on Scott, we usually hear from his wife. This poor guy's wife really runs a tight ship. If he comes to a card game and he loses money and we talk about it on the air, his wife yells at him.

If I tell him that he's going to die unless he cuts out those cigarettes, his wife yells at him.

If he even gets invited to one of our bachelor parties at Scores, he's afraid to go because he might get yelled at.

Maybe that's why we never see Scott. He figures the more he hides back in his engineer's studio, the less chance he has to get in trouble. *Out of sight, out of mind, out of breath.*

STUTTERING JOHN

John's got so many wacky stories that I gave him his own chapter. I'll say this, the motherfucker makes a good-looking babe. Look at those legs.

INTERN HALL OF FAME: *MY GUNGA DINS*

In some ways, my interns perform the most important function on my show—*handling my food.* With my obsessive-compulsive problems, food handling is a major concern. I used to eat two potatoes a day during my air shift, so learning how to properly prepare my potato became a major job. I had very specific rules about the potato preparation. I make few demands and I know this sounds spoiled and rotten, but I work hard and I want my lunch handled just the right way. By the time lunch comes around I'm as hungry as a horse. Lunchtime is ten A.M. because of my early hours and I don't want my goddamned potato fucked with. I want the potato microwaved and delivered on time. Nothing worse than being on the air hungry and waiting for that potato.

I eat the potatoes hot out of the microwave with no butter or oil because I diet obsessively and don't want any extra calories. I wrap pieces of turkey around the potato and shove them in my mouth as fast as possible during commercial breaks. The whole meal is about 300 calories and very satisfying. I usually eat so fast that I swallow tons of air with my food and as a result I belch and fart through the rest of the show. ROBIN CANNOT BELIEVE THE AMOUNT OF GAS PRODUCED BY TWO SMALL POTATOES.

I also burn the entire inside of my mouth every day as I shovel this meal in at incredible speeds. People who have seen me eat this shit get absolutely nauseous. My hair ends up getting filled with pieces of potato and turkey as I gobble it down in a four-minute commercial break. After I eat, I am covered in potato. I am **disgusted** with myself that I eat this **mess** so fast and don't take some time to enjoy the fucking meal. Robin can barely look at me during this process. The potato is the most important ritual of my day.

At first, I made it Gary's responsibility to wash my potato and microwave it. But like most of his tasks, he delegated this, which upset me. Then I got to thinking about Gary's smelly teeth and gums and hands and moustache and germs and I let him pass the baton. Sometimes I would see him washing the potato in the bathroom after he peed and he didn't wash his hands that good. I figured the microwave would burn off all the fucking germs from **Gary's stinky doody hands** so I ate the fucking thing anyway. But his stinky doody hands were in the back of my mind the whole time.

Plus, at least twice a week Gary was late with the potato. I told him he was a FAILURE not only as a producer but as a waiter as well. I always felt strange yelling at another adult about how my potato was not prepared on time. I sounded like Joan Crawford throwing a tantrum about wire hangers. But I came to ***understand*** Joan Crawford. Hey, she wanted her kids' clothes hung on a nice fucking hanger. Is that too much? I wanted my potato handled properly.

"My fucking potato should be as important to you as it is to me," I would say to Gary.

"Bauf," he would say. He has trouble saying the word "boss" because of his giant teeth, lips, and gums. "Bauf, I'm sorry, I just forgot the potato today."

"Forgot? Then you know what, Gary? BUY A FUCKING ALARM CLOCK and get me the potato on time."

"But, Bauf, I was busy producing the show," Gary would reply. I hate when he calls me "Boss." I hate when he argues with me. As far as I'm concerned producing the potato is part of producing the show.

"There is nothing more important in your day than my potato. I really know this sounds demanding, but *I pay you a salary and all I really want is my damn potato. I don't care if you never do another thing right, just get me that fucking potato.*" Joan Crawford had nothing on me.

"You've never been on the air, Gary." I continued beating a dead horse. "You need to fuel yourself to be funny."

Despite all my valuable lectures on food preparation Gary was still showing up late with my potato. Stuttering John was the next person to inherit the potato preparation chore. He handled the potato detail for a while, but then I was forced to remove him. I got word that John would take my potatoes into the bathroom and wash them in the sink. After they were washed, he made the cardinal error of placing the clean potatoes on the filthy sink while he retrieved a paper towel to dry them off.

Who knew what was going on on that sink? Our bathroom was *dirty, filthy, and disgusting.* The radio station bathroom was shared by hundreds of people and some of them were real foul. Lots of foreign guys worked with us who had the strange habit of using the sink at work to wash, shave, and shampoo. We used to come in and find fucking head lice in the sink, crawling around. John put my potato on a sink filled with head lice.

But firing John from potato detail was difficult. I never liked changing the guard because it meant I had to train a whole new person. We'd get an intern to admit on the air that he was jerking off like a jackrabbit at night and all of a sudden I'd start thinking about him handling my potatoes. I needed a celibate intern.

Over the years, two interns have stood out because they've managed to stretch their internship over six years. Mike Gange and Steve Grillo both managed to major in *The Howard Stern Show.* Both Mike and Steve have handled the potato detail. I would surprise-check on them while they were making potato preparations and they always handled this detail with reasonable efficiency. They came to me to learn all about the radio business. They learned the most important rule about radio. They learned that radio sucks. They wasted their entire college careers majoring in a fucking potato. It's fucking insane. Their degree should say **Magna Cum Potato.**

FUCKIN' MIKE GANGE

It's incredible, but Gange has a very high opinion of himself. This is a guy who graduated from one of the world's worst shitholes, C.W. Post, and as a reward his parents threw him a $25,000 party. He was the first Gange to graduate college and his parents were proud. Meanwhile, most of his credits were in microwaving my food. If your kids ever tell you they want to intern somewhere ***tell them to drop fucking dead.*** What a waste of money.

GANGE'S ALL-TIME BIGGEST FUCKING BLUNDER: Gange was good with the potato, so it was time to elevate him and give him a new responsibility. My wife and I had a friend who was very ill. Since she was bedridden, she spent most of her time watching television and was a big fan of the *Seinfeld* show. I had a tape with every *Seinfeld* episode on it and I wanted her to have it. This woman and her husband were church-going, respectable people. The husband had even studied for the priesthood. I felt good about sending a little happiness to this woman who had been so kind to us. It was a small gesture but I knew she would really appreciate it. Howard Stern, giving of himself, the good Samaritan, I liked the sound of that. Gange was helping me out at my house answering phones and doing some light clerical services. I told him to make a copy of the *Seinfeld* tape and send it off. Gange took an old tape of mine and used it to make the copy. The prick forgot to push the record button and he sent the tape to our friends. The next day I get an irate call from the husband.

"If this is your idea of a practical joke, it's really not funny and it's SICK! SICK! SICK!" this guy told me. It turns out that Gange had taken one of my old porno tapes and used it to make the copy. This beautiful couple had gotten a Japanese enema tape. Some listener sent me a video of Japanese guys running around on a beach in Japan somewhere, trying to get girls to shit on a surfboard. If the girls couldn't shit these guys would give them enemas. So this straight, unsuspecting couple sat down for a night with Jerry, Elaine, and the gang **and got a bunch of jacked-up Orientals shitting on surfboards.**

Our friend passed away a short while later. Thank you, Mike Gange, member of the Intern Hall of Fame.

STEVE GORILLA GRILLO

Grillo makes Gange seem like a Rhodes scholar. He is now in charge of my food and has served in this capacity for at least four years. It took him a long time before I trusted him with the potato. Grillo begged for years to handle the potato. He had to work his way up to this position.

HALL OF FAME ANECDOTE: He sent us a handwritten résumé on lined paper that was ripped out of a notebook. I'm no Hemingway but I've never seen a funnier, and more BADLY CONSTRUCTED LETTER than this. When we saw this letter we swore we would never hire this guy because he had to have some mental disorder. But we were desperate and he would work for free.

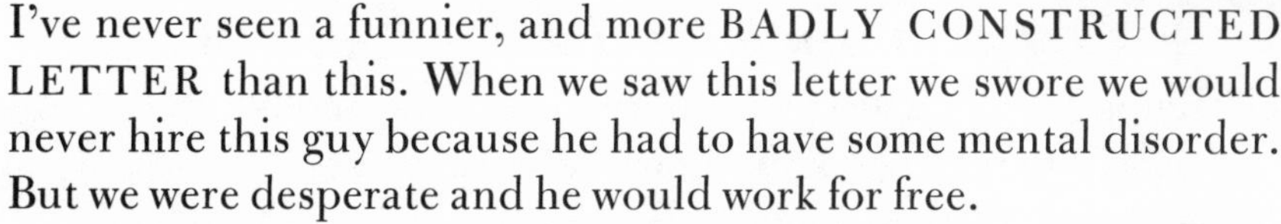

A desire that eats inside of me? Not only was this thought insane but the letter had at least **eleven spelling errors** and a hundred grammatical errors. I figured we

I am going to try to get Right to the point. I am writting this letter, hoping you will feel my sincerety. I know I have to start out on the bottom and what better place to start out on the bottom than with a show that's on the top. I have this desire inside of me that eats at me everyday should hire him and let him compete with my daughters in a spelling bee.

So I put him on the air and got my eleven-year-old daughter on the phone. Grillo's first word was "ridiculous." He got it right. Emily then spelled "separate" correctly. Then Grillo drew the word "compliment." He spelled it wrong and Emily nailed it. His next word was "definite." "D-E-F-I-N-A-T-E," he guessed. Emily got it right.

I decided to level the playing field. I had Emily get her eight-year-old sister, Debra, on the phone. Debra's in the third grade. She was half asleep when she contested Grillo. It was nip and tuck for a few minutes. Debra scored with "gauge" and "straighten." Grillo nailed "pamphlet" and "receive." It was time for the tie-breaker. The word was "relevant." Grillo got as far as R-E-L before he gave up. Debra spelled it correctly and won. But I feel pity for Grillo. Next year, I'm sure he'll still be at Hunter College so I'll have him go up against Ashley, my two-year-old. It'll be close. She already knows how to spell "Da-da."

RALPH CIRELLA, BERRY BOY

Ralph Cirella is a very good friend of mine and is just a peripheral part of my show yet he generates more hate mail than any other person on the show, including the Ku Klux Klansman Daniel Carver. Ralph first started working for me on my first TV show and created some great special-effects makeup. But his greatest contribution was when he began dressing me and taking care of my hair. My hair was like a POODLE POOF. On a humid day it would frizz and add six inches to my height. I used to moan that here I was a guy who was lucky enough to have hair and yet my hair made me look like Louis XVI. Ralph talked me into growing out my hair and dropping my stupid King Louis look. He also figured out that all my clothes were too short for my lanky body and he began buying all my clothes. He comes out to my house and picks out all the clothes I'm going to wear. The son of a bitch even trims

DEAR HOWARD the GreaT,

I have listened to your show for as long as it has been on the show. But I can't stand Ralph the Homo. He makes my skin crawl. His voice makes me sick to my stomach. I want to turn the volume down till he leaves. And I am a Homo, and can't stand him. Fire his ass + get a ~~Real~~ REAL HAIRDRESSER.

The Homo must go!

DAMN FAGGOT

Love your Show
~~Homo~~ Don + Tom

my nasal hairs. How's that for a job? He loves doing it and **laughs like a mongoloid** every second he cuts through that thatch in my big crooked schnozz.

PROM KING

I receive hundreds of hate letters a week about Ralph. Log on to Prodigy computer service any night and you'll see at least three "I Hate Ralph" bulletin boards. And it's not just strangers who hate Ralph. Whenever I decide to bust Ralph's chops on the air, everybody in my radio family runs into the studio to get a shot at him.

There are a lot of theories circulating on why Ralph is HATED so much. Ralph's theory is that he is hated because everyone is **jealous** that he's become a close friend of mine. Stuttering John says that even before Ralph got close to me, everyone hated Ralph. It is incredible to me that I am fought over like a high school **promqueen.**

Before I became famous everyone was fighting to get away from me. Now that I'm the prom king it seems to truly bother everyone that I like Ralph. Ralph laughs at Ralph hate mail. He thinks it's a pisser that a lot of people think he's a homo because he does my hair and dresses me.

Ralph is my closest friend. I hardly ever hang out with guys but when I do it's with Ralph. We have almost identical interests in everything. We like the same music, movies, and we both watch *Baywatch*, MTV, *Star Trek, Beverly Hills, 90210,* and *Melrose Place.* I mostly like that Ralph knows how to be unobtrusive around me. If I get sick of him and I want to disappear for an hour, Ralph'll just sit in the living room and *amuse himself* while he waits for me. He's always available when I need him. He's the perfect friend for me. He's my Kato Kaelin.

DISINFORMATION HIGHWAY

I MAKE SURE EVERYONE IS AS *MISERABLE* AS ME, that's what makes me happy. I've also managed to turn the work place into a jungle. The way to get on my good side is to give me information concerning other show members. Stuttering John tells me that Ralph is sleeping in my office on my couch. Scott the Engineer tells me he overheard Gary on the phone screwing up.

Gary tells me one of the interns has a gambling problem.

I've created a network of informants among all my coworkers. Grillo tells me that Jackie fought with his wife at a beer fest promotion and ***called her a cunt***. Gary tells me that Robin was late for an appearance even though she vowed she wouldn't be late. Robin gets revenge by telling me Gary **fucked** one of our listeners and she **VOMITED** on his bed while he had sex with her.

At one time or another, Jackie, Robin, and Fred have all walked off the show. Bits of information supplied by informants get these angry moments going. A tattler gets rewarded with my praise, for bringing me ***juicy, embarrassing information*** about a coworker. Everyone likes turning someone in because that means you are assured airtime. It's like having **MY OWN PRIVATE HITLER YOUTH.**

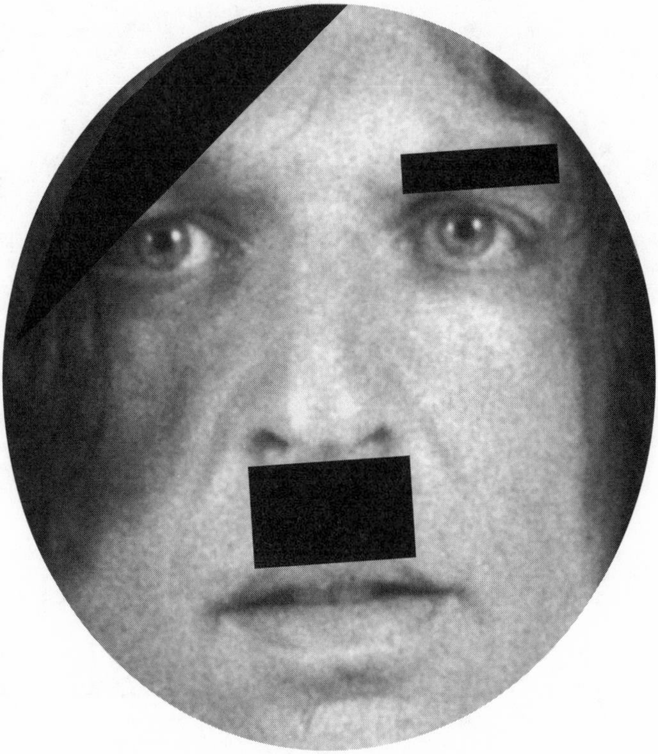

CHAPTER 6

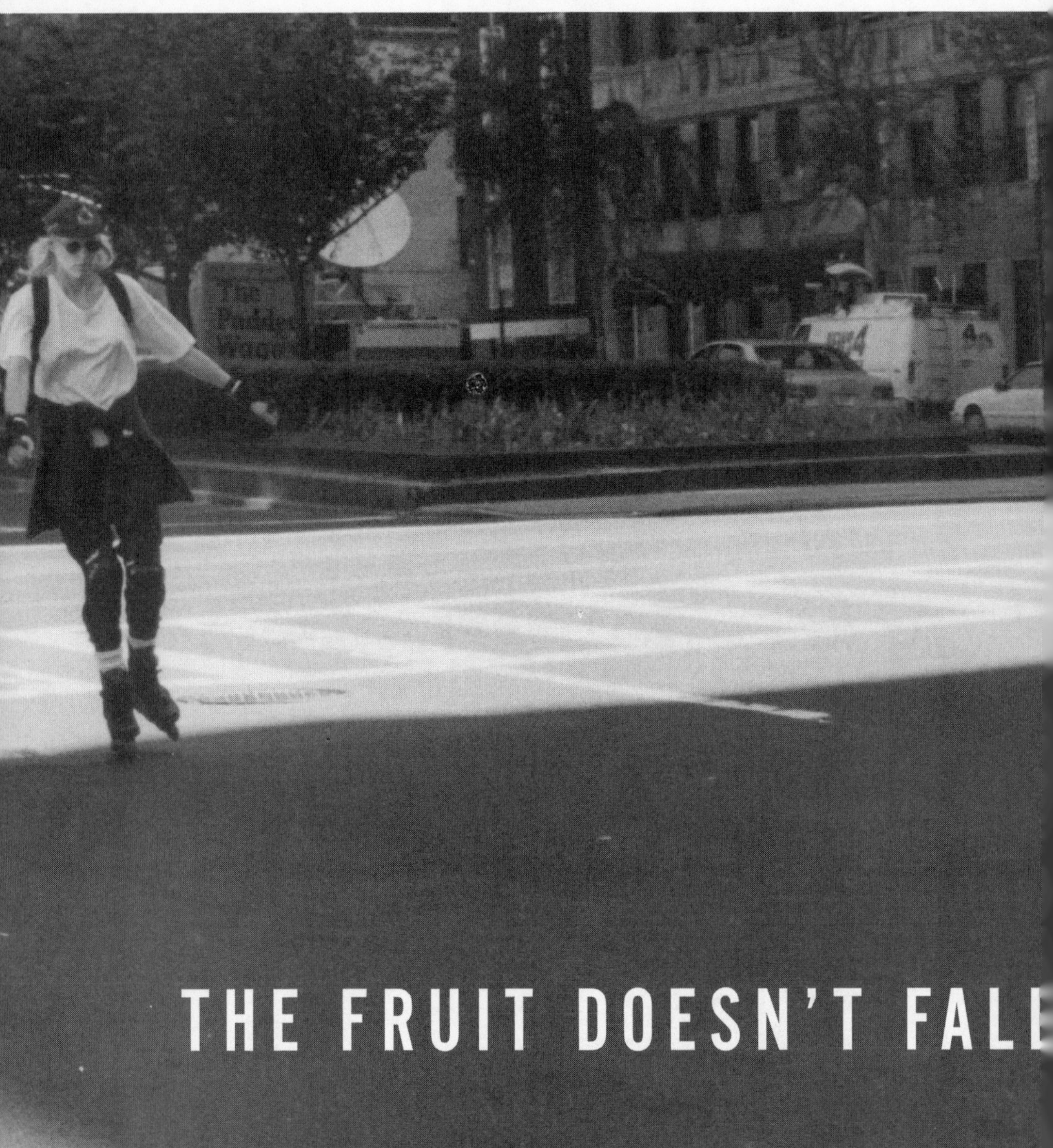

THE FRUIT DOESN'T FALL

I am one angry, fucking-pissed-off asshole.

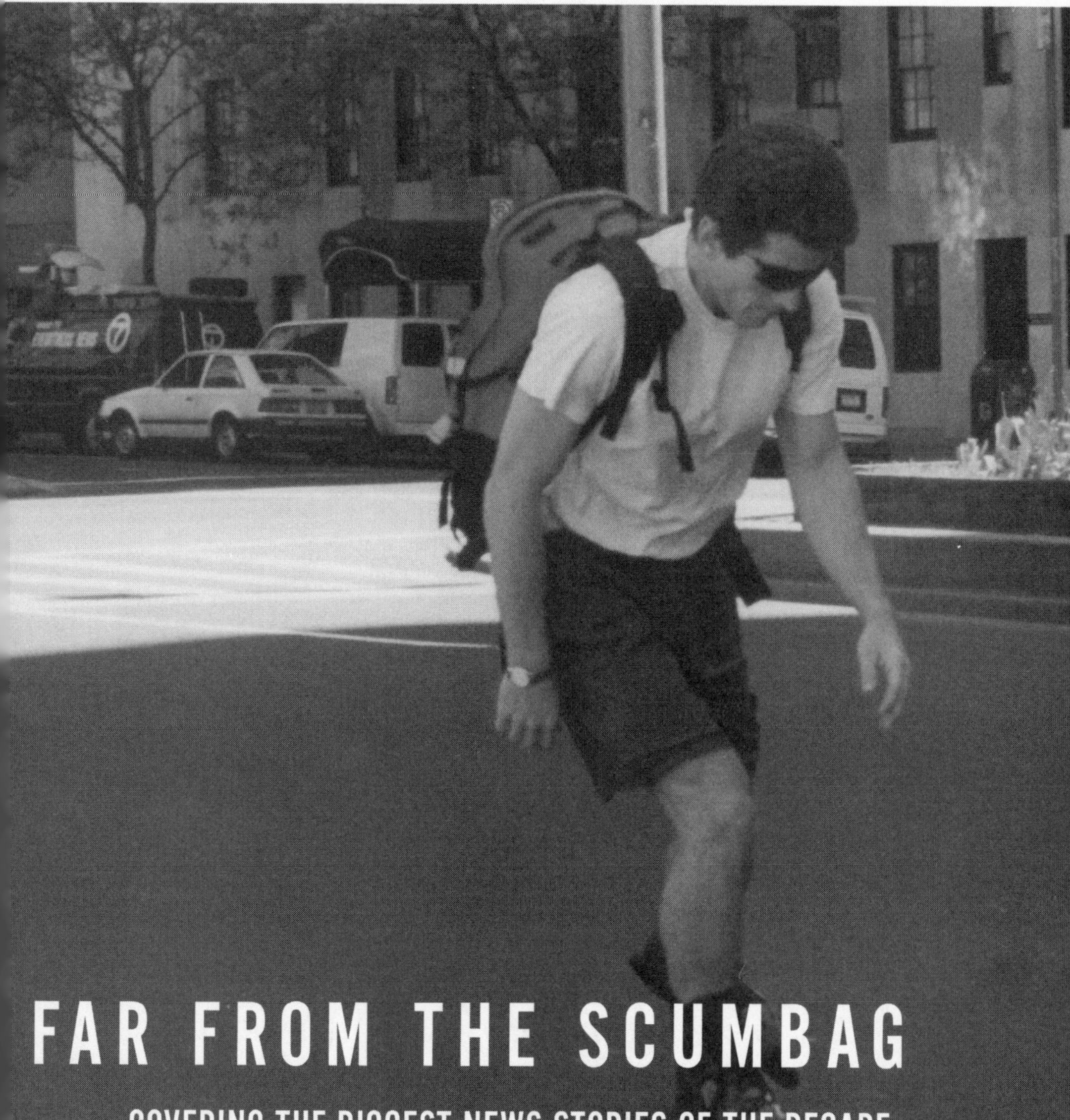

FAR FROM THE SCUMBAG

COVERING THE BIGGEST NEWS STORIES OF THE DECADE

WHY? BECAUSE I WASN'T BORN RICH.

If I was born rich I would know how to play it. Take the Kennedys, for instance: Born with fucking silver spoons in their mouths, what did they ever do to deserve their wealth? Joe Kennedy snuck booze over the border and poisoned half of America—why is he worshipped? Why am I *not* worshipped? I tell a few vagina jokes to make people laugh on their way to work and everybody's pissed off. As the old saying goes, sticks and stones can break your bones, but vagina jokes can never hurt you.

The Kennedy men bother me enough, but the idolization of the Kennedy women makes me berserk. People always get pissed off when I blast the Kennedy women, but they should thank me for all the hypocrisies that I point out.

Let's start with Rose Kennedy: What kind of a role model is that? Here's a woman who buried her head in the sand and sat idly by while **her husband fucked every Hollywood bimbo on two feet.** The whore-meister General Joe Kennedy would even bring home Hollywood starlets to sit at the dining-room table with the whole family while

Rose Kennedy ***kept her stupid mouth shut.*** And this was *before* the strokes she had in the eighties.

Now if I brought Pamela Anderson—no, never mind her—if I even brought THAT COW Sally Struthers (the one who is trying to feed half of Biafra, and, by the way, if the Biafrans just ate *her* they wouldn't be starving anymore, in fact they'd be ***downright bloated)***—if she walked in the door, here's the scene: My wife would tear out EVERY SNATCH HAIR AND EYEBALL FROM ME, never mind from Sally. And that's the way a woman should be. That's who people should be worshipping: Alison Stern. Rose Kennedy should not be an icon. Alison Stern should be an icon.

And this woman should be ***ashamed*** of herself. No wonder her sons grew up and couldn't keep it in their pants. Just remember: *The fruit doesn't fall far from the scumbag* (and by the way, a poster with that slogan will soon be available from ReganBooks, and nobody steal it or I will sue you).

So finally Rose Kennedy decides to do something. Her daughter is having sex, something her father was doing to everybody at the dinner table no less, and Rose runs out and ***removes half her brain*** and gets her a lobotomy. She should have gotten Joe's brain removed. And back then, remember, it wasn't fun being retarded. There was no Special Olympics.

So here is my open letter to the whole fucking family:

AN OPEN LETTER TO ALL THE THIRD GENERATION KENNEDYS (EXCEPT FOR MY FRIEND, ARNOLD SCHWARZENEGGER)

Dear Kennedys,

You don't know what it's like to grow up in the real world, to actually have to work for a living.

You have never worked.

You have never wanted for anything.

You have never created anything.

You are not in touch with what real people think.

You've probably never risked your life taking a subway.

I wish my grandfather was a famous bootlegger like yours was, but I had to work for a living.

My grandfather wasn't a criminal who passed down his money to a series of leeches who are so nonproductive that they've just about pissed away the family fortune.

My grandfather never brought his mistress, Gloria Swanson, home for dinner and flaunted her in front of my grandmother.

My grandfather and grandmother never lobotomized my aunt because she was a bit of a rebel.

My uncle never drowned a poor young woman and got away with it.

My aunt never married an old Greek just so she could raid his coffers.

My uncles never gang banged Marilyn Monroe.

And, last but not least, my family uses birth control, so there'll be enough room on the frigging planet for everyone else.

Thank you very much.

Yours truly,
Howard Stern

JACKIE

Rose Kennedy was admired by the American public, but nothing compared to the way they worshipped Jackie O.

I could never understand why the whole world worships this

woman. What has she ever done?—aside from editing that piece-of-shit-nothing-fluff-book by Michael Jackson, *Moonwalker.* It should have been called ***Turd Burgler.***

They say that Jackie O was a great first lady because she brought style and class to the White House. What were they talking about? She wore a pill-box hat—which isn't even a hat. IT'S A BOX. And she redecorated with our hard-earned taxpayer's money. I couldn't care if she lived in a shithole with that damn hat and her pills. To me a great first lady would be one who didn't waste my money redecorating.

And what about the whole sickening Jackie-death-watch scene? Hundreds of reporters and people who apparently have no lives spent endless hours staring up at Jackie O's window like zombies, lining the street outside her Fifth Avenue apartment. I wish I had that kind of time. What did these people expect? Did they think they were gonna shove her body up to the glass? Hold her hand up and wave? Blow a kiss through those hard, cold lips? I'll tell you what happened, nothing happened.

Except that John John and Daryl Hannah, the mermaid from *Splash* and THE 50-FOOT WOMAN, Rollerbladed into his mother's lobby. Jesus Christ. I can't stand that John John. I'll be damned if I'm going to sit around for hours waiting to get a glimpse of some loser who flunked the bar exam twice. What has he ever done? God, I wish I could get pussy like that. And what a great ass. Daryl's too.

Then the funeral comes. And John John and this babe **ROLLERBLADE TO THE SERVICE.** Isn't that disgusting? You know, if I Rollerbladed to my mother's service the press would kick my ass up and down Fifth Avenue. But all the fucking news analysts got on the news and excused it by saying it was a way for John John to blow off steam and deal with grief. What a bunch of bullshit! He's an exercise freak. On the day of his mother's death he's too busy worrying about whether or not he has a piece of cellulite on his ass. I wish a boil would grow on his ass the size of his mother's pill-box hat. I was surprised that John John didn't hang-glide into the burial at Arlington.

So they buried Jackie O next to John Kennedy—right?—with that stupid eternal flame. Fuck that flame! It's a waste of taxpayers' money. Why don't we just set up a video fireplace like they used to do at Christmas time on Channel 11?

But back to my point: I was fascinated with how the media was covering this story. Everyone was getting interviews with the thousands of Kennedy offspring—***offspring of the demon seed Joe Kennedy***—and I couldn't get Au Bar's favorite patron, William Kennedy Smith. I got on the air and complained that now that Jackie had died everyone had all sorts of cool information but me. One paper even reported that if Jackie weighed 115 pounds, she would weigh 57.5 pounds on Mars. On Jupiter, Jackie O would weigh about 3,657 pounds . . . almost as much as Rush Limbaugh.

Now, Cindy Adams is the biggest vulture on two feet. I hate her—not only because of her beehive hairdo that's so out of date it actually has bees in it—I hate her because when she was a young reporter—back in the nineteenth century—she was invited to the palace to have a viewing of the shoes of Imelda Marcos, that sneaky thief. No matter how many reports there were about Imelda Marcos taking food out of babies' mouths to feed her shoe habit, that Cindy always had a glorified essay praising Her Highness. So I open up the paper one day, and Cindy Adams writes about her exclusive with Jackie O's butcher. *Butcher?* Eat *my* meat, Cindy. Now I was really pissed. If that old hag could get an interview with the butcher, surely one of the pathetic creeps in my audience must have had an interaction with a Kennedy.

Well, after yelling at my audience for days, I finally hit pay dirt! THE EMBALMING-FLUID DELIVERY BOY! I immediately put him on even though I had no idea if there was even such a thing as an embalming-fluid delivery boy.

"Of course there's embalming-fluid delivery boys," he protested.

"Did Teddy try to drink the embalming fluid?" I wondered. I asked him how Jackie looked.

"She looked about eighty years old, very thin," he reported.

"Did she look as bad as Johnny Carson?" I asked.

"It was sad," he said.

"Was she nude?"

"No. You're perverted, but I like it," he said.

"Was she wearing garters?" I pressed. "Wait, I hear JFK Jr. Rollerblading over here to beat me up. Thanks, dude. You know more than Cindy Adams. You should go deliver her some embalming fluid. She looks like she's been dead for years."

The Cock-Meat *Sandwich*

Jackie O's death was a big story, but the biggest story of the decade, the one that was the topic of conversation at every water cooler on Monday morning, had to be **the woman who found a whole penis in her sandwich**—100 percent human cock meat.

All this other celebrity bullshit doesn't really affect you: Jerry Garcia or Mickey Mantle dies, big deal, but you find a penis in your sandwich and I guaran-fuckin'-tee you, *that* will change your life.

A New Jersey woman made the news when she discovered the severed penis in her sloppy-joe sandwich at the Atlantic City casino where she worked. Gary got this woman on the phone. I offered to serve as the woman's attorney.

"When you bit in," I asked her, "did someone yell 'Ouch!' Were there testicles in your salad? I want to know what kind of case we have here."

"I was cutting the sandwich up and I looked to the side and it was lying there," the victim said. She said it was about an inch long . . . circumcised.

"Did you suck the sloppy Joe sauce off it?" I asked. "DO YOU BELIEVE YOUR LUNCH HAD SYPHILIS, CLAP, OR HERPES?" I asked.

"No," she said.

"Too bad. That would make the award bigger."

She told us that she carefully placed the penis in a napkin and it was taken into custody by the Atlantic City police.

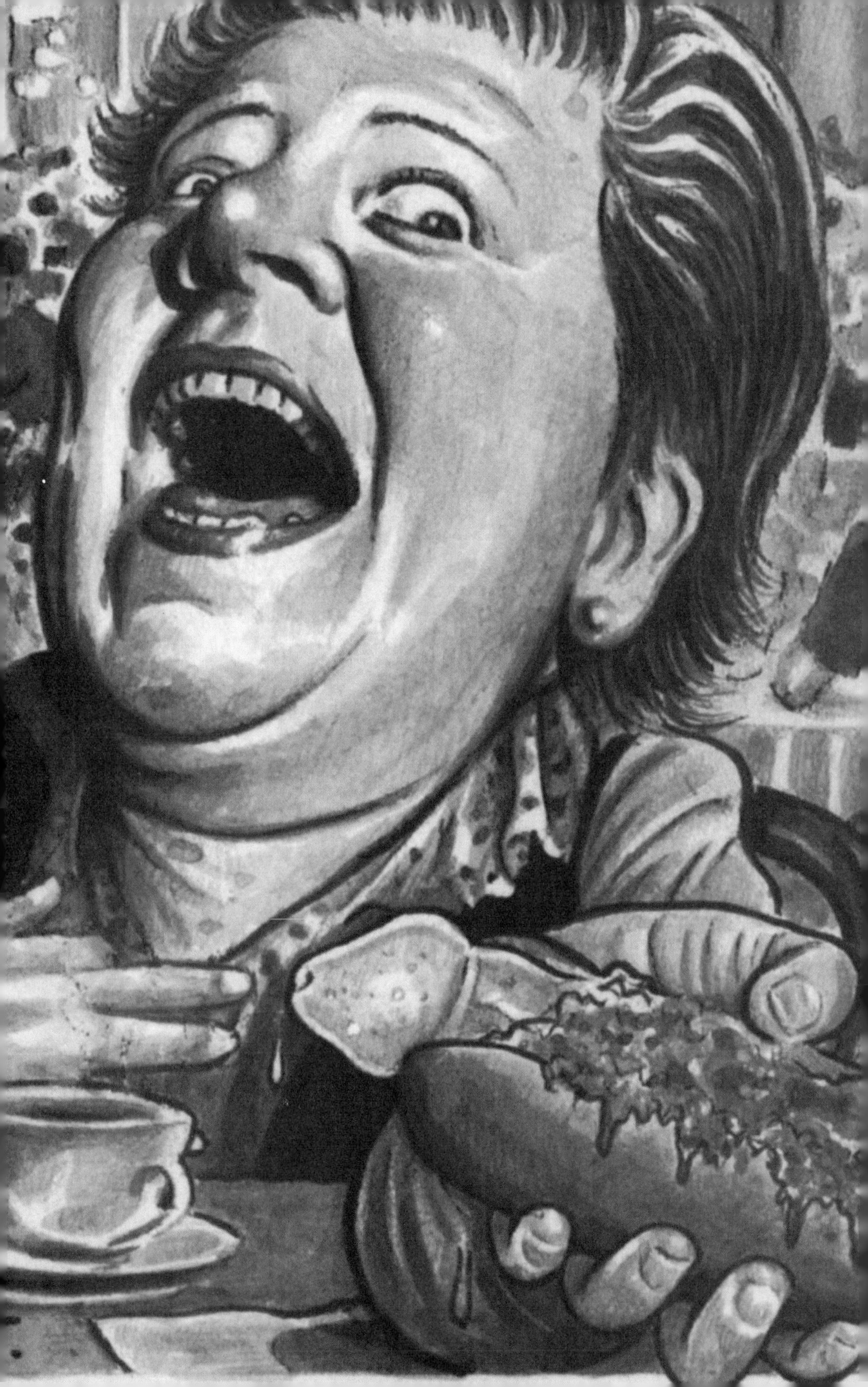

"Do you believe this evidence will stand up in court?" I had to ask. "At any time did your food squirt at you? Do you ever want to sleep with a man again?"

"I don't know," she said.

"AHA, NOW YOU'RE THINKING OF BECOMING A LESBIAN. That will make your award even bigger. You need a real lawyer. A man who knows something about food and the law. ***You need the kind of lawyer who would eat a sloppy joe with a penis in it.***"

So I called **the bloated attorney Dominic Barbara,** even though I was afraid he might eat the evidence. He came on the line, and I filled him in on the details of the case.

"She says when she hears the Oscar Mayer jingle, she breaks out in a sweat," I told Dominic. "She's very confused. She wants to divorce her boyfriend and marry her lunch."

"This sounds like an excellent case," Dominic said. "The hotel can be sued. And since this case involves a small penis, Howard could be an expert witness."

UNCLE ED

Close runner-up in my best-news-stories-of-the-decade category is **the shit-worshipping, urine-sipping pervert** Uncle Ed of Philadelphia. Robin found an item that an elderly man was arrested in Philadelphia for buying soiled underwear from neighborhood kids. They confiscated 312 plastic trash bags filled with soiled socks and underwear, along with five-thousand photos of nude boys.

So I wasn't at all surprised when Gary came in and said that one of the guys who sold his underwear to Uncle Ed was on the line.

"We didn't do anything sexual with the guy," the caller explained. "IT WAS AN EASY WAY TO GET CASH ON FRIDAY NIGHT."

***"Didn't you ever hear of collecting pop bottles for the deposit money? Or selling* Grit?"** I asked.

"The guy was actually a nice guy, believe it or not," he explained. "He wouldn't say much. He would stare at you. You didn't even have to take off your underwear in front of him. I went into the bathroom."

A second guy called in. He told us he was fifteen when he used to visit Uncle Ed, but now he sounded like a gravel-voiced truck driver.

"Some friends of mine told me to go up to the queer's house for tickets," the politically incorrect caller said. "My friend says if you urinate on him and slam his member in the door, he's got all kinds of tickets."

"So you went over and slammed his weenie in the door?"

"We go over there and he gets in the tub and both of us urinate on him. Then he says, 'Can one of you guys slam it in the door?'"

"He sticks it in the door and you slam the door and it slams *shut*?" I couldn't believe this.

DF

"No, the door wouldn't close. The door popped back open. Like if you had a dishtowel stuck in the door," the guy said.

"Was he in pain?" I asked.

"He didn't even wince."

"He had a big sausage, didn't he?" the first caller remembered.

"Uncle Ed, man, you could slam a door on his weenie and he wouldn't wince." I was impressed.

"Howard, he was at least ten inches," the first caller said.

Why do all the perverts get big dicks? Here I am a regular Joe with no dick and all my life no one ever asked me to slam their penis in a door.

I would love to make money doing that. How easy is that? I wish guys liked me. Guys are not attracted to me. I used to watch *Midnight Cowboy* and think how great it would be to get paid to let someone suck your cock. But that would never happen. No, I have to get up at four in the morning to make a buck.

Gary put a third caller through.

"In 1975, I went over to Uncle Ed's, and he had me do the thing with the erection in the door, then he gave me fifty dollars if I could throw up in his mouth," the guy said.

"That's a radio exclusive," I bragged.

But that was just the tip of the iceberg, so to speak. The next day, another client of Uncle Ed's called in. This guy was a cab-driver who was invited in by Ed after he dropped him off at home.

"We went in his bedroom and he had an oversized potty chair. He asked me to sit on it and go potty and he'd give me a hundred dollars," the guy remembered.

"A hundred dollars to go pooh-pooh?" I was ready to drive down to Philly myself.

"Yeah, but before I got on the potty chair he got down on the floor and stuck his head in the part where the potty goes and I pottied right in his mouth."

"Oh, my God!" I said, as I fantasized my bowels being emptied into this pervert's mouth.

"Stop it!" Robin yelled.

"That's the truth. I started going there three times a week," said the cabbie.

"Let me get this straight. After you were done, he'd give you a hundred dollars and you'd get up and leave?" I asked.

"Well, he would clean you up before you got up," he said.

"He would wipe you?" I asked.

"No."

"Oh, my goodness. I see. You're not gay are you?" I asked.

"No, I was in the army in Germany," the caller said. **"THIS IS NOT UNCOMMON IN GERMANY AT ALL."**

"Did he tell you what to eat before you came over?" I asked.

"After the fourth time he did. He told me specifically what to eat. The more consistency it had, the better. He told me to eat a lot of cheese. This went on for three years."

I feel compelled at this time to say that for the first time in my career I was speechless. Who knew that eating cheese makes good pooh-pooh? ***Aren't you glad you bought this book? You won't be reading any good shit-eating stories in that Colin Powell's book, even though he was stationed in Germany and he's named after a sphincter.***

Woody Allen

Everyone was shocked when Woody Allen and Mia Farrow announced that they had split because Woody had a problem with his woody around Mia's kid, Soon-yi. I was not surprised or

shocked. I had this *meeskite*'s (an Italian word for "UGLY MAN") number many years ago.

Woody Allen always struck me as a pathetic and sad man. **I refused to kiss his ass** like all those suck-up Hollywood types. All of them hold benefits and charities for children and not one of them condemned his low-life, amoral habits.

And Woody Allen's been seeing a shrink for twenty-five million years—that's a malpractice suit waiting to happen.

And of all the women that this guy could have, who does he choose? Soon-yi, Mia's adopted daughter, whose ***FACE LOOKS LIKE A CATCHER'S MITT.*** Is that face enough to make a guy go temporarily insane and violate one of the most sacred trusts between human beings? This father figure watched that kid grow up, and now he's taking naked pictures of her behind Mia's back—and fucking her? What kind of an asshole is he? But he's not the only one. What drives me crazy is these Hollywood people who defend perverts like this.

I couldn't get one guest to come on the show and bad-mouth Woody Allen, so instead, I invited one of the most boring individuals on the planet onto my show: Dick Cavett. I've never seen him rock the boat or say anything bad about anyone in show business—except me, of course. He finds me base, lowbrow, and amoral, but he constantly calls me to be on that dumb cable show he has.

I had him on because he's Woody Allen's friend. In fact Dick idolizes Woody so much that he even wears the same hat. When Woody switched from a cap to a fishing hat, guess what? Dick switched too.

Dick represented all of Hollywood when he walked through

the door. And I was ready for the kill. Anyone who would tolerate what Woody Allen did and not stand up to him is not a man and would have to stand up to me—God. Little did he know that he would have to defend that heathen, Woody Allen.

So I jumped right at him the second he came in.

"Hey Dick, do you have any daughters I can bang?" I fired at him. He didn't respond.

"Do you think it's wrong that Woody Allen dates the daughter of Mia Farrow?" I asked Dick, point-blank. "*Yes* or *no*? Do you think it's morally wrong?"

"No, I don't see anything intrinsically wrong in the things you name," he said. *Groupie.* I was sure this Yale intellectual would have higher standards.

"Do you ever say to him, 'Hey, dude, out of all the women in the world you could get, maybe it would be a better idea to stay away from Mia's offspring?'"

"Whenever I say 'Hey, dude' to Woody, he gets annoyed," Cavett said.

"Hey, Dick, do you ever go out for chinks? Not food, young girl chinks. Does Woody like to play fortune cookie with Soon-yi? You know where he hides a hundred-dollar bill? In his underpants—and Soon-yi has to find her fortune. DOES WOODY GET PISSED IF HIS NAKED PICTURES OF SOON-YI ARE BLURRY?"

"For a while I thought this might be tasteless, but I'm relieved to see this," Dick said.

I decided to hit him where it hurts. Since Dick was a manic-depressive and ***had undergone electroshock therapy,*** I knew how to torture him.

"Stick your finger in a wall socket, Dick. You're getting depressed," I said.

Dick was as wooden as an Indian. I had to get Dick out of the room, not because I felt bad for him, but because I know an audience can only take so much Dick.

Let's face it. Dick had ninety-seven canceled television shows, and all of them were canceled because **the audience lapsed into a coma.** I wasn't staking my career on a long Dick Cavett appearance. "Hey, Dick, did you ever have any of your cancellations predicted by fortune cookie?" I asked. "SAY SOMETHING FUNNY, YOU'RE AS FLAT AS MIA'S CHEST." And with that, we pushed Dick out of the studio.

Woody was cleared of the molestation charges against his own daughter, but he continued his custody battle. Can you imagine giving this guy custody of children? This is a guy who was telling Mia he couldn't have sex with her because of God knows what kind of outlandish reasons—***meanwhile, he's taking nude pictures of her kid.*** Then when she finds out he's schtupping the girl, he tells Mia he fucked her daughter to instill confidence in her.

THAT'S HOW *MY* FATHER INSTILLED CONFIDENCE IN ME, TOO. IT WAS ON MY FIFTEENTH BIRTHDAY. I THOUGHT HE WAS TAKING MY TEMPERATURE. BUT, I'LL TELL YOU, TODAY I'M ONE CONFIDENT SON OF A BITCH.

What is wrong with everybody? Years ago, just dating Soon-yi would have been the end of his career. Just ask Fatty Arbuckle. Today, it's easier to find a black person who thinks

O.J. is guilty than to find a show-business person who thinks Woody is even a little bit wrong.

But let's face it, being the hypocrite that I am, if Woody were to call tomorrow and offer to direct *my* film, **I'd jump at the chance.** Who cares if he's a pervert? As long as he doesn't fuck around with my kids.

‘I hope he dies’

CHAPTER 7

LONG LIVE THE BEAST!

NO ONE ELSE HAS A RIGHT TO BE ON THE RADIO BUT ME

Somewhere deep in my bosom—yes, I do have a bosom. I have a bosom because I've done nothing but sit at a computer for months writing this book, and I've actually developed flabby breasts.

Yes, somewhere, deep in my bosom, deep in my soul, deep in my heart, lives . . . "THE BEAST." For the most part, THE BEAST never emerges and never rears its ugly head. I keep THE BEAST buried, deep inside. On most days you'd say I was a model citizen: I am kind to my parents, faithful to my wife, and loving to my children. But make no mistake, I have a dark side, and that dark side is evil and mean. I am capable of true terror, but it is THE BEAST who drives me to do those cruel and unthinkable acts.

I still remember the day that THE BEAST called to me and forced me to do wicked acts: March 25, 1986. I remember it well. THE BEAST was so strong within me that it forced me down on my knees to pray to God. I never ask the Lord for favors because I think God has better things to do than listen to the wishes of a big-nosed, whiny, scraggly-haired, half-Jewish asshole. I didn't want to ask for something superficial like money, health, or peace on earth because I wanted something better than all that. I wanted something much more delicious. I wanted God to give me what any self-respecting DJ would want: *I wanted to beat that shithead Imus in the ratings.*

Now maybe you think that asking God to help you kick the ass of a washed-up loser is a bullshit thing to ask the Almighty for, but nothing in my world was more important to me at the time. I wanted complete victory over this no-talent skunk. Very simply, I wanted to fuck the dead-and-rotting skull of Imus, and I wanted . . . God's help. What's wrong with that? Why shouldn't I have God on my team? I was on the right side of a holy war.

WHAT THE HELL

I had just been fired from WNBC and had moved to my new radio home, 92.3 K-Rock. I wanted my victory to be so complete that Imus would suffer a quick and embarrassing ratings slide. That lizard-skinned piece of garbage deserved to be punished publicly! This Imus who had muttered insults under his breath when he saw Robin in the halls of NBC, this braying-jackass Imus who ignored me when I was the new kid on the block, deserved to have his ratings-blood sucked out of him until he lay drained of listeners. THE BEAST demanded that I humiliate him.

"Dear God," I whispered into my smelly microphone. I should have asked God why my mike stinks so bad, but I knew the answer. Twenty-four hours a day this microphone was utilized by smelly disc jockeys with coffee, cigarettes, and onion breath. I had often begged management to change the wind sock that soaked in the smells of the various radio performers, but they were too cheap.

There I was, getting distracted with thoughts of shitty-smelling breath, when THE BEAST got me back on track. "Dear God, I ask of you a small favor. Make it so that we destroy Imus's career. I beg of you, destroy all the jackasses at NBC, those scumbags who fired me."

It was a powerful prayer and, quite frankly, it was a lot to ask for. I probably shouldn't have bothered God with such trivial matters, but as long as I had God's ear I thought I'd ask for a few more things.

"God, don't think me too pushy. I thought that you, O Great Holy Spirit, could give Scott Shannon cancer. . ."

What the hell. At this point there was a lot of morning competition, and why not fix Scott Shannon as well? We're talking almost ten years ago, and I had no idea that Scott Shannon had absolutely zero talent as a performer and no chance of beating anyone in the ratings. Who knew wishing death on him was unnecessary? I continued on with my prayer. Maybe God was still listening and I could sneak in a few more suggestions.

"I pray Jim Kerr gets AIDS. And that Soupy Sales stays just the way he is on the air. If he stays that way we're sure to get huge ratings. I also pray you put a curse on the Incubus, our former general manager, John Hayes. Let's pray that Imus never gets back on cocaine, because he was a little bit interesting when he was on coke. Now, he's completely boring."

"Yes, Lord," Robin seconded me. She must have a little of THE BEAST in her, too.

"So let me recap, dear Lord." I wanted to make sure God had my laundry list of requests straight. "God, remember:

- Scott Shannon: **cancer**
- Jim Kerr: **AIDS**
- Soupy: **stay the same**
- And Imus: **stay off cocaine**
  and just keep repeating my old material."

I was on a roll. Having God's ear made me delirious.

"And God, please, one last thing, cure the breath of Boy Gary, my producer. But on second thought, I don't think that's within your power."

Well, there it was: an ugly prayer, a prayer that should never have been brought to God's attention, a prayer so selfish and trivial that it should never have been said out loud and certainly not broadcast over public airwaves. Yet there it was, a prayer filled with wishes of cancer, AIDS, and ratings. THE BEAST had forced me to become a heathen.

LET ME EXPLAIN

"Howard, how could you wish cancer and AIDS on your opponents?" my biggest fans said to me. How is it that a nice, intelligent man could plummet to the depths of humanity and depravity and wish death on others?

Well, to answer that I have to look deep inside my soul and give the most truthful answer I know. After much introspection, I can honestly say the answer is: "I DON'T KNOW." What the fuck, do I look like a psychiatrist? I know you paid a lot of money to find out the answers to these questions, but I can't figure out why I'm such a prick. And if I knew I probably wouldn't tell you anyway. IT'S NONE OF YOUR FUCKING BUSINESS.

What I do know is that I get good and pissed off when I see others stealing my material. It makes me nuts when a freak like Imus slowly pilfers parts of my act and then won't own up to it. In 1986, Dickwad was on the air, playing twelve records an hour, doing traffic, weather, and news updates. He spoke for thirty seconds at a time and never had a guest. His bits were corny and canned. He was old and tired.

Then, slowly, Imus changed, adapting all of my ideas, the ideas I started creating when I was five years old, playing with the tape recorder my dad brought home for me. Imus was taking credit for my ideas. Instead of praising me he tried to pass himself off as an original!

So I became irate.

THE DEMON, THE BEAST, festers inside of me and then pops out like a freshly squeezed pimple and explodes into a vicious tirade, forcing me to wish death and destruction on all my enemies. I wouldn't mind Imus stealing from me if the mindless dolt would just thank me once in a while for revolutionizing the airwaves.

But I hated the corporate slugs who fired me from NBC even more. I had done a good job, I had been a good soldier, and my only reward was a swift kick in the ass and a one-way ticket to Nowhere Land.

The pencil-pushers who ran NBC thought they could just

replace me with a Howard Stern clone. They were hoping the other radio stations would see me as damaged goods and a liability. Even after they fired me they offered me money to stay off the New York airwaves. BUT I WASN'T GOING TO BE VICTIMIZED!

I WAS GOING TO FIGHT BACK!!

STERN CHILD, THE VICTIM

When I was a little kid, I was a victim. Many times I would turn the other cheek when I should have stood tall. I was overly polite when I needed to be firm. There was something in my personality that avoided confrontation because I always felt I would lose in a two-way struggle. I never excelled at anything. Fat Johnny, the neighborhood bully, used to see me walking down the street and would call out my name.

"STERN! COME HERE!" he would roar with the self-confidence of a tiger scoping out his prey. Then Fat Johnny would punch me in the back, push me down, and jump on me, crushing me with all his weight . . . and I just turned the other cheek. Do I have your sympathy yet?

Why didn't I stand up to the prick? Why was I such easy pickings for the neighborhood vulture? My parents took me to judo class to learn to defend myself, and I dropped out after one lesson. I must have enjoyed being the victim, the weakling, the coward. All the other kids in that self-defense class seemed so athletic and capable, and I couldn't do a simple somersault. If only I had mastered the ancient Japanese arts.

"*Johnny San, come to Grasshopper Howie for your asskicking*," I would have whispered to Fatso as I prepared to kick him in the nuts using the powers that had been handed down to me by my Oriental masters.

It would have been glorious if I had been born with a backbone. In school I was beaten and rejected by black thugs who hated me because I was white. Why didn't I stand up to those racist fucks? I was a victim, that's why. I had "victim" written all over my freakish face. I was a gawky lamb available for slaughter. I had lived my entire young life as a sniveling coward. I was the half-Jew who bowed his head and walked into the gas chamber without putting up a fight. I was the woman who never leaves her husband, despite the beatings and abuse. I was Captain Picard from *Star Trek,* who blindly followed Starfleet Command's prime directive of noninterference and was captured by the evil enemy of mankind, the half-robot, half-human diabolical race known as the Borg. It was Picard who almost caused an end to humanity because he was a victim. . . .

Oh shit! Now I've really lost it. I'm a fuckin' Trekkie! Next thing you know I'll be running around in Mr. Spock ears and waiting for the next rerun of the Tribble episode. Talk about losers! Assholes waiting in line for Mr. Sulu's autograph and learning how to speak Klingon. Those *Star Trek* conventions should be outlawed and all Trekkies sterilized.

But when you think about it, who am I to call Trekkies losers?

I was a loser. Not quite a Trekkie or a postal worker, but I was the guy who lost at every competition. I choked under pressure. I was the camper picked last at softball games. I was the junior-high gym-class toady too uncoordinated to play baseball. I was the one tall teenager who sucked at basketball. I wasn't good at anything. Now, I must *really* have your sympathy, having utilized a brilliant literary device called "manipulation." I sucked with women, and my Friday nights were filled with endless card games, pizzas, and stinky cigars. I was rejected by the *in* crowd, the *out* crowd, and the *in between* crowd. I hung with the dipshits. I wasn't the king of the dipshits, I wasn't even his second in command. I was just a follower, a Friday-night-poker-playin' asshole.

I was the guy afraid that one of the other dipshits would get a girlfriend and leave me behind sitting next to an empty chair at the card table. Even at the card table, I was humiliated. I couldn't bluff. For a dipshit who played cards that much you'd think I would have developed some skill. You remember the Kenny Rogers song "The Gambler": when he talks about knowing when to hold 'em, fold 'em, walk away, and run? Well, I didn't know when to hold 'em, and I didn't know when to fold 'em, and I sure as shit never walked away, ran away, or fuckin' flew away, for that matter. ***Suck my dick, Kenny Rogers***. I bet that *Hee Haw* hillbilly can't play cards either.

You saw what a loser I was on my second video release, *The U.S. Open Sores*, when I played tennis against Gary, my producer. He whipped my ass in front of twenty thousand people, even though I am a much better tennis player.

That's me. Choke Artist Howard Stern, the loser, the uncoordinated oaf. I hate that part of me. Pint-sized Nils Lofgrin was a guest on my old WOR television show and he whipped my ass in basketball. A guitar player half my size, almost a midget, humiliated me in front of an audience of millions. I tried to brush it off, but it really bothered me.

Women even beat me in basketball. On my E! television show Martin Landau's girlfriend played a friendly game of one-on-one and beat my ass so bad she left me scoreless except for one lucky basket. The final score was 21 to 17 and she spotted me fifteen points. Fifteen fucking points. *Hello?* Anybody still here, or are you ready to hang yourself from the depression that is setting in?

How's that? Pretty fucking humiliating. I suck at almost everything. I said I suck at *almost* everything. You see, I am good at one thing—actually, I'm not just good at one thing,

I'm *extraordinary* at one thing—and that's radio. I'm not just good at it, I'm the *best* at it. I can broadcast my ass off. Put me in front of a mike and leave me a four-hour blank canvas, and I become Picasso, da Vinci, and that one-eared bastard who mutilated himself rolled into one. I can fuck you up your ass six ways till Sunday and pick your corpse clean and you won't know what hit you. When I'm behind the mike I can open up your brain and suck the snot out of your nose. What the hell am I thinking about? *Suck the snot out of your nose?* I am one intense motherfucker when I'm on the air. I can size you up in a split second, pick out your secret weakness, and beat you to a pulp. I am Superman, Batman, and the fucking Hulk rolled up into one, and if you don't believe it, then try to take me out. I dare you! I FUCKING DOUBLE-DARE YOU, YOU TWISTED PIECE OF SHIT!!!

You have never known a competitor like me. The way I see it either you're on my side or you're dead. It's that black and white. It's either yin or yang. It's either Bob or Ray, Jack or Jill, Bob or Booey. Any way you slice it or dice it I will kick your ass if you oppose my show. I always thought I would grow tired of killing off the assholes, but the competition still thrills me.

In the beginning I thought I was so competitive because I wanted money, power, and fame, but it has nothing to do with that. What drives me is that I can finally do something *perfectly*, and I like doing it well. Babe Ruth could hit the ball, Einstein could write equations, and Stern can, well, *Stern can make you laugh while you're stuck in a traffic jam.*

I am the strongest radio vampire in the world and I am obsessed with one simple notion:

NO ONE ELSE HAS A RIGHT TO BE ON THE RADIO BUT ME!

How sick is that?

But, I am an inventor. Now I know it's not the lightbulb, and I know it ain't the gas-powered engine—hell it's not even the Clapper—but it's my invention. I invented saying PENIS and VAGINA on the radio, and I'll go to my grave proud of that accomplishment.

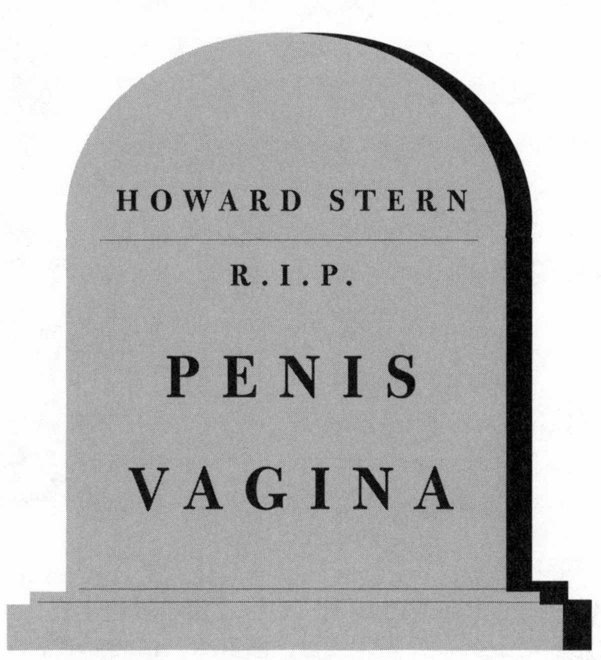

DESTRUCTION, A NECESSARY EVIL

THE DESTRUCTION OF IMUS: my great battle, my Waterloo, my Alamo . . . my God, I want to fuck the blonde in the thong on *The Grind,* the MTV dance show. Sorry, I shouldn't write while watching the tube. I'm turning this shit off and getting down to the business at hand. Okay . . .

So now maybe you understand why I prayed to God that day for the total destruction of IMUS. Now you understand why THE BEAST within me is a necessary evil and a thing of beauty. THE BEAST had transformed me. No longer was I a mousy victim. I was now a lean, mean fighting machine and Imus was to die an embarrassing public death. Death by humiliation. *Imus was going to pay for what Fat Johnny had done to me!* I wasn't that geeky kid anymore. I was now . . . a geeky adult, with a mission.

God must be on my team because he answered my prayers in a big way—he answered them with the ratings book of the century. We blew that shitbag's brains out in less than three months.

Stern on Imus: 'I hope he dies

R.I.P. NBC, OR THE THRILL OF THE KILL

The Beast was fed for the moment, satisfied with the kill. I had vanquished my mortal enemies—the assholes at NBC. Not only had we trounced alligator-face in the morning, but the entire radio station crumbled. The guy they brought in to replace me had sunk to an all-time low. Imus had no listeners left, and NBC never had ratings the rest of the day, anyway. Now a $55 million radio station was worth under $20 million. I sent a funeral wreath with the words R.I.P. NBC to be hand-delivered to the main desk.

It was particularly gratifying, though, to beat Imus. Sounding more stupid than usual, Imus had boasted that he would eat "a dead dog's dick" if I beat him in the ratings. Well, it was time for a little "Poodle Penis Parmigiana," hold the fur. Little details about Imus flooded my memory: I remembered how he used to strut around the radio station declaring, "*I'm number one, on the number one, in the number one!*"

The first time I heard this I just blew it off as the ramblings of a broken-down addict who couldn't handle his booze or cocaine. But what Snaggle Tooth was bragging about was the fact that he was the number-one disc jockey, on the number-one station in New York, the number-one city in the world. Like most of Imus's statements, you needed an interpreter to even come close to understanding what he was saying. Now his slogan would have to be ***"I'm number twenty-seven, on the dead last, lowest-rated radio station, in New York."*** I love it!

Another annoying thing he used to do was whip out a big wad of bills and talk about all the money he had. Fucking braggart. It was pathetic the way he had to buy his young girlfriends expensive jewelry to keep them happy. He would run around the station bragging about the fact that he just spent ten grand for a pearl necklace. Most of the folks at NBC who worked desk jobs weren't making much more than that, and he had no idea what a jackass he sounded like to them.

THE BEAST in me loved bringing him down to the gutter. All the time I had been at NBC, the suits there had constantly been after me to be like Mr. Imus, that great radio icon. The big man whose idea of a radio show was to open the mike and utter the now-forgettable phrase "*How's your donkey kong?*" and then cut to a record or a traffic report.

It struck me that this was too important an event to let pass without ceremony. I needed to gloat. I needed to party with the people who had made me whole. I needed to stick it in Fat Johnny's, *oops,* I mean, Imus's face. When I became number one in Washington it was certainly a milestone, but this New York victory was intensely personal. We immediately made plans for the first of many funerals that we would hold to bury our competitors. Holding a public funeral was divine inspiration. I had THE BEAST to thank for that.

We decided to conduct the funeral in front of the Beanstalk restaurant, one of our loyal sponsors, which was within shouting distance of the NBC offices. It happened quite spontaneously and without much planning. I got on the air the day of the funeral and told our listeners to meet there after my show. No big buildup, no great fanfare. I wanted it to happen quick. I needed instant gratification.

I also knew that if I waited days to plan this shindig, the city would get wind of it and refuse us a permit, and I didn't want to get caught up in a sea of red tape. I wanted my funeral in front of the NBC building, and if I waited, NBC would find a way to thwart me. You'd think I was General Rommel planning World War II the way I carried on, but I had a plan. My plan was ...**TO ACT STUPID**.

Even if the police complained about the lack of a permit, I would just plead *stupidity.* (I'm good at pleading that.) I would say I didn't know what I was doing. Of course, I knew exactly what I was doing.

When I casually told our listeners to meet me at the Beanstalk restaurant after my show, I had no idea if anyone would show up.

What if I gave a funeral and nobody came?

UH, *SHE'S* IN CHARGE

I sent Gary out as our advance man. We had rented a hearse and put a coffin labeled IMUS in it. Robin and I were going to arrive around noon in a huge stretch limo with a sun roof. We'd get out, pull the coffin out of the hearse, conduct a ceremony around the coffin, and then split. It had to be hit-and-run because we had no permits, and I knew there would be trouble the instant I started carrying on.

Apparently, NBC considered the sidewalk in front of the restaurant part of their jurisdiction, so they started to threaten to arrest Gary as he was setting up our PA system. I told you those fuckers would try to mess me up. They had called the police and told them we were setting up for a mass demonstration and we didn't have a permit. I could see the hand of the Incubus, my former general manager, John Hayes, all over this. He was just itching to arrest me and sabotage the funeral.

Everyone at my new radio station, K-Rock, was telling me to forget the whole idea and cancel until we could get permits, but THE BEAST started to well up inside me with images of all the times I had run away from confrontation. Images of the bully Fat Johnny, the racist black thugs in Roosevelt, the girls who beat me at basketball, and those shitty card games. THE BEAST spared me the image of my father calling me a moron, and I was glad for that.

I called everyone in for a quick meeting. I spoke up and inspired the troops. "Don't be afraid to hold the funeral! NBC ain't gonna do shit! I ain't letting a little thing like a sound system defeat me! I am prepared to hold this funeral without a PA, and I will shout at the top of my lungs if I can't have a microphone."

Everyone mobilized. I was having a funeral despite the fact that the police were now saying that they would arrest me if I set

foot on Rockefeller Center property with a PA system. I was prepared to go to jail.

The cops finally suggested that we set up the PA on the corner of Sixth Avenue and Forty-ninth Street, since that was a public street. By that time about seventy-five people had shown up, and things didn't seem that out of control.

Within a half hour, about four thousand people were massed around the corner. The police barricades had been totally overrun. The hearse was engulfed. It was a total mob scene.

Robin and I got to within a block of our destination, but when I stuck my head out of the sun roof, the crowd went berserk. They surged toward our car and spilled out into the street. The cops had to close Sixth Avenue to all traffic. It took us at least ten minutes to go the final half block.

I was wearing a black hooded robe. I wanted to look like Death from those stupid Ingmar Bergman films I had to watch at Boston University. I'd graduated magna cum laude in "movie watching." I also had a megaphone that was programmed to play certain songs, and it beeped out "Taps." This only incited the crowd. They were screaming and bowing to our limo.

Finally, Robin and I somehow managed to get out of the limo. Robin was a vision, dressed head to toe in white except for a black veil. I stepped to the mike, and the crowd started chanting:

"HOWARD! HOW-ARD!"

The sudden rush of seeing my audience and realizing they cared about beating Imus just as much as I did was powerful.

Why had this mob shown up? Maybe they needed to see a guy who didn't back down and got to fuck his old boss in a big way. MAYBE THEY WERE THERE BECAUSE THEY LIKED

TO SEE A GUY FIGHT BACK. Maybe they didn't give a shit about any of that and they were just there on a lunch break. Who cared? The funeral was a success. I opened the mike and spoke.

"All right, friends. Now remember, this is a serious occasion, because someone has died. In fact, an entire radio station has died. And now a reading from Sister Robin."

Robin stepped up to the mike, clutching a big black Bible. She pulled up her veil, revealing her face. The crowd went wild. She opened the Good Book and began reading.

"They have acted ruinously, and they have acted unrighteously. Because of that, God has looked down on this situation and no one is getting ratings at NBC!" I didn't know what Robin was going to say and quite frankly her religious fervor took me by surprise. If you read her book, *Quivers: A Life*, you know there are definitely a few demons living inside of her, and she was having fun blasting away at the enemy.

"Thank you, Sister Robin!" I screamed. It was time to get Imus's coffin, but we couldn't even get close to the hearse. I assessed the situation. Sixth Avenue was totally shut down. The cops were fuming. People were hanging out of the windows at NBC, checking out the funeral. The entire NBC security force was lined up outside the building, afraid that our hordes were about to invade. I realized I had better cut the ceremony short.

"Friends, death can be an ugly thing, but in this case it's beau-

tiful," I said. "Before I enter my car again and spread the ashes, I want to say unto you, I WISH THE TEN PLAGUES ON NBC!"

The cheers of thousands filled up the street.

"*Locusts! Boils! And low ratings upon all of them!*" I said. They cheered again. I had run out of plagues. I told you I was unprepared. No one seemed to be counting. This group wanted blood. I quickly moved on. "You guys did it! You made these guys die!" The crowd exulted. I got swept up in the moment and called upon that great Stern wit to say something profound.

"FUCK NBC!" I screamed.

I brought Robin back to the mike, and we finished with a rendition of "Amazing Grace." We tried to get back into our limo, but an irate police officer blocked our way.

Our promotions director, a smart woman named Sharon Rosenbush, made the mistake of identifying herself. The cop grabbed her and pulled her off to the side. I was sure she was going to be arrested. He had his nose pressed up against her face and he started screaming at her.

"Is this over? Are you done?" he asked with a menacing tone. "Who's in charge here?!!" he screamed.

Without hesitation, without blinking an eye, as the leader and hero of this group, I answered that cop. I gave him an icy-cold stare and bravely said, "Uh, *she's* in charge." Then I quickly

jumped in the limo and locked the fuckin' doors. Hell, I didn't want to go to jail, I had better things to do. It was a perfect day to be poolside.

Before I hightailed it out of there, I poked my head out of the sun roof and gave it one last poetic shot. I LIFTED MY MIDDLE FINGER AND SALUTED NBC. Four thousand fingers went up in unison.

The Imus funeral was a lot of fun, but later, when I had time to reflect, I realized that I had blown it. I hadn't cashed in enough. What was I thinking? This funeral could have been a ratings bonanza on the radio! I didn't even have a visual record of it because my friend Neil was supposed to videotape it with his camcorder but he got crushed by the mob.

This, of course, was all before I became a sophisticated manipulator of the media. You can see how much I've grown at being a crass and conniving opportunist over the years.

THE HOLLOW VICTORY

I thought THE BEAST would be satisfied, but I still felt tortured. Yes, it was a good feeling to whip NBC's ass and take down an entire radio station, but I knew it wasn't just Imus who was bothering me. The truth was that there were a thousand Imuses out there, all ripping off my material and building careers off of my style and approach to radio.

Now, how funny is this? Take a minute to laugh at my

unusual illness. Do you realize how fucked in the head I am? *When I win, I'm empty*. I'm never satisfied. This is my fate, *my private hell*, this is why I have to get the fuck out of this business.

I was driving myself crazy. I needed to be heard all over the country, but the industry I worked in was filled with pea brains who couldn't accept a network broadcast in morning drive. Once again I was frustrated and annoyed with radio because of the resistance to new ideas.

Outside of the tristate area, I was a nobody. I would go to visit my wife's family in Boston, and they had no idea I was famous. They knew I was in radio and would talk about their local morning man and how wild he was, quoting jokes that I had done the week before. They were laughing at *my* material. Man, I would fume. My nostrils would flare. (And I have *huge* nostrils—so big I can pick my nose with my thumb, and when they flare, it's pretty scary.) Alison's Great-Aunt Emma was bedridden and very old. She heard I was in radio and asked me to come into her bedroom to talk privately. I assumed she was anxious to hear about my exciting life. She turned to me and said, "Howard, you are in radio, aren't you?"

"Yes, Auntie Em," I said proudly. Finally, a woman who wanted to hobnob with greatness. "Auntie Em, what would you like to know about radio?"

"Howard," she said, "I have a problem. I can't get my radio to work. I was wondering if you could fix it. I want to hear the Boston Red Sox game."

The old woman thought I was a radio repairman. *Oh shit!*

I looked over the radio and saw that she had it on FM and she needed to switch it over to AM. The damn thing wasn't broken. I pretended I was fixing it. I fixed it in a minute.

"You certainly are good at what you do," she said, congratulating me on a job well done.

Some superstar I was!

HOWARD STERN, RADIO REPAIRMAN.

ME, THE BIG HOLLYWOOD SQUARE

From time to time I would go out to L.A. to cover big events like the Academy Awards and the Emmys, and I would run around the red carpet trying to get celebrities to answer goofy questions. (All the shit Stuttering John now does.) While every half-baked actor was being mobbed, I was just ignored. In L.A., I was a zero.

One time I flew to L.A. to tape *Hollywood Squares.* The show was so incredibly lame and wimpy that I accepted because I knew I could goof about it on the air for weeks, but the goof was on me. I was filling in for Shadoe Stevens and sat directly under Jm J. Bullock. That's not a typo, this dude Jim actually spells his name Jm. What the fuck was that about? I could only guess. Quite frankly, I didn't care to know and from where I was sitting old Jm J.'s ass was directly above me and I was getting a view only his gynecologist had seen.

All the so-called celebrities who did that show were backstage waiting to be introduced to the live studio audience. It was a collection of people who either were on their way down the show-biz ladder or were already on the last rung along with circus performers.

As each celebrity was announced, the person would come running out onto the stage and climb into his square. The crowd went wild every time one of these third-rate celebs came out.

"Ladies and gentlemen, please welcome Princess Zsa Zsa Gabor," the announcer boomed. Wild applause. The fucking crowd was reacting like Jesus H. Christ himself had come out and turned water into wine.

"And now a warm *Hollywood Squares* welcome to Leslie Easterbrook."

W h o ?

She was the chick from *Police Academy,* the tall blonde with the giant tits. The fucking place broke into a standing ovation. Tile was falling off the ceiling because of Easterbrook.

EASTERBROOK? EASTER *BUNNY!* Yeah, show me the Easter Bunny, then maybe I'll applaud.

The cast of *Police Academy* was obviously very available 'cause the next guy up was the black guy from *Police Academy* who makes the funny sound effects with his mouth. They introduced him as Michael Winslow, but I think he should have been introduced simply as "The-Black-Guy-Who-Makes-Sound-Effects from *Police Academy*."

Anyway, the dude came out and the studio audience broke into a thunderous ovation. People were jumping up and down. I double-checked the monitor. Maybe Elvis had walked out with him. Nope, not the case.

One after another, a parade of the obscure trotted onstage, Dr. Joyce Brothers, followed by Ross Schafer—yes, the one-and-

only Ross Schafer. Anybody got a *Who's Who*? He was a comedian who hosted *The Match Game* for ten seconds.

Glen Campbell was next—you know, the guy who had those legendary domestic disputes with little Tanya Tucker. The audience was doing a wild foot stomp like *The Arsenio Hall Show* was back in town.

Now, it was my turn. GOD'S GIFT TO RADIO was all set. The women were expecting a hot hunk 'cause I was filling in for Shadoe Stevens, the beefcake announcer. They sat there, legs akimbo, getting wet, waiting to see the hunky fill-in choice.

"And now, Ladies and Germs, all the way from New York, Disc Jockey Howard Stern!!"

The curtain opened and . . . *Hello? Oops!* I must have gone through the wrong door. I must be on the set of a nature movie 'cause all I hear is the sound of crickets. Wait a second, I just heard a pin drop.

N O T H I N G .

You could see the people in the audience opening their mouths and forming the words "Who the fuck is that?"

Damn, it was embarrassing. The women were retching, *en masse.* Instead of a hunk, they got the fifty-foot gork from planet nine. It only got worse. We taped a whole week of shows, and I only got called on three times. Even the contestants were looking at me like I was a mistake. I was such an unknown that I could have been a contestant.

And not once was I chosen as the good-luck secret square.

Can you believe it? The contestants get to pick a good-luck charm to stand up on the stage with them while they put a key in a car to see if it started. Damn it! Now I wasn't a lucky secret square, and the whole country knew it. Fucking Jm J. got picked every fucking time.

Jm J. was King Shit and I was nobody. If this show had been taped in New York I would have been the fucking good-luck secret square and Jm J. would be dodging rotten apples! I was a nobody! *A NOBODY!*

The other celebs even felt bad for me. *Princess* Zsa Zsa trotted her FAT ASS down between taping sessions and looked at me with doughie eyes and said, "Dahlink, I don't know who you are, but you are absolutely vile."

Well now, I felt right at home. She was right. I *was* vile. The three times I was called on, I answered the stupid *Hollywood Squares* questions with a vicious tirade. I was so wickedly outrageous that the audience thought I was a psychopath.

Now this was good television! It was so good that they edited out most of what I had said, because my comments didn't fit a family format. *No shit, Sherlock.* All I know is that by the end of my vile week as a Hollywood Square, I had formed a new powerful alliance with a princess.

Princess Zsa Zsa came to my dressing-room door on the last day and said, "*Dahlink, you are vile . . . but you are funny. So I love you.*"

I fantasized putting my finger in the princess's pussy, then I came to my senses. I had had a bad week, but it wasn't that bad.

TO THE CITY OF BROTHERLY LOVE

I was a nobody in Boston.

I was a loser on *Hollywood Squares* and a zero in L.A.

It was time to implement phase one of my plan to take my show national. So I set my sights on another stupid disc jockey.

This disc jockey, JOHN DEBELLA, was blowing horns and running idiotic contests and answering the phone "Yazoo!" on his top-rated morning-zoo show at WMMR in Philadelphia. I guess he felt safe, ninety miles away, but he was about to be cornholed by yours truly, right there in the City of Brotherly Love.

Once again, the geniuses of my industry said that the Philadelphia audience would never embrace an out-of-town show, especially one coming from New York. Conventional wisdom was that the radio personality had to know the local streets and the names of area high schools to have a successful show. Aaaagggghhhh! Does David Letterman?! WHY SHOULD RADIO BE ANY DIFFERENT!!?

This was like starting all over. And I was running out of patience. I wanted to flip a switch and be heard all over the United States, but instead I would have to prove myself, market by market, and delay my dreams of national recognition and eventual world domination. I would have to prove the pundits wrong. It was my boss, Mel Karmazin, who finally had the balls to say, "I'm putting you on the Philly station, and I don't care what my management people think."

It was time to go to war.

THE BATTLE PLAN

I began by analyzing the situation. If this was to be war, I needed a game plan. Well, one look at the Philadelphia ratings and I had all the game plan I needed: Standing on top of the ratings like a giant Colossus was this bald-headed morning zookeeper, John DeBella. He had been undefeated in over fifteen straight ratings books. For over four years he had dominated the Philadelphia radio scene. If I was to win in Philadelphia, I'd have to dethrone DeBella.

THE BEAST inside began to well up.

"Howard," he called to me.

I tried to ignore him.

"*HOWARD,*" THE BEAST bellowed.

I kept on ignoring him.

"Sexy Boy Howard," THE BEAST said, using a softer, more feminine voice. Oooh, methinks THE BEAST is trying to sweet-talk me. Maybe THE BEAST was light in the loafers, a bit fey.

THE BEAST dropped the jokes and got real loud. The familiar mantra was being recited!

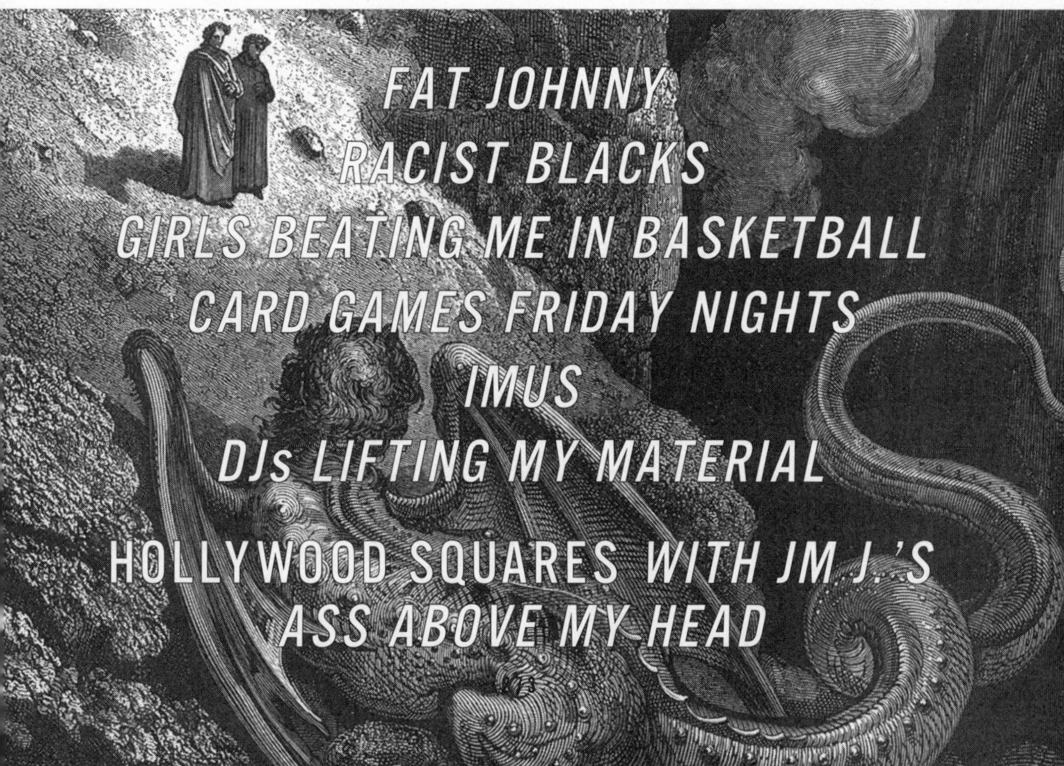

THE BEAST reminded me that if I was ever going to be national I would have to smash DeBella into the ground. I needed to fuck him up good—dissect him. Suck the life right out of him. I was getting good and worked up. DeBella was doomed. I needed one more thing. I needed a reason to hate him . . . on a personal level.

I found my reason in Gary, my producer. Gary had once worked with DeBella at WLIR in Long Island. At the time, DeBella was the star disc jockey and Gary was a lowly intern. Gary told me that DeBella was so arrogant that the interns, as part of their standard orientation, had been instructed not to talk to DeBella in the halls. They were told they weren't even allowed to look him in the eye. That was enough to get me going.

WHO THE FUCK DID THIS ARROGANT PRICK THINK HE WAS?!!

It didn't matter if it was true. It was all I needed!

I called Andy Bloom, our program director in Philadelphia, and he sent me a whole DeBella package: articles, interviews, tapes of his show. I reviewed the material, and I was amazed at how ordinary a performer DeBella was. Not horrible, but not a superstar. I was equally amazed at how great a performer DeBella *thought* he was.

His show followed the typical morning-zoo format: a couple of guys sitting around, hooting, clapping, blowing horns, and hitting a cymbal to punctuate a bunch of lousy jokes, in between playing plenty of lame music. I had given that up years ago when I was still in Washington.

Every day had to have a little gimmick. On Monday he'd play that Boomtown Rats song "I Don't Like Mondays" *ad nauseum.* Wednesday was Hump Day because you get past Wednesday and the week is almost over. Friday was Hawaiian Shirt Gonzo Friday. Everyone was urged to wear Hawaiian shirts to work. *This* was my great competition?

I studied DeBella's physical appearance, looking for weaknesses. First of all, he was bald. And it must have bothered him, because he wore funny hats to cover it up. Then he had a big fucking walrus moustache. He looked like a demented Jerry Colonna. Plus he had one of those smiles where you could see a lot of his gums. He had a real pompous attitude, always flashing those smug smiles. I had a lot to work with.

Then I found out he had actually married one of his own listeners. I couldn't believe it. Jackpot!! Lots of DJs picked up girls on request lines and banged 'em, but they never *married* them. I, of course, have never even kissed the listeners I've talked with on the request lines. I got married so fucking young that I never had the opportunity to experience that God-given right of the broadcaster: to have wild monkey sex with his audience.

Without having seen her, I knew DeBella's wife would be way too beautiful for this character and that once his ratings disappeared ***she would be gone with the wind.***

No way was DeBella prepared for the storm that was coming. He was about to feel my rage because he had broken my rules:

THOU SHALT NOT BE ARROGANT OR SMUG.

THOU SHALT NOT MARRY ONE OF THY LISTENERS.

THOU SHALT NOT STEAL HOWARD'S BITS.

I was preparing to drop heavy artillery on this zookeeper. I had my ammunition. Whenever I'd hear the word "DeBella" I'd pull up the program:

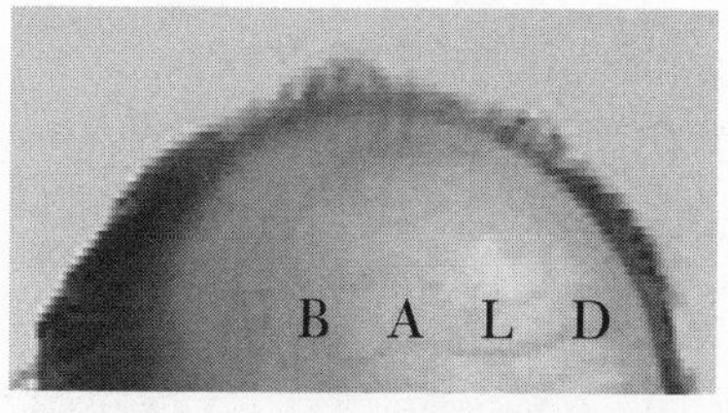

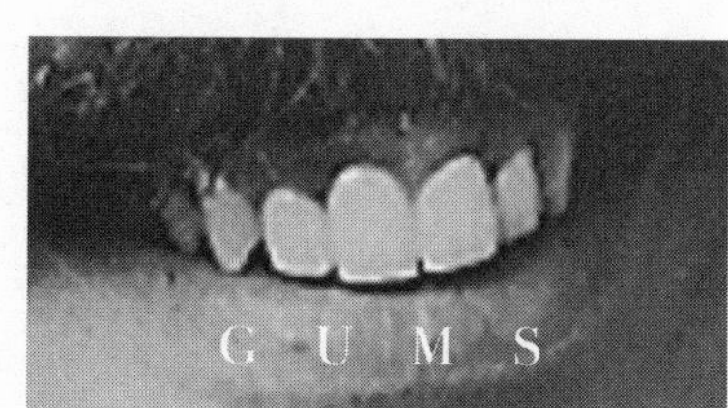

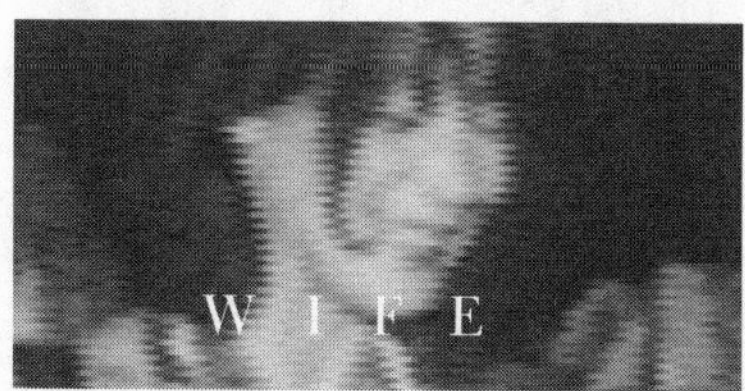

The Beast continues on page 276

HOWIE WOOD

Listen, stop busting my balls asking where's my big Hollywood movie. There's going to be a *Private Parts* movie and it's going to be done right. I've learned my lesson.

I've been flirting with Tinseltown for years. I've met with the heads of development at every studio. They all loved me. They all wanted me. We took meetings.

"I've never done a movie before. What film should we do?" I asked these geniuses.

"Howie! Baby! Honey! Darling! We want to be in bed with you. We'll make anything you want. Fill up our plates. Name your movie."

I was on the spot.

"OK, uh, let's do *The Adventures of Fartman,"* I said off the top of my head. I was kidding around.

They all vomited.

I even went on the Jay Leno show and announced that I was going to do a Fartman movie. Again, I was joking. But that night, J. F. Lawton, the hottest screenwriter in Hollywood, was watching. This guy had just written *Pretty Woman* and *Under Siege.* He heard me say "Fartman" and a bell went off in his head.

"That's my next movie," he proclaimed.

Within months we were set. We had a deal with New Line Cinema, the people who brought you Freddy Krueger and the Ninja Turtles. And soon, Fartman. Everyone loved the script. But, at the last moment, the project was scrapped because New Line wanted the lion's share of the merchandising rights. They had been burned by both Krueger and the stupid Turtles. I didn't care. I wasn't about to give them my merchandising. The deal fell through over Fartman coffee mugs.

So, for anyone who never believed me, what follows is the world premiere of the first five pages of the Fartman script. It's in comic-book form, so you can visualize the stunning work of genius it would have been.

THE ADVENTURES OF
FARTMAN
TOM MORGAN
STORY/ART
BONGOTONE
COLOR
ADAPTED FROM THE MOVIE SCREENPLAY BY
J. F. LAWTON
BASED ON A CHARACTER
CREATED BY
HOWARD STERN

WEST 42ND STREET.
HELL'S KITCHEN.
NIGHT.
ZZZZIP!
VRRROOOM
ANOTHER SATISFIED CUSTOMER.
MAN, LOOK AT THE SIZE OF THOSE DENOMINATIONS!
EASY MONEY, BLOODSHOT.
SHUT UP, BONEY FINGERS!
WHAT'S THAT?!
HEY, BABY, COME TO PAPA!
TERROR!
RUN!

TOO LATE, STREET QUEEN!
SLAM!
MMMF!
RRRIPP!
GET THE MONEY!
LET'S GO!
BASTARDS!
HELP! HELP! SOMEBODY HELP! PLEASE!
MEANWHILE, HIGH ABOVE THE CITY STREETS--
HMMM, SMELLS LIKE TROUBLE.
OR IS THAT ME?

NOT BAD FOR A C-CUP.
YOU SHOULDN'T HAVE PUSHED HER-- IT SO HARD. YOU COULD'VE HURT-- IT.
YOU KNOW WHAT'S BEEN HAPPENING TO OTHER MUGGERS LATELY-- HE GOT THEM!
LOOK, I'M TIRED OF TELLING YOU! HE DOESN'T EXIST! IT'S JUST ONE OF THOSE URBAN LEGENDS... LIKE BABA BOOEY'S TEETH!
WHAT'S THAT SMELL?!
NOTHING... JUST GARBAGE. THERE AIN'T NO--
FARTMAN!!

I THOUGHT I GOT THE WORD OUT THAT SCUM LIKE YOU WERE THROUGH!

WE'RE SORRY! WE'LL GIVE THE MONEY BACK! WE WON'T EVER--
SHUT UP! I'M NOT TAKING SHIT FROM A QUEER IN YELLOW TIGHTS!
BEHOLD MY AWESOME ASS OF POWER!
THE FARTMAN STRIKETH!

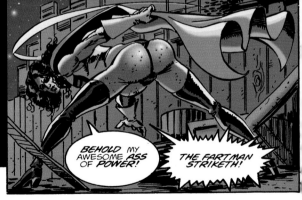

BLAFRRRRRTT!
DON'T HURT ME! PLEASE--
LISTEN, PUNK. TELL YOUR FRIENDS. I'M GIVING THESE ROTTING STREETS BACK TO THE HARD WORKING PEOPLE OF NEW YORK.
PARASITES LIKE YOU BETTER FIND A NEW PROFESSION.
OTHERWISE YOU'LL ANSWER TO FARTMAN!
I BELIEVE THIS BELONGS TO YOU.
OH, FARTMAN, AT LAST THE STREETS ARE SAFE FOR US GIRLS.
ANY TIME YOU WANT A FREE ONE--
JUST ASK FOR BRUNO.
SHE'S A HE!!
OH, CHRIST!! I'M PUKING ALL OVER MY NIFTY COSTUME!!
FARTMAN TURNS THE OTHER CHEEK...
BLAFOOM!
AND IS GONE WITH THE WIND.

REJECTED BOOK COVERS

You think it's easy coming up with a cover for your book? I spent hours and hours and went back and forth until I was nauseous. I was so attached to the ones that were rejected that I thought I'd share them with you.

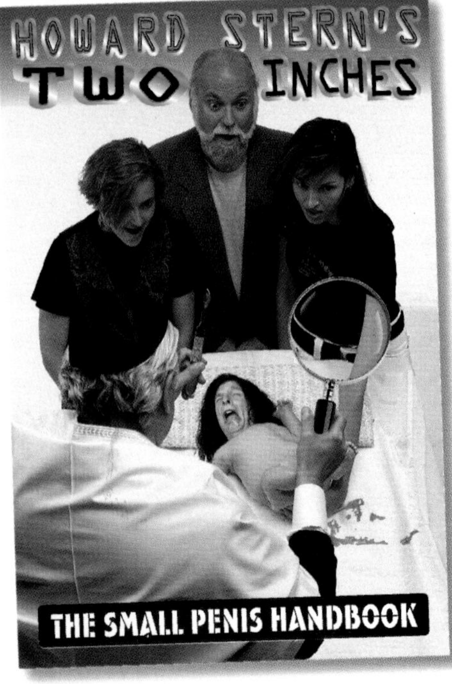

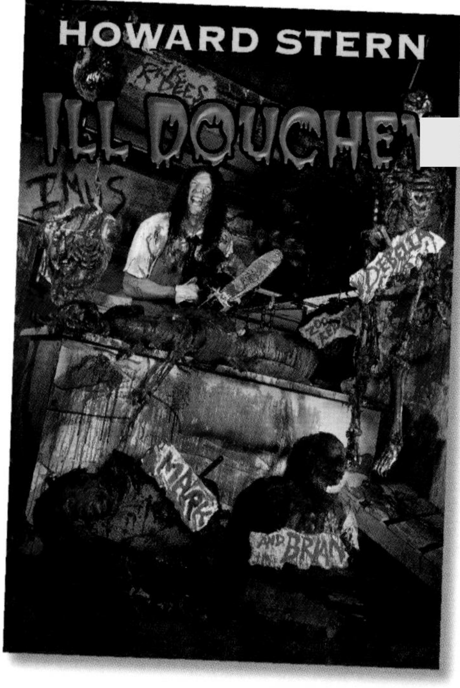

HOWARD STERN'S
Clinic for Behavior Modification

Tongue Foo
HOWARD STERN

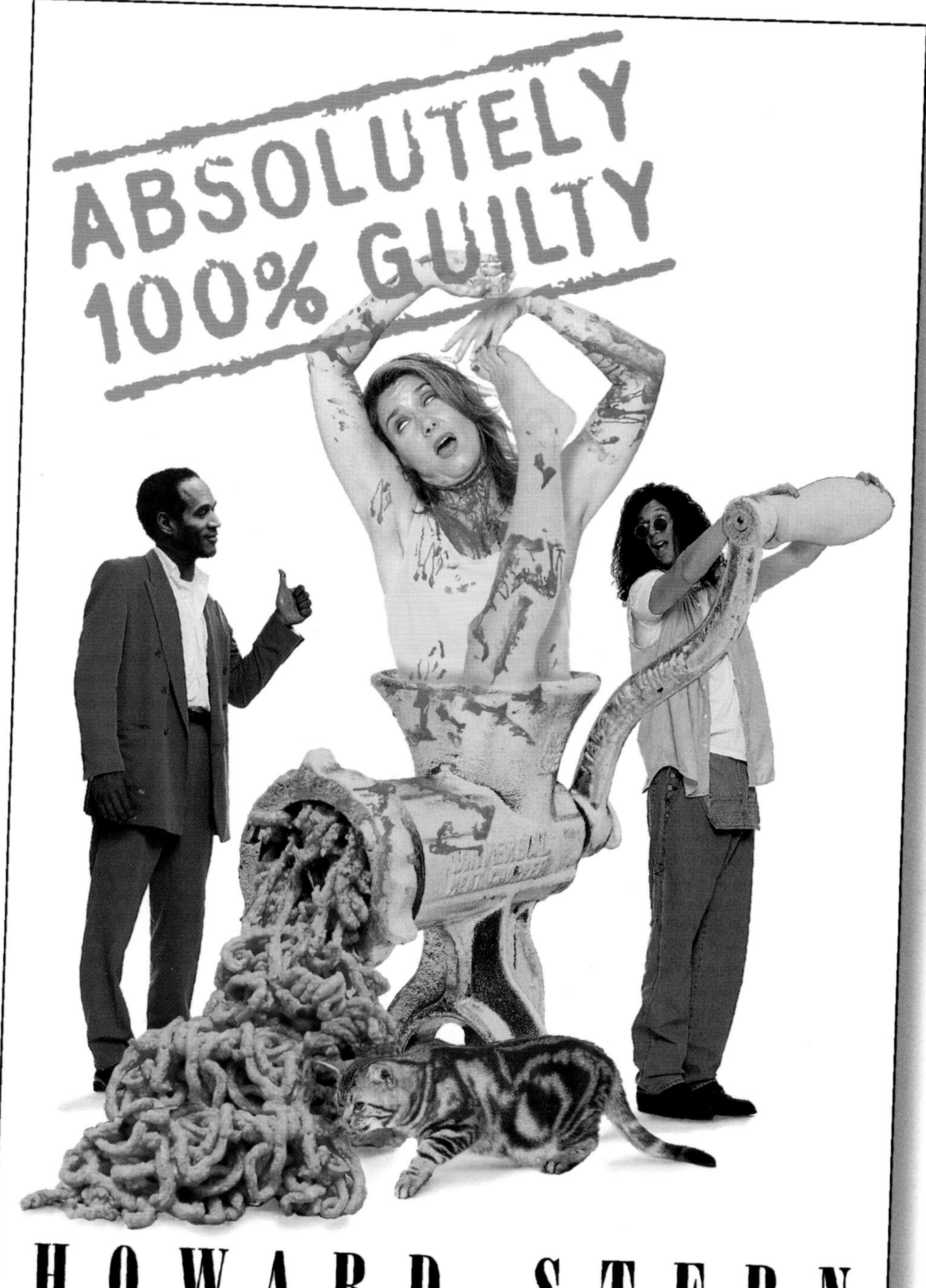

HOWARD STERN

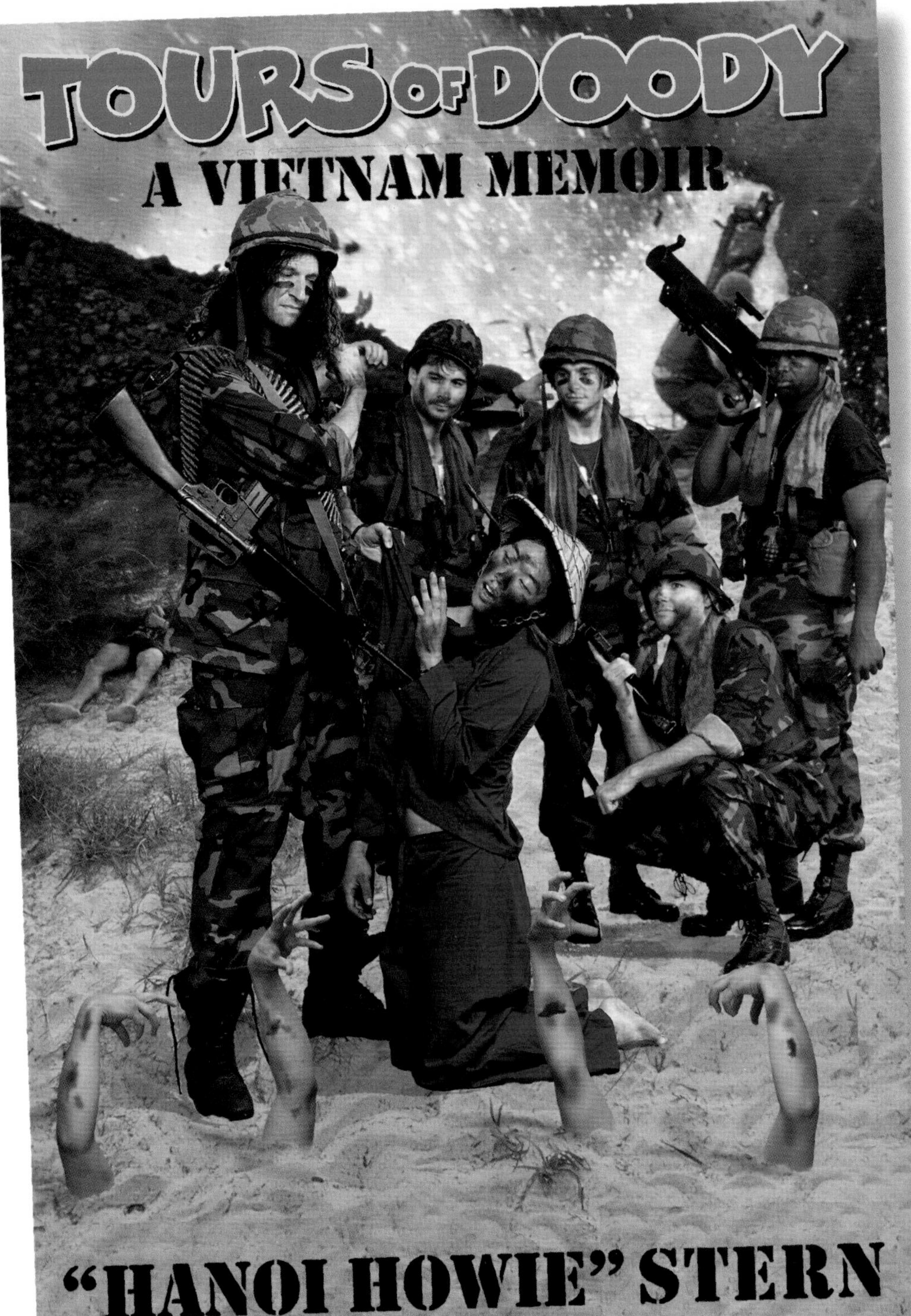

Judith,
Do you think anyone will know that I've buried the villagers and left their arms out so they can wave goodbye to me?
Howard

HOWARD STERN

SMELL
MY
FINGER

The 7 Steps To Enlightenment

Ba Ba Buddha Stern

HOWARD STERN

BIG
NOSE
LITTLE
HOSE

Scratch
here

Scratch 'N Sniff
HOWARD STERN

Scratch
here

HOWARD STERN

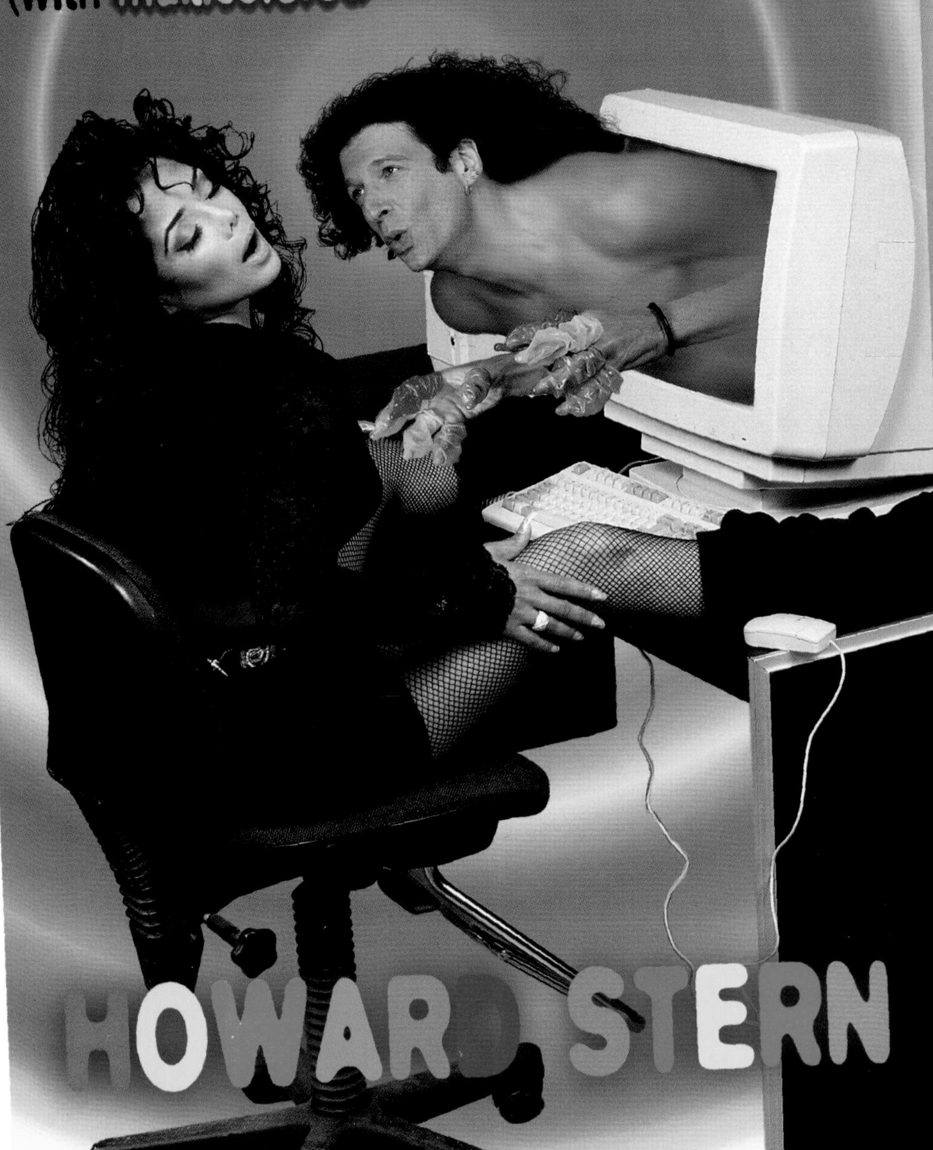
MY HEAD COMING OUT OF A COMPUTER
Into LaToya Jackson's Lap
(with multicolored condoms on my fingers)
HOWARD STERN

GOVERNMENT RELEASES NEW CONDOM AD
HOWARD STERN
FCC

HOWARD SPERM

Boom, boom, boom, just like a nuclear bomb.

On August 18, 1986, when we debuted in Philadelphia, I was ready for the battle.

"HELLO, PHILADELPHIA! Welcome to your worst nightmare! And get ready for some good radio because I know you've been listening to some ***scum-head***, some *bald* **dickface** up there. Radio's become a dismal thing, and I'm here to fix that."

I made three predictions that day on the air.

1. I WILL DEFEAT THAT STUPID ZOOKEEPER IN PHILADELPHIA.
2. HIS WIFE WILL LEAVE HIM.
3. HIS HUMILIATION WILL BE SO PROFOUND THAT HE WILL COME BEGGING TO ME TO GET PERMISSION TO WORK AGAIN AFTER I DRIVE HIM OFF THE AIR.

Hey, this was war.

I wanted to shock the shit out of Philly that first day. They were gonna learn the difference between my show and every other zoo straight off. We started talking about butt-fucking, but to be clean on the air, we called it ham-slamming. I got the harmonizer out, and I made my voice high and interviewed "Ham" and "Slam"—the two gerbils who lived up Boy George's ass.

"HEY, IT'S REALLY HOT IN HERE!" Ham said.

"YEAH, AND IT'S *WET*, TOO," said Slam.

Then Robin did a news story about a testicle transplant, and I jumped on it.

"Oh, man, I'd love a testicle transplant. I'd like the balls of an elephant transplanted onto me. Hey, isn't technology great? Could a penis transplant be far off?" I asked.

"I'm sure they could do it right now," Robin said.

"I'm gonna find me a dead black man with the largest schlong ever—and elephant testicles. No, skip the black guy—a horse. Ever see a horse's penis, Robin? That's what I want. I'd be pulling down my pants every ten seconds. I'd threaten women with it. My wife wouldn't let me be with other women, so I'd get into horses. Actually, I wouldn't even use it to get laid. I'd just go to health clubs and shower next to other guys. For once in my life I'd be able to shower in front of other guys. That's like driving a new Mercedes."

It was time to cut to do traffic. Susan *Beserkowitz* Berkeley came on. We took great delight in tormenting Susan. And she would always go berserk, that's how we named her. Every Friday, the program director would tell us that Susan couldn't take it, she was quitting. But Monday rolled around and there was Susan on the other end of that satellite feed. So I wanted to make that day's session special for the new Philadelphia audience.

"Hey, Susan, did that testicle transplant story interest you?"

"That's pretty interesting," Susan said, trying to hide her disgust.

"Hey, isn't it true that your mouth is a testicle bank?" I asked.

She, of course, claimed it wasn't.

I began talking about that feminist health book *Our Bodies, Ourselves.* In the book, they advocate women examining their vaginas using hand mirrors.

"God, that's like watching a horror movie," I said. "If Susan looks, it'll be seven years' bad luck. Hey, did the mirror fog up, Susan? Did you touch yourself?"

"Would you just cram it?" Susan said.

"Hey, Susan, when you break wind in the bathtub, does it upset you if the bubbles go up your back?"

I think we drove her off the line before she could even do the traffic report. Susan was a good sport and was quite good on the air. The Margaret Dumont of the show. I miss working with her.

Then I started in on a masturbation rap. Robin wanted to know if I still jerked off.

"Robin, I'm thirty-two. I'm still doing it," I said. "I'm just like my dad. My father used to do it four times a day—twice to me and twice to himself. Everybody does it. Hey, I'll bet ya people do it while they *listen* to us."

"Watch out for those tolltakers," Fred said.

Like I said: "Philadelphia, WELCOME TO YOUR WORST NIGHTMARE!"

I was showing off for Philly. I knew reporters were listening and the whole city was focused on me because the news media, both print and TV, were counting down the days to my arrival. Of course, every newspaper critic predicted I would fail because "Philadelphians don't like New Yorkers and New York radio shows." Same old shit. Shows you how well the critics know what they're talking about. Never listen to critics, they're the last to know what's going on.

THE SYMPATHY FACTOR

I would do anything to get ratings in Philadelphia. Before the first ratings book was due, I revived an old routine I had done in New York. I got on the air, and I told my audience that my grandparents had been killed.

"I just want you to know that it's gonna be hard for me to get through today's show," I said in a monotone. "My grandparents were killed in a car accident last night. I'm not saying I want your sympathy or anything. But if you could give me ratings I'd appreciate it. Okay?"

"What kind of thing is that to say?" Robin chided me.

"I just want to say I'm having a tough morning and I especially hope the people in Philadelphia, aged twenty-five to fifty-four, with an income of over $35,000, have sympathy for my family." I started weeping.

I took some phone calls. My fans were playing along with me.

"You have my sympathy," one said.

"Before my grandparents went in the car they had a Cup-A-Soup. I'm serious, Robin." I started whispering. "*Damn Cup-A-Soup. Cup-A-Soup,* I HATE YOU!"

"Who knew they were going to go for a ride after drinking soup?" Robin said.

We broke for commercial—probably Cup-A-Soup. When we came back, I pretended I was talking to my New York listeners only.

"Hey, you people in New York—Philadelphia's still in a commercial break. I know I did this *shtick* before about my grandparents dying, but these rubes in Philadelphia are really going for it. It could help our ratings, so play along, will ya?"

Then I went back into my sad voice.

"When they brought my grandparents to the hospital my grandmother was barely alive but the last thing she said to me was, 'Booby, I'm so proud of your radio career. Please get the big ratings in Philadelphia.' See, she was from Philadelphia."

I lied just in case the good people of Philadelphia really hated New Yorkers. Couldn't hurt if Grandma was from Philly.

I continued: "My grandma's last words were, 'If there's a heaven, I'm gonna be smiling when I see a big share for you in Philadelphia, because that means you could end up syndicating all over the country in the morning. So if you come in with a ten share in Philly—' "

"Your grammy was a real radio maven," Robin interrupted.

"She said, 'I'd like to see you with a fifteen share of adults twenty-five to fifty-four. Or, even more astounding, a twenty share of eighteen-to-twenty-five-year-old adults, like you did in New York. That would make me so proud!'" I continued.

I broke down and started sobbing again. I took a phone call.

"Hey, that grandmother *shtick* always gets big ratings," this guy said.

"HEY, MAN! GRANDMOTHER *SHTICK*! THIS IS NO PUT-ON! WHAT ARE YOU TALKING ABOUT? YOU SUCK, YOU KNOW THAT, MAN?"

I was indignant. I took another call. This listener was more sympathetic.

"I can't believe that happened. Did they hit a tree?" he asked.

"They jumped the divider—and this is unbelievably ironic—they hit a Snapple truck. None of the salt-free or all-natural soda or juice was hurt, but my grandparents went to their just reward," I said. Snapple was another huge advertiser.

We took another phone call. It was a woman who suggested that I bury myself in my work and keep on going.

"Hey, you sound cute," I said.

"I am cute, but we're talking about your dead grandmother," she said.

"What's your breast size? I know that sounds crazy but my grandmother told me as she breathed her last breath: ***'Only talk to ladies with huge cans.'***"

This caller told me she had just woken up. I asked her if she was nude, and she said she was wearing her husband's shirt.

"Do you sleep with panties?"

"Mmm-hmm," she said.

"So what do you have on, like little panties and a T-shirt?"

"Howard, I know you're mourning but . . ."

"ACCIDENT, *SCHMACCIDENT*, I HAVE SEXUAL NEEDS," I told her. I pulled the pertinent facts out of her: five foot nine, 125 pounds, with blond hair and C cups. I asked her to start making love with her husband on the air, but she said her husband was a DeBella fan and he wouldn't get on the phone.

"I'm telling you, he'll do it. Just keep the phone on the pillow. I want to hear you moan."

"No, no," she said.

"Please?" I begged.

"NO!" She was insistent.

I hung up, in search of new prey.

The next Philadelphia caller blew the whole bit. He told me our Philly station had come back in the middle of the commercial and heard me conspire with my New York audience.

"You knew it? You bastards!" I yelled. "You rubes! You were going for it. Hey, Philly, Mr. DJ? Whoever's running the show there, use your brains. Run a promo until I'm done. But, listeners, give us the ratings anyway. My grandparents *did* die—several years ago. Although I do have one step-grandmother locked up in an old-age home somewhere."

HOWARD WILL COME

I kept up my attack on DeBella every day. I had to make this campaign important to the audience. What could be in it for them? I promised them that if we overtook DeBella, I would come to Philadelphia and hold a funeral there for him. I told them it would be the greatest outdoor party Philly had ever seen. The management at WYSP, my station in Philly, was telling me I should start to make appearances in Philly sooner because I would be accepted much quicker, but I resisted. I wanted my first appearance to be when I was number one, even if it meant I had to wait *years*.

I had huge battles over this issue with management but I refused to budge. It became almost a mythical quest: HOWARD WILL COME. The Philly audience didn't even know who the fuck I was, but I was planting seeds. It was like, "Build this and they will come." Pretty soon the audience was as vested in me becoming number one as I was. Every day, someone from Philadelphia would call in and go, "Howard, man, when are you coming to Philly?"

"Not till we're number one," I'd invariably say.

Meanwhile, I kept the heat on DeBella. And it was working. About six months after we started in Philly, I got a report that he was booed in public. I immediately reported on the air, with sadistic glee, "I just heard they booed him off the stage at that comedy club he hosts on Friday nights. Evidently, he's having a mini nervous breakdown, too. I wonder if that young wife of his is giving him any sexual satisfaction? See, he married one of his listeners who's supposed to be a hot little fox, and she's got to be a little angry now that this guy's not so happening. That zookeeper's gotta be pulling what little hair he has left in his head out."

I began to call DeBella while we were both on the air.

"*Yazoo!*" He answered all his calls that way.

"Hey, this is Howard Stern. Why don't you get on the air with me?" I asked.

Click. Hang up. I tried again. Busy. I'd try another day. It got so bad that he changed his hotline number. But within a few days, I'd get the new one and start in again. I'd keep calling and they'd keep hanging up. Then one of his zoo idiots came up with a great idea: The next time I called, they put me on hold. When you're put on hold on WMMR, you hear what's being broadcast on the air. So they figured that I'd call and be put on hold and then K-Rock would be playing WMMR. Well, that was exactly what happened.

But they didn't figure that I'd just talk *over* their show and make fun of how stupid it was. *This was my dream come true!!* It was illegal to play another radio station's signal, but here they were giving it to me! I was so happy to be on hold, just listening and goofing on everything they were doing. The brainiac who came up with that idea almost got fired when WMMR's general manager found out what had happened.

JANKS THE MERCILESS

Shortly after I began tormenting DeBella, I got my first recruit. And what a kamikaze he turned out to be. His real name was Tom Cipriano, but he went by the name of Captain Janks, which was the name of his commanding officer in the army. Janks was a shipping clerk in Philadelphia who listened to DeBella but then switched to us when we came on.

Janks took my calls to DeBella and turned them into an art form. He became totally obsessed with making DeBella crazy. I had good reason to try to bring DeBella down—he was standing between me and national syndication. But Janks's motivation was much more bizarre. Apparently Janks had attended a DeBella appearance at some Philly mall and had asked his zookeeper to play some cuts by his favorite group, Sweet. According to Janks, DeBella told him that the zoo was a fresh, innovative morning show and Sweet wasn't worth listening to. Then DeBella made some joke about Janks's height.

That one incident turned the diminutive Janks into a madman. He began to call DeBella obsessively to torment him. These tapes didn't air anywhere, and Janks was doing this just for the sheer enjoyment of listening to the zookeeper go slowly crazy.

Every morning, like clockwork, Janks would get up an hour early and go to work on the phones. He had two lines, both set to speed-dial DeBella's studio. He tape-recorded each call and mailed us the tapes. Gary and I would listen to them before we went on the air. I, of course, was intrigued by this maniac and instantly wanted to make him part of my radio family. His motivation made no sense: I mean, so DeBella hated Sweet? Who gives a rat's ass about some fucking group? But I loved Janks's dedication. He was as obsessed and irrational about the zookeeper as I was. He was willing to fly into a fucking wall for his emperor.

"Yazoo!" DeBella would answer the phone.

"*Baldy!*" Janks would scream, then hang up. Two seconds later, Janks would call on the other line.

"Yazoo!"

"You suck!" Janks would yell. "HOWARD RULES!" Then he'd hang up and go back to the first phone.

"Yazoo!"

"What's Yazoo?" Janks would yell.

"Why don't you get a life?!" DeBella would scream, slamming the phone down.

Janks had DeBella so crazed that sometimes DeBella would answer the phone and just yell "Get a life!" before he even heard who was calling. God knows how many listeners he alienated that way.

Janks was relentless. And for some reason I still can't fathom, DeBella would actually talk to this raving lunatic. If it had been me, I would have hung up on him. No words. No nothing.

"Yazoo!" DeBella would say.

"WOULD YOU MARRY ME?" Janks would reply.

"Really, you're absolutely ridiculous," DeBella would answer.

"*And you're bald*," Janks would say.

"Well, so what? I'm bald, I'm a little overweight. I'm forty years old, but I have meaning in my life. You've got nothing. Your whole life revolves around calling me on the radio and trying to get me upset. But you're invited to do so every day. It's your phone bill. What do you do? Do you have any friends?

Guess what, pal? I knew I was gonna be bald when I was twelve. I've got a great job, a fantastic salary, a wife who loves me, a great house. And what do you have? NOTHING!"

Why was DeBella wasting his time? Why was he taking it so *personally*? He should have been putting his energy into creating great radio, not bragging about how wonderful his life is to some crazed phone stalker.

I knew that it was just a matter of time before DeBella would fall.

HOWARD FOREVER, BALDY NEVER

After a year and a half, I had made significant inroads into DeBella's huge lead, but I still wasn't number one. I still couldn't come to Philadelphia to thank my fans. So I did the next best thing: In 1988, I decided to disrupt DeBella's largest annual WMMR promotion—the "Louie Louie" Parade. Every May, thousands of people would show up in stupid costumes to play kazoos and march down the streets of Philadelphia singing that stupid song "Louie Louie." It was just an excuse for most people to get drunk and make asses out of themselves, but because the event raised money for charity, it was supposed to be *w o n d e r f u l.*

So about two weeks before the event, I got on the air and asked my listeners in Philly to disrupt the parade.

"We should get the crowd to chant my name at his parade," I suggested. "This guy goes into nightclubs in Philly and people chant my name. Maybe he'll have a nervous breakdown. Look, even if we don't disrupt his parade, the psychological pressure on the guy will be intense."

I got our station program director, Andy Bloom, to make up thousands of HOWARD FOREVER, BALDY NEVER posters for my fans to hold up while they lined the parade route. The next day a listener called in to report that some of my fans were calling DeBella on the air and asking him where they could get HOWARD FOREVER, BALDY NEVER posters. I immediately called DeBella.

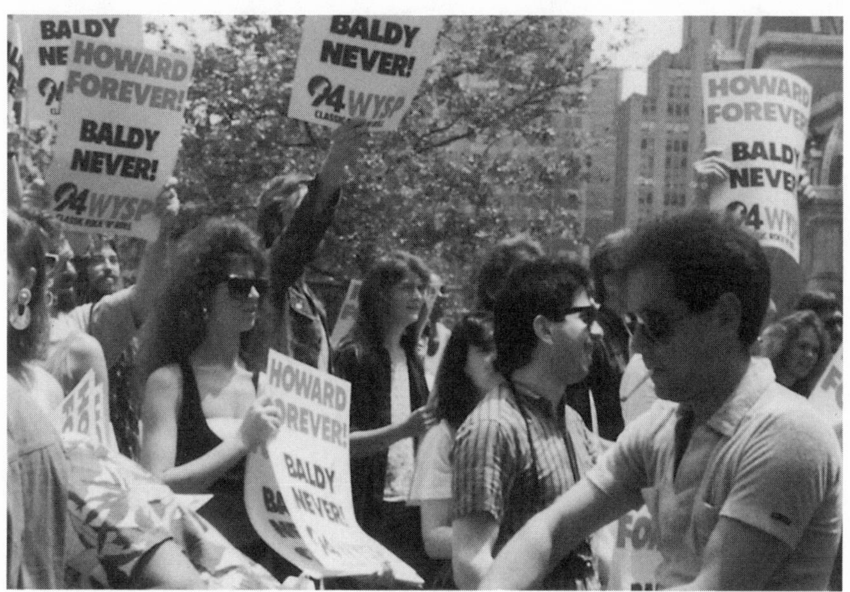

"Hey, Baldy, it's Howard Stern. You're on the air!"

DeBella hung up.

On the twentieth of May, two days before the parade, the latest ratings came in. We were third, but we had stolen so much of DeBella's audience that for the first time in years, DeBella wasn't number one. He had slipped to second place. I exulted over the air.

"Evidently, the zookeeper is screaming and ranting at the program director to do something about this!" I told my audience. "Then the general manager pulled in the program director and yelled at him because they weren't number one anymore."

I called DeBella again.

"Hey, Baldy, it's me, Howard Stern," I said.

"Thanks for dialing 976-PUSSY," DeBella said, in a mock black voice. "You have reached the pussy hotline." Then he hung up.

"Ooh, that was outrageous," I mocked him. "I suppose we're supposed to be shocked now. They're doing shock radio now. I hope he's having a nervous breakdown."

On the day of the parade, my troops mobilized. Throughout the parade route, there were pockets of people holding up their HOWARD FOREVER, BALDY NEVER signs. No matter where DeBella looked as he cruised down the streets, waving from his convertible, wearing his stupid Nehru jacket and dumb jester's cap, he saw a sea of Stern fans.

UGLY MAN. AN UGLY MAN.

Throughout our war, DeBella's strategy was to ignore me. Maybe that was a valid tactic when he was sitting on a 15 share and I had a 2. But now I was creeping up on him, and I'd even knocked him out of the number-one slot by continuously calling him a ***freaking-Jerry-Colonna-bald-headed-bastard-whose-wife-only-married-him-because-he-was-on-the-radio,*** and *still* he wasn't responding.

Behind the scenes, he was going berserk, but his ego wouldn't allow him to talk about me on the air. But during interviews he would say interesting things about me. We got a copy of a profile of DeBella that a local Philadelphia TV station ran, and it was fascinating—so fascinating that we played it again and again on our radio show.

PICTURE THIS: DeBella's sitting in the backyard of his home in a fashionable section of town. In the background, you can hear birds chirping. He's wearing a black-and-white op-art shirt. The only thing missing is his trademark big, fat, I'm-better-than-you-are cigar. DeBella is pontificating on the radio world when the interviewer asks him about his wife.

"Annette doesn't like publicity. That's *my* department. *Her* department is us—home life. She's not in this business, *I* am. *I'm* the one you're talking to. She's up there trying to keep the dogs quiet."

What a *skeevosa*! I would never answer a question like that. He sounded like the King of Siam, carrying on like a sheik with a concubine. Then DeBella was asked the toughest question of his career:

"Howard Stern?" his interviewer asked him quizzically.

Disdain crept over DeBella's face.

"Ugly man. An ugly man. Like how can anybody go through life . . . I can't do anything about the hair falling out of my head but he could do something about that nose."

The interviewer sounded shocked. "Oh! What does he do that you wouldn't do?"

DeBella leaned back. "The difference is simply this," he pontificated. "We do a show." He paused. "*He's an a-a-a-act.* An act grows tired." Then he smiled smugly.

"Offensive?" the interviewer continued.

"Offensive? Nah. Not really. He doesn't really do anything for his audience. What he does, he does for the press, and the press has a tendency of buying it all."

"'Howard Stern will find his first defeat at the hands of John DeBella. I don't lose,'" the interviewer read. "*Your* quote."

"I don't. I don't!" DeBella insisted.

"You really are that self-confident?" the host asked.

DeBella paused. You could hear the birds chirping in the silence. "I'M THAT DAMN GOOD," he pronounced.

If I ever needed motivation, if I ever lacked an ounce of inspiration, all I'd have to do is play that tape and I'd instantly want to destroy him again. This is a guy who thinks it's the height of creativity to wear an ugly Hawaiian shirt and do birthday announcements and lame zucchini jokes. I wanted him humbled. This guy's ego was out of control (as if mine wasn't) and I felt it was my mission to teach him. God had put me on this earth to humble DeBella.

THE FLY CAUGHT IN MY MISERABLE WEB

I love watching animal shows on TV. Nature seems so cruel when the deer is brought down by the lion, but nature isn't cruel. Nature is indifferent. It's survival of the fittest, natural selection.

DeBella was just a fly caught in my miserable web. This is how I react when my back is up against the wall: like an animal. Sometimes I'd feel a pang of regret for the way I was going after DeBella. He was a Queens boy, and his family still lived in New York, so they'd hear my ranting. One day, Gary told me that DeBella's grandmother had called the station.

"Stop talking about my grandson!" she yelled at Gary. "You talk so mean about him. He's a nice boy."

That jolted me . . . for about a day. But then we'd hear stories about how pompous he was and that would drive me nuts again. Only I am allowed to be pompous.

So I'd say, **"Fuck his grandmother,"** and I'd pull out all the artillery again. He had to be humbled. I had to dethrone him and ride triumphantly into Philadelphia to preside at the funeral.

But my plans were almost thwarted by my own management. They were going to offer DeBella a million dollars to come to our Philly station and do afternoons.

I turned beet red. I was on fire. Screw my management.

"You're going to deny me my moment!" I screamed, "I WANT THAT FUNERAL! Don't you see? I'm destroying this guy. He is going to be unrecognizable, a fucking laughing stock. And you're going to ruin the image of your station by putting on a guy who I've painted as a fucking loser?"

I had to catch my breath.

"A MILLION FUCKING DOLLARS! IN A COUPLE OF MONTHS, HE'S NOT GOING TO BE WORTH TEN CENTS!"

My own company wanted to take the thrill of the kill away. We were two years into this thing, and I hadn't defeated him yet. I knew the momentum was with us. They just needed to be patient. My tirade, though, did no good. They went ahead and offered him the money. *Amazingly,* DeBella turned it down because he was so confident that he'd kick my ass. What a fucking mistake! A blind man could see I was going to win this battle.

ASSASSINATION RADIO

In the meantime, because of my success in Philly, I convinced the management to put me on their Washington station. On September 29, 1988, I made my triumphant reentry into the Washington market. Infinity had changed the call letters of their station to WJFK, so we came on that first morning and I said, "Welcome to WJFK. Assassination radio." Then Fred played three gunshots.

That caused a nice little stir right off the bat.

By October 1989, I was on the verge of dethroning DeBella. Our ratings came in and we were at a 7.7. DeBella was slightly ahead with an 8.1 share. But in the all-important Males 25–54 category—the demographic everyone wants because these guys spend money—we were winning with a 16 share.

The handwriting was on the wall.

Meanwhile, back in New York, my ratings were soaring. I was beating every other morning show. The only station that was ahead of me was WINS, the all-news station.

Imus: **history.**
WNEW: **irrelevant.**
WPLJ: **not a factor.**
The morning zoos: **dead.**

I was on top, but no one was proclaiming my victory. The New York newspapers were silent about my success. The geniuses who wrote all those columns saying I was going to fail were afraid to eat some crow. So it was up to me to celebrate my success. I picked up a hand-held mike and did an on-air victory walk around the station.

I walked into the promotions department, but there were only interns there. Then I saw Ed Moir, our sales manager, in the hall.

"What do you want to say to me—the King of New York radio? KISS MY ASS," I ordered.

"Beautiful, Howard. I love it," Ed tried to get away from me.

"All the sales guys are running away," I announced. "Hey, if it weren't for me you guys would be selling *disco music*."

I collared Ed again.

"You're wonderful. What the hell do you want us to say?"

I was disappointed in the salespeople. I walked farther on and found Denise, Tom Chiusano's secretary.

"It must be unbelievable working in the same building with me, knowing I'm the King of New York radio," I said.

"Am I supposed to comment on that?" Denise replied.

"Seriously, don't you get questions all day about me? What's the most-often-asked question?"

"Is he really as sick in person?" Denise said.

This was some tribute. I walked down the hall and entered the offices of our sister station, the AM all-Spanish station. I found the receptionist.

"You want to say something nice about me?" I hoped.

"I think you're taking unfair advantage," she said. "You know little about us. Maybe you could come down here one time when you're not on the air and find out who we are and what we do."

"WHO CARES? I'm busy carrying the whole company," I scoffed at her. "This is some victory walk, Robin. I'm getting out of here."

I found Tom Chiusano, our general manager. He knew what to say. "You are definitely King of Morning Radio in New York. No question!"

"Don't you believe I saved your job?" I said to him.

"Before I go to sleep every night, I pray to Howard," Tom admitted.

Just then Mark Chernoff, the program director, walked by.

"Mark, crawl into your office," I screamed. "How dare you look at me like that? Keep your eyes averted when I walk around here! KEEP YOUR EYES DOWN! I GOT A 6.7!"

Then I turned to Robin.

"You know, I'm not getting my rocks off. This victory walk SUCKS."

"Try the financial department," she suggested.

"You mean all those Indians back there?"

I figured they would love me, but despite all my success, no one would give me my due. Everyone was saying it was a team effort. Except for one woman in the commercials department.

"Howard, I have to tell you something. I think you're a pain in the ass. You know why? Because with this power comes more commercials. And more work for me. YOU SELL, YOU SELL, YOU SELL."

There was someone who knew how to greet her King.

THE FIRST PREDICTION

It was harder not to give me my due when the ratings came in six months later. Once again, I was *numero uno* in New York. But a day later, we got the Philly ratings. I had trounced DeBella by two full ratings points! I HAD THE NUMBER-ONE SHOW IN NEW YORK AND PHILADELPHIA!! It was the first time in the history of radio that a morning show was number one in two markets. I took to the air and read with glee a column by Stu Bykofsky, one of those jerky radio pundits who had predicted that Philadelphia would reject me.

I have made a big mistake. When the Berlin Wall came down, that should have warned me. If that could happen, anything could happen. The sun could rise in the west, penguins could fly in the tropics, and Howard Stern could be number one in Philadelphia morning radio. No, please, dear God—anything but that. But that's what happened yesterday. John DeBella was handed a crushing defeat. You know what that means? It means the Stern gang, led by the old original freak beak himself, will be coming to Philadelphia. Lock up your daughters and your sheep.

Victory! At last! After three and a half grueling years, it was the moment we had all been waiting for. But what good was beating DeBella? I still had no national prominence.

"Asshole," THE BEAST yelled at me, **"you are still unknown."**

On the air, I was jubilant. We were coming to Philadelphia! We would swoop into town and claim the just fruits of our magnificent victory! On May 10, 1990, we set up a stage in Rittenhouse Square, just yards from the window of the zookeeper himself, and we had our long-awaited funeral.

This time I did it right: We took a bus down to Philly the day before. That morning, we started broadcasting before the funeral even began. We began by rehearsing our funeral songs with a black choir we had engaged for the day. Then we did a live press conference.

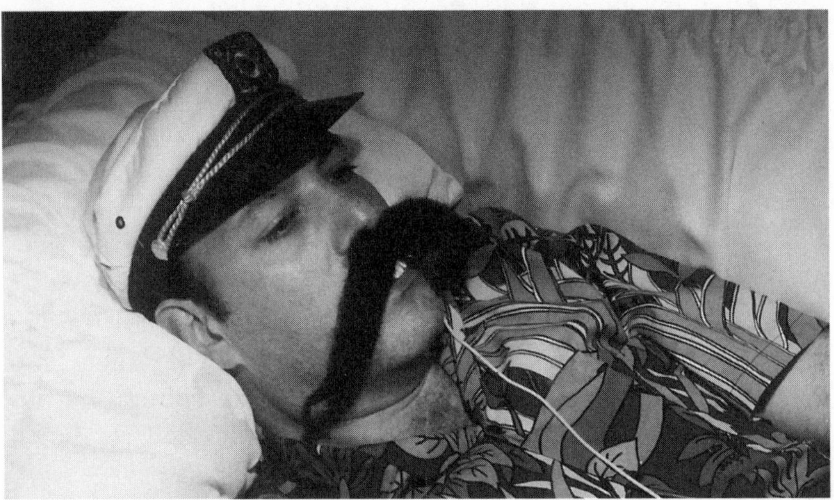

Over a hundred media people showed up. We dressed Scott, our engineer, in a Hawaiian shirt, sailor cap, and fake walrus moustache and we had him lie in an open coffin. Then I started the press conference with a formal opening statement:

"Sshh! Quiet down! I want to hear DeBella's head hit the pavement in Rittenhouse Square when he jumps out the window."

The room fell silent, except for the clicking of the still cameras. "First of all, as I look out among you, as I look at your faces, thank God you're all behind the camera! In all seriousness, I've thought about this a long time and what I want to say to the press is—EAT ME! You guys have mistreated me for so long. Anyway, we're proud to be number one, because what we do is, dare I say, revolutionary? It's been a bumpy road but we're thrilled to be here."

Thousands of people braved the rain to celebrate with me. I was genuinely moved when we took to the stage and saw all these people delighting in our success. I felt totally triumphant.

Fuck beating DeBella, I had proved to this lame fucking industry of mine that radio could be so much more than what they ever imagined. I grabbed the mike and addressed the crowd. I was wearing a Cardinal's outfit, a long robe and one of those funny pointed hats.

"How's the zookeeper feeling this morning? That guy sucks! He sucks! He sucks!" I started chanting.

It was now time to reveal to the audience my innermost thoughts. I wanted to say the words they needed to hear. I approached the mike.

"Now as I stand before you, victorious," I told the crowd, "I can only think of two things:

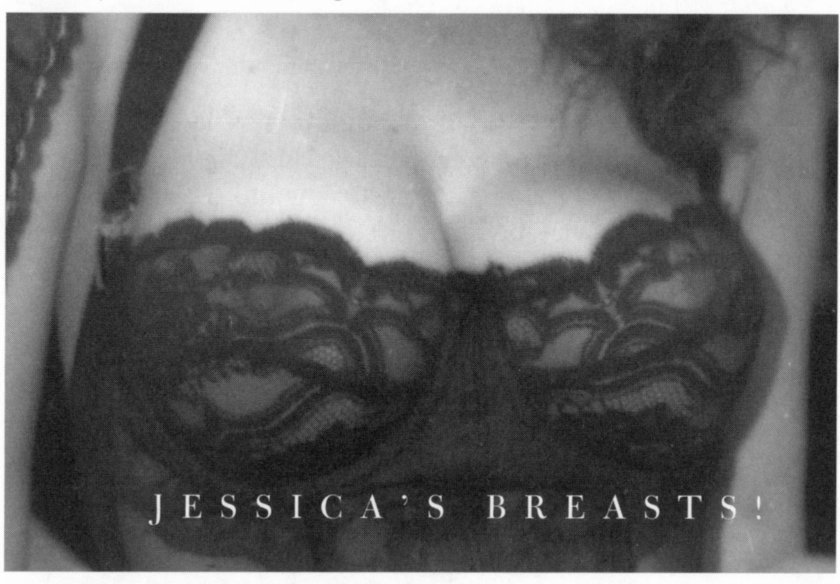

The crowd roared approval.

It was time to deliver the eulogy.

"An endangered species is now extinct! The zookeeper is finished! We have stomped him into the ground. In fact, I understand his moustache is now sticking out in China somewhere. I didn't want to tell you this, but as we speak, his wife is packing her bags. She might even be in this crowd."

Because I was now victorious I decided to take the high road for once. I did something out of character: I behaved like an adult.

With my new-found maturity, I lowered a huge painting of the zookeeper's face, grabbed a can of paint and defaced his image. Then we lowered the picture of the new King of Philadelphia radio—*me*. Jessica came out and, at a loss for words, just showed the crowd her body and everyone went nuts.

I broke into a dead-on Elvis impression with a parody of "Are You Lonesome Tonight?" retitled "DeBella, Are You Lonesome Today?"

> Are you lonesome today?
> All your listeners went away.
> You dumb butthead, they're listening to me.
> Your station is dead
> Like the brain in your head
> They've come over to my family.
> Tell me, DeBella, are you lonesome today?

We had pumped the volume so high that we later got reports that our funeral was leaking out over WMMR's feed. I left the stage while the song was still going strong and the audience was jumping up and down, cheering, but . . .

There was a hollowness to this victory celebration.

The funeral was great, but I wanted everyone in the whole fucking world to hear me.

WHO DO I HAVE TO BLOW TO GO NATIONAL?

DeBella was finished after the funeral. We had literally buried him. Of course, he showed his characteristic bravado in the face of his stunning defeat. Minutes after our funeral ended, he invited the press up to a room at WMMR. There was a closed coffin and pallbearers surrounding it, and then the lid popped open and DeBella emerged. He had a bottle of champagne and he poured glasses for everyone and declared, "I'm not dead yet."

But he was. Largely because we said so. I was amazed at the way that DeBella and the management of WMMR reacted to our victory. DeBella's weakness was that he couldn't be honest with his audience about his emotions. He should have spoken about the hell all this was. It would certainly have been more interesting than Hawaiian Suit Tuesday. But DeBella panicked, WMMR panicked, fucking Westinghouse, the station's owner, panicked.

At the time, I crossed my fingers and hoped that these idiots would continue to perceive themselves as losers. Because, in reality, they were still winners. They had the number-three rated show out of almost forty fucking stations. Most stations would have given their *left nut* for DeBella's rating.

But they panicked and brought in consultants and started restructuring the show—which made me intensify my efforts against this guy. I wanted him off the air.

Remember, it was war and you don't turn your back on somebody just because you've knocked them down. Of course, I had my kamikaze: Janks actually started harassing DeBella *more* after the funeral. The phone calls were a given, but Janks went out of his way to get to DeBella. When DeBella did a radio stunt and dressed up like a sheik and pumped gas while doing a live remote at a Philadelphia gas station, Janks jumped in his car, drove to the gas station, and got in line. When it was his turn, he struck.

"FILL ME UP. NOW! And squeegee my window when you're done," he barked at DeBella.

"Hey, asshole, get outta here," DeBella growled, when he recognized it was Janks.

Then Janks went home, took the tape of the show that he made, and transcribed the portion of the show where DeBella called him an asshole. Then he sat down and wrote a letter to the FCC:

> Dear Sir,
>
> I am registering a formal complaint against Philadelphia radio personality John DeBella on the basis that he used disgusting dialogue on his program the other day (May 16, 1991). My wife and my four year old little girl were having brunch with me on 5/16 while listening to radio station 93.3 WMMR. At approximately 8:45 AM Mr. DeBella used the word ***"asshole"*** during his on-air broadcast. I happened to have tape

rolling and, by chance, did catch his disgusting, vile comment on tape. I hope that the FCC will do everything in their power to remove Mr. DeBella's broadcasting license, and perhaps fine him. I look forward to swift and speedy justice in this matter.

Sincerely,
Thomas Cipriano

Of course, the FCC failed to act on this complaint. Who cared, though? The constant humiliation had to be numbing.

SHE'S LEAVING HOME

Along with Janks, I also kept the pressure up on DeBella. I wouldn't rest until all three of my predictions came true. I was confident that as his ratings plummeted, his relationship with his wife would deteriorate, **AND I WAS RIGHT**. Two years after the funeral, my second prediction had come true.

Then it hit me. "Why don't we have DeBella's wife on Dial-a-Date?" I said on the air. "I'll offer the spoils of my victory to my audience. Well, there it is. Total destruction. No ratings, no wife, and no money soon. The only thing left is to get his driver's license revoked."

After the show, we immediately got to work on some song parodies. The next day, I decided it was time to play music again on my show. And what a lineup of tunes I'd selected:

She's Gone
Runaround Sue
I'm a Loser
Bye, Bye Love
I'm Just a Lonely Boy
I Miss You
Who's Sorry Now
I'm Sorry
How Do You Mend a Broken Heart?
I Fall to Pieces
Bits and Pieces

Then I played "She's Gone" over and over again, singing along: "She's gone, your ratings are gone, your hair's gone, your house is gone, and your job'll be gone in October. He's bald, bald, he's bald." I was having a great time.

"This is what I live for," I crowed. "I get no sex from my wife.

I eat nothing but turkey and baked potatoes and oat-bran cereal. I can't even watch TV. I have to go to bed at eight. I sit at home, alone in my house waiting for days like this. You have to allow me my moment of happiness. It's my party, and I want everyone to join in."

Everybody joined me and sang along to "She's Leaving Home." I was having so much fun that I even made two gorgeous lesbians wait outside while I trashed DeBella some more.

GANG BANG

So there I was swatting DeBella around like a lion picking at fresh kill and so thrilled by this turn of events that I felt we had to have another celebration. So we rounded up the gang and headed south on the turnpike again. This time we would convene across the street from the Liberty Bell. WMMR had moved and we wanted to be right under DeBella's nose when we broadcast his Divorce Party live.

An astonishing crowd of fifteen thousand people jammed the outdoor courtyard. Before we began the rally, I held another press conference. "Even though I made this guy's hair fall out," I announced, "even though his wife divorced him, and even though I took his listeners, his ratings, and his 'Louie Louie' theme—I vow not to rest until the zookeeper is passed out drunk in a puddle next to a curb, and the other bums are playing tic-tac-toe on top of his bald head."

I answered a few more stupid questions and then it was time for the rally. We were all dressed as victorious gladiators. We took to the stage and the crowd went wild.

"He is bald! He is bald! She is gone! She is gone! He is screwed! He won't be renewed! He is through! He's not funny! He's washed up! He's a loser! He is hairless! He is hopeless! He's a bitter, broken man!"

"By the way," I added, "let me remind you that we are in Philadelphia today for a reason. And the reason that we have gathered is to look at Jessica Hahn's jugs. Jessica, come on up here . . ." Then I introduced Captain Janks to the crowd. It was unbelievable to watch a loser like Janks get up and have the audience give him an ovation. Janks was every bit the superstar that DeBella thought he was.

THE ULTIMATE EVIL

I still needed more. I wouldn't be happy until DeBella's wife was in my studio, playing Dial-a-Date. I called to her like a vampire in the night. "Look into my eyes, you are getting sleepy," I would say in the worst Bela Lugosi impression ever done on radio.

Every day on the air I called to Annette to join me, to join the dark side. And, once again, Baldy played his part perfectly in driving his wife into our open arms. Apparently their divorce got so rancorous that DeBella canceled all her credit cards and froze their bank account. She desperately needed cash. Gary was contacted by Annette's lawyer, and he negotiated a fee of five thousand dollars and a hotel room in exchange for an appearance on my show. She didn't commit to a Dial-a-Date but I was sure that once she was on the show, she'd consent.

That morning, I was beside myself. I would have a new ally.

"**We are so evil**," Robin said.

"The ultimate evil," I agreed. "I'm the guy in *Hellraiser 3*. The zookeeper's wife is with us. She is now completely mine."

I called Annette into the studio.

Our eyes met. She was drawn to me. She was all alone in her battle with the zookeeper. She needed to be loved . . . by THE BEAST.

"Look how cute you are. Nice body. Don't feel bad. ***The guy's a dick***. He deserved this." These were the words she needed to hear. "Don't worry, you'll clean him out," I assured her. "You deserve every penny for sleeping with that guy. How many years did you sleep with him?"

"Nine," Annette said.

"She's almost crying when you make her recall that," Robin joked.

"Yeah, you'd cry too if he was on top of you," I added.

"At least I didn't slide out of bed from the moustache wax," she said. She was falling under my spell. She was now cracking jokes. My conversation relaxed her. My tone was soft and loving, something women today rarely experience but hunger for from men. I knew it was time to pop the big question. I would not be denied . . . my destiny.

"Will you . . ." I asked oh-so-gentlemanly, "play Dial-a-Date?"

"Yes," she replied.

This was my ultimate triumph! She was mine. I *was Nostrildamus!* All my twisted predictions were coming true.

"I love it! I love it! This is the greatest show ever! I said that once we took away his ratings, I'd have the zookeeper's wife, and we do! She's mine!" I rejoiced.

Then I addressed DeBella.

"I told you to get out of town, you stupid ass. Philadelphia's my town now. You do what I say, you're my dog. ***Bark for me***. I have nothing to live for except beating you into the ground. All I do is wake up in the morning and dream of

MY PRIZE, THE ZOOKEEPER'S WIFE, ANNETTE

humiliating you. And now your own wife is on my show." I turned back to Annette.

"By the end, did you hate spreading for him? You did, didn't you?" I couldn't stop.

"I don't remember doing much of that at the end," she answered.

"Let me describe Annette to my listeners. She's 107 pounds. five foot six, a sweet face, a tight body, a punk, black hairdo. A B cup, but they look bigger because she's small. A nice ass. And one of our lucky Philadelphia listeners will have a date with her. I love this. The humiliation is complete."

I asked her if she wanted a back rub. She agreed, so I went behind her and started rubbing her back. My long thin fingers caressed the soft flesh of my new comrade. My princess. My new soldier in the dark war. It was an electric moment. The joining of our forces. She was now part of my legion. Then I asked her if I could kiss her neck and she agreed. She craned her neck for me to taste. I would take the zookeeper's wife in my arms for the first time.

"Hey zookeeper, I'm rubbing your wife's back and kissing her neck, YOU STUPID BALD IDIOT!"

Had it not been for my marriage I probably would have gone further right then and there. I would have laid her out on the floor, entered her and come within seconds . . . probably leaving her completely dissatisfied, like I do with all women.

THE SPOILS OF WAR

But it was time to play Dial-a-Date. Just by chance, Captain Janks had gotten through and we made him bachelor number one. Bachelor number two was a bouncer who claimed to look like Jean-Claude Van Damme. Bachelor number three was a salesman who claimed to make six figures and possess a large penis.

We started with Janks. He began describing his ideal first date with Annette, but he didn't get far before I started ranking on him for living with his parents, never getting laid, not owning a car, and being short. Thank God I didn't say anything derogatory about Sweet or he'd probably be hounding me to this day. Janks, though, had actually written a love ode to Annette:

Annette, my dear, let me kiss your sweet face.
Let me discover your charms, and leave John in disgrace.

The two other bachelors made their pitch for Annette, but I wanted to see Janks on that date with her. Imagine how awesome it would be for Captain Janks to actually take DeBella's wife out on a date.

Y a z o o !

"Whenever we destroy the lives of our most hated competitors, these are the spoils. Our legions of Philadelphia fans grew and grew, and they came out to greet us every time we came to town. So now, I offer them the spoils. We took the zookeeper's woman, and now I'm giving her to a listener. My gift to you, the beautiful Annette DeBella."

I turned to Annette.

"If you pick Captain Janks, you would drive a *shiv* into the zookeeper's heart, so deep . . ." My voice was hypnotic, menacing, strong.

"I'll pick Captain Janks," Annette agreed, there for revenge, not romance.

"He used to tell Janks to 'get a life' and now Janks can say, *'You told me to get a life, but I got a wife–your wife.'*"

The humiliation was almost total. It was bad enough that Annette was going on a date with her husband's tormentor. But what was worse, we were going to follow them and film the entire evening for my *Butt Bongo Fiesta* video.

Then the press accused me of being a sore winner. *Hard Copy* called me "Sick Sick Howard." The narrator sounded like he was right out of the film *Reefer Madness*:

Howard Stern hasn't gotten to the top of the entertainment C list without taking victims: Handicapped people. Fat people. Bald people. And people like John DeBella. Then he did the cruelest and most heartless thing any radio host could imagine. He put John DeBella's wife on display on "The Howard Stern Show." He went so far as to auction off Annette DeBella to the highest bidder. JUST REMEMBER THERE IS ONE MAN WHO WILL NEVER BE THE SAME AGAIN. A MAN WHO BROUGHT PEOPLE JOY WITH THE SIMPLE WORD "YAZOO."

The press never understood the true nature of what was going on. I was the only person who was trying to shame this poo-poo head of a husband into behaving.

Besides, it was great radio.

I'M DRINKING THE ZOOKEEPER'S BEER

Gary picked up Janks in a limo and drove to the zookeeper's house. But Janks made them stop on the way so he could buy a box of chocolates and some flowers. What a romantic. They got to the house, and Annette was there with her girlfriend. She invited them in and gave them a grand tour of the house. Then she went into another room to get ready to go out.

Janks went berserk. Of course, we were filming all of this.

He'd whisper to the camera, "HEY, C'MERE. I'M TOUCHING THE ZOOKEEPER'S WALLS. HEY, I'M PETTING THE ZOOKEEPER'S DOG." He took an apple out of the refrigerator. "I'm eating the zookeeper's food." The only thing he didn't do was **take a dump** on the zookeeper's floor.

Finally, Annette was ready to go out. Before they left, she taped a short segment on her back porch. "This is the worst week of John DeBella's life and I am not finished. The things he keeps doing to me. I don't care if I end up in a tent in Homestead, Florida."

This was one bitter divorce!!

Annette took the gang to a nearby bar and restaurant where she was a regular. We filmed her and Janks feeding each other cake, toasting with champagne, and we even caught Captain Janks sticking his tongue in her ear. Everybody was having a great time. As the evening progressed, Annette got progressively more intoxicated. By the time the crew stopped filming, she was slurring her words. They drove her back to her house and turned the cameras on one last time to record Captain Janks's goodnight kiss. The little bastard actually grabbed her ass.

In the middle of this hostile, bitter divorce, Annette tragically died. According to an article published months after the fact in *Philadelphia* magazine, she was furious with DeBella over

a $130,000 IRS refund check made out to both of them that DeBella had deposited into a separate bank account. She also suspected him of taking her ten-thousand-dollar engagement ring back for spite. I was glad this article came out because it backed up everything I had been saying.

Apparently, she was so upset that she threatened to call Baba Booey and invite our show down to broadcast live from the zookeeper's house. Her attorney told her to hold off on that until he could square away these issues with DeBella's lawyer.

But they were never resolved. That same day, Annette went back to the same restaurant where we had filmed the Dial-a-Date, drank until she had more than twice the legal limit of alcohol in her blood, and then drove home. She entered the garage, automatically closed the door behind her, and then passed out with the car still running. When her new boyfriend woke up and found her in the car hours later, she was already dead of carbon monoxide poisoning. A few days later, the coroner issued a controversial report claiming she killed herself.

Of course, the media tried to blame me for killing her. I was outraged because we had nothing to do with her death. We were the ones to give her a little **self-respect** in the final days before her death. Her brother said that both her psychiatrist and her lawyer urged her to do the show. In fact, her parents contacted us and told us that they appreciated how nice we were to her before she died.

GOODNIGHT, PHILADELPHIA

The end came quick for DeBella. Finally, they scrapped his format totally and teamed him up with a sportscaster and created a hybrid sports-rock show. That was the final straw. That show pulled such lousy ratings that they moved the once-mighty zookeeper to an afternoon slot. They slashed his salary to about one-tenth of what he was making at the height of his popularity.

But he still didn't get it. Just to fuck with his head, I replayed my morning show up against his afternoon show the day his show debuted. And then he started issuing challenges to me, claiming he'd beat me in the afternoons.

DeBella debacle ends

Difficult year closes with departure of former Zookeeper

Mercifully, he didn't linger long. Within six months, WMMR refused to renew his contract. On the last day of September 1993, DeBella was history. He claimed that he was the one who decided to call it quits, that "the business had changed." His type of radio wasn't "hip no mo'," he said. "What is hip is based on humiliation and shock and degradation." He said it was time to do something other than "play silly songs, jump up and down and throw pumpkins."

Of course. **That's what I had been saying for the last five years.**

DeBella added that he wanted to get in touch with himself and pursue landscaping and gardening. "He wants to get in touch with himself, he should go down to his cesspool and visit his hair," I said. "If he's gonna plant stuff, why doesn't he plant some seeds in his head and see if anything grows."

Then one listener called in who actually went to a ***tag sale at DeBella's old house.*** Incredibly enough, DeBella was selling Hawaiian shirts, promotional albums, and the coffin that he jumped out of the day of our funeral.

A TAG SALE

Friday 9AM to 3PM
Saturday 9AM to 2PM

Fine Partial Contents
Must Go

Custom Chippendale pickled pine entertainment center, carved mahogany king 4 poster bed, Chippendale high chest by Virginia Galleries, L+J.G. Stickley mahogany 10 drawer chest and matching lingerie chest, Henredon lamp tables, Queen Anne corner chair ca.1740, several small maple chests (one w/bookcase unit), never used Sealy posturpedic twin bed, maroon velvet sofa, oak & smoked glass tables, 4 Buehl chairs, sev. upholstery chairs, occasional tables, etc. etc., large selection of outdoor furniture incl chairs, lounges, etc. Fine bric-a-brac incl Lenox gold band china, Lalique, Baccarat, Lladro, Waterford incl lamp, Xmas decor, etc., Boehm Royal Copenhagen, much stemware, pottery, S.P. mod Battersea boxes, large selection kitchenwares, fireplace equipment, many fine lamps, prints, books, mirrors, antique tea tin, Majolica box by Mottahedaa, frames, baskets, brass incl sconces, fine crystal & brass chandelier, wrought iron fixture w/matching sconces, custom window treatments, linens, large silver framed mirror, much more. ALSO, Fender Stratocaster elec. guitar (both new), ladies bike, floor model radio, stereo speakers, Orthopod gravity mach., computer desk, so much more.

DeBella left the airwaves with a twenty-minute tearful goodbye to everyone at the station. Then he put the final spin on our long battle.

"A lot of you are probably asking yourselves now, 'Why the hell didn't DeBella say anything back in all those years of getting trashed?' It's real simple, folks. The show was for you, the listeners . . . You, my listeners, matter the most . . . You, the listeners, were there. You held me up. I thank you for that . . . I love you. Goodnight, Philadelphia. Don't take any shit from anybody." Is this guy more pompous than any ex-President? It was done. It was survival of the fittest, and flabby me was the fittest.

And that was it. After seven years of battle, my victory was complete. I had taken this arrogant disc jockey and turned him into an arrogant landscaper.

But, like a ravenous addict, I still wasn't satisfied. I craved more—and then it hit me: I would get some vans, and paint "Howard Stern's Landscaping Unlimited" on the side of them. They'd cruise Philadelphia and offer a full array of landscaping and gardening services—all at half price.

Believe it or not, the third prediction came true. Yes. The zookeeper came to me for his next job. Infinity had an opportunity to hire DeBella for afternoon drive on their Philly station. He had been off the air for a long time and it looked like the gardening business wasn't working out too well.

My bosses at Infinity came to me and said they would only hire him if I approved it. I loved it.

Grovel time for DeBella

Ex-Zookeeper for WMMR to apologize on air to Stern

The Beast welled up. Now this was truly the spoils of war! I could kill him all over again. He lay paralyzed, awaiting my decision. The monster in me was now in the position of ultimate power. There was only one judge, one jury, and one executioner . . . ME.

ETERNAL HELL

I held the zookeeper's fate in my hands. His professional life dangled on a thread. I could forever have him banished from radio. Forever doomed. Eternal Hell as a gardener. Or I could breathe a fresh blast of oxygen into his dead lungs and give him back some dignity.

He truly was my bitch, and I was his daddy. My boss told me to take a few days to think about it. I looked at him and wasted no time giving him my answer.

"That won't be necessary," I said, looking him directly in the eye. "Give him a job," I said.

The owners were shocked that the decision was made so nonchalantly, but it was never personal with me. It was all business. He was no longer a threat, and it was never a thrill for me just to kick a guy when he was down. That would have been evil, and I'm only **half** evil.

In the end, THE BEAST had a heart.

The rest of the story seems pretty obvious, right? I had done the impossible and become the number-one, undisputed champ of New York and Philly radio. Now, it was Miller time. Time to kick back and receive all the good things in life.

My dreams of an L.A. radio outlet and eventual world domination were at my fingertips.

The tough times were over and the world was my oyster.

I marched into the office of my boss, Mel Karmazin, president of Infinity, and I said with mucho confidence, "Mel, may I now have the honor of serving as the morning man for your station in L.A., KROQ?"

He looked at me, smiled, and said, "N o ."

It was that simple. He told me I'd never be number one in L.A. and that was final.

I looked at him, fresh from my victory and said,

"THEN I QUIT!"

And then I walked out.

CHAPTER 8

THE PATH OF THE WARRIOR

Then I walked back in. Why shouldn't I walk back in? I'm not that crazy. I was making a lot of money on three stations. But my bosses at Infinity were adamant that they didn't want me on their L.A. station. Once again, they said L.A. is different from New York or Philadelphia. Scott Shannon, a New York disc jockey, had gone out there and bombed. But the real reason they didn't want me on in L.A. was that they were afraid that if I did well there, in the entertainment capital of the world, I'd become a bigger star and Infinity would lose me to television or the movies.

What my bosses failed to realize was that THE BEAST had to be fed. If they kept throwing obstacles in the way of my planned national domination of radio, I'd just quit and go out to L.A. and start all over again at another radio station. I needed L.A. bad.

My contract was just about to expire when we compromised. Infinity allowed me to sign a syndication contract with a competing station in L.A. They got to keep most of the syndication fees, without the headache of ownership. I finally got a chance to broadcast my radio show to the most influential audience: the movers and shakers in the entertainment business in Hollywood. Everyone was happy.

Then, with THE BEAST at my side, I started plotting my plan to conquer L.A.

Destruction of my rivals was at hand. Mine was the path of the warrior.

ALL RADIO PEOPLE BEWARE!!!

THE ROCKY ROAD TO NATIONAL RADIO SUCCESS!
ILLUSTRATED BY DREW FRIEDMAN
SWAT
QUACK
START
LOS ANGELES
7/91. I FINALIZE NEGOTIATIONS TO GO ON IN LOS ANGELES AND PLAN MY ATTACK. I DECIDE TO IGNORE RICK DEES. HE'S A NO-TALENT LOSER WITH A 12 YEAR OLD AUDIENCE. HIS CLAIM TO FAME WAS MAKING STUPID DUCK SOUNDS OVER SHITTY DISCO MUSIC ON HIS SINGLE, "DISCO DUCK". I DECIDE TO TARGET TWO LAME-O'S FROM OKLAHOMA, MARK AND BRIAN. I WILL ATTACK ON TWO POINTS: THEY DO STUPID RADIO STUNTS AND THEY MARRIED EACH OTHER ON THE AIR.
ECCHH
7/25/91. WE DEBUT ON KLSX-FM IN LOS ANGELES. I TELL THE AUDIENCE THAT UNLIKE THOSE UNHIP MORONS, MARK AND BRIAN, I WON'T DIVE INTO JELLO OR WALK AROUND IN MY UNDERPANTS. HOWEVER, TO ATTRACT LISTENERS, I PROMISE THAT ROBIN WILL HAVE SEX WITH A MEMBER OF THE L.A. AUDIENCE IF WE GO TO NUMBER ONE.
7/26/91 I TELL MY AUDIENCE THAT ANYONE WHO LISTENS TO TWO GUYS WHO MARRY EACH OTHER IS A HOMO.
8/91. AFTER TWO WEEKS ON THE AIR IN L.A., I RENAME MARK AND BRIAN MARGE AND BRIANA. I TELL THE AUDIENCE THAT THEY ARE NOW MY TWO BITCHES AND WHENEVER THEY'RE SEEN IN PUBLIC, THEY SHOULD BE CALLED BY THEIR BITCH NAMES. I REVEAL THAT MARK AND BRIAN GO TO THE BATHROOM LIKE GIRLS-- THEY SIT ON THE BOWL WITH THEIR BIKINI PANTIES WRAPPED AROUND THEIR ANKLES AND THEY WIPE THROUGH THEIR LEGS.
11/91 MAGIC JOHNSON REVEALS THAT HE HAS TESTED POSITIVE FOR THE AIDS VIRUS. I INFURIATE ALL OF L.A. BY NOTING THAT MAGIC IS NO HERO OR ROLE MODEL, JUST AN IRRESPONSIBLE GUY WHO STUCK HIS UNPROTECTED PECKER WHERE IT SHOULDN'T HAVE BEEN ONE TOO MANY TIMES. MY PROGRAM DIRECTOR, ANDY BLOOM, GETS DEATH THREATS. WITHIN WEEKS, COMMENTATORS ARE PARROTING MY TAKE ON MAGIC.
OOPS!
LETTERING BY: PHIL FELIX

8/31/92 WE DEBUT IN CLEVELAND ON WNCX-FM. WITHIN A MONTH, AN ANTI-STERN GROUP CALLS FOR A PUBLIC RALLY AGAINST MY SHOW. I SEND STUTTERING JOHN AND FRED THE ELEPHANT BOY TO ADDRESS THE RALLY. THE EVENT DRAWS TWO ANTI-STERN PROTESTERS AND FOUR HUNDRED OF MY FANS.
LONG LIVE HOWARD
HOWARD
GIVE US
TA TA TOOFY!
BA BA BOOEY!
WE LOVE
DOWN WITH HOWARD!
WE LOVE HOWARD
HOWARD FOREVER
#1 STERN
HOWARD!
HOWARD
CLEVELAND LOVES HOWARD
HOWARD SUCKS!
HOWARD RULES!
KING OF ALL MEDIA
WE WANT HOWARD
HOWARD IS GOD!
OH MY GOD!
CRACK!
OOGA!
10/92
MARK AND BRIAN ROLL OVER LIKE THE BITCHES THAT THEY ARE. I'M NUMBER ONE IN LOS ANGELES, NEW YORK AND PHILADELPHIA SIMULTANEOUSLY, A RADIO FIRST.
WLUP Contract
10/15/92 WLUP, WE DEBUT IN CHICAGO ON AN EVERGREEN STATION. BUT I HAVE MISGIVINGS. THE GENERAL MANAGER, LARRY WERT, PROMISED TO PUT ME ON FM BUT THEN HE CHANGED HIS MIND AND I'M CARRIED ON HIS AM STATION. AFTER A FEW DAYS OF ATTACKING THE OTHER DISC JOCKEYS ON THE STATION, WERT CALLS ME AND TELLS ME THAT LUP IS ONE BIG FAMILY AND I SHOULDN'T MAKE FUN OF THE OTHER ON-AIR PERSONALITIES. I TELL HIM THAT THOSE OTHER GUYS ARE CLONES OF ME BUT THAT DOESN'T MAKE THEM FAMILY. I CONTINUE ATTACKING THOSE ASS-HOLES.
11/22/92. WE GO TO L.A. FOR THE MARK AND BRIAN FUNERAL. THE NIGHT BEFORE THE FUNERAL WE HIRE TWO GIRLS WHO CLAIM TO BE SISTERS TO COME TO THE HOTEL AND DO A LESBIAN SHOW. AFTER GIVING A SHORT SPEECH, CLAIMING THAT THEIR DEMONSTRATION WAS FOR EDUCATIONAL PURPOSES AND NOT TITILLATION, ONE OF THEM STRAPS ON A DILDO AND FUCKS THE OTHER ONE IN THE ASS. AND OF COURSE, WE SEE JESSICA HAHN'S FAKE TITS AND REAL PUSSY ONCE AGAIN IN MY HOTEL ROOM FOR AN IMPROMPTU LINGERIE SHOW.
11/24/92 WE HOLD OUR GALA FUNERAL OUTSIDE OF THE PALACE THEATER. MARK HARRIS, MARTHA RAYE'S EFFEMINATE HUSBAND, SINGS "CALIFORNIA, HERE I COME" AND GETS PELTED WITH FRUIT BY THE AUDIENCE. AFTER WE GO OFF THE AIR, JESSICA HAHN HAS A CAT FIGHT WITH ANDY BLOOM'S GIRLFRIEND AND GETS PUNCHED IN THE TITS.
KLONNK
...OPEN UP THAT GOLDEN GATE...

FCC FINE
PAY:
$600,000
PENIS!
VAGINA!
BA BA BOOEY!
12/18/92
THE FCC FINES ME $600,000 IN AN ATTEMPT TO DETER OTHER MARKETS FROM PICKING UP MY SHOW. IT DOESN'T WORK. WITHIN TWO YEARS, I'M ON IN BALTIMORE, LAS VEGAS, CLEVELAND, DALLAS, ALBANY, NEW ORLEANS, BUFFALO, ROCHESTER, OSTON, SAN SE/ SAN FRAN- CO, ORLANDO D MIAMI.
2/19/93
WE DEBUT IN ROCHESTER ON WRQI-FM. THE STATION HAS A WEAK SIGNAL EVERYWHERE IN THE AREA, EXCEPT FOR THE MUELLER FARM. THE MUELLERS LIVE NEAR THE TRANSMITTER AND THEY PICK UP MY SHOW ON EVERY ELECTRICAL APPLIANCE IN THEIR HOUSE, INCLUDING THE TELEPHONE. MR. MUELLER BLAMES ME FOR THE LOSS OF NINE HEIFERS IN THREE YEARS. MRS. MUELLER WORRIES THAT HER MINISTER WILL CALL WHILE I DISCUSS "VAGINAL SEX."
3/93
WE'RE HEADED FOR NUMBER ONE IN CLEVELAND UNTIL THE MEDIA VICIOUSLY ATTACKS ME FOR SINGING A SPOOF OF THE "GILLIGAN'S ISLAND" THEME SONG AFTER TWO DRUNK CLEVELAND INDIANS PITCHERS DECAPITATE THEMSELVES BY PLOWING THEIR SPEEDBOAT INTO AN UNLIT DOCK IN SPRING TRAINING. AGAIN, MY GENERAL MANAGER GETS DEATH THREATS.
8/12/93
I'M FINED ANOTHER $500,000 BY THE FCC, WHEN I DISCUSS THE MERITS OF SHAVING VS. WAXING PUBIC HAIR.
8/20/93
USING THE FCC FINES AS A PRETEXT, LARRY WERT CANCELS MY CHICAGO SHOW. OBVIOUSLY, HE INTENTIONALLY SET ME UP TO FAIL SO HE COULD ELIMINATE ANY COMPETITION FROM THE CHICAGO MARKET. WERT REFUSES TO PAY OUT MY CONTRACT SO I SUE THE STATION.
NOTHER FCC FINE
PAY:
$500,000

11/15/93 WE DEBUT IN MYRTLE BEACH, SOUTH CAROLINA ON WYAV-FM. FIVE DAYS BEFORE WE BEGIN, THE GENERAL MANAGER GETS PHONE THREATS THAT THE STATION WILL "BURN TO THE GROUND" IF MY SHOW AIRS. A GAY AND LESBIAN GROUP FROM ATLANTA, GEORGIA BUSSES IN 150 PEOPLE TO PICKET THE STATION. WITHIN ONE RATINGS BOOK! WE GO TO NUMBER ONE.
6/10/94 CLEVELAND FORGETS ABOUT THE BOATING ACCIDENT CONTROVERSY AND WE GO TO NUMBER ONE. WE HOLD A FUNERAL FOR LANIGAN, THE ONE-EYED DISC JOCKEY WE DETHRONED. WMMS, OUR COMPETITION, JAMS OUR BROADCAST AND CUTS OUR WIRES. THEIR ENGINEER IS ARRESTED AND CONVICTED. AFTER AN INVESTIGATION, THE DISTRICT ATTORNEY ALSO ARRESTS THE STATION'S PROMOTIONS DIRECTOR, HEIDI KLOSTERMAN A.K.A. HEIDI KRAMER, FOR ATTEMPTED DISRUPTION OF A PUBLIC SERVICE. SHE PLEADS GUILTY. IT'S THE FIRST TIME MY SHOW IS DECLARED A PUBLIC SERVICE BY OFFICIALS.
3/29/95 I'M BACK ON THE AIR IN CHICAGO ON WCKG-FM, A COX-COMMUNICATIONS STATION. I IMMEDIATELY TARGET MY COMPETITION, A TALENTLESS HOWARD STERN CLONE NAMED MANCOW. I PROCLAIM MYSELF MANCOCKS BECAUSE IT'S A COX-OWNED STATION AND I PROMISED MY LISTENERS THAT WHEN THEY MAKE ME NUMBER ONE IN CHICAGO, I'LL HOLD A FUNERAL AND PUBLICLY FIST MANCOW.
6/28/95 AT THE SENTENCING OF THE WMMS ENGINEER WHO CUT OUR BROADCAST WIRES, THE JUDGE, TIMOTHY McGINTY, CALLS ME A "CRUDE AND OBSCENE RABBLE ROUSER", BEFORE GIVING THE CRIMINAL ENGINEER A SLAP ON THE WRIST. I VOW TO DEFEAT THIS JUDGE IN THE NEXT ELECTION. MY PRELIMINARY RESEARCH REVEALS THAT JUDGE McGINTY HAS TWO DRIVING WHILE INTOXICATED CITATIONS TO HIS CREDIT.
8/95 I INTENSIFY MY ATTACKS ON MANCOW AND LARRY WERT. I CHANGE MANCOW'S NAME TO GIRLCOW AND I PROMISE TO FIST BOTH HIM AND HIS DEAD FATHER. I PRAY THAT LARRY WERT GETS CORNHOLED BY THREE GAY BIKERS IN A BATHROOM ON A TURNPIKE AND HE CONTRACTS THE AIDS VIRUS, AND THAT NIGHT, HE DIES AND THE FAMILY DOG EATS HIM.
10/95 COX ASKS ME TO TONE DOWN MY ACT. I SAY I'LL NEVER SELL OUT MY AUDIENCE AND I DECIDE TO SWITCH STATIONS IN CHICAGO. THE FISTING OF MANCOW IS PUT ON TEMPORARY HOLD.
BULLETIN: RATINGS JUS IN—WE ARE ONE POINT AWAY FROM BEATING HIS ASS— GOODNIGHT
ONE WAY
HIC
DEEPER... DEEPER.
NO! NO--! NO! PLEASE! NOOO--
WYAV-FM
5000

I ♥ NY
STERN FOR
AL FOR
D.F.

CHAPTER 9

THIS COUNTRY IS OUT OF ORDER

HOWARD STERN FOR GOVERNOR

MY PLATFORM:

1. Fix the roads at night

2. Kill the criminals

3. Resign after accomplishing #1 and #2

I'm sick of government. I don't know anything about the economy. I don't know anything about foreign affairs. I don't know anything about the deficit. (By the way, what the fuck *is* a deficit?)

But I do know one thing. When I'm driving to work, **I don't want to sit in traffic. PERIOD!**

This is an issue that affects me—the fucking deficit doesn't. I don't care if we're $50 billion in debt. A lot of politicians say that we're mortgaging our children's future. They say that if we keep spending, our kids won't have Social Security or health care. Who gives a shit if our kids have Medicare? That's *their* problem. I'll be dead by then.

Look, I don't want to know what *I* can do for my country, I want to know what my country can do for *me*. When I'm coming home on the Long Island Expressway every miserable weekday of my life and it takes at least two hours to get home because two guys are shoveling asphalt while eight other guys are leaning against their shovels watching them—that's when I ask what the hell is my country doing *to* me, not *for* me.

I just want some jackass politician to worry about the small picture. The shit that affects me on a daily basis. Here's what affects me. I suspect it affects you too:

- **Traffic.** Let's be smart and fix the roads at night. Night time is when people **don't drive to work.**
- **Crime.** I'm scared to walk the streets so let's kill everyone who's scaring me. ***Don't tell me the death penalty's not a deterrent. It's the ultimate deterrent. Death works.***

Simple, huh? I would be the greatest politician that ever lived if I could solve these two problems. People would pray to me. Children would salute me every morning in school. I wouldn't try and solve every fucking issue—just a few important ones. So after sitting in bumper-to-bumper traffic two hours for a nineteen-mile ride, I got right on the air:

"If somebody elected me to some high office—maybe made me governor—and I wanted to win the favor of the people of this state, I would not allow construction during the day when people are trying to get to work."

Robin asked me if I was actually announcing my candidacy.

"Yes." I shocked myself. "I don't say that I'm the world's greatest thinker, but I know one thing: *Traffic sucks.* You won't have traffic if you elect me."

I made one more promise that first day that I announced my candidacy. If elected, I would make Nicole Eggert from *Baywatch* the official state girlfriend.

I was amazed at the initial reaction to my offhand comments. We got hundreds of faxes urging me to run. It seemed that I had struck a raw nerve. New Yorkers were fed up with Governor Mario Cuomo. He was a big zero. He had been in office for twelve years and nobody could remember one thing he had accomplished. The guy was a friggin' hermit. It used to piss my father off that every year New York would host the Belmont Stakes horse race and Mario would be a no-show. Governors were supposed to show up at things like that to promote their states.

Somehow, Mario had bamboozled us into thinking that he was a great philosopher and a wonderful statesman. What statesman? He did nothing. He spent all his time up in his ivory tower, pondering. "Hey, Matilda, bring me another meatball. I got to ponder if I should run for president."

"But Mario, it's two in the morning. Come to bed."

"No, I must ponder."

It only took him about three friggin' years to make up his mind. And after all that, he decided not to run.

But the death penalty was a real black-and-white issue, no pun intended. The vast majority of New Yorkers wanted it. Every year the state senate and assembly would vote a new death

penalty bill in, but this philosopher would sit in his ivory tower and veto them.

When it came to my own problems, once again, Cuomo was nowhere to be found. Sure, he'd halfheartedly say he believed in free speech, but he never did anything to help me in my battle with the FCC. He'd never come on my show. Then Robin found out why: A friend of hers knew somebody who was close to Cuomo. One day, Cuomo visited this guy and the guy had a copy of my book *Private Parts* on his desk. Cuomo saw my book.

"Why do you have that piece of garbage lying around?" Cuomo asked his friend.

So that was it. He hated me. *Fuck him.* It was war! I was going to the mattresses! I would run against this motherfucker—*and win!*

I'd take the death penalty, his most vulnerable issue, and make that the cornerstone of my campaign. And why not? I was incensed that New York didn't have the death penalty. A friend of mine from junior high school had recently been slaughtered by a creep who claimed he was suffering from multiple-personality disorder. Right now, this guy was sitting in prison, picking his ass and laughing his balls off while my friend was being eaten by worms.

What did Cuomo ever do to get rid of murderers in New York

State? Nothing. It got so bad that murderers started migrating to New York and killing more people here because they knew that Cuomo would never let them be extradited.

On March 10, 1994, I took to the airwaves and made an impassioned appeal:

"Elect me governor and I'll bring the death penalty to New York and then I'll resign. Fair enough deal? Just write down my name. I'm not gonna run on a party ticket or anything. I'll just bring the death penalty and fix the roads."

"You'll be governor of the roads," Robin said.

"I would go out and get competitive bids. I'd put more toll collectors on. I'd make it so your cable company would have to compete with another cable company. The things that affect people are TV, tolls, and getting to work. I'd give you these things, bring you the death penalty, and then I would resign."

Again, my on-air comments brought a firestorm of activity. I had obviously connected with the electorate. Among the many responses was a letter from a member of the Libertarian party who suggested that I run as a Libertarian. I really didn't know much about the Libertarians. I knew they were for less government and more individual freedom. I liked that. And I liked the idea of having an actual political party backing me. That way, I wouldn't have to do anything. I'd go to a few debates, shoot my mouth off, and I'd get a substantial vote. That would be better than being a write-in candidate. Who knows how to write in? I get flustered just trying to close the friggin' curtain on the booth when I vote.

On March 21, I went on the air and expressed interest in running as a Libertarian. Immediately, I received a call from a guy named Joe Brennan, who was second-in-command of the New York Libertarian party. He was thrilled that I wanted to run as a Libertarian.

That day, I added yet another plank to my platform: I promised that, if I was elected, married men would be allowed to date strippers and if they were caught, their wives would not be able to collect alimony. I knew that was a risky position to take. I might alienate a large number of female voters. But I refused to compromise my principles for mere political expediency.

The next day, I received a call on the air from **LUDWIG VOGEL,** who was the state chairman of the Libertarian party. The beauty of my campaign was that I was bringing the normally behind-the-scenes political process out into the open. In front of millions of listeners, I negotiated for the top slot on their ticket.

"I can win. Whatever guys you got out there aren't gonna win. If you want me, I'll do it," I told him.

"If we want you, you've got to get sixty percent of our convention vote," he said.

"Listen, I don't have time for conventions. Are you interested or not?"

"I'm interested," he admitted. "But you've got to sell the membership on that. Running for governor isn't the same as describing how loud you can fart on the air."

"Hey, I'll back out of the race," I threatened. "I'm offering you an incredible candidacy. You guys wanna stay in obscurity? How do I get sixty percent of the vote?"

"Pitch the membership at the convention. It's at the Ramada Inn in Albany on April twenty-third and twenty-fourth," he explained. "Saturday and Sunday."

"Oh, I can't do that," I decided. "Dude, by then I'm poolside."

"If you really want to win, tell all your friends to come and vote for you," Ludwig said. "They have to pay their dues first."

"Nah, I'm not gonna do that." I played hardball.

"Wait a minute," Robin screamed. "Don't throw your candidacy away yet."

"The way you get our nomination is to pack the convention with three hundred friends and win two-thirds of the vote," Ludwig admitted.

"Forget it," I said.

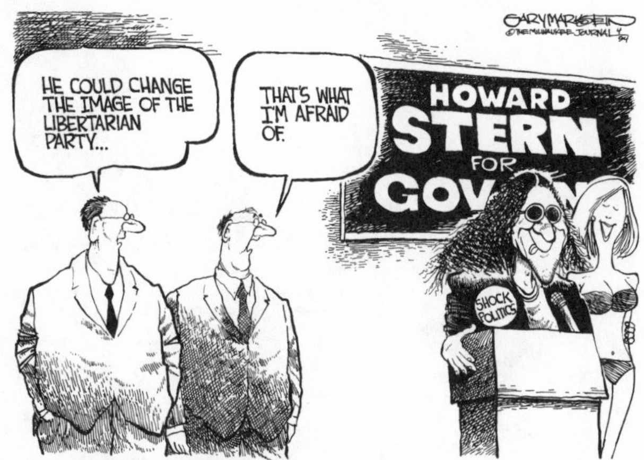

"What are the dues?" Robin asked.

"Fifteen dollars," Ludwig said.

"See, this is the Libertarians creating a bureaucracy," I said. I was offended that this guy didn't just hand me the nomination on the spot. Who wanted to go to freaking Albany? I don't even like going around the corner.

"This is easy, Howard," Robin said. "All we have to do is get three hundred people to pay fifteen dollars and go to Albany to vote for you."

"And then you have it made in the shade," Ludwig agreed.

I was beginning to like this Ludwig guy. He was giving me the blueprints to take over his party. I knew that it would be no problem to get three hundred listeners to pack the convention. We were number one in Albany already. We resumed our negotiations. I tried to get Ludwig to switch the convention from Albany to Long Island, but he wouldn't budge. He did agree that I didn't have to show up for Sunday's sessions.

It was a deal. I told Ludwig to get Joe Brennan and be at the studio the next morning. It was time for a major press conference to announce my candidacy for governor on the venerable Libertarian line.

A VOLT FOR EVERY VOTE

I was up late that night, writing my speech on a brown paper bag, just like Lincoln. Overnight, we had five thousand HOWARD STERN FOR GOVERNOR buttons made up. By the morning, the media had jumped on the story. I was on the cover of *Newsday*. Mario Cuomo had issued a statement saying that my entrance

HOWARD STERN
FOR GOVERNOR
HOWAR
FOR GO

into the race added "excitement and a spectacular quality that I didn't think the campaign would have." Some pundits even went so far as to say that I would be the difference in a close race. Fuck them. I wasn't content with being a spoiler. I was in this to win.

I couldn't *wait* to be governor.

I would get to kiss babies.

"I'll kiss every baby. Even before they're born," I exulted.

"You'll be kissing bellies," Robin laughed.

"I'll kiss a little more than that, Robin," I said.

We were almost set for the big announcement. CAROL ALT, my scheduled guest that morning, was enlisted to introduce me to the press, who had jammed the corridors of K-Rock. Joe Brennan and Ludwig came in too.

Ludwig told me that since yesterday's show, the Libertarian phones were ringing off the hook. But then he told me that the Libertarians had only two phones—one in Albany and one in New York.

"You Libertarians ought to kiss my ass in Macy's window," I told them.

It was time for the press conference. We were expecting Carol to come with her husband, former New York Rangers great, Ron Greschner. I had written great speeches for both of them. But Carol showed up alone. And she refused to read my favorite line from her speech: "We need to spread Howard Stern's word like I spread for Gresch." But she did endorse me, and she made a plea to fellow supermodels Christy, Paulina, Claudia, Elle, Cindy, and even Kate Moss to follow her suit.

"Help us make history here. You've heard of the New Deal, the Fair Deal . . . here's the Stern deal."

I walked up to the lectern.

"Thank you for that beautiful speech, Carol." I grabbed her and kissed her.

"Let me go," Carol yelled, struggling to get my hands off her ass. God, it felt good. I faced the assembled press.

"People want to know the answer to one question: Is Howard Stern serious about his candidacy? This is no disc jockey *shtick.* I swear to you that I am a serious candidate for the governor of New York."

I explained my three major issues again. I was especially eloquent talking about the need for capital punishment.

"Believe me, criminals will be convicted. I say electrocute them now and then give them the trials later. People who commit violent crimes against the police and honest citizens will be put in the electric chair. We'll take these misfits and we'll fry them like fish. That's why my campaign slogan will be 'A Volt for Every Vote.'"

I told the press that I would find a suitable honest lieutenant governor and then step down right after I enacted the death penalty.

"I recognize my faults. I say to you that I'm not perfect, but I am here to be your next governor," I concluded.

"What *are* your faults?" a reporter asked.

"I've got a few faults: I'm forty years old and I masturbate. Maybe I talk about sex too much. I don't think that's a horrible thing. But I'll tell you what my assets are. I am totally honest. There will be no backroom dealings on this. Everything will be done on the radio. I'm embarrassed I'm so honest. Who else would admit to the size of his genitals being under two inches? Would any of you here admit to that? I didn't think so. So I'm saying that I'm an honest person—and I have the hair to be the governor."

I opened the floor to more questions.

"What role will Stuttering John play in your administration?" the woman from *Inside Edition* asked.

"I'm not making a joke about this. Stuttering John's an idiot.

"THAT'S IT—ONE MORE THING AND I'M MOVING TO JERSEY!"

He will have no place in my administration. I am going to appoint responsible people."

Another reporter argued that the death penalty wasn't a deterrent, but I told him that I didn't care. I thought it was great for the family of the murdered to get revenge.

"IF I REALLY HAD MY WAY, FIRST I WOULD KILL THESE GUYS IN THE ELECTRIC CHAIR. THEN I WOULD USE THEIR CRISPY REMAINS TO FILL UP THE POTHOLES."

"Will you file a financial disclosure form?" **Penny Crone,** that nudge from Fox TV, asked me.

"I will *not* file a financial disclosure form," I said.

"Why not?" Penny persisted.

"Because who the hell wants you knowing what I make, Penny? You'll be blabbing it all over town."

"How much did you make on your book?" Penny shouted.

"How dare you? Tell me how much Fox pays *you*."

"Thirty thousand a year," she lied.

"You poor woman. No wonder you can't afford a good haircut. Who's shaving your head? Sinead O'Connor?"

After a few more questions, it was over. We went back into the studio. My entire radio crew was impressed by how serious my speech had been. That was intentional. I really was in this race to win. My father called up. This was his dream come true. He has always wanted me to run for elected office.

"I always thought there was a diamond under that rough coat and it has finally come out," my father said. We exchanged a few pleasantries and then he hung up.

"The first person to get the death penalty: my father," I announced. "He treated me like a rat bastard my whole life. Don't think that I forget. He'll be strapped into that chair

numero uno. Fry him up nice and crispy. Now he's on board. When I was a little baby and craved love, where was he?"

I played the tape of my father screaming at me as a young child. "I told you not to be stupid, you moron," Ben's voice rang out over the years.

Carol Alt looked real nervous. She decided it was time for her to leave.

"My poor father, I'll zap him till his nuts explode, with my mother on his lap," I fantasized.

Carol was definitely ready to go.

"Then Gresch and my wife are next to get the chair," I decided. "Yeh!"

Carol ran out of the studio.

THE SEARCH FOR *A RUNNING MATE*

I was now a legitimate candidate. I was even the subject of Jay Leno's opening monologue:

> Howard Stern says the first thing he would do as governor is reinstate the death penalty. That's a great combination—Howard Stern and the death penalty. Boy, you felt sorry for people on death row before, imagine a guy walking his last mile. He gets strapped in that chair. There's a phone call. It's the governor. "Hey, you wearing any underpants?"

Aside from Leno, the media was taking my bid very seriously. I was discussed on CNN panels. The *Daily News* had a poll that showed nine out of ten respondents were in favor of me running. In *USA Today*, columnist Joe Ershel gave me a left-handed compliment:

Howard Stern, the radio shock jock, has announced his candidacy for governor of New York, but no one it seems, is taking it too seriously. Is it that people figure a wealthy, sex-obsessed bore who is under investigation by a federal agency is not a legitimate candidate? So what makes him different from all of the other guys running for office? When voters in the Commonwealth of Virginia go into the booth in the next election, their choice for Senate will likely be between Chuck Robb and Ollie North. They'll choose between a man famous for getting nude back rubs from Ms. Virginia and one who lied to Congress and now presumably wants to go there to be lied to by others. I don't know about you, but I'd take the loudmouth on the radio any day.

I even began picking up some endorsements. Art Thompson, the mayor of Freeport, Long Island, was the first politician to hop aboard my bandwagon. The actor Daniel Baldwin called in, while comedian Richard Belzer was a guest on the show, and they both offered me unwavering support. I had Yankee owner George Steinbrenner on and I promised him that I would make the Bronx safe for his Bombers by electrocuting the entire population of the Bronx, leaving only Yankee Stadium still standing. Since Steinbrenner was in delicate negotiations to keep the Yankees in New York, he couldn't come right out and endorse me but I could tell that he was a huge supporter of my campaign.

The grassroots appeal of my candidacy was captured perfectly by a letter to the editor of *Newsday*. Michael J. Hunt of Long Beach, Long Island, spoke for millions when he wrote:

Attention, mainstream America. Howard Stern is not the enemy. He's a lot like you—suburbanite, father of three, goes to bed early, gets up early, goes to work, doesn't go out of the house much and doesn't smoke, drink, or consume drugs. He supports the death penalty, abor-

tion rights and also, like you, is fed up with crime and the decay of American values. And he wants to do something about it. Howard Stern is going to be a serious candidate for governor this year, SO GET USED TO IT.

Great letter, huh? Too bad it was from a wiseguy. Michael J. Hunt. Get it? Mike Hunt. My cunt.

Meanwhile, I was having trouble with my newly adopted party. It seems that a Stern backlash had formed, centered on my major opponent, a thirty-six-year-old upstate New York trial attorney named **JAMES OSTROWSKY.** His spokesmen were making veiled threats that they would invoke Libertarian laws that would make it impossible for me to win the nomination. This from a party that was supposed to be for less government interference. We had also heard that Ludwig and Joe were in trouble for supporting me.

Of course, Joe Brennan called in constantly to deny all these rumors. What he couldn't deny was that the Libertarians were so inept that our listeners were having a hard time getting enrolled as members. We heard horror story after horror story of being unable to contact the party. No wonder they were for less government. They couldn't even run an answering machine.

"You gotta understand, you're dealing with a volunteer organization," Joe tried to calm me when he called in. "None of the people are paid to do this."

Great. I was attempting to win the endorsement of a party that was run by a bunch of interns. That's like running for a party that was led by Gange and Grillo. But as the date for the Libertarian convention loomed nearer, I had other worries. I had to find a suitable running mate.

As with everything else about this campaign, we conducted our search for lieutenant governor on the air. I consulted my inner circle and came up with a short list: Gary was pushing

RUTH MESSINGER, the borough president of Manhattan. He had met her several times and he thought she'd be excellent.

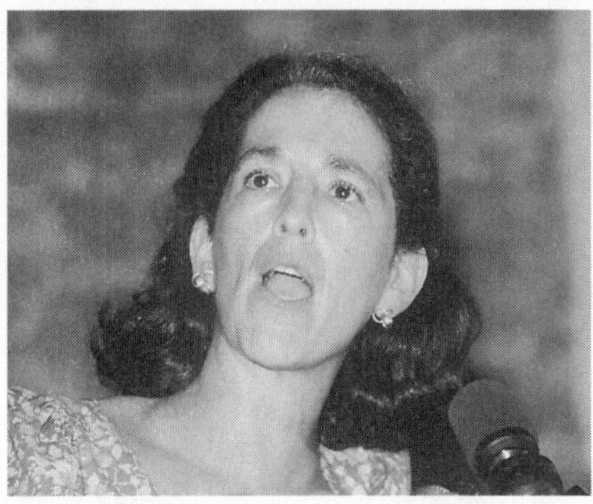

In fact, he said he voted for her because she was black. We got her on the phone and within minutes, we determined that MaMa Monkey was out of his mind: Not only was Ruth *not* black, as I had suspected, *she was a bleeding-heart liberal to boot*—and she was against the death penalty.

"So you're saying to me that if I offered you the lieutenant governorship, you would decline?" I asked.

"That's right," she said. A huge collective groan filled the studio.

A bunch of other politicians turned me down, then a listener called in and suggested that I contact JFK Jr. Robin thought that we could get a great slogan with him as my running mate: THE SKUNK AND THE HUNK. But I was more skeptical. I didn't even know if JFK Jr. knew how to dress himself. The only thing he'd done was Daryl Hannah. I was about to settle for James Dillon, an unknown Queens conservative Republican who had lost his only bid for a city council seat, when Gary rushed in to tell me that we had one last candidate for lieutenant governor: **STAN DWORKIN,** a Democrat from Rockland County. From 1985 to 1993 he was an elected county legislator. Gary also told me he was a self-employed leather-goods manufacturer. This guy sounded great. I told Gary to get him on the phone.

The more we probed, the better Stan looked. He had served on the New York chapter of the Arthritis Foundation. He was on the board of directors of the Rockland County Association for the Visually Impaired. Charity work is good.

"I should mention, Howard, that I have no history of electroshock treatment. I've never had any extramarital affairs . . ." Stan said.

"You *are* married?" Robin asked.

"Married with two sons, Robin," I read from Gary's notes.

Stan was coming through with flying colors: pro death penalty, pro abortion, history of cutting county taxes—and, finally, he told us he'd be proud to accept the position if I offered it to him. Now I was in a bind. Dworkin was perfect except for one thing: *He was Jewish.* With him as my running mate, we wouldn't have a balanced ticket. Dillon, on the other hand, was Irish Catholic.

Now this was *real* politics. In the past, behind some closed door, in a smoke-filled room, someone would say, "Hey, Stan's a Jew. We can't run one and a half Jews on the ticket." I was putting that secretive process out on the open airwaves, for millions to hear.

"Stan, if we run would you mind changing your name to Stan McDworkin?" I asked.

Stan said he had a proposal. He knew that I was in favor of eliminating some of the highway tolls, so he proposed that we legalize gambling in the Catskills as a way to maintain the revenue.

This was a man with initiative.

"What did Dillon propose? Nothing," Robin noted.

"Yeah, Dillon was just glomming onto my action. He's a bachelor, he's in it for the babes."

My mind was made up. Dworkin was just the kind of guy I was looking for. A hardworking public servant who toiled in obscurity but could do a great job if given the opportunity.

We finally had our running mate, only an hour before we

were ready to board the bus that would take us to Albany and to our date with destiny—accepting the nomination of the Libertarian party for governor of the great State of New York.

THE *TWISTED* ROAD TO ALBANY

We decided to broadcast not only the convention, but our trip up to Albany. So we assembled a decidedly motley crew for the journey. Of course, Robin, Fred, Jackie, Gary, and Stuttering John were aboard the bus. Scott the Engineer was behind his portable soundboard. But to make the journey a little more palatable, I brought along some of my favorite girls: Miss Howard Stern, Elaine Marx, was on board. Accompanying her were two other runners-up from the New Year's Eve pageant, Elaina Beastie and Debbie Tay, the lesbian space alien. For good measure, I invited Tempest, one of my favorite strippers. Unfortunately, Fred the Elephant Boy was also on the bus. He was going to put my name in nomination. Meanwhile, he was putting some very noxious fumes into the stagnant bus air. I was sick as a dog with a stomach virus to begin with, but Elephant Boy's farts were driving everyone over the edge.

About a thousand fans congregated to bid adieu to us. It was a very festive atmosphere. By the time we hit the thruway, we had attracted a whole convoy. Ronnie the limo driver followed in his car. Tom Cheapasano, Superagent Don Buchwald, K-Rock Promotions Queen Peggy Panasch, and Larry "Ratso" Sloman were in another car. Ludwig Vogel was driving up in his own car. Corky, Miss Howard Stern's husband, their baby, and their nanny were in Corky's BMW. The whole trip up, Corky kept cutting off other cars so he could drive right alongside the bus and peer into the window. Talk about a jealous husband. It was no shock when Elaine left him a few months later.

Besides our friends, there were at least a hundred cars filled with wacky fans following the bus. Whenever we'd come to a tollbooth, there were scores of cars that had pulled over and their occupants were waving and bowing to the bus. It was an incredible sight. But the trip up to Albany turned out to be a disaster. Gary had orchestrated a few stops along the way so I could enjoy some photo ops with the press, who were also part of our large cavalcade. Our first stop was at a Burger King in Newburgh. Gary had chosen this as a wonderful place for me to meet my black constituents. He assumed that there would be blacks here because a) it was a Burger King and b) this had been the site of some of the press conferences during the Tawana Brawley fiasco.

Leave it to Gary. When we got to the Burger King, *there wasn't a black face in sight.* I made a short speech out of the window and we moved on.

Our next stop was just as disastrous. We went a few blocks down the road to a strip club called Goldfinger's. Our entire entourage poured into the club only to discover two bored dancers and two customers. But the show must go on. I jumped onto the stage and addressed my constituents. One of the customers turned out to be a fan who had come to the club only because he knew that I was going to be stopping there. He wanted to shake my hand, but I refused. Who wants to shake hands with a guy who's been in a strip club for hours?

I turned my attention to the other potential voter. He was sitting at the bar in the back of the club, hiding his face from our E! cameras—and giving me the finger. Turned out this guy was an

Imus fan and he hated me. I decided to leave the bar before I got my ass kicked. So far Baba Booey was two for two.

The only good thing about Goldfinger's was that Ludwig Vogel managed to get bronskied by that night's headliner, Colt 45. We were interviewing Ludwig on the bus and he was answering in his usual robotic tones when this woman started flashing her enormous tits outside the bus. Of course, we invited her in and we found out that she was this famous stripper. Without any prodding, **SHE WHIPPED OUT HER 34HHH JUGS AND SANDWICHED LUDWIG'S FACE BETWEEN THEM.** That was the first time Ludwig ever seemed awake.

Our last stop before we hit Albany was at a small town called Saugerties. I had wanted to meet with some local officials and discuss serious matters like a real candidate. The mayor of Newburgh had turned us down. The Woodstock town supervisor also passed. But Gary had convinced the mayor and some officials of Saugerties to meet with us.

Oddly enough, by the time we got to Saugerties, the mayor was nowhere to be found. But Gary located two town officials. He escorted them through the large and very enthusiastic crowd that was waiting to greet our bus. Once they were aboard, we immediately got into a serious discussion of the problems facing Saugerties. They told me that the major problem was a lack of jobs. High taxes were another concern.

I suggested that they build some new strip clubs.

I told them that Saugerties was one of my favorite philosophers. They didn't seem impressed.

I asked them to endorse me, but they said they weren't ready to do that yet. We began negotiating. I promised I would bring them electric bowling alleys. They still held out. By the time they left the bus, I hadn't gotten an endorsement, but I felt that I truly understood the problems of my constituents from Saugerties. I addressed the crowd:

"I am aware of your problems. My advice to you is to move. There are too many problems here. Just give me your votes, your tired, your poor, your women. I can only close with those immortal words, Baba Booey, Baba Booey. Farewell, Saugerties."

We made our way to Albany. I was feeling miserable. I went to the back of the bus and took a nap, something I had done between each of the stops. So I felt a little bit more energized when we pulled up in front of the Omni Hotel in Albany.

I was even more energized by the enthusiastic crowd that was waiting for us outside the bus. I grabbed my megaphone and addressed the mob. After an opening greeting, I spotted an old man on the edge of the crowd. Realizing that the elderly vote in disproportionate numbers compared to the rest of the population, I directed my comments to him.

"I see a very old man there and I want to reach out to senior citizens. I never thought much of senior citizens in the past. Quite frankly, I think you guys are always looking for handouts. When my parents get as old as you, I'm gonna send them to an old-age home and they'll eat dog food. But I'm here to say that if you elect me, I will give the senior citizens free dog food and Geritol on Sundays."

Gary brought a black man drinking a beer to the front of the crowd. This guy wanted to talk to me.

"Salaam Haleckem, Haleckem salaam," I greeted the brother. "Sir, I have spoken to the residents of Harlem from my bus, and I

am aware of the problems of the black man now. But please, do me a favor. Give the old man his wallet back. I will not tolerate crime. Is there anything that you want me to know about the black community of Albany?"

"Yeah, we want Robin in the black community more often," the guy said.

"Thank you very much, sir. You are a good man. I love you. Just stay out of the hotel tonight."

We made our way through the crowds and into the lobby. I went straight to my room and passed out. I was wiped. From all accounts, I missed a pretty wild party that night at the hotel bar. My general manager, Tom Cheapasano, was actually buying everyone drinks. All my wacky listeners were there, including Elephant Boy, who wound up getting invited up to a room by a couple who wanted him to watch them have sex.

"THIS IS A PUTSCH!"

We were back on the bus by eight the following morning, on our way over to the Italian American hall, where the convention was to be held. There was incredible excitement in the air. So much excitement that Debbie Tay revealed to us that she had already masturbated twice that morning, just to release all that excess energy.

On the way over, I got the opportunity to finally meet my running mate, Stan Dworkin. I was shocked when I first saw him. He was overweight. He was wearing an ill-fitting suit that went out of style in the seventies. Hair was streaming out of his ears. He had a large bushy silver moustache and a thick shock of silver

ELAINA BEASTIE, MINISKIRT, HIGH HEELS, PIERCED CLITORIS

hair that resembled a hair helmet.

"Stan, you really owe me," I said. "It's good that you brought your wife and kids along. I only brought strippers." We both looked around the bus. Tempest was wearing a sexy black Lycra minidress that was connected by garters to thigh-high black boots. Miss Howard Stern wasn't wearing any underpants beneath her dress. I asked Elaina Beastie if she had any underwear on.

"No, my clit ring's hanging out," she said.

Debbie Tay unzipped her shorts to reveal a red, white, and blue thong.

I thought Stan was going to go into culture shock.

"Stan, are you wearing underwear?" I asked.

"Yes, Howard, I'm very conventional," he said.

"I like Stan," I told Robin.

"Yeah, but he's got to shave that moustache." Robin wasn't beating around *that* bush.

Stan was worried since his wife had never seen him clean shaven. I asked the girls what they thought.

"If he lets us shave *him*, I'll let him shave *me*," Miss Howard Stern purred.

After a few minutes, we arrived at the Italian American hall. It was an amazing sight: thousands of fans camped out in the parking lot. My local station had rented a flatbed truck and they were broadcasting from the parking lot. Miss Howard Stern Albany—Jackie Campbell, the lesbian ice sculptress—was dancing topless on the truck along with another big-titted friend of hers.

'Can you believe someone like Howard Stern has the nerve to run for governor?'

Our bus was immediately surrounded by a cheering crowd. Once again, I had to grab the microphone and greet my constituents. As soon as we opened the window, the crowd started chanting "HOW-ARD, HOW-ARD."

"Who will be your next governor?" I asked.

"HOW-ARD," they chanted back.

"You know, as I look out on your faces, I have to say one thing: It is shocking that they let you people vote."

After a few more words, I introduced each person as they left the bus. It was like a football pep rally. Everyone got off and said a few words to the crowd. Everything was going smoothly until I introduced Elephant Boy.

"You know him, but for God's sake, you can't understand him: *Elephant Boy*," I yelled.

Elephant Boy got so excited that he literally spit in my face when he addressed the crowd. It was awful. He hocked such a huge looie that I had a spiderweb of saliva running from my dark glasses onto my hair. I'm so germphobic—I was paralyzed with fear. Thankfully, someone gave Gary a tissue and he wiped me off.

Inside the building, the hall was packed with a few Libertarians, a lot of press, and hundreds and hundreds of my supporters. As we made our way to the back, where our broadcast booth had been set up, a huge deafening roar went up, followed by the by-now inevitable "HOW-ARD" chant. There were handwritten signs bobbing in the air. This was really like a convention.

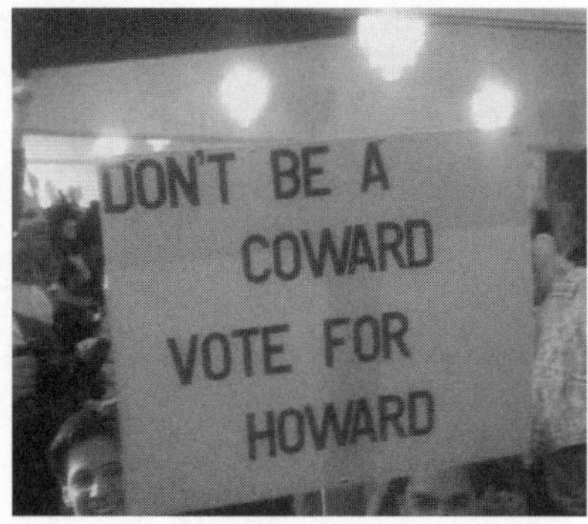

The old-time Libertarians were freaking out. They were used to having twenty people at a convention. This was like Hitler taking over at the beer hall—except, to Jackie's dismay, there was no beer. The Libertarians had never seen anything like this. They had all abandoned traditional political parties because they all wanted to be stars. Now they were being pushed aside by a bunch of hooligans.

Even I felt bad for them.

Robin and I started broadcasting from the back. We equipped Gary with a handheld mike and had him roam the hall and file reports, just like Dan Rather used to do at the presidential conventions. Right after we arrived, the nominating speeches began. Ludwig was onstage, presiding over the convention. He listed the candidates for governor: Joe Brennan, Dottie Lou Brokaw, Ed Jowitt, James Ostrowsky, Norma Siegel, Howard Stern. When he mentioned my name, the place went ballistic. I stood up at the booth in the back and waved to the crowd. My ovation was about a hundred times louder and lasted ten times longer than all the other candidates' combined.

Scott started playing my campaign song. Elephant Boy took the stage to nominate me. Kenneth Keith Kallenbach was there to second the nomination. In case you've forgotten, Kenneth Keith is the nut who used to blow smoke out of his eyes on my old TV show. He also lit firecrackers and threw them down his pants, nearly blowing his balls off. Then he sent me videotapes of himself shitting in a box.

We hadn't prepped either Elephant Boy or Kenneth Keith. Whatever they would say, they would say from the heart.

"Sha' up, si' down," Elephant Boy barked incomprehensibly. Thanks to his monumental speech defect, no one understood a word he said. "Reifhte thtid regirt, Howar' tihtwexe."

Elephant Boy droned on.

"I'm ruined," I moaned from the back.

"If you could only see the looks on the faces of some of the hard-line Libertarians," Gary reported.

I decided to pull the plug.

"Gary, get him off! Get him off!"

Mercifully, he finished.

"Oh, my Lord, was that a disaster," I said.

Kenneth Keith Kallenbach stepped up to second my nomination. "Not briefing Kenneth Keith may have been a major error," Gary warned.

"Hi, I'm Kenneth Keith Kallenbach," he began. "I'm here to second the nomination of Howard Stern. I don't read the newspaper, I don't watch TV, but I know when a good governor should be elected. Howard Stern for governor!"

"All right." I was amazed that Kenneth Keith was coming through.

"Hey, I drove all the way up here from Philadelphia. I hardly slept at all. I'm tired. When I woke up, I wanted a turkey sandwich, but I didn't get one . . . "

"Oh, no." I realized I had spoken too soon.

". . . When I was taking a shower this morning, I fell out of the bathtub I was so excited. People think I'm a wacko. I'm here to say *I'm no wacko.* I know when there's a governor. Howard Stern's a governor. You think I feel like having violence? I don't want no violence. That's why Howard Stern should be elected governor. I hardly had any sleep. Look at me, I'm dead tired. Hey, any questions? You got questions?"

"Get him off, Gary!" I shouted.

"Hey, who wants to

see my dildo? Look, I got a dildo." Kenneth Keith whipped a huge dildo out of his pants and was waving it in the air.

"GARY, GET HIM OFF THE STAGE!!!" I yelled above the roar of the crowd.

"Who wants to see my dildo?" He was still ranting like a madman. Robin was laughing hysterically. Finally, Kenneth Keith jumped off the stage and sat down. I was mortified.

It was James Ostrowsky's turn next. Just before his name was put into nomination, Captain Janks ran up on the stage and grabbed the mike.

"JAMES OSTROWSKY SUCKS! YOU BETTER VOTE FOR HOWARD!" Janks yelled and ran off the stage.

"I am so embarrassed. Oh, my Lord, I am getting out of here," I moaned. "I no longer want to be governor. I am under the table. How can I go up onstage?"

Gary reported that one of my nuttiest fans, Melrose Larry Green, who spends his days and nights wandering around on Melrose Avenue in Hollywood holding up HOWARD STERN signs, almost got into a fistfight with an old-time Libertarian because Melrose was wearing a big, stupid, floppy green Statue of Liberty headband and he was waving his signs in some guy's face.

Then Gary reported that my fans were heckling the woman who was seconding James Ostrowsky. We turned up the volume from the stage. "How many of you laugh as you hand in all the information the IRS asks you every April fifteenth?" she asked.

Gary reported that Melrose was laughing like a madman.

"How many of you laugh when your neighbors' children are taken away from them because the state has decided they are unfit parents?" Melrose led a much larger laughing section.

"How many of you laugh when your guns are taken from you and people are able to mow you down because you have no way to defend yourself?"

"THESE PEOPLE ARE ALL PARANOID," I said.

This woman finally finished. It was now time for the statements from the candidates. I was almost embarrassed to show my face.

"The crowd is going wild, Robin," I reported on the air, as I made my way to the stage. "Lots of champagne is being opened.

The convention hall is wild with energy. Robin, I can barely make my way up to the stage. Thank you! Thank you!" I greeted the crowd and sat down on the dais. Robin joined me.

The old-time Libertarians were disgusted by the behavior of my loyal fans. They were getting their first look at me, the next leader of their party, and they were nauseous. Ruination by the evil King of All Media was at hand. I felt so evil that day. I was destroying their little political party. They all took themselves so seriously and, in my own inimitable style, I was making fun of them.

I got up to address the crowd.

"I am very impressed with the Libertarian party. And if you're asking me if I'm a serious candidate, I didn't drive six hours to come up here because I'm jerking off! I'm damn serious."

Then I made my pitch for Stan. The old-time Libertarians didn't like Stan because he was a Democrat. To them, he was a carpetbagger. They were threatening to hold the whole convention over another day. There was no way I was going to spend another day in Albany, dicking around with a bunch of dreamers. I appealed to their common sense.

"Already I have twenty percent of the vote against Cuomo. I'm taking this thing all the way to the top. While Stan Dworkin is not a Libertarian, when you talk to him, you'll see that his views match those of the Libertarians in this room. I am going to run as a Libertarian and I am going to win as a Libertarian, and in order to win, I have to have a legitimate candidate running alongside me, one that the mainstream will accept. The only way we'll win this election is if I have Stan Dworkin at my side!"

I finished with a flourish. The crowd leapt to its feet, chanting "HOW-ARD, HOW-ARD." I sat back down. Robin and Baba Booey were impressed that I had given such a serious speech. Hell, I actually started to believe that I had a chance of winning.

"I was going to go for jokes, but I decided that I have to get this nomination on the first ballot so we can get massages on the bus on the way home," I explained on the air.

I asked one of my opponents, Norma Siegel, how I did. She said that she felt much better about my candidacy. She also started pushing herself on me for lieutenant governor. She knew she wasn't getting the nomination, and I was her only hope. Imagine me being your only hope—that's pretty sad.

Now it was time for a few questions from the audience.

A woman stood up and screamed, "I am the parent of a murdered child. I want nothing more than the bastard that killed my son to be dead."

"Good," I agreed.

"I want the death penalty," she said.

"I'm the only candidate here for the death penalty," I answered. "I empathize with your situation. I have three children."

I was seizing the moment. The other candidates were speechless. I was a master politician! Whatever the audience wanted to hear, I would feed them.

"Is that murderer in a cell right now?" I asked.

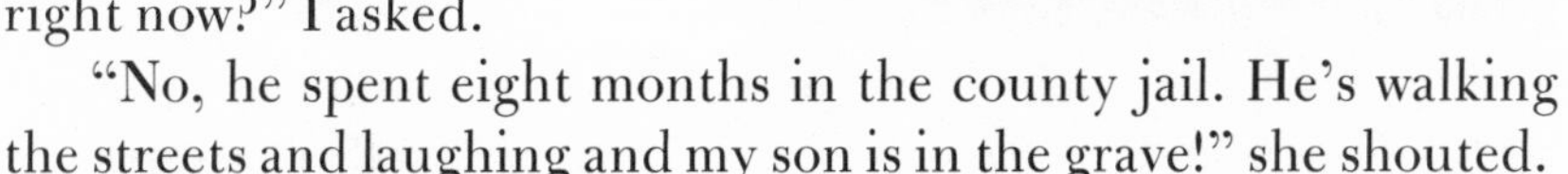

"No, he spent eight months in the county jail. He's walking the streets and laughing and my son is in the grave!" she shouted.

The audience went wild.

"LET'S GO GET HIM!" someone screamed. It felt like a lynch mob. It was time to vote. Suddenly, all the Libertarians

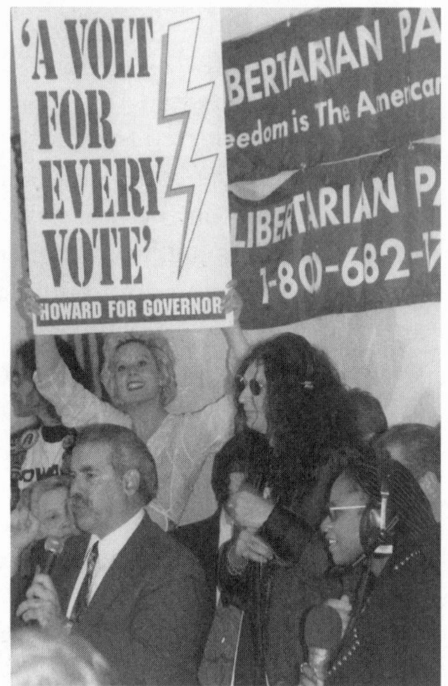

were fighting over how to conduct the vote. We were pushing for a simple voice vote. I really wanted to get the hell out of here. Some of the old-time Libertarians were livid, screaming at Ludwig. James Ostrowsky's people were demanding paper ballots. Someone took the mike and basically told the crowd that it didn't matter what we did because I was going to win.

At that, a nerdy-looking guy in a suit leaped to his feet.

"THIS IS A PUTSCH, THIS IS NOT A MEETING," he shouted.

A huge gob of mucous flew out of his mouth and nearly hit Baba Booey.

"THIS IS A DISGRACE. *YOU'RE* A DISGRACE!" He was shouting and pointing at the podium.

"*YOU'RE* OUT OF ORDER!" Ludwig yelled at him.

It was total chaos. They argued some more and then they finally decided to have a paper ballot. That meant we'd be there at least a few hours more. The convention couldn't drag on too long. There was a wedding booked for the same hall that night.

We decided to eat some lunch during the voting break. Our contingent moved upstairs to a private room. While I was picking at my salad, Gary raised an interesting point.

"Boss, as soon as you leave, all your fans'll go and then Stan won't have the votes to get in."

I had a headache from all these noisy Libertarians. What was all this fuss about? This was a party that had nothing going on. "Get Stan on the ticket! Lock this thing up! I'm out of here." Without me, they didn't have a party. I was the life of their party.

I was ready for a backroom deal.

the backroom deal

I had an idea. I decided to call the top four candidates into a private meeting and offer them patronage positions in my new administration, as long as they would endorse Stan Dworkin for lieutenant governor. This was great. I was already acting gubernatorial. Gary ran out to round them up.

We met in a nearby backroom.

"I'd like to propose on the floor that Stan be lieutenant governor and that you four people would have important positions in our administration," I pitched to the other gubernatorial hopefuls.

"It would be such a strong thing if I could hold up Stan's hand and say we're in this together. Can't we do this today instead of tomorrow?" I pleaded.

After a few minutes' discussion, it seemed that everyone was agreeable. Except for my archrival, Ostrowsky. He had been sitting in the corner, away from the rest of us.

"Jim, are you comfortable with that? You haven't said anything."

"I don't want to rain on your parade, but I don't know this man." He nodded toward Stan. "I think we should get people with a track record in the Libertarian party to be our candidates."

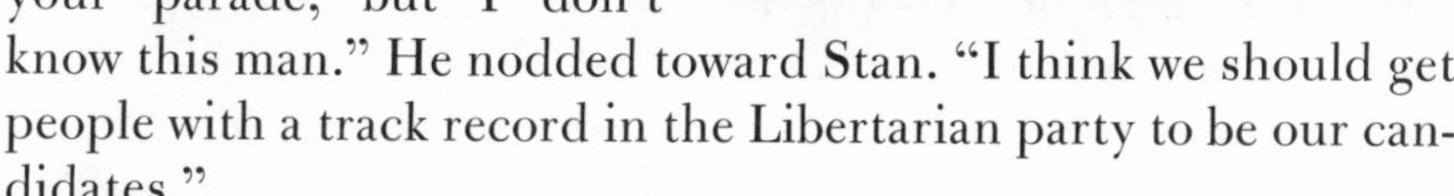

"Wouldn't it be better if we win this thing and actually have a shot at appointing Libertarians to office?" I asked.

"You're a very shrewd political analyst. But I also have been in politics since I was twelve and I just can't see you winning the election," Ostrowsky said.

"But you can't win either, and I can pull at least 200,000 votes, which ensures you a place on the ballot for the next election," I pleaded.

After all of this political maneuvering, I had won three of them over. Ostrowsky was still a holdout, but I had a feeling he had no real power base. Mission accomplished. We started walking down the hall toward the convention room.

The convention was reconvened by Ludwig. They had the tally of the voting for the gubernatorial nomination. This was the big moment. There were a total of 381 registered voters present. I needed 253 for a first ballot victory. Ludwig began the tally:

"Robin Quivers, one vote . . ."

I asked Robin if she had voted for herself.

"Ed Jowitt, 1, Joe Brennan, 10, Dottie Lou Brokaw, 22, Norma Siegel, 24, Jim Ostrowsky, 34, Howard Stern, 287."

The place went wild. That was it. I had captured the nomination on the first ballot. Debbie Tay and Elaina Beastie had stripped down to their thongs and they leaped up on one of the tables on the stage. They started a lewd bump and grind. Stan took one look at them and turned to me. "I just lost all of my credibility," he moaned. Now it was time to ramrod Stan through. I took the mike for an acceptance speech.

"This is only the first step. We must all go forward as Libertarians to win this one for the Libertarian party. And to make sure that not only am I the governor but that Stan Dworkin is the lieutenant governor—*and that the Libertarian point of view is represented in my administration.*"

I thought that was very magnanimous of me. After all, we had just stolen their party. It was the least I could do to assure them that some of their ideas would be represented.

"I would like right now to ask you to give support to Stan as my lieutenant governor, by acclamation . . ."

The crowd roared. Ludwig asked for a second. Dottie Lou Brokaw, my future cabinet member, grabbed the mike.

"I have talked with Howard and Stan and looked into their

eyes. I will second the nomination of Stan Dworkin."

Ludwig tried to get a voice vote to acclaim Stan but some of the old-line Libertarians were furious. Another fight broke out. The same guy in the front row leaped up and screamed that I was creating a coup d'état. He was shouted down again. Melrose went over to him and they started pushing each other. Someone wanted to nominate someone else for lieutenant governor, but Ludwig told him the nominations were closed. Someone tried to move to adjourn. Nine people were screaming, holding up little copies of *Robert's Rules of Order*. It was sheer insanity.

Ludwig ruled that a show of hands for Stan was enough. Someone in the audience demanded to hear Stan speak before they voted. I thought that was a good idea, so we brought Stan to the mike. "Here's the next lieutenant governor, my running mate, Stan Dworkin!" I shouted.

"I appreciate the confidence that Howard and everyone has shown in my background, my position . . ." Stan began.

Suddenly that same guy in the front row sprang to his feet again. He was a little guy but he had a booming voice.

"WE DON'T KNOW YOUR BACKGROUND! TELL IT TO US!" he screamed.

"And I promise . . ." Stan tried to go on.

"THIS IS NOT NAZI GERMANY 1928. YOU TELL IT TO US FIRST. WHAT IS YOUR BACKGROUND? WHO ARE YOU? I DON'T KNOW. YOU DON'T HAVE A CLUE AND I DON'T HAVE A CLUE."

In the middle of all this frenzy, I looked out at the audience. Melrose was holding up a large sign. It read DON'T BLAME ME. I'M A COLGATE GRADUATE. The most embarrassing guy in the world was embarrassed by what was going on.

"I made the same promises that Howard has made . . ." Stan tried to continue.

"WHICH WAS WHAT?" the annoying guy yelled.

"I have spoken with Dottie and other members of your party all day—*our* party, my mistake, *our* party," Stan corrected himself. "This is all new to me."

"YOU'RE JUST A CARPETBAGGER. YOU'RE THE PIED PIPER OF THE HIPPIES!"

The crowd started chanting "DICK" at this ranting old-time Libertarian. Stan was allowed to finish his speech. Then Ludwig asked for a show of hands.

Stan's nomination passed.

"Thank you for coming and on to victory in Albany. We're gonna do it. We're gonna win this one," I shouted.

Thank God it was finally over. I was still feeling like shit from the flu. I was looking forward to getting a nice massage on the way back but, as usual, since we weren't taping for the radio show, the girls all disappeared. Airtime hogs. I dragged myself to the bus and collapsed.

But I had some solace. I was riding back home as the new gubernatorial candidate of the Libertarian party.

> "THIS IS THE GREATEST POLITICAL SATIRE OF OUR TIME."
>
> —A CBS PRODUCER,
> AFTER SEEING FOOTAGE OF THE CONVENTION

STAN'S
MAKEOVERS and WITHDRAWALS

The convention was exhausting, but all the hard work was still ahead of us. We had a crucial meeting several days later at the radio station. My think tank surrounded me: Robin, Fred, Jackie "the Joke Man" Martling, and, of course, my press secretary, FaFa Flowlie, Boy Gary.

"Friends," I said, acting more gubernatorial already. "We have the nomination now, but it's time to address a very important issue."

Everyone was glued to my every word.

"We have a serious problem on our hands," I said earnestly.

"The fact that the FCC doesn't allow candidates to have radio shows?" Robin asked.

"No," I said.

"The reality that if you're going to stay in this race, you'll have to reveal your finances?" Jackie crowed.

"No," I answered. **"The problem is—Stan Dworkin has so much hair coming out of his ears, nobody'll vote for him."**

Everyone in the room moaned. Stan's ear hair was a major concern. How do you tell your lieutenant governor that his ears are a major turnoff? Seeing as how I didn't have the balls to confront anybody face-to-face, it was decided that I would tell Stan about his problem on the air. I read the riot act to him, and he reluctantly agreed to an enforced makeover.

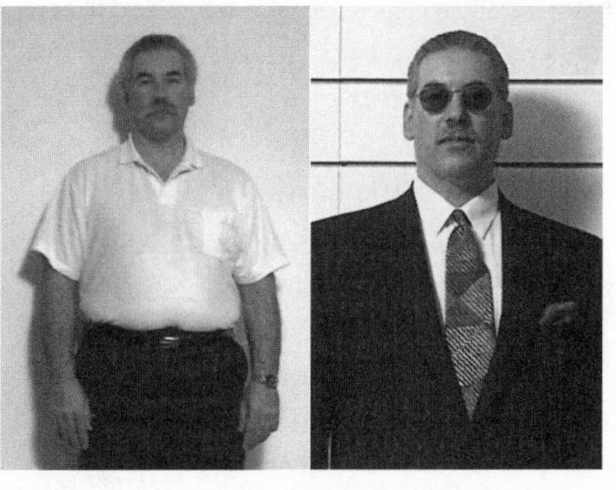

STAN DWORKIN

BEFORE EAR HAIR REMOVAL — AFTER EAR HAIR REMOVAL

Then I told him he had to go on a major diet.

A few days later, we took Stan to a salon where they cut and highlighted his hair, trimmed his moustache, and plucked any stray hair from his ears and nose. Then we took him to NBO and got him a suit that actually fit him.

I was serious about this campaign.

I was so serious that I even rented a house in Plainview, Long Island, just so I could use the address for my official filing papers. They wouldn't allow me to put down my P.O. box. But if I put my real address down, it was part of the public record and any wacko could look it up and pay me a visit. So I actually paid rent for a house that I'd never use.

That's how serious I was about running.

Unfortunately, the Libertarians didn't seem to be. Instead of getting the necessary signatures to put me on the ballot, all they did was call me up so they could debate arcane Libertarian ideas. Of course, each of those dudes thought that they represented the party, so we were getting calls from fifteen different people asking to speak with me. I told Gary that under no circumstances would I speak to any of them, including Joe Brennan and Ludwig.

NO JOKE – STERN WILL HAVE IMPACT

By RITA DELFINER

Radio shock-jock Howard Stern is Gov. Cuomo's secret weapon in the gubernatorial race, according to The New York Post/Fox 5 poll.

In fact, in a close election, Stern's decision on whether to stay in the contest "could very well determine the outcome," pollster Frank Luntz predicted.

The bad boy of the airwaves would do Cuomo a good turn if he remains in the battle, Luntz said.

That's because Stern would draw anti-Cuomo votes that would go to Republican challenger George Pataki, the poll shows.

HOWARD STERN
Potential kingmaker.

If Stern yanked his name off the ballot, his supporters would break for Pataki over Cuomo by better than two to one, the poll found.

"In percentage terms, that's an extra 2-percent to 3-percent advantage to Pataki, depending on turnout," Luntz said.

Stern could find himself a kingmaker

Meanwhile, the hardcore Libertarians threw Ludwig out the day after we left Albany. The new chairperson was aligned with Ostrowsky's group. They were threatening to have Stan dumped from the ticket. I was fed up with the Libertarians. All they had to do was go out and get me the signatures like they promised. Without doing any campaigning, I was back up to 18 percent of the vote. Cuomo only had 36 percent. I was sure that I could rally the goofy vote in the last three days of the election and sweep to victory.

But I was facing a few other problems besides the wacky Libertarians. There were two major obstacles to my getting elected.

The first was the equal-time provision. Since I was a broadcaster, it was felt that I had an unfair forum that the other candidates didn't. It didn't matter that I didn't plan to even talk about the election till the last few days. Early on in the campaign, Mario Cuomo had waived his equal-time rights. I guess he thought that I would take votes away from the Republican candidate since we were both for the death penalty. So Mario desperately wanted me in the race.

The Republicans felt the opposite. They would have done anything to get my ass booted. So they were going to mount an equal-time fight. A few of the other wacky minority-party candidates were also threatening equal-time suits. But I hired a lawyer and we discovered a loophole: I wasn't a bona fide candidate until all my signatures had been filed and approved by the state attorney general. We figured that that might take until October 15. That would mean that I would have to leave the air from only October 15 to election day.

'Baseball's on the rocks, O.J.'s fading out, imagine what a yawner this summer would be if Howard Stern wasn't running for governor.'

Of course, that idea horrified my bosses at Infinity. October was one of their highest-billing months in terms of ad revenues. They were looking at losing millions of dollars of business.

I didn't care. I was *serious* about running and *winning* this fucking election.

There was one other problem that wasn't as easy to overcome. There was a law on the books that stated that every candidate for statewide office had to file a financial disclosure form. This was one of those ethics laws that were intended to cut down on corruption among elected officials. In theory, this was a great thing. As long as we knew who the elected officials were doing business with, we could make sure they didn't throw any state business their way and have a conflict of interest.

But in my case, this law was a nightmare. None of the other candidates were celebrities. If I disclosed my assets, the repercussions would be staggering. Immediately, that noodnick Penny Crone would broadcast my net worth all over Fox TV. Every other media person would pick up this story too. If I had less money than people thought, I'd be perceived as an idiot. If I had more money, I could never get a vacuum cleaner fixed again without being robbed.

Either way, I knew that Jackie would have a heart attack and demand more money.

Forget about Jackie. Who wanted my *kids* to know how much money I had? My daughters would find out how much I was worth and suddenly I'd be saddled with lazy, spoiled kids like Johnny Carson's or the Menendez brothers.

So I offered to compromise. I was willing to disclose what stocks I owned. That was simple. All I had was stock in Disney and Philip Morris. But it was nobody's business to know how much I had.

This financial disclosure law was weird. I hired a few teams of lawyers, and each team disagreed about its interpretation. Finally, we retained some of Cuomo's top lawyers. These experts told me that there were many cases in which people never filed the financial disclosure forms. Al Sharpton ran for senator and never filed. But it was a law that failure to file could be punishable by a year in jail and a ten-thousand-dollar fine. Just my luck, they'd go after me. I considered doing the time. I certainly could catch up on my reading and I'd get to jerk off a lot. But I didn't like the whole idea of filing. Hey, I was a Libertarian. Fuck the government. So I sued. My lawyers, for a very substantial fee, filed a challenge to the Financial Disclosure Act. They argued that my case, as a celebrity running for office, was unique. They asked that I be exempted from this law. On August 3, the judge handed down his verdict. He didn't even address my concerns. He just dismissed the case and told me to file or else.

A tearful farewell

And so it was with a heavy heart that we called a press conference during my show the next day. That was it. The bastards had won. I had been worn down. New York was about to lose what would have been its most dedicated, although short-lived, governor in history.

We had a huge turnout for the press conference. I had intern Steve Grillo's Uncle James introduce me. I chose him because he suffered from throat cancer and he could only speak through his voice kazoo. He held this machine up to his cheek and emitted some high-pitched beeping sounds. It was impossible to understand a word he was saying, but I was employing the handicapped. Hey, I couldn't be criticized for that.

Finally, mercifully, Uncle James stopped. The crowd applauded. I took my position behind the microphone.

"I want you to know that I spend twenty-five hours a week

telling you all the most intimate details of my life. Name another candidate who gives you such disclosure. Has Mario Cuomo ever told you the size of his penis? Has he talked about the stains in his underpants and burying those underpants in his backyard when he was young? And this guy Pataki, has he ever shown you his face on camera, much less his ass at the MTV Music Video Awards? Only *I* have done these things."

I went into the whole background of the financial disclosure law. I told them about the lawsuit and the verdict.

"While I've told you everything about myself since the first day I started broadcasting, there is only one fact I never revealed: I never told you how much money I have in the bank. And the reason I never told you how much money I have in the bank is that ***it's none of your business.*** It has nothing to do with me running for governor, that I know.

"I had countless meetings over this thing and now I've lost. The legal geniuses feel that no matter how many times I appeal, no matter how much money I go through, eventually I will have to file financial disclosure. These laws are obviously a conspiracy to keep good people out of the race. Anyway, with much regret, I have to tell you now that I am resigning from the campaign. I am stepping aside, but I will run for pope."

It was all over. My campaign had come to an end standing in front of these cameras in the K-Rock lobby.

Looking back, I'll never regret my short-lived flirtation with public office—standing up and fighting for positions that I thought were right. It's funny, but since the campaign, I've come to change some of my views. After watching the O.J. trial, I've now come to the conclusion that justice is *not* dispensed evenly in this country. If you're rich it doesn't matter how guilty you are, you can avoid getting fried. If you're poor you'll get railroaded right into that chair. It's a two-tiered justice system.

For that reason, I am now firmly *opposed* to the death penalty except in cases where there's no doubt, like Colin Ferguson's assault on innocent passengers on the LIRR.

I guess that I've realized that I can't trust the same assholes who come after me for allegedly "indecent" broadcasts to decide who should live and die.

But I'll always remember that wonderful time that I spent

campaigning for the highest elected office in New York State. I'll never forget reaching out and touching those two strippers' lives at Goldfinger's in Newburgh.

I'll never forget Ludwig getting bronskied by Colt 45's 34HHH beauties on my campaign bus.

And I'll never forget Elaina Beastie's beautiful bare ass cheeks undulating to the beat of "Howard Stern for Governor."

I may have been denied the opportunity to serve the great people of New York State, but those scenes will live in my memory forever.

WHAT MIGHT HAVE BEEN

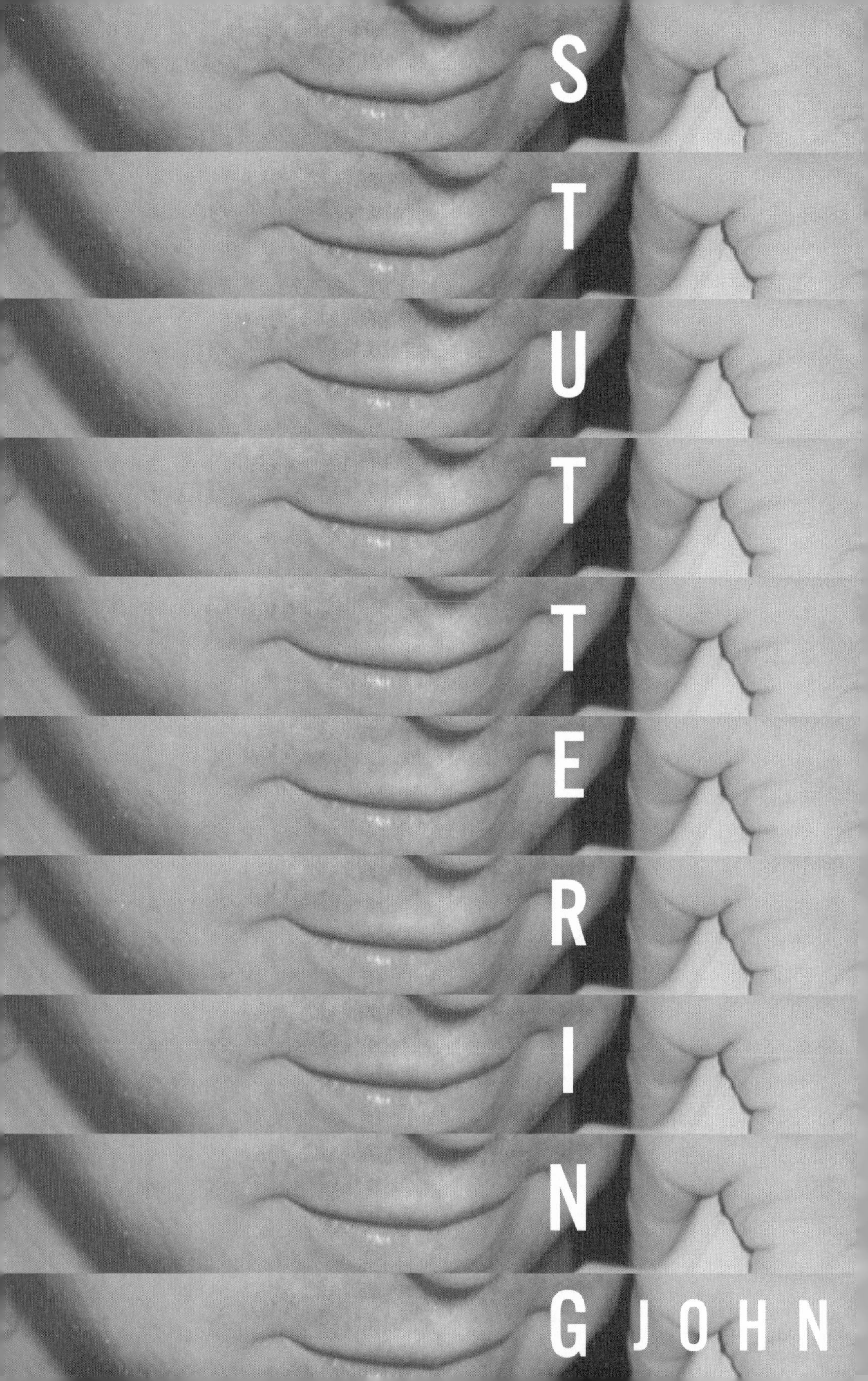
S
T
U
T
T
E
R
I
N
G
JOHN

CHAPTER 10

I LOVE STUTTERING JOHN. Who else could take so much abuse from us in the studio and then go out into the real world and get harassed ten times worse? To me, John has ***the scariest job imaginable***. He has to approach celebrities and, armed only with a microphone and a list of cleverly engineered questions that we write, **verbally terrorize them** into revealing their true essence to the world.

Twenty years of flapping his tongue and machine-gunning his words is nothing compared to the humiliation John experiences at the hands of the handlers, publicists, security guards, and assorted hangers-on whose very jobs are to preserve the aura of ***IMPORTANCE*** and ***DIGNITY*** around the celebrities who are John's prey. **HE'S BEEN SCREAMED AT, PUNCHED, PUSHED, SHOVED, ELBOWED, SPIT ON, SLAPPED IN THE FACE, PICKED UP, THROWN OUT, AND PUSHED DOWN A FLIGHT OF STAIRS.** Yet, like a stammering Energizer bunny, he comes back for more, and more, and more. This year, Stuttering John celebrates his seventh year as our celebrity interviewer. Here are some of his latest achievements.

MR. ROGERS

John collared everybody's favorite children's show host, Mr. Rogers, when he made a public appearance at FAO Schwarz, autographing his latest children's book.

"Would you like to machine-gun Barney?"

"Pardon me?" Mr. Rogers seemed incredulous.

"Would you like to machine-gun Barney?"

"Would you?" Mr. Rogers said, in his best Mr. Rogers voice.

"Why is Captain Kangaroo so bitter?" John followed up.

"Do you find him bitter?" Mr. Rogers was all concern. "That's strange. I never found Captain Kangaroo bitter."

Mr. Rogers's handlers had to grab his arm and lead him away. He seemed baffled that someone like John could exist.

DR. SPOCK

Dr. Spock was about to sign copies of his latest book when John showed up to interview him.

"What makes kids h-h-homo?" John sputtered.

Spock actually went into a long-winded explanation of the dynamics of family structure in the origins of homosexuality. John stared at him blankly, then asked the second question on his sheet.

"Which is better punishment for children—**SPANKING OR ENEMAS?"**

John was immediately escorted out, but Dr. Spock felt compelled to answer. "Neither! Neither!" he stood up and yelled at the departing journalist.

F. MURRAY ABRAHAM

It looked like the actor F. Murray Abraham was going to **cornhole** John when John interviewed him. He was laughing and playful and throwing his arm around John, answering every dumb question. When John asked him when was the last time he picked his nose, F. Murray went **DIGGING INTO HIS CONSIDERABLE SCHNOZZ,** picked a huge booger, and smeared it on John's back.

"If I paid you a hundred dollars to kiss me, would you do it?" John asked next.

"Oh, no, man. I'd do it for nothing," F. Murray gushed and grabbed John and planted a wet one on his cheek.

Elle, Naomi, Claudia, and Cindy

Lately, John's been getting a lot of mileage out of tormenting supermodels. It's really something special to listen to John ask a

supermodel a question AND THEN HEAR THE WIND WHISTLING THROUGH HER EARS.

John caught Elle MacPherson going into an Oscar party at Elaine's.

"Elle. Elle. Who's our vice president?"

"Are you trying to make fun of me?" she snapped. "You think I'm a stupid model or something?" She stormed into the restaurant. Meanwhile, she hadn't answered the question.

John had previously snared Elle when she was teaching a course at the Learning Annex in Manhattan.

"ELLE, HOW HARD IS IT TO HIDE YOUR TAMPON STRING DURING SWIMSUIT PHOTO SHOOTS?" he shouted. She looked at him with great revulsion.

At a press conference announcing the opening of the Fashion Cafe, Elle, Naomi Campbell, and Claudia Schiffer were sitting ducks as they sat on a podium and faced their tormentor.

"Who's smarter? Christie Brinkley or Forrest Gump?" John had to know.

"You're Forrest Gump," Claudia retorted, creating a battle of the nitwits.

"Girls," Stuttering John shouted. **"Have you ever farted on the runway?"**

"What?" Naomi was incredulous.

Stuttering John was escorted out.

When we heard that Cindy Crawford was going to appear at a charity event we dispatched John immediately. When we later found out that it was to announce a fund-raiser for pediatric AIDS, even I had second thoughts. Until I learned that the name of the group was DISHES—Determined, Involved Supermodels Helping to End Suffering. **Fuck 'em.**

John stood there and listened to a series of sad speeches. He told us later that he was beginning to really bum out at having to interrupt this serious event, but he reminded himself he was there for the celebrity, not the cause. Is this guy a robot or what? Since Cindy was only going to meet the press one-on-one, John actually blurted out his question in the middle of Cindy's speech.

"Cindy, when was the first time you saw Richard Gere's disappointing equipment?" John interrupted.

Cindy was taken aback but plowed right on.

"Uh, I just want to say thank you all for being here."

Three men surrounded John and watched as he packed his bags. They started walking him out.

"Hey, Cindy, do models take vomiting lessons?" he managed to scream before one of the guards put his hand over his mouth and dragged him out.

Michael Caine

One time John attempted to catch Michael Caine at a book signing. He bought a book and waited in line. When it was his turn, he whipped out his mike and managed to get a few questions in before he was removed. But he wasn't satisfied. He heard that Caine was going to do another book signing three days later at an uptown store. So John put on a disguise and positioned himself behind a cement column near the bookstore. He timed it perfectly. Just as Caine was two feet away, John lurched out from behind the column and caught him again. A few days later, Caine was being interviewed by Pia Lindstrom on WNBC. They went to a commercial break.

"You know this guy, Stuttering John?" Michael asked Pia. "I fought in the trenches in the Korean War and before a battle, I'll always remember smelling that putrid smell of the enemy. That's what I smelled right before that guy got me the second time."

IVANA

John snared Ivana Trump when she was meeting the press before her appearance at the Learning Annex. About six reporters surrounded Ivana. These cretins were asking her about her Pizza Hut commercials with the Donald and her stupid line of clothing.

"How many rooms in the Plaza did you think Donald cheated on you in?" John yelled out.

"Oooh," one of the other reporters gasped, as if she'd been shot.

"I have no idea. You'd have to ask him," Ivana answered coolly.

"I think we should leave that one out," one of the publicists said.

"Are you a citizen?" John followed.

"Of course I'm a citizen," Ivana fumed.

"What country?" John asked.

"America," Ivana said. The publicist finally realized it was John but it was too late.

"I have no problem with a man which tries to offend me," Ivana said. "I can answer you."

"You're an inspiration to so many women..." Another reporter tried to steer the session back to the mundane but it was too late.

"IVANA, IS YOUR NEW GUY BIGGER IN THE LAP THAN DONALD?"

She just smiled blankly. It was all over. John reached out and shook her hand.

"Take care, Ivana. **BIG FAN**," he lied.

RAQUEL WELCH

Sometimes celebrities react very strongly to John. Morton Downey Jr. overturned a table and threw John to the floor. At a Brentano's book signing, Eric Bogosian grabbed him and slammed his head up against a wall before bookstore security dragged John down a flight of stairs, by his neck. Then they threw him against the wall and knocked down a bookcase. Lou Reed put his hands around John's neck, ***trying to***

strangle him. But his most embarrassing moment had to be when Raquel Welch whacked him right in the nose. We'd better let John relate that story.

Stuttering John: I caught Raquel Welch as she was leaving a celebrity auction. She was walking toward her car and I fell into step right behind her.

"Hey, Raquel. Are they drooping yet?" I yelled out.

She didn't stop walking but she just swung back with a short karate chop and hit me with the back of her fist right on my fucking nose. I was stunned. Man, I had that fireworks feeling. I'd never gotten hit by a woman before. Meanwhile, she got into the limo and took off.

The next day, my nose was killing me. I had to go to the doctor's and get it X-rayed. I was so pissed off that I was thinking about suing her. But then I spoke to Andrew Dice Clay.

"Hey, John, what are you gonna do, sue her? Tell the whole world that **YOU GOT YOUR ASS KICKED BY A CHICK?"**

BURT REYNOLDS

John got Burt just as he was sitting down to sign copies of his new book at a mall in Connecticut.

"What's the best thing about dinner theater—the dinner or the theater?" John started with an innocuous question.

"I don't have the dinner theater anymore. Sorry," Burt said.

"What's the closest you've been to Dom DeLuise when he c-c-c-cut the cheese?"

Burt got that look. He was trapped. But the security guards moved in and pushed John away. He retreated to the back of the small group of reporters but then three security guys surrounded him.

"John, Burt doesn't want you around," one of the guys said. They picked John up and started physically removing him from the mall. John fought back. They wound up almost crashing through the plate-glass window of one of the stores.

"Stop fucking pushing me!" John screamed. "I don't have a gun. It's a microphone."

John was told he had to leave the mall. But he thought on his feet. He started walking away and then he took an escalator to the next floor up. John realized that if he leaned over the railing, he would be directly above Burt's head. The E! crew framed both Burt and John in the same shot and then John let them rip.

"Hey, Burt! Burt! How long before you start hosting *Those Amazing Discoveries*?" John shouted out. His words reverberated throughout the enclosed mall. There were hundreds of people watching this classic encounter from all levels.

Burt looked up at his antagonist.

"*You'll* be hosting *Amazing Discoveries*." What a comeback.

"Burt! Burt!" John's voice boomed down. "Will Loni get a free book? ***Burt! Did you avoid Ned Beatty after he got raped in* Deliverance?** Burt! Are you from Jupiter? If yes, are you vulnerable to Kryptonite?"

John blew these last questions out like machine-gun fire. As he spoke, security was bearing down on him from all directions. Meanwhile, most of the people there were cracking up at John's questions.

"Burt! Did you ever nail Marilu Henner? Burt! How do you respond to the charges that you are hot-headed? Thank you, ladies and gentlemen. Goodbye!!" John saluted the crowd with a flourish. Then he started running to escape the cops. He may stutter but he sure can run.

Stuttering Vic

The only problem with John stalking celebrities is that sometimes he gets the ridiculous notion that he's a celebrity too. Right about the time that John's record came out, he started to act a bit too highfalutin. He delegated most of his intern responsibilities to Gorilla. He started making appearances on shows like Conan O'Brien's and Ricki Lake's. He even got a short-lived gig as the show buffoon on Brandon Tartikoff's folly, *Last Call.* Thank God only about ten people saw that show. I was furious that other shows were trying to take Stuttering John's persona and water it down in totally unfunny contexts. I had to get John back in line before his ego became insufferable. So I hit John where I knew it would hurt the most. We found another intern who stuttered and was Indian, to boot.

Stuttering Vic was a computer nerd who was hired by my assistant Cathy Tobin as a show intern. At first, we didn't even know that he stuttered. But once we found that out, and we brought him on the air to ***bust John's balls,*** I fell in love with his unique speech impediment. With John's stutter, you'd get instant gratification. But Vic's was different. You had to wait and wait and wait for it. In the meantime, Vic would speak in the precise, clipped tones of the educated Indian merchant caste. But all of a sudden he'd go into this wild putt, putt, putt and it was LIKE A SLOW ORGASM. And when we had them both in the studio, it was heaven. Vic was **PUTT, PUTT, PUTTING** and John was **AH, AH, AHHING**. Stereo stammering.

We never really had any intention of replacing Stuttering John with Stuttering Vic. But I told John that if he screwed up, Vic would have to step in and replace him, so I forced John to take Vic out on a number of assignments and show him the ropes. It broke John's heart to reveal all his secrets to someone who he feared would replace him, but John did it anyway. And one time, it actually came in handy that Vic was around. He was able to do something that John had long dreamed of—**he nailed Kathie Lee**.

Kathie Lee and her co-host Regis Philbin were set to do a dual appearance, signing their new cookbook. We immediately dispatched John, along with his trainee, Stuttering Vic. John knew there was little chance to get to Kathie Lee once she was inside the bookstore, so he hid behind a post a discreet distance from the store's entrance. When the limo pulled up, John pounced.

"Have you stolen Oprah's hairdo?" he shouted at Kathie Lee as she was hustled into the store. She acted as if she didn't even hear John. Then he made an executive decision that would forever endear himself to me. He finally managed to sacrifice his own ego for the good of the show. He sent Stuttering Vic, an unfamiliar face, into the store to confront Kathie Lee.

Vic waited patiently in front of the table that had been set up for the signing. Regis and Kathie Lee were busy personalizing autographs for the old biddies who watch their show. Finally, Stuttering Vic summoned up his courage and opened up his mike.

"K-K-K-K-Kathie? C-c-can we ask you a c-c-c-c-couple of questions for WXRK radio?" He was stuttering like a crippled banshee.

"Yes." Kathie Lee seemed confused to hear a stutter and not see John.

"Don't you think it's strange that someone who has a cuh-cuh-cuh-cook writes a cuh-cuh-cuh-cuh-cookbook?" Stuttering

Vic's motorboat stammer boomed out in the bookstore.

He was immediately surrounded by publicists.

"No more questions," one of them said.

But this was Vic's big chance. While they were escorting him away, he turned around and addressed Kathie Lee. He was close enough to drown her in his stutter spittle.

"WOULD YOU EVER ABORT A CHILD IF YOU KNEW HE WAS GOING TO BE A RETARD?"

"Would you ever have Howard on your morning show?"

Vic's stuttering sounded like a helicopter coming in for a landing. I felt proud when they came back to the station and we played this tape. Now there were two. Stuttering Vic finished his internship and went back to college, but the competition energized John.

CHARLTON HESTON

—JOHN'S CROWNING ACHIEVEMENT

John pasted his silly fake moustache on and waited for Heston to come out of the NBC building.

"Charlton, do you think Ronald Reagan r-r-remembers who you are?"

E V E R Y T H I N G F R O Z E .

"He's not doing any interviews." One of Heston's publicists tried to put her body between Charlton and John. But Charlton was ***livid.***

"That's an outrageous question," he muttered. He continued signing autographs and then he turned toward John. He GRABBED John's mike and held it down.

"Jesus Christ!" he swore. The veins were popping out of his neck. His eyes burned into John with an intensity that was chill-

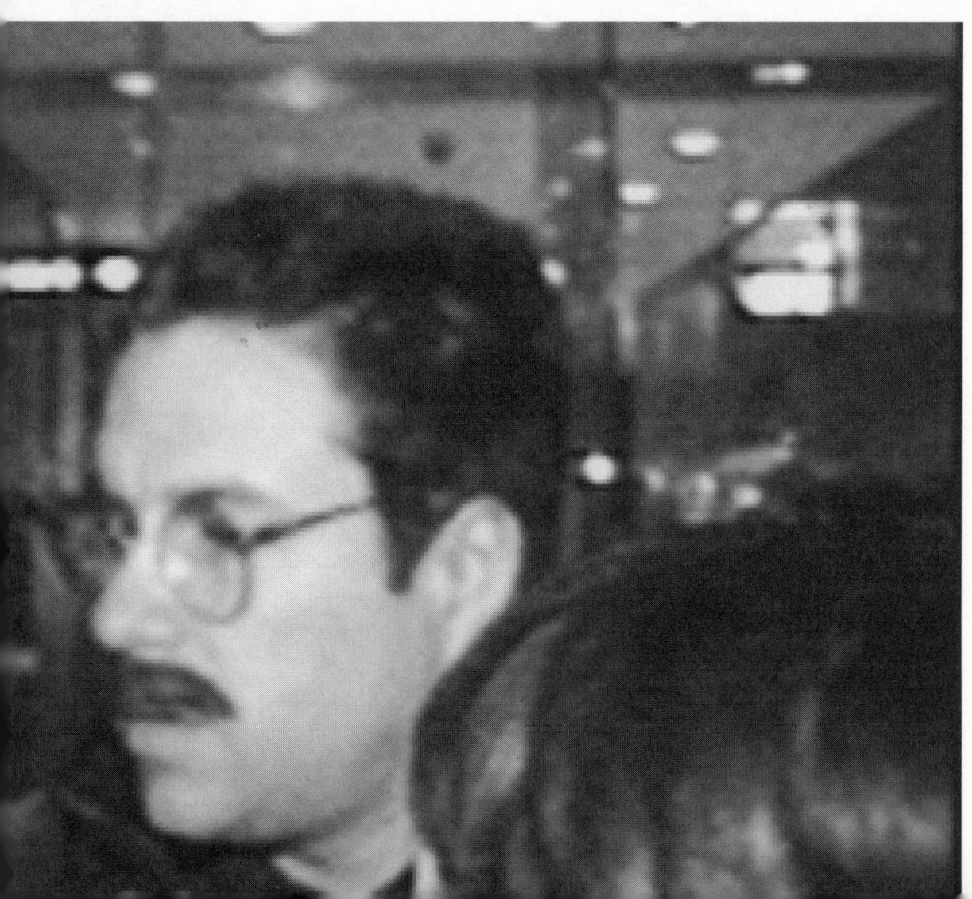

ing. He was Moses, scorned by his people. If he had had a tablet, he would have broken it over John's head.

"Don't do that," he commanded John.

"Do what?" John asked, the picture of innocence.

Heston released the microphone and **SHOVED** John to the side. He **STORMED OFF,** almost knocking over an autograph seeker. One of the publicists started **SCREAMING** like a banshee, a bloodcurdling out-of-this-world howl. The other publicist started **THREATENING TO CALL THE POLICE.** But John was undeterred. He followed Heston to the outside sidewalk, where Charlton was bolting for his car.

"Take care, Charlton." John waved. And then he smiled the smile of the totally content.

FORGIVE ME,

CHAPTER 11

FOR I HAVE SINNED

THE UNLEASHING OF THE MAD PHONE STALKERS

Forgive me, Father, for I have sinned, and I need to make a confession.

I have unleashed an epidemic on the world. It's a cancer that can't be stopped. The chain reaction is sheer madness. I came into an innocent world and I corrupted it. Shit! I am the Anti-Christ.

It all started out **innocently enough** with one phone call.

"Hi, My name is Robert, and I'd love to piss up your asshole. I'd like to wet your sphincter with my hot golden urine. Do you want to be my little piss boy?"

Ah, there I was, having fun as usual. Making my prank phone call for the day . . . in my office alone, a forty-one-year-old man with three people waiting outside to see him, my agent on the other line, and everyone's on hold—because *this* is the biggest thrill of my life.

Some people go to the gym.

Some people get a massage.

Me? I get on the phone.

I'm not doing this as a radio bit. I'm doing it for my own private enjoyment. I'm calling a GAY party line and picking up BOYS!!!

"Do you want to play laundry?" I asked the willing anonymous bone smuggler on the other line. Who knows? It could have been another disc jockey. It could have been a senator. It could have been Rush Limbaugh.

"I've never done that. What's that?" he asked.

"That's where I take a hot iron and I burn your testicles," I said.

"Man, you're ***too freaky*** for me," he said and hung up.

I used to make phony phone calls when I was a little kid, which was fun, but this is better—my humor is so much more sophisticated now. When I was nine I didn't know about pissing in a man's asshole. So many people my age have forgotten how to have fun. I know guys who play golf. Golf? WHAT A BUNCH OF DIPSHITS AND HOMOS. I'm not going to play golf when I know there's a telephone waiting for me where I can reach out and goof on any unsuspecting **NITWIT** who stays on the line with me.

The King of the Cranks

My listeners have followed my lead and taken the genre of phony calls to new heights. My dedicated fans have made it virtu-

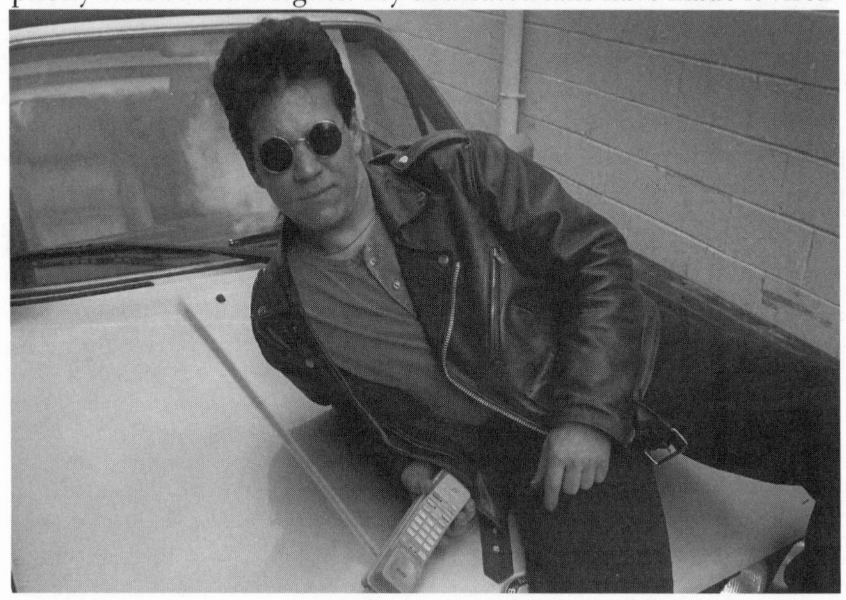

ally impossible to watch a call-in television show without hearing at least one caller who delights in scamming the host and mentioning my name. And the King of the Cranks is Captain Janks, who is far and away the most important Stern show phony phone caller. He singlehandedly started the phenomenon of calling up talk shows and mentioning my name. When it became harder to get past the show's screeners because of the large number of people who followed Janks's lead, he consistently came up with new, creative ways to get through the gatekeepers and get his message across. He has served as a mentor for a whole new generation of phony phone callers, unselfishly giving them tips and encouragement.

Janks's story is amazing. He's an odd little guy who ***lived with his parents*** when he first started calling in to my show in 1989. But with a phone in his hand, this guy became invincible. His first calls were to *Larry King Live!* He would simply ask the guests what they thought of Howard Stern. If Larry King would have acknowledged my greatness the first time Janks called, he would have saved himself years of torment. But he refused and BLEW JANKS OFF. Like DeBella before him, **he had created a monster.**

Early the next morning, Janks called us up and we played the tape. Even though I explained to my audience that this was not behavior I could condone, I LOVED IT! I LOVED hearing my name on other shows. EVERY SHOW ON THE PLANET SHOULD BE ABOUT ME. Let's face it, I don't get much advertising. And this was free publicity. The best kind you could get. This was guerrilla theater. Come to think of it, Larry King looks like a gorilla. How he gets these women to marry him is beyond me. And they marry him ***again and again.*** Women must be desperate.

Giving Janks publicity fueled him even more. He went to war with Larry King. He called on the regular lines. He called on the international lines. It got to the point where Larry King couldn't say, "Amsterdam, you're on the air" and be certain that the next voice wouldn't be Janks screaming, **"WHAT DO YOU THINK OF HOWARD STERN?"**

Larry King was the perfect foil. His whole body would tense at the mere mention of my name. Then he'd lash out and hit the phone button to disconnect the call. Then he'd regain his composure and nonchalantly say, "We've seem to have lost that call," and quickly change the subject.

Janks opened up the floodgates. Soon, people were calling Larry King every night and mentioning my name. This led to increased vigilance on the part of the show's screeners. But Janks loved the challenge. He bought a voice alterer and got past the screeners by calling as a woman. Not content to get on the show, he began placing phony phone calls to Larry King in his office. Then he started making prank calls to King's guests while they were in the green room, waiting to go on the show. If Janks had been a doctor he probably would have discovered the cure for AIDS by now. ***But, in his demented mind, he had more important work to do.***

When Larry King had Perot and Gore on to debate the proposed NAFTA treaty, Janks spent all night trying to get through. When he failed, he came up with an ingenious scheme to embarrass King.

He called all the major news outlets and claimed he was an audio technician on the *Larry King Live!* show. He said that the King show was so afraid of getting crank phone calls from Howard Stern fans that the producers had actually used staffers to plant fake questions during the debate.

To back up his contention, he sent along a tape. The tape

purported to contain a conversation between Larry King and a producer named Pat.

VOICE: Hey, Larry. Pick up line two, please.

LARRY: Hello.

JANKS: Hey, Larry, it's just me calling back.

LARRY: Is this Pat?

JANKS: Yeah, Larry.

LARRY: Hey, Pat.

JANKS: All right, listen. We have staff members on lines two and three continuously through the night with questions lined up. So don't worry about Howard Stern calls. Take as many calls as you want, okay?

LARRY: Yep.

JANKS: Okay.

Janks played the part of the producer, Pat. To get Larry's voice, he spliced together soundbites of Larry King's real voice that Janks had recorded previously. His prank worked. A number of newspapers picked up this story. In fact, Tom Johnson, the president of CNN, had to call a press conference the next day to categorically deny Janks's charges.

Janks is a great innovator. **I DON'T CONDONE ANYTHING ILLEGAL** but I must admit that a little phone fun is harmless. He was the first phony phone caller to use soundbites from my show on his calls. He used weird Jackie sounds. He threw in the first "Baba Booeys" on some calls. One day, when Fred left a message on someone's answering machine using the sound effects of a car crashing, Janks took it one step further. He called a local cable cooking show and pretended to be calling from his car phone.

MALE HOST: Let's go to North Wales and Bill. Hi, Bill.

JANKS: Hello, Frank. Hello, Mary. I'm in my car right now and I'm trying to find a nice Cajun restaurant to go to around this area.

MALE HOST: Uh, a good Cajun . . .

Just then, Janks played the sound of a horrible car crash.

FEMALE HOST: Is he in an accident?

MALE HOST: Are you all right?

There was a long, silent pause.

FEMALE HOST: Bill?

MALE HOST: Bill?

FEMALE HOST: Oh, dear. ***That sounded terrible.***

MALE HOST: Oh, boy. Uh, we're hoping that he calls back, all right? I'm sure he's all right.

FEMALE HOST: Oh, dear.

MALE HOST: I've got my fingers crossed, that was a little bit scary. Okay, let's go to Irene, in Arlington. HI, IRENE!

Howard Stern Thinks You're a Fat Pig

Janks would take amazingly elaborate measures to get a call through. He spent almost three hours impersonating Jim Carrey's manager and then Jim Carrey himself to get a thirty-second shot at Ed McMahon when he did the *Today* show. What I love about Janks is that my enemies are his enemies. I've always hated that fat, no-talented load, Ed McMahon. So when Janks saw that he was booked for the *Today* show and that Jim Carrey was promoting a new movie, he seized the opportunity. He called the *Today* show posing as Jim Miller, Jim Carrey's manager.

The *Today* show producers had no idea what Carrey sounded like. So Janks/Jim Miller told them that at the start of his career, Jim Carrey had been a guest on *Star Search* and had **LOST**.

Jim thought that it would be a nice surprise to call in and say "Hi" to his old friend Ed.

Janks bullshitted as Jim Miller with the producers for two hours. Finally, he produced "Jim Carrey." It was Janks with his voice altered slightly. They put him right on the air:

MATT LAUER: Somebody else who's doing okay, Ed, is on the phone with us right now. As a matter of fact, we were talking about him a second ago. He called in. I believe he was a *Star Search* loser. Is my caller here?

JANKS: Yeah, hi!

McMAHON: (pretending to recognize his voice) Jim! How are you?

JANKS: Hi, Ed. Hi, Matt.

LAUER: I'm fine, Jim. How are you?

McMAHON: Do you believe this guy, what's happening to him?

LAUER: You actually lost on *Star Search*?

McMAHON: Well, you don't lose. He was in competition and someone else exceeded his performance. How's that?

JANKS: That's right. Hey, Ed?

McMAHON: Yes.

JANKS: Howard Stern thinks you're a fat pig. Is that true?

McMAHON: No, no, no. That's what he thinks about himself.

JANKS: Well, you are a fat pig!

McMAHON: YEAH, OKAY.

LAUER: Apparently, that's not Jim Carrey, and we apologize for that.

OKAY, WE'VE BEEN HAD

The most elaborate prank Janks ever pulled was when he convinced the producers of the Jerry Lewis telethon that he was Larry King and that he wanted to call in live to Jerry during the waning hours of the telethon. The amazing thing is that Janks pulled off the whole stunt off his home in Pennsylvania. He and his friend, Kevin Renzulli, spent hours and hours preparing this prank. First of all, Janks got a local call-through number in L.A. So whenever the producers of the telethon called him to make arrangements for the phone call, the L.A. number rang in Pennsylvania.

Whenever the phone rang, Janks answered, "Larry King's office." Then they covered each angle of their story. Larry was allegedly flying into L.A. to see his daughter, so in case the producers checked with the airlines, Janks made plane reservations in King's name. When it came time to produce Larry on the phone, to convince the telethon people the call was legitimate, Janks created another phony tape of Larry, using old soundbites. It worked. The producers thought it was Larry. Meanwhile, Jerry hadn't been taking any calls during the entire telethon. They had to patch in a special line for "Larry King."

Jerry was EXHAUSTED BUT EXCITED when he announced this special surprise call:

JERRY: We have Larry King calling me on our phone . . . which should be on the line . . .

JANKS: Hello.

JERRY: Hello.

JANKS: Hello, Mr. Lewis. What do you think of Howard Stern, the radio personality? How do you like them apples?

Jerry looked ***immensely pained***. He **faked** a laugh, but you could see that he was furious.

JERRY: I don't think we got Larry King, no. I think it was a phony. Well, you know, we do this show, it's life and death,

and it's important. But you're always going to get a SCHMUCK out there. That's okay, what the hell. It's what makes the world go round. They *sucked you in* pretty good, folks. If Larry King was really going to call me, he would have called me on my private phone in the dressing room. Okay, we've been had.

Jesus died for you

My favorite calls are the ones that Janks makes to a nun named Mother Angelica. She's got a cable call-in show on a religious network. She's a big, fat woman who wears that huge bonnet-type habit. She's got a cross around her neck that's bigger than the one Jesus was hung on. Janks's calls to Mother Angelica were so popular that all the other phony phone guys started calling her too. But what's great about Janks's calls to her is that he makes them as a woman:

JANKS: Mother Angelica, how are you?

MOTHER ANGELICA: I'm fine. And where are you from?

JANKS: I'm calling from Skitback, Pennsylvania.

MOTHER ANGELICA: And what is your question?

JANKS: I was wondering . . . would you let Howard Stern ***light your fart?***

MOTHER ANGELICA: (LONG SILENCE) Now, why would you say something like that? It's always amazing to me that women can ask such FOUL questions on this program. You really need to examine your conscience. Jesus died for you. Do you know that? And instead of being grateful that you have the opportunity for salvation, and the great gates of Heaven are open to you, you take the beautiful soul that God gave you, and you keep piling garbage, and mud, and disfiguration on it. A soul with that kind of mud and your kind of mouth cannot enter heaven.

One of my favorite impersonations was the time Janks posed as a **black girl** named Clorese:

MOTHER ANGELICA: And what is your question?

JANKS: My question is . . . ***would you spread for Baba Booey?***

MOTHER ANGELICA: Would you what? That's one of those bad calls again. (LONG PAUSE) I think so many of you out there are so sick. **So sick. Cheap.** I hope and pray that you will look at yourself and think again of the dignity and love with which God made you and that you are REDUCING YOURSELF TO AN ANIMAL. I think we need to pray for you. I blame the people of all denominations that have not preached the Good Word, the Good News. ***You've allowed people to become homosexual.***

And you in the media allow Satanic people to take the airwaves. We are more satisfied with garbage than the Lord God. May his mercy cover all of you. Do we have a new call?

THE KINGS

Soon we were inundated with phony phone callers who followed Janks's lead. One of them happened to be Alice Cooper's road manager. He was the first listener to follow my lead and dub himself King. He called himself **THE KING OF ALL VCRs,** since he spent a great deal of his time recording programs on his five VCRs.

For a while, the King of All VCRs was incredibly active. He regularly hit Larry King. He once called Larry on the international line and posed as a Dane to ask Cindy Crawford if she

would ever consider having plastic surgery to look like Howard Stern. When Larry King had an HIV positive woman on who was prominent in the Bush reelection campaign, the King of All VCRs called up posing as a HIV positive homosexual. When he got on the air, he asked her why, as a gay man with AIDS, he should vote for Howard Stern. Larry King got so flustered that he went, "Ignore that call. But let's ask that question. Why should people vote for Howard Bush? I mean, George Bush."

THE KING OF ALL VCRs unleashed a flood of imitators. Everywhere you looked, some phony phone caller was calling himself KING OF SOMETHING. One guy would just record other people's phony phone calls and call them in. He named himself KING OF ALL RECORDERS. There was a KING OF ALL EAST COAST VCRs. A guy named KING OF ALL SOUNDBITES specialized in calls where he'd make the Howard Stern mention and then play a succession of soundbites from my show. One guy even called himself the KING OF ALL SUBPOENAS because he was engaged in a bitter divorce battle with his wife and she had tried to subpoena his phony phone call tapes to prove to the judge that he was too sociopathic to get custody of their children.

My King, Bob of Bowie

It was an anonymous caller who made the one phony phone call that propelled the Howard Stern calls into national prominence. It happened when Ross Perot visited the *Today* show on June 11, 1992. Katie Couric, the host, went to the first caller:

KATIE: The caller is Bob of Bowie, Maryland. And he has a two-part question.

CALLER: Mr. Perot, is it realistic to believe an outsider can go to Washington and convince the Congress to make major changes in the government? And secondly, **HAVE YOU EVER HAD THE DESIRE TO MINDMELD WITH HOWARD STERN'S PENIS?**

KATIE: All right, thank you very much. Not a great second question. . .

The reaction was instantaneous! Every newspaper in the country reported the exchange the next day. TV commentators decried the perversity of the "Howard Stern callers." But what was worse, my father called me that night and bawled me out.

"What are you doing?! Don't you know that that man could be president of the United States? Do you want to cultivate an enemy like that?" he lectured me. My father must have been high. I had nothing to do with that call.

The next day, I asked the caller to call into my show. He did. He was a little shocked by the reaction. He said he knew he was going to do a prank call but that the penis mindmeld question just came to him spontaneously. He also asked Gary, off the air, if he was going to win anything for his call. He was angling for a CD player. We should have given him one. But we're too cheap.

We never heard from him again.

The King of All Messengers

The King of All Messengers is, in many ways, the most unique of all these guys. First of all, he's in his fifties. He's married with two kids. He owns his own messenger service. He's got a relatively expensive art collection. To look at him, you'd think he had a life. But in reality, he drives to work, does his payroll, and then goes straight home to his basement. Sound familiar?

But at least I get paid. He puts on his King of All Messengers hat and T-shirt and he turns on his satellite dish. Then he sits and makes phony phone calls.

The King of All Messengers has his own unique style. He's the kinder, gentler phony phone caller. He won't shout out obscenities. He asks very long-winded, literate questions, throwing in as many names as he can from the show. Then he'll shout out "Baba Booey" in rapid, machine-gun-fire attack style.

The King of All Messengers got the most notoriety from a

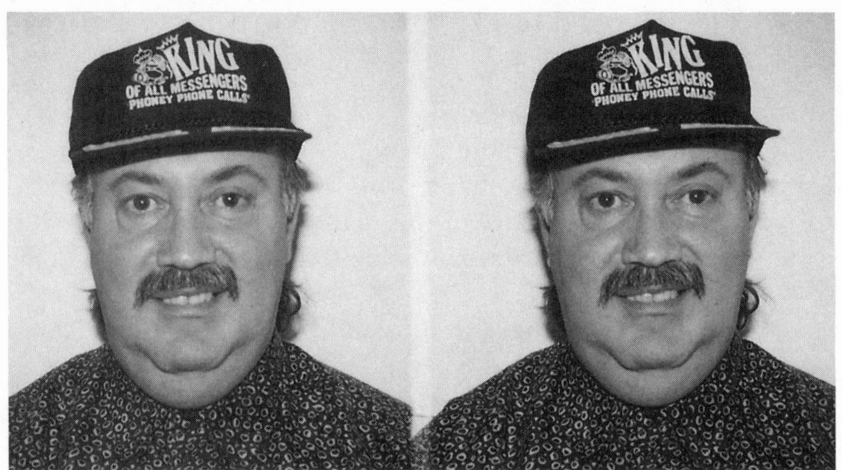

phone call he made to CNN during the aftermath of the World Trade Center explosion. He had been on the line, waiting to prank *Sonya Live,* when they broke for coverage of the bombing. Despite his moral qualms, he stayed on the line and got through to CNN. The rest is history:

ANCHOR: . . . people trapped in the rubble. A number of . . . what? Excuse me, Gary Dellamonte is on the phone. He's stuck in the World Trade Center. Gary?

KOAM: Hello.

ANCHOR: Where are you?

KOAM: I'm in Building Number 2. I work for a customhouse broker, and there were reports of a gas leak. That's what we heard . . . and we felt the explosion up on the eightieth floor.

ANCHOR: Eightieth?

KOAM: And we heard that the gas was from Howard Stern's Fartman movie.

ANCHOR: Say again?

KOAM: We felt the gas was from Howard Stern's Fartman movie.

ANCHOR: Oh, I see.

KOAM: They're filming that here . . .

ANCHOR: Well, that's another element. We have not been able to determine either through emergency services or anyone else what caused the explosion, but that's all being looked into. Are you still on the eightieth floor?

KOAM: Yes, I am.

Any human being who wasn't a trained puppethead would have hung up by now. This proves that anchorpeople don't listen.

ANCHOR: We understand the building is being evacuated. Why are you not evacuated?

KOAM: Well, I wanted to call. I was looking to see if I could speak to Stuttering John and Baba Booey.

ANCHOR: Well, we don't know those folks. [Obviously, not a fan of my show. Prick.] But we do understand that the building is being evacuated, and some people on the upper floors like yourself may not be willing to evacuate because of smoke and darkened stairwells. Can you verify that?

Of course, he couldn't. He had already been disconnected by somebody at CNN who had half a brain. But that call was awesome enough to win our F-Emmy that year for Best Phony Phone Call. We gave the F-Emmy to the King of All Messengers just to get Captain Janks crazy. It worked. Janks started a feud with the King of All Messengers that lasted for months. Janks enlisted

another prankster, ***the King of All Song Parodies,*** to call the King of All Messengers at work, posing as an FCC employee:

KOA SONG PARODIES: Chris? My name is David Gill and I'm from the Federal Communications Carrier Bureau. We're calling to inform you that you are in violation of Federal Statute 127J. If convicted, you may have to pay up to $8,000 in fines and/or serve up to six months in a Federal prison. We have a phone log of over 70 calls that you've made to a variety of different stations between December 11th and February 8th interrupting the public airwaves. You go by the name of either the King of All Messengers and/or Captain Janks.

KOA MESSENGERS: Me? Not me? (NERVOUS) How did you get my name?

KOA SONG PARODIES: We obtained a federal court order. You usually don't have to go to jail, but you can end up paying a big fine.

KOA MESSENGERS: For what? I haven't made any calls. I don't make calls.

KOA SONG PARODIES: Well, we have a lot of tapes that say differently. We have a tape where you call CNN allegedly from the Twin Towers. And these are all in reference to the Howard Stern radio show.

KOA MESSENGERS: I think you're mistaken.

KOA SONG PARODIES: And you go by the name of King of All Messengers, Captain Janks, King of VCRs . . .

KOA MESSENGERS: Not me. (STUTTERING) Uh, not me. I think you have the wrong person.

KOA SONG PARODIES: We have people at the radio station who have confirmed that it is in fact you.

KOA MESSENGERS: Who did you talk to?

KOA SONG PARODIES: Steven Grillo, Michael Gange . . .

KOA MESSENGERS: Strange, I don't know those people.

The King of All Song Parodies hinted that all charges would be dropped if the King of All Messengers cooperated and ratted on the other phony phone callers. But, to his credit, the KOAM just kept denying his involvement. Right after the call, he made a frantic call to Baba Booey to find out if he had committed any crime by making prank calls. He didn't find out that he had been scammed until he heard his call on the air. He was such a good sport about the whole episode that Captain Janks called off the hostilities and they are once again united with a single purpose: to drive every talk show host in America crazy by mentioning my name.

PONCE DE LA PHONE

Ponce de la Phone is one of the second generation phony phone callers. And, judging by a consensus of the scammers themselves, next to Captain Janks, he's the best. Ponce is a twenty-one-year-old Hispanic college dropout from Alhambra, California, who wanted to raise the level of phone graffiti

to new artistic heights. Unlike the older, more staid King of All Messengers, Ponce likes to work rude. He's tormented Charles Grodin a number of times about **his bad rug**. He's asked both Daisy Fuentes and Kathleen Sullivan if they wanted HOWARD STERN'S MEAT. Interestingly enough, Kathleen hung up on him in disgust, but Daisy seemed interested. ***I'll call her as soon as Alison dies.***

Ponce is best known for a remarkable innovation in the phony phone call technique. Ponce has taken tapes of my father yelling at me as a child and cut them up. He has actually managed to use these cuts in his phony phone calls. His first call was to a black cable show:

HOST: Ben, from Pasadena.

BEN STERN: I don't want any foolish answers from you. Otherwise, don't answer.

HOST: OK, Ben. From Cal . . . you're from . . .

BEN: I don't . . . well, how do you feel about religious services, and why children should attend them?

HOST: Where?

BEN: (SCREAMING) SHUT UP, SIT DOWN!!
(THEY HANG UP)

HOST: OK, we've got a *loco loco* here.

Ponce has done amazing things with soundbites from my show. He's used my voice to call into a local show about cable TV. He's called in to a Korean cable show as Jackie and apologized for the Jessica Hahn bathtub incident. Once, he called an astrology show as Robin:

MALE HOST: We're going to go to line one, Robin in Santa Monica, who's been waiting patiently.

ROBIN: I think I'm not of this planet.

MALE HOST: Oh, okay.

FEMALE HOST: You and Howard Stern, huh?

Ponce then played a tape of Robin's laugh, repeated endlessly on a loop. I loved that call so much, I played it four times in a row.

I like Ponce because not only is he creative, but he can think fast on his feet. One time he called a local show that deals with cable TV problems. After my mention, the host threatened him:

PONCE: **WOULD YOU EAT HOWARD STERN'S TOE CHEESE OR WOULD YOU RATHER STICK YOUR HEAD BETWEEN ROBIN QUIVERS'S BREASTS?**

HOST: Wait, wait. Oh, man. Do you believe this? A Howard Stern caller. I'm sorry. David, find out who this person is. Line number two. Let him know that the police are actively tracing this call at this very moment. That's right. Let's bring in another call while the authorities are doing their job.

Ponce was so incensed that this host was **bullshitting** about tracing the call that he got a friend to call the same show a little later that same night and impersonate an LAPD officer:

HOST: All right, you're on the air.

FRIEND: Uh, this is Officer Rosales of the LAPD, Hollenback Division.

HOST: All right. Good deal.

FRIEND: I just wanted to make a comment. There was a young gentleman on earlier, I don't remember the exact conversation, but you told him that you were tracing the call. I just wanted you to know that it is illegal to say that over the air . . .

HOST: Is it really?

FRIEND: Oh, yes, sir.

HOST: Well, then I'm going to apologize. I've been a listener to call-in programs for many, many years and when the hosts get someone who says profanity, a lot of times the host will say their call is being traced to discourage others. If I actually said 'by the LAPD,' I must actually bend over backwards and say that is not any of the truth. Maybe it might be traced by a member of our own staff. They're looking for that caller right now. *Probably they won't find him.* But if I ever do choose to say that certain line again, maybe I should actually qualify it a little better. Officer, uh, Rosales?

FRIEND: No, this is Baba Booey.

HOST: Oh, boy. This is the problem with talk television today. We have people out there who ***don't take it seriously***. We have people who like to play games with Larry King. People who like to play pranks on Charles Grodin. People that think it's funny to fool around . . .

People like Ponce de la Phone! A TRUE GENIUS at his craft.

THE KING OF CABLE

The King of Cable is our youngest but in many ways most inventive, phony phone caller. He started sending calls to our show when he was fifteen. Like Ponce, the King of Cable is a Janks disciple. He's way too radical to enjoy the more cerebral calls of the King of All Messengers. But in his short career, he's shown tremendous versatility.

The range of his calls is truly astonishing. He's affected a Chinese accent to call a Chinese talk show and ask them HOW MUCH IT COSTS THE HOSTS TO HAVE SEX

WITH HOWARD STERN AND BABA BOOEY. He put on a great Amos and Andy voice when he called C-Span and ***told the director of the NAACP that he "smelled like Howard Stern's ass."***

The King of Cable is incredibly persistent, too. He once single-handedly disrupted a pledge drive by his local Virginia PBS station. He made so many crank calls to their pledge lines that they traced his number and were about to prosecute him until they learned he was a minor. They contacted his parents and the King of Cable was grounded. He wasn't allowed to use the family phone for two weeks.

But the King of Cable's most ingenious prank came at the expense of the Black Entertainment Television (BET). While visiting Washington, he called up the offices of BET from a plush phone booth in the Ritz-Carlton hotel. He claimed that he represented Spike Lee and that Spike wanted to make a visit to the station to promote a new film. At the last minute, the King of Cable called again and canceled the visit, claiming time pressures. He promised that Spike would call into the station soon.

After a few more calls to the station in the intervening days, he finally struck. While BET was broadcasting a live call-in show with guests Darryl Strawberry and musical star Babyface, the King of Cable called in as Spike Lee:

DARRYL: Everybody was shocked, but I had to come public with it because I wanted everyone to see how serious a drug addiction problem can be for you.

HOST: Caller, are you there?

KING OF CABLE: Yeah, wassup?

HOST: Hey, and uh, what's your name, caller?

KING OF CABLE: Hey, man. It's Spike Lee.

HOST: SPIKE LEE ON THE PHONE, Y'ALL!!! (BIG APPLAUSE FROM THE STUDIO AUDIENCE)

KING OF CABLE: Hey, Black Entertainment Television, wassup?

HOST: We all right.

KING OF CABLE: Hey, wassup, Darryl Strawberry . . . Babyface.

DARRYL: Hey, Spike.

HOST: What's on your mind, Spike?

KING OF CABLE: I'd like to tell the black youth of today to listen to Howard Stern and Baba Booey. You know what I'm saying, brother? Howard Stern's a brother. You know what I'm saying? Howard Stern's a man, brothers. Wassup?

HOST: Okay, thank you. Goodbye. That was just a tripping caller. Okay. That's all he was.

After a commercial break, even the host had to acknowledge the genius of the King of Cable. He introduced each of his guests and then he turned to the camera, "And let's give that Spike Lee impersonator a big hand. He had us fooled."

WHEN DISASTER STRIKES

We get the most reaction from the phony phone calls that our listeners make to news outlets during natural disasters. Even the on-air anchors respond most strongly to these calls. "**Now is**

NOT THE TIME FOR CALLS OF THIS NATURE," they typically say. ***Yeah, like there's a right time for those calls?*** I'm of the opinion that disaster calls actually play a worthwhile function. They point out what idiots run our media. These guys call up established news organizations like CNN, claim that they're mayors of local towns affected by the disaster and, without even checking, boom, they put them on the air.

Our callers have a field day during disasters. Janks goes crazy everytime there's a natural disaster in California. He's made calls during floods, earthquakes, fires, you name it. During the forest fires a while back, he posed as a Ventura County Fire Department spokesman and alerted the media that the fires were caused by someone burning Howard Stern's *Private Parts* book.

The King of Cable is totally prepared when disaster strikes. He knows the name of every spokesman for every public agency that deals with crises. When tornadoes threatened the Washington, D.C., area, he called News Channel Eight and told them he was a spokesman for the National Weather Service:

HOST: And now, for a look at the storms that moved through the region, we turn to Pete Morris from the National Weather Service.

KING OF CABLE: Well, it seems like the tornadoes have moved up near the Chesapeake/Cape County area. We advise everyone to go in a safe place, and we believe they'll be out of the region pretty soon. Thunderstorms will be coming in.

HOST: Okay, does that mean we're out of the woods for the rest of the night?

KING OF CABLE: That means that Baba Booey will be coming in. Baba Booey. Baba Booey. Baba Booey. Baba Booey. Howard Stern rules. You suck.

HOST: All righty. Well, certainly those things happen. Moving along to serious news tonight . . .

The King of Cable made his biggest splash when he called CNN shortly after a USAir plane crashed in North Carolina. As soon as he heard about the crash, he rushed to his room and pored over his aeronautics library. For years he had been collecting aeronautics research in anticipation of a disaster like this. He quickly got all the specifications of the plane in question. He would be prepared for any questions they might throw at him. Then he called CNN:

ANCHOR: On the phone with us now is Jim Hall of the National Transportation Safety Board. Jim, what can you tell us at this time?

KING OF CABLE: Good evening, how are you doing?

ANCHOR: Fine, thanks.

KING OF CABLE: Well, it's hectic right now. It seems the flight went down while heading into the Raleigh-Durham airport. So far we believe that there are survivors, and everyone on the plane was too busy listening to Howard Stern and Baba Booey . . .

(IN THE BACKGROUND, THE TV FLOOR CREW MOANS)

ANCHOR: Jim? Did we lose the call? We'll try to get some more information from the NTSB as the evening goes on.

One call that even I had trouble playing was Captain Janks's call right after the Oklahoma City bombing. But I realized that you cannot censor a phony phone call. Those outrageous calls are the ones that ultimately go down in memory.

In fact, Gary felt in some way responsible for Janks's call. Just earlier that day, Gary had rejected a few calls that Janks wanted to air. He told Janks that his calls just weren't up to par. Apparently, Gary drove Janks right over the edge:

CNN: I understand that we have a person who is near downtown in Oklahoma City. Howard Carr, businessman, who happened to be in the area, and joining us now by telephone. Mr. Carr, can you tell us exactly where you were and what happened when this first occurred this morning?

JANKS: Well, I own a Radio Shack next door to the Federal Building, and when we first heard the explosion, we ran outside and thought it was a sonic jet or something like that. The whole side of the building is devastated. And there's a woman lying in front of me on the ground, her leg is pretty badly damaged. The building just totally exploded. I don't understand how it happened, but I think it was the aftereffect of Robin Quivers's new book, *Quivers: A Life.*

CNN: Okay, we . . .

JANKS: Baba Booey, y'all.

CNN: Okay, thank you very much. We're going to shut that down . . .

Janks told me that to this day, some of his relatives still don't speak to him because of that call. Thank God they didn't hear the other call Janks made the day of the bombing. He also called a local Oklahoma City TV station and actually got interviewed as the Mayor of Oklahoma City. That same day, the King of Cable went on local Oklahoma TV as Congressman Frank Lucas and told the viewing audience that the suspects were Islamic men and one of them was believed to be Howard Stern.

WHAT'S AMAZING IS THAT THESE GENIUS PHONE ARTISTS CAN GO RIGHT ON THE AIR AS PUBLIC OFFICIALS AND NO ONE EVEN BOTHERS TO CHECK THEM OUT.

The King of All Rednecks

We even have a phony phone caller who specializes in calamities. He calls himself the King of All Rednecks. He's a utility worker from California. So far, he's done six phony phone calls and they've all made the air. He called as Sgt. Jack Marlow of the LAPD Bomb Squad when a bomb was found in the Glendale Galleria. He was Jack Marlow (a name I call my writer, Jackie Martling) of the South Coast Air Management District when

there was an oil refinery fire in Wilmington, California. But his funniest call came **during a freeway bomb scare.** He posed as a California Transit employee, Kenneth Kallenbach (the guy who blew smoke out of his eyes on my old WOR-TV show).

FEMALE ANCHOR: On the phone right now, a man from Cal Trans, his name is Kenneth Kallenbach, he's at the Sautel off-ramp right now. What do we know about the other side of the freeway, sir?

KING OF ALL REDNECKS: Well, the other side of the freeway should be moving shortly. But, one of the motorists had discovered what was purported to be a pipe bomb. We believe at this time it still may have been a bomb. *It was one of Chevy Chase's movies. Baba Booey. Howard Stern. Baba Booey. Howard Stern . . .*

MALE ANCHOR: Aw, get him off the air. Get him off the air. Just get him off the air.

KING OF ALL REDNECKS: *Baba Booey. Baba Booey. Baba Booey. Baba Booey. Howard Stern. Howard Stern. Baba Booey.*

Maury from Brooklyn,
the King of Them All

In my estimation, the greatest phony phone caller is a guy from Brooklyn who didn't even bother to give himself a phone name. He won't prank any call-in shows because he feels they're too easy a target. In fact, he's only made two phony phone calls in his life, both times when breaking news events have interrupted a program he was enjoying. He got so angry that he spontaneously called the TV station. Yet each call is a classic and got national coverage. Maury is a twenty-three-year-old Syrian Jew who works in his family's mail order business. To me, he's the King of Them All.

Maury's first call came during the coverage of **THE LONG ISLAND RAIL ROAD MASSACRE.** Colin Ferguson, a Jamaican, opened fire and killed or injured scores of people on the train. Meanwhile, Maury was at home with his family in Brooklyn, settling down to watch *Jeopardy!*, his favorite show. Just then, Channel 7 interrupted the show for live coverage of the Long Island Rail Road massacre. Maury was so pissed off that he called Eyewitness News. He affected a thick, obviously phony Jamaican accent.

"Hello, ABC."

"Listen, mon, I was on de train. I witnessed the whole murder," Maury said. Within seconds, he was on the air as Dexter, being interviewed by **the shriveled-up newscaster Bill Beutel:**

BEUTEL: Dexter, you were a passenger, tell me what you saw.

MAURY: Yes, I was on de train. He starts yelling, running around, shooting up all these people, the most frightening ding I ever seen in my life.

BEUTEL: Tell me more about it. What did the other passengers do? What did you do?

MAURY: All of a sudden I'm asking de man, I'm askin' him, wha' you doing this for? And him sayin', "Baba Booey, Baba Booey, Baba Booey."

BEUTEL: **What did that mean? "Baba Booey"?**

MAURY: I don't know what it mean. "Baba Booey, Baba Booey, Baba Booey." It's de most scary thing I've ever seen.

BEUTEL: What were the other people doing?

MAURY: I don't know. All he kept saying was "Baba Booey."

BEUTEL: If called upon to do it, would you be able to identify the shooter?

MAURY: No. I've got to go.

BEUTEL: That was Dexter.

Maury hung up. His brothers were cracking up. **HIS MOTHER WAS AFRAID HE MIGHT BE ARRESTED** but they all told her to calm down. Within five minutes, he was inundated with about thirty phone calls from friends of his who recognized his stupid accent. For the next few hours, there were serious news reports that the gunman had shouted "Baba Booey" as he slaughtered the passengers. ***For a few minutes, I was worried that one of my listeners had snapped and flipped his wig.*** But by the next day we realized that it had been a hoax. Even still, we got a call from an Israeli guy who thought the gunman might have been saying "Abbaboohee," which was some kind of Islamic war chant.

But Maury's next call was one of the greatest phony phone calls in history. It had all the elements that make for a home-run call:

- He got through to a network show.
- He kept them on the line for a long time.
- He got one of my mentions in.
- He used a stupid *Amos 'n Andy* black voice.
- And he got Al Michaels to explain to Peter Jennings that it was a Howard Stern call.

Yes, Maury made the infamous "I see O.J." call to ABC news during the Bronco chase.

Again, Maury had no intention of making a phony phone call. He was happy to be watching his beloved Knicks. But then NBC interrupted their coverage of the NBA playoffs to go live to the O.J. chase. Maury was so incensed that he decided to call NBC and prank them. He couldn't get through to NBC, so he looked up the ABC number that he had called when he made the Long Island Rail Road call. He reached the newsroom at ABC in New York.

"I'M A PRODUCER FOR ABC IN L.A. WE'VE GOT A NEIGHBOR OF O.J. ON LIVE REMOTE. PATCH ME RIGHT THROUGH," he screamed.

The person who answered the phone hesitated.

"Listen, you got five minutes to put me through. If we're not on the air in five minutes, I'm giving this to the Chicago affiliate," he threatened. In the background, he could hear people shouting, "What? Five minutes?" Then he heard someone yell, "Patch through line seventy-six. Seventy-six, go with it."

Suddenly, another guy was on the line. This guy was determined to get the call through. I guess he thought this exclusive was going to make his career. The guy gave Maury Peter Jennings's direct line. Within seconds of calling it, Maury heard someone shout, "Go with it!" and he was live on the network with Peter Jennings:

JENNINGS: We're asking everybody to be quiet for a moment. We have on the phone with us Robert Higgins, who lives in the neighborhood, and is on the ground, and can see inside the van. Mr. Higgins?

Maury, slipped into a thick black dialect that made Kingfish seem like a Rhodes scholar.

MAURY: Uh, yes, how are you?

JENNINGS: Just about as tense as you are, sir.

MAURY: Oh, my Lord, this is quite tenses.

Right now, if Jennings wasn't a wooden Indian, he would have realized that this guy was a fake. First of all, his dialect was obviously phony. Second, a shucking and jiving black man is obviously *not* O.J.'s neighbor. All Jennings could see was his exclusive!

JENNINGS: What can you see?

MAURY: What I'm lookin' at right now, I'm lookin' at de van, and I see O.J. kinda slouchin' down, lookin' very upset. Now lookee here, he look very upset. I don' know what he gon' be doin'.

JENNINGS: Can you see him doing anything specific? Is he merely sitting there?

MAURY: He is jus' sittin' aroun', you know? Uh, jus' lookin' like he be very nervous.

JENNINGS: Can you hear anything, Mr. Higgins?

MAURY: There's jus' too much commotion. I be in the back of a news van, so I can't really hear dat good, but I can see it all. And I see O.J. I see O.J., man, and he looks scared. And I would be scared, 'cause they's cops all deep in dis.

JENNINGS: Thank you, Mr. Higgins.

MAURY: **AND BABA BOOEY TO Y'ALL.**

Look at this fuckin' puppethead. He still didn't have a clue. What's the matter with him? Doesn't he listen to my show?

JENNINGS: The driveway to the O.J. Simpson home in Brentwood. Clearly an effort to be made to have him come out of the vehicle . . . in the doorway of the house, his friend, Al Cowlings.

MICHAELS: Peter, by the way, just for the record, this is Al Michaels. That was a total farcical call. (SILENCE) Um, lest anybody think that that was somebody who was truly across the street, that was not. He said something in code at the end that's indicative of the mentioning of the name of a certain radio talk show host.

JENNINGS: Okay, thanks Al.

MICHAELS: So he was not there.

JENNINGS: Well, we have them on every coast. Thank you very much. *That's not the first time, nor the last, we will have been had.*

THE KING OF ALL PRINCES

We recently got our first overseas Howard Stern phony phone call. In some ways it surpassed even Maury's brilliant O.J. call. We have no idea who engineered this brilliant prank—he didn't want credit. All we know is that Gary received a fax from a guy in London: "I WILL BE SENDING YOU IN TWO DAYS ONE OF THE GREATEST PHONY PHONE CALLS EVER MADE. I HAVE TO REMAIN ANONYMOUS BECAUSE I WORK IN A NEWS ORGANIZATION."

It was probably Peter Jennings.

After we got the tape, we got a call from this guy. He called himself The Ambassador from London. Prince Charles had made a rare television appearance and he took some phone calls. The Ambassador, using a technique perfected by our phony phone callers, got the show on his regular line and his call waiting so he would be TWO callers in a row. We sat back and listened:

HOST: When the Sovereign dies, and if you are alive and healthy, will you lead the country?

CHARLES: I would certainly imagine so. And it's not going to be because I decide I'm not going to do it. All my life I've been brought up to try to carry out my duty to the country, to lead as well as possible.

HOST: I'm going to stop you there, I'm so sorry. If I could squeeze in one more caller. In London. Hello.

AMBASSADOR: Hello. My name is Mr. Abbooey. Bob Abooey. Am I through to Prince Charles?

HOST: Yes.

AMBASSADOR: Ah, God bless you, Your Royal Highness. I'm indeed most honored to be speaking to you on the telephone. And a very good afternoon to you as well, Jonathan.

HOST: Good afternoon. And welcome to *Any Answers.*

AMBASSADOR: Thank you. Baba Booey. (BELCHES) **EXCUSE ME, I'VE GOT A HAIR STUCK DOWN IN MY THROAT. I'VE SPENT ALL NIGHT WITH PRINCESS DIANA.**

HOST: What do you mean?

AMBASSADOR: I'm sorry—it's a very bad line. The actual question I want to put to His Royal Highness is, Baba Booey, do you think, Baba Booey, you'll ever get to be King of England?

CHARLES: Yes, absolutely.

AMBASSADOR: All right. Well, I believe very strongly that

the House of Windsor and your throne will be challenged by an under-endowed American gentlemen very, very soon. That's my theory.

HOST: When you say very soon, what do you mean, sir?

AMBASSADOR: Well, I say very soon, and I speak with some authority. I'm an Earl, and an OBE, that makes me an Earlobe, and speaking as the British Ambassador to Howard Stern, I can announce that Mr. Stern will not only be Governor of New York, but he'll become the King of England next.

HOST: What makes you say that?

AMBASSADOR: BABA BOOEY MAKES ME SAY THAT. BABA BOOEY, BABA BOOEY. PRINCESS DIANA SCREWS THE ELEPHANT MAN WITH THE QUEEN MOTHER WATCHING AND THEY DO IT WITH. . .

They cut the Ambassador off. But little did they know, he was on the next line too.

HOST: Rupert Cavanaugh, from Hampshire.

AMBASSADOR: Hello, Jonathan and Your Royal Highness. I'd just like to say that I thought that last call was an absolute disgrace. And do calls like that upset you?

CHARLES: Oh, I . . . not very much. You can't avoid something of this unfortunate nature.

AMBASSADOR: People like that are a nuisance. **My question is, why don't you stick your head up a dead bear's asshole?**

HOST: Ummm . . . let's go to Liverpool, and Rita Bellon next.

I don't think the Prince will be doing television any time soon.

"Am I in Trouble, Daddy?"

I was sitting in my basement, working on this book, when Alison came rushing down.

"It's Dial-A-Mattress on the phone. Did you just order a bed?" she asked me.

"What are you talking about? I'm writing my friggin' book. Why would I order a mattress?"

I picked up the phone. The guy had no idea it was me. It seems they had Caller ID and someone from my number had just ordered a mattress and then hung up. I told him it was a mistake and then I hung up. Then it dawned on me. I called my twelve-year-old daughter Emily and her friend downstairs.

"Emily, did you just call Dial-A-Mattress and order a bed?"

The two girls looked at each other. Then Emily, with tears in her eyes, confessed.

"Yes, we did it, Dad." I was in shock. Why was I in shock? After all, my genetic code was strong. The shocking thing is that Emily had no idea that I was the King of Phony Phone Calls. By her age, I had already logged thousands of prank calls. Endless scams. Beautiful masterpieces!! But now, I was a father. I was Ward Cleaver with a Joey Ramone haircut. I needed to teach her right from wrong.

She confessed that she and her friend had been making phone calls all day. They started out calling a disc jockey on Z-100, acting like two hot babes, asking him out on a date. They tied up his phone for hours.

Secretly, I was proud. She instinctively knew the now ancient arts. I wanted to run upstairs and make calls with them and show them my secret powers. But, alas, I was Ward Cleaver now.

Emily then told me she'd called Dial-A-Mattress, one of my dear sponsors, POSING AS A RESIDENT OF ATLANTIS (that's the underwater city for you dolts who don't read very much). She'd ordered one hundred waterbeds for her buddy King Neptune.

When the guy asked if they wanted boxsprings, too, they hung up. They didn't know what a boxspring was.

I faced a real dilemma. How could I, the King of All Phony Phone Callers, chastise my daughter for making phony phone calls? On the other hand, I couldn't let her fuck with my livelihood.

"Are we going to get in trouble now?" Emily asked.

"No, you're not in trouble. But do me a favor. Don't call Dial-A-Mattress anymore. That's one of the companies that Daddy does business with. Hassling them isn't funny," I explained. "**BUT CALL THOSE IDIOTS AT THE ZOO ALL YOU WANT.** Here's a great idea. Call the disc jockey up like you're going to make a request. Then instead of asking for a record, ask him if Johnnie's there. Do that for about twenty straight times. Then after he's totally freaked out and screaming every time you call, call him back and say, "'This is Johnny. Did I get any calls?'"

Then I changed my mind. Ward Cleaver, Ozzie Nelson, Dick Van Dyke, and Robert Young from *Father Knows Best* all flooded my mind. And so did the voice of Ben Stern:

"I TOLD YOU NOT TO BE A MORON!"

I turned to my daughter and said, **"It's kind of funny, but it's really not right to be hurting people. So I don't want you to do it again."**

I had done the right thing. I had finally risen above my basest impulses. I was Über Dad, a great teacher.

I couldn't help but reflect as my daughter and her friend left the room that they had learned a valuable lesson.

But I hadn't.

I picked up the phone and called a Gay Party line.

"Hi, I'm Robert."

CELEBRITIES

Roseanne

Jim Carrey

Tori Spelling

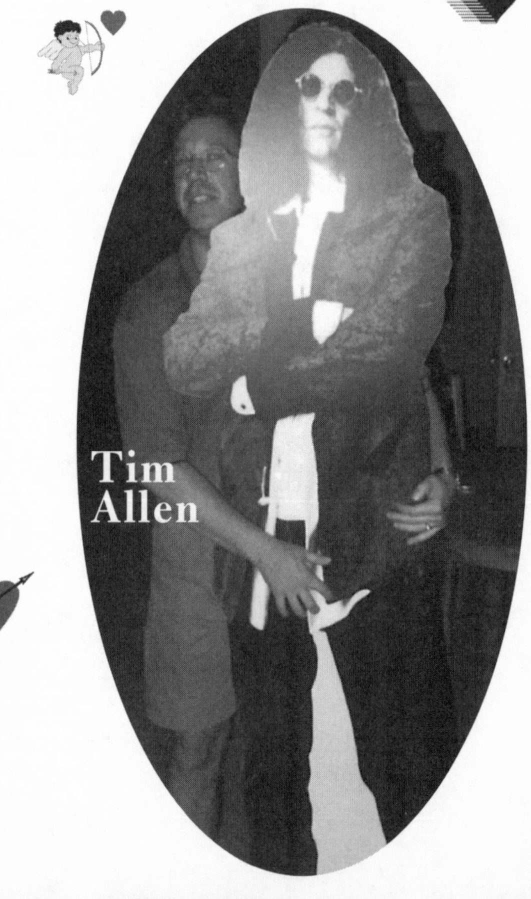

Tim Allen

I LOVE

Tom
Arnold

Nicole
Eggert

Yasmine
Bleeth

Heather
Locklear

THE STERN INQUISITION

CHAPTER 12

TOM ARNOLD

My loyal listeners must have fainted when I had both Tom Arnold and Roseanne on my show within the space of a month. We had been enjoying one of the most **bitter feuds** in the annals of show business. Tom hated me because I had identified him as the Yoko of the Nineties. He banned the entire *Roseanne* cast—even my friends like Sandra Bernhard and Sally Kirkland—from appearing on my show. Roseanne gave interviews where ***she called me "a fucking asshole, racist, sexist, homophobic fucking pig.*** He's uglier than Joey Ramone."

I really didn't know why Roseanne was so mad at me. I was the only person who was willing to call Tom a gold digger. Maybe she heard the commercial I did for Fortunoff, advertising Tag Heuer watches. These watches are so good that you can skin-dive up to six hundred feet and they still work. To prove these claims, I pretended to be Roseanne's gynecologist wearing a Tag Heuer during an exam. I put the echo chamber on.

"Hey, the watch is still ticking and **WE'RE THREE HUNDRED FEET INTO ROSEANNE.** It's still going! Four hundred, five hundred, we're six hundred feet in—and the watch is still going!

and **ROSEANNE**

(insert last name here)

NOTHING'S EXPLODED!"

I don't know about Roseanne, but Fortunoff got completely incensed.

Everything that Tom and Roseanne did became fodder for this great feud. When Roseanne surfaced with her molestation charges, I suggested that HER FATHER ACTUALLY DID HER A FAVOR, because **no one else would have touched her.** When she claimed to have been a hooker while she was still a struggling stand-up, I said I would have paid to have sex with an elephant first. When ABC threatened not to run the *Roseanne* episode that featured that infamous lesbian kiss, I got on the air and demanded that they screen that segment.

"Hey, it's amazing that they found a woman who'd kiss that water buffalo. I say 'Air it!'"

I must have bugged the shit out of Roseanne by putting her mother on the air to thank me for casting doubt on her ***SORDID INCEST STORIES.*** Then we'd regularly have Bill Pentland, her first husband, as a guest.

He was still financially involved with Roseanne, so he couldn't really give us dirt, but it was still fun to have him on while we said things like:

"Hey, did you get nose bleeds from climbing on top of Roseanne?

"Isn't balancing on top of her like making love at a party on top of a pile of coats?"

I continually made fun of the way Roseanne was polluting the airwaves of America with her no-talent husband. I particularly loved the short-lived sitcom where Tom played a dirt farmer. I got on the air and gave my version of how the plot *should* have gone:

"So Tom Arnold's a dirt farmer who can't make a living off the dirt. A lightbulb goes off over his head. 'Wait a second, there's this big, fat, ugly comedienne. She's heinous. ***She's got big, fat legs and fat, smelly everything else. I don't care. She's filthy rich and she needs a man.'*** So he goes to the Comedy Club and he nails her. IT'S HORRIBLE but at least he doesn't have to wash because he's a dirt farmer. So he's on top of her, and he's bouncing and bouncing and he bounces all the way to the moon and back. And he's going at it. Dust is flying off him. And Roseanne's digging the sex: '*Oh, Tom, this is great, you stud! I'm gonna marry you and make you a big star!* **By the way, I'm still a virgin. You missed. Keep looking. Wrong fold.'** And by the end of the show, he's so disgusted doing it with Roseanne that he digs a hole in the dirt and has sex with it."

But we really had fun when Tom and Roseanne announced their three-way marriage to Tom's sexy assistant Kim Silva. I immediately asked my wife, Alison, to check into a mental institution and then agree to our having a three-way marriage with the girl of my choice. Then I gave it to Tom. "In the privacy of her own house, she's got to sit down and have a conversation with herself. I don't know if she hears voices in her head, but she ought to talk to the voices and say, 'Is this someone who loves me?' Because **THIS IS PATHETIC. SHE IS NOW FINALLY STUPIDER THAN SHE IS FAT."**

When the whole three-way thing blew up in their faces and Tom and Roseanne separated, I was only too happy to gloat.

"Roseanne should apologize to me. So I was right all these years, calling Tom the Yoko of the Nineties. I guess after Tom chose the assistant fifty straight times over her, she got the clue. The fat was finally pulled back from Roseanne's eyes."

Now that Tom and Roseanne were publicly duking it out over their divorce settlement, I felt that it was inevitable that one of them would use my show for the ultimate fuck-you forum. "The first Arnold in is a new friend," I promised.

I guess I gave Tom the inside track after I saw *True Lies*. I got on the air and admitted that Tom was pretty good in that movie. He played well off Arnold Schwarzenegger and kept the picture going. Here everyone in America is bad-mouthing Tom, and I finally had some nice things to say about him.

About two weeks later, we had a mystery guest on the show. We determined that he was in an action-adventure film. Robin and I both guessed that it was Keanu Reeves. You can imagine my surprise when I took off my mask and there was Tom, sitting in my studio.

"Gary, erase all the old tapes of things I've said about Tom," I began, backpedaling on the run. "This is the biggest slap to Roseanne's face. He must be ready for a divorce. Actually, Tom, this will be most shocking to Roseanne because Roseanne hates me, right?" I said. A shrewd maneuver to imply that Tom was my friend.

"I don't know that she hates you . . ." he mumbled.

"She has said she thinks you're talented," Robin reminded me.

"And you said nice things about her," Tom suggested.

"I did." I remembered. Except for liking *True Lies* **I couldn't remember one nice thing I ever said about Tom.** But operating on the assumption that the first one in was my friend, I demanded that Roseanne gladly give half of her assets to Tom.

"You're entitled to half of Roseanne's money, fair and square. Women can't have it both ways. Tom is now a multimillionaire and that's the bottom line!"

Every time I tried to get Tom going off on Roseanne, he deflected my opening. He said Rosie was a fun person, Rosie was brilliant, and he fell in love with the whole package. I asked him about her twenty-seven personalities, and he said that was true of all women.

All he had were nice things to say about her.

Except that **he was saying all these things with a *hot, luscious, twenty-one-year-old broad on his lap* at the time.** Her name was Julie, and Tom had met her at the Viper Room in L.A. They had been going all around the country since that meeting, helicoptering backstage at Woodstock '94, fun stuff like that. She was a knockout, sitting there with her little belly shirt exposing a sleek, firm, just-past-her-teens physique. WHAT A FUCKING BURN ON ROSEANNE.

A few hours later, Gary got a call from Allan Stephan, a friend of Roseanne's. He started pumping Gary for information about what Tom said on the show, and then finally he asked Gary to hold on. After a few seconds, Roseanne came on the line.

"Yeah, me and my new boyfriend are taking a helicopter to Altamont," she cracked.

"That fucking prick."

"It wasn't that bad, he didn't say anything bad about you," Gary said.

"Oh, I love Rosie so much." Roseanne imitated Tom. *"Rosie's the greatest."*

"Are you upset with what he said?" Gary asked innocently.

"No, you fucking moron," Roseanne cracked. ***"I'm happy as a pig in shit!"***

Amazing—it only took her two seconds to figure out that Gary was a moron. I always said she was smart.

Alan requested a videotape of the show, probably for Roseanne's lawyers. Then he promised that Roseanne would come in and do the show.

True to her word, Roseanne came in a few weeks later. "This would only be a bigger event if JFK himself came in," I said as Gary ushered Roseanne and Allan Stephan into the studio.

It took a little while to break the ice. Roseanne and I were like old gladiators, wary of the other's punching ability. We circled each other slowly.

"I'm staring at Roseanne, saying, 'Is this moment really real?'"

"Tom would get transcripts of the show, and I'd read 'em and I'd think they were funny. I laughed at them a lot, and he would get really upset," Roseanne said.

"You blasted me in the newspapers," I said, like I was the victim.

"I had intense rage that year, and I was faxing the meanest things about everybody. It made me feel better." She smiled.

"I liked when you said things about me," I admitted. "It's kinda complimentary."

"LIKE WHEN I SAID YOUR FANS WERE PLUMBERS MASTURBATING IN THEIR TRUCKS ON THE WAY TO WORK?" Roseanne laughed.

"But you were right," I said.

"I should know, I was married to several of them," Rosie said.

"I always thought you were the most talented. Let's be honest, I made fun of your weight because I'm not bright," I said.

"And I made fun of your face, and it's the obvious thing to do," Rosie observed.

"How you fell in love with Tom is unbelievable to me. I saw it, the whole world saw it. He was not the guy for you. All the sycophants in Hollywood wouldn't tell you, except me. When did it finally dawn on you that this guy didn't love you?" I persisted.

"Who knows . . . ?" Rosie sighed.

"Are you dating your brains out now? Having good sex?"

"I have a really good boyfriend."

"And he really gives it to you?" I asked.

"Gives me what?"

"Sex."

"*Sex?*"

"Intercourse. *Coitus.*"

"He's very sweet, and, yeah, he's real good," she finally admitted.

"All three inputs?" I had long dreamed for the day when I'd get to ask Roseanne that question.

"Oh my. *What* did he say?" She played dumb.

"I was wondering if he uses every opening he can get his hands on. In other words, is all of you available if a guy goes to bed with Roseanne? Is the sky the limit?"

"I refuse to answer that," she said.

"I can't believe it. You're so open usually," I said.

"Well, I'm very happy. Does that say it?"

"We had Tom in here with his girlfriend—" Roseanne cut me off.

"Don't talk to me about him," she said.

"Why? Can't handle it?"

"Well, the more I talk about him, the more money I'll probably have to give him."

We were bonding. Before long, Roseanne admitted that she had had sex with Sam Kinnison and that she doesn't use a vibrator when she masturbates.

"Do any of your personalities want to kick me in the balls?" I wondered.

Roseanne said no, and that's when I knew that our rapprochement was a fait accompli. We even kissed and hugged, and then she left the studio.

My audience flooded the fax lines.

Unbelievable! I have new respect for Rosie.

Howard, this has been the greatest show ever.

Howard, go brush your teeth. They must be brown from all the ass kissing.

CHEVY CHASE

Since my last book, Chevy's done really well for himself: He was pulled over by the Beverly Hills cops for **driving drunk**. His blood alcohol level was .18, more than the legal limit in California to operate a vehicle—it was also double his Fox ratings for that ***failed late-night show he did for twenty minutes.*** I couldn't believe the judge ultimately let him go with a slap on the wrist. **They should have beaten him twice as hard as they did Rodney King.** Hey, put that out on video, I'll bet you it grosses a lot more than *Cops and Robbersons.*

QUESTIONS I ASKED LOU DIAMOND PHILLIPS AFTER HIS WIFE LEFT HIM FOR MELISSA ETHERIDGE:

1. When your wife first went lesbo, did you smell it on her breath?
2. **Did you smack her around when she told you?**
3. Did the marriage counselor you both went to start giggling when you told him the story?

JOHN WAYNE BOBBITT ON REALIZING HIS DICK WAS JUST CUT OFF:
"I opened my eyes, barely, and I see Lorena sitting there and I felt a jerk, a pull. I sprung up like **'Wow, this hurts.'** I wanted to scream but nothing came out. I caught her leaving out of the corner of my eye. Then I looked down and I said, 'Shit!'"

WHY WILLIE NELSON IS A GREAT GUEST

When I asked Willie if he ever got caught cheating on one of his wives, he smiled.

"Yes, I have. So I said to her, 'Are you gonna believe what you see or what I tell you? I know what you think you see.' But **my first wife tried to beat me up.** She found me. I came home drunk one night and passed out in the bed. She wrapped the sheet around me and took a needle and thread and sewed it up meticulously. Then she took a broomstick and started beating the hell out of me. I woke up, and there's a lot of white things coming at me. BANG, BANG, BANG. Then she packed all my clothes and left. So when I finally tore my way out of the sheet, there I was, buck naked with no clothes. So that's why you never should do these things."

Hey, sex stories and a public-service announcement at the same time. What more do you want from a guest?

HOW I WOULD HAVE CONVICTED

LORENA BOBBITT

If I were the prosecutor, Lorena Bobbitt would be in prison for life right now. I would have been in front of that jury slicing up bananas, salamis, hot dogs, whatever. I would have beaten that jury into submission. I would have asked them, *"How many of your sons have penises?"*

ALEC BALDWIN

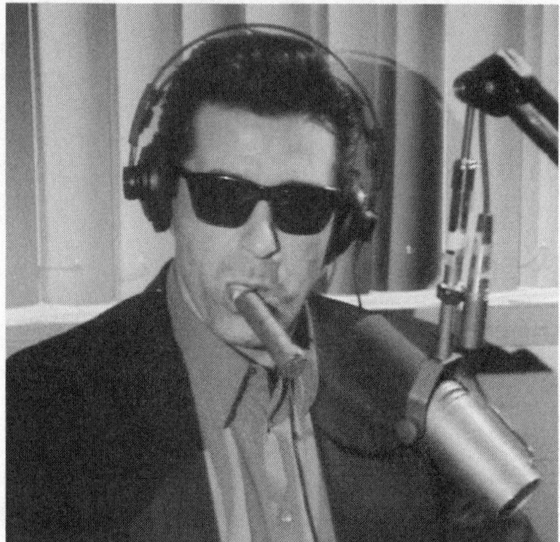

I'm thrilled that he's a huge fan of our show. He's smart, articulate, and socially conscious—but most important, he's married to one of the greatest pieces of ass on the planet. Oh, what I would do to that Kim Basinger. In fact, whenever Alec's on the show, we have this cat-and-mouse game. He wants to talk about funding the National Endowment for the Arts or supporting PETA—People for the Ethical Treatment of whatever.

Me, ***I JUST WANT TO TALK ABOUT WHAT IT'S LIKE TO FUCK HIS WIFE.***

He was a hard nut to crack, but Alec finally came in to promote *The Shadow*. As soon as he entered the studio sporting Ray-Bans and smoking a big fat Cuban cigar, I had him.

"You are a big star. Wait a second, don't say a word yet. **Let me see if I can smell Kim**, right from here. ***Mmmmmm."***

"Right to the groin, right away. You're a pig, Howard," he said.

I let him babble a little about *The Shadow* and then I struck.

"Are you faithful to Kim?"

"I am."

"You never even *look* at any other women?" I was incredulous.

"Never. Never. Never. Never look at other women."

"There is a certain joy to having a woman put her hand down your pants for the first time. Do you know that joy?" I asked.

"Uhh . . ." Alec was stunned. He tried to change the subject.

"Let me smell your hand. I'll give you five dollars right now. Hey, did Kim ever have sex with a black man?"

Alec groaned.

"I think I may have hit something, Robin," I gloated.

"Jesus, Mary, and Joseph . . . There's a board in this studio with words that light up. That just lit up on the board: 'Sex with a black man.'"

"Was she a lover of Prince?"

"I have no idea," he laughed.

"You didn't ask?"

"You know what it's like when you're in love with somebody? Everybody that went before doesn't matter. That's how you stay in love. Do you tell your wife about the other women when you're laying in bed?"

"Of course," I said. "It's the only thing that gets her off."

"I'm working from another manual entirely, Howard."

"So you never asked about Prince? You didn't find a purple condom or anything?"

"So ugly, so ugly," Alec moaned.

"Will she ever dress up in outfits to make you aroused?"

"Now it's games you're into, Howard?"

"Yeah, you ever handcuff her to the bed? I'd like to handcuff your wife to a bed."

"You ever play dead girl by the side of the road?" Alec asked. He was getting into this. "You're like a logger in the Northwest woods. And you're driving your truck along and there's a car accident on the side of the road. ***AND YOU PULL OVER AND YOU MAKE LOVE TO THIS DEAD GIRL'S BODY."***

"Oh, really! Kim does this with you?"

"Sure."

"And she'll . . ."

"NO, SHE DOESN'T . . ." he tried to backtrack.

"Oh yes, she does," I insisted.

"Ever play best friend's mommy?" Alec was showing his true colors. "You're a little boy and you go to Tommy's house to have lunch. And Tommy's not there yet and ***his mommy seduces you."***

"No kidding!

"Did you last a long time the first time you nailed Kim? Be honest. **YOU EXPLODED FAST, RIGHT?"**

Alec cracked up.

"Oh, come on," I persisted. "When there's a knockout human Barbie doll lying there doin' stuff? And she was very loving in the sense that she's never had to really put out that much because she is so good-looking . . ."

"You are just filled with these predispositions about people's stamina and Barbie dolls lying in beds. It's unbelievable," he said.

"Come on. This Kim Basinger's the best-looking girl on the planet. I got to learn about this. You say you can hold out? ***And Kim doesn't just lie there like a lox.*** She puts out. She cares about pleasing you."

"What do you want me to say, Howard? Do you want the truth or a good show?"

We took a vote. It was three votes for the truth. Two for a good show. But Alec didn't care.

"She was an animal, Howard. It was like being in the bed with the entire circus—**FLIPPING, TOSSING, ROLLING, BOUNCING, FIRE, ANIMALS, LEASHES, WHIPS."**

That probably meant he exploded in two seconds.

"Your wife is fantastic. Oh, that movie, *9 1/2 Weeks*. ***I'D LIKE TO DRAG HER BY THE HAIR RIGHT AROUND THE ROOM."***

"She's listening to this right now," Alec said. "Send out a love message to her. She's a big fan of yours."

"Look, Kim, Alec is a good-looking guy, but let me tell you what I'd do to you. If I had you in the sack, what I don't have in my pants . . ."

"This is a selling point?" Robin interrupted.

"I'm being up-front with you. When I take my pants down, you're going to be a little shocked," I warned her.

"YOU GOT HER, HOWARD," Alec cheered me on. "REEL HER IN, MAN. BRING IT OVER THE TRANSOM, BABE!"

"If I had you in the sack, first I'd handcuff you to the bed. Feet completely spread apart . . ."

"That's just pro forma with you?" Alec interrupted.

"You're spread-eagle. I'll have nine-and-a-half tongues. Start at the feet and move up the legs. I'll be all over you and then when you're aching for you know what, I'll walk out of the room—now you're in a psychological sweat. And believe me, ***IF I CAN'T SATISFY YOU WITH WHAT'S IN MY PANTS, I'LL USE ONE OF ALEC'S CIGARS.*** Look at the size of that cigar!"

I slumped down in my chair and caught my breath. I had just seduced Kim Basinger, with the assistance of her husband.

JIM CARREY

I liked Jim Carrey when he was on *In Living Color*. But when I saw those ads for *Ace Ventura* I went on the air and predicted it would be a big bomb.

It opened to $23 million. Biggest hit of the year.

When I finally saw it on video, I loved it. Since I'm a big man in at least one respect, I got on the air and admitted I was wrong, that Jim Carrey was brilliant, and he carried the movie. Jim was so appreciative that he came into the studio to promote *The Mask*.

"Ahh, big star, big star, Jim Carrey," I greeted him. "Listen, how did you have such great timing to **dump your wife** right before you got $7 million for *The Mask*?"

"Well, I woke up one morning, and I looked over at her, and I just thought, ***'I WISH HER BUTT WAS HAIRIER,'"*** Jim started lisping. "I realized that I was living a lie. If I wanted that I'd go to the seaquarium, know what I mean?"

JULIETTE LEWIS

Is this girl sexy or what? She's not typically pretty, but she looks like a real fucking hose bag. ***MAN, I'D LIKE TO FUCK HER, CHOP HER HEAD OFF, AND THROW IT OUT THE WINDOW.***

She called in when she heard me talking about what a hot bod she had.

"Sometimes," I said, "I see you as ugly, but I want to do stuff to you that would knock the ugly out of you and make you beautiful. Know what I'm saying?" How could she? *I* didn't know what I was saying.

"I'd approach you from the back like a tiger. Ever see those animal programs?" I asked her. "Why don't you come in here? I'd have some sex with you on the air. I'd give you rug burns. I'd take you by the hair and drag you around." I was out of control. "You ever do two guys at one time?"

"That's not even an interest of mine," she demurred.

"I'm like being with two guys at the same time. I'm like an octopus. I could be working the top of ya and the bottom of ya. Ever get into lesbianism?"

"No. Get off the sex subject. It's so boring."

"Are you into autoerotic asphyxiation?"

"What the hell's that?"

"That's where I tie myself up and choke myself to the point where I'm almost dead . . . you know what? I'd tie you up and you'd be naked, spread-eagle on the bed and then I'd . . ."

Now that's what I call seduction. She hung up on me, and I never heard from her again.

MARK HARRIS, MR. MARTHA RAYE

Mark Harris is probably one of my top-five all-time great radio guests. Mark is so flamboyantly homosexual that ***you become gay just listening to him.***

What's great about Mark was that he wouldn't admit he was gay the first few times he came on. I guess that was because he had recently married Martha Raye, the **aging comedienne,** and he didn't want to fuck up the inheritance. About his fourth visit, under relentless interrogation, he admitted that he was "bi." I suggested that meant **he liked both men and boys.**

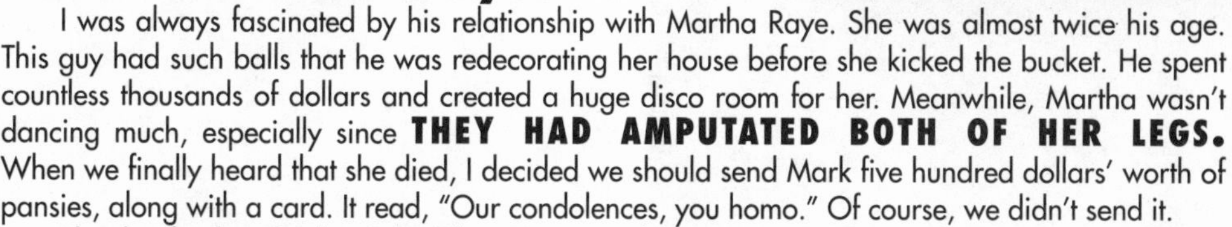

I was always fascinated by his relationship with Martha Raye. She was almost twice his age. This guy had such balls that he was redecorating her house before she kicked the bucket. He spent countless thousands of dollars and created a huge disco room for her. Meanwhile, Martha wasn't dancing much, especially since **THEY HAD AMPUTATED BOTH OF HER LEGS.** When we finally heard that she died, I decided we should send Mark five hundred dollars' worth of pansies, along with a card. It read, "Our condolences, you homo." Of course, we didn't send it.

Shortly after her death, we had the grieving widow in.

"You will now get the mother lode—at least a million dollars from Martha Raye," I suggested. "All that from ***ONE QUICK SCHTUP.*** You only made love to Martha Raye once."

"Twice," Mark corrected.

"Up and down," Jackie said.

"When was the second time?" I asked.

"Who remembers? There's so many things in my mind," Mark said.

"When you make love to a ninety-year-old woman, you remember," I said.

"Will you let her rest?" he hissed.

"Did you make love to her after her legs were removed?"

"NO!" he said.

"Was she awake when you did it?"

"She was well awake."

"Did you need grease?"

"What kind of grease? Poli-Grip? We didn't need grease, and we didn't use K-Y jelly either," he said.

"I have a forty-year-old wife, she needs grease. At seventy-five, that's a crack in the sidewalk. Be honest," I said.

"You need motor oil," Robin added.

Mark was out the door because he was scheduled to have his testicles lifted.

JAMES GARNER ON HOWARD STERN:

"Howard Stern is the epitome of trailer trash. **He's absolute slime.** Every time I see him, I'd like to slap him in the mouth and say, 'You sit down, little boy, and shut up.'"

HOWARD STERN ON JAMES GARNER:

"I can't believe this guy wants a war with me. ***HE SHOULD BE BUSY WORRYING IF HE'S GONNA HAVE A SOLID BOWEL MOVEMENT."***

ME AS SATAN TRYING TO SEDUCE KATHIE LEE

"Come to me, Kathie Lee. You know you want me. **Hold my horns and ride me.** Don't you want Satan's baby? Put my tail in a bad place. I love you, Kathie Lee. **I LOVE THE EMPTY BEACH BALL THAT SITS ON YOUR NECK.** Satan loves phonies, and you are the Queen of All Phonies. Arrrrgh. Yes, Kathie Lee. I will pump you full of evil. YES, TAKE IT ALL. Put your mouth on Satan's worst place and ***accept his wet gas.*** It is Satan's aphrodisiac.

"Kathie Lee, this Halloween, dress as a witch and put the broomstick in Satan's favorite spot, bristles first, and ***fly all around the Tristate area.*** You know you're attracted to me because I have more scales than anyone except Giff. Does Giff eat Branola in between his monthly colon checkups? Sleeping with Satan is better than going through one of his coloscopies. Come to me. I'll make your eyes roll to the back of your head. *I WILL BECOME A BACTERIA AND VISIT YOU IN PLACES PERVERTS CAN ONLY DREAM OF."*

RUSH LIMBAUGH

When Limblow's not ***sucking up to the Republicans,*** he's shilling for Pizza Hut. He looks like that shitty stuffed-crust pizza. **JUST POKE HIM AND I'LL BET THAT GLOPPY CHEESE'LL COME OUT OF HIS EARS.**

Everything on this blimp's body resembles food:

- Each of his fat fingers are like individual salamis.
- **He's got dingleberries the size of Swedish meatballs.**
- HIS BREASTS ARE LIKE TWO LARGE PUMPKIN PIES.

I'll bet you when he gets hungry and he can't Rush to the fridge, he starts eating his own body parts. Check his underpants, **I'm sure he's got skidmarks as wide as radial tires.** Ooofah.

I personally know how much this human snowman eats. Baba Booey used to live in the same apartment building as Rush, and sometimes Gary would have to squeeze in and share an elevator with ***that fat pig.*** One time, Gary came home, and he saw a huge oversized Lincoln Town Car with the presidential seal parked out front. It was Rush's car. Rush's limo driver, this black guy with the hat and uniform, was unloading his groceries. They actually filled up one of those giant hotel luggage carts with all his D'Agostino bags.

That was only lunch.

I couldn't believe it, but Rush managed to drag himself away from the dinner table to get married recently. He wed an aerobics instructor he met while he was online on Compuserve. Any idiot knows that you have sex with girls you meet online, you don't go off marrying them. What was he thinking? Did he think this woman would have communicated with him if he was still off the radio and **SELLING SCOREBOARD ADVERTISING FOR THE KANSAS CITY ROYALS?**

(CONTINUED...)

RUSH CONTINUED...

THE STERN

I can imagine that computer courtship:

```
Dear troubled woman,
 I am a big fat know-it-all. I am typing to you on
a special keyboard for my huge fat fingers. I am
typing even though it is virtually impossible to
keep my huge head up. Did you know that my head
alone weighs 67 pounds? So, will you marry me?

RL

 P.S. I lied. I am typing this with my toes so
that my hands are free to stuff my face. Hey, have
you ever had a stuffed-crust pizza pie? Marry me and
I'll show you the right way to eat it.
```

It worked. They got married by Supreme Court Justice Clarence Thomas. **I guess he pulled himself away from his Johnny Wadd porno tapes** long enough to conduct the service. It was a short ceremony—fifteen minutes—exactly the same amount of time Rush goes between meals.

I wish I could see videotape of their wedding night. How does a woman look at that ***nude hippo*** and say, "That's for me"? Maybe she's a chubby chaser.

Still, this guy's got fat in places that don't even exist on most humans. His ass looks like the surface of Mars. **He doesn't have folds of fat on his body, he's got closets.** She must have to attach ropes to his body and mountain-climb up there to have sex with him. Then she's gotta kiss that mouth with all the smells from the food and his stinky cigars.

I'M GONNA VOMIT FOR THAT POOR WOMAN.

RICHARD JOHNSON

NEAL TRAVIS

LIZ SMITH

esday: New York's best gossip columnists every day in The Pos

NEW YORK POST

LATE CITY FINAL

DAY, SEPTEMBER 3, 1995 / Sunny and pleasant both days, 75-80 / Details, Page 22 ★★ 50

HOWARD PAYS $1.7M

Associated Press

Howard Stern

Shock jock's boss settles FCC indecency charges for cash

See Page 3

CHAPTER 13

EXTORTION

HOW THE U.S. GOVERNMENT FUCKS YOU AND ME

MAKE IT IN UNMARKED BILLS IN A PLAIN PAPER BAG PLACED IN A TRASH CAN OUTSIDE 1919 M STREET, WASHINGTON, D.C.

You ever get fucked in the ass by a wiseguy? I don't mean literally. Well, if you *did* literally get fucked in the ass, I'd be interested in hearing about it because I need to learn more about this amazing phenomenon. No way that LITTLE EXIT should be able to handle ***a big, full cock*** and yet it does. That kind of butt fucking is interesting, and maybe in my next book I'll devote a chapter to it. In this particular instance I'm talking about a different kind of butt fuck. I'm asking you, has anyone ever screwed with you real bad when you were 100 percent in the right and you still couldn't win? When you were absolutely 100 percent not guilty and **you lost anyway?**

I'll give you an example of what I'm talking about: I have a friend who's been going through a divorce for two years. They are arguing over child custody and money. She hired lawyers and private detectives but her husband keeps hiring more lawyers and outspending her and then she has to turn around and hire more lawyers and more private detectives. Her legal bill is now half a million dollars and rising and she's going to DECLARE BANKRUPTCY just to get her creditors off her back.

After two years, she has three confused kids, no child support, an endless cycle of court appearances, and she's broke. She's not a bad woman and she hasn't committed a crime. She just wants to get on with her life and raise her children. The judge couldn't give a shit that this woman is almost destitute. The judge couldn't give a damn that all of this money is being spent on lawyers and the children are living in a dump. She's a loser, her husband is a loser, the kids are losers, and the lawyers win. She's getting fucked in the ass and there ain't a person who can help her.

The whole system is set up to fuck you. Judges are former lawyers. Judges want the system to keep going so they can go into private practice and make a killing. Congress is filled with lawmakers who are former lawyers. **Seventy percent of the world's lawyers live in the United States.** We are all getting fucked in the ass, directly or indirectly, by lawyers.

I've been getting fucked in the ass since I was a mere child. I learned at a young age that sometimes no matter how right you are, you still can get fucked in the ass by a wise guy. My sister and my mother fucked me in my ass when I was six. How's that for a confession?

YOGI BEAR, MY GOD

Here's how it happened. My favorite show on television was Yogi Bear. All I wanted to do with my life when I was six was watch that goddamned bear **AND THAT HOMO BOO BOO** play tricks on that ***dumb-ass cracker***, the park ranger. Yogi was God to me. The motherfucker could steal your picnic basket and smile like he was your best friend. Life would have been a little

bit easier for young Howard if he could have watched that show every day, but my parents only had two TVs in the house. One TV was downstairs in the playroom and one was upstairs in my parents' bedroom. The one in the bedroom—or, as we called that room, Love Central—was off limits to me and my sister Ellen. My mother didn't believe in watching TV in a bedroom. Don't ask me why, but the woman had a laundry list of rules and regulations. She didn't want filthy dirty shoes and feet up on her bed. I think that was the reason. She also believed that children should not be isolated from one another.

Who the fuck knows? WHO THE HELL CARES? All I know is that Ellen and I had to share one TV. We used to fight over that TV set all the time. The two of us got along great except for the daily fight over the TV shows. I wanted Yogi Bear and my sister, who was nine, wanted to watch love movies. My dad was no Nelson Rockefeller but buying another TV would have been a small price to pay for a little peace and quiet around the house.

So I went to my mother for some help and guidance with this difficult situation. I told her I wanted to watch the fucking bear cartoons and my sister wanted love movies.

"You sit down there and work it out with your sister," my mother scolded me. "The two of you must learn to watch together."

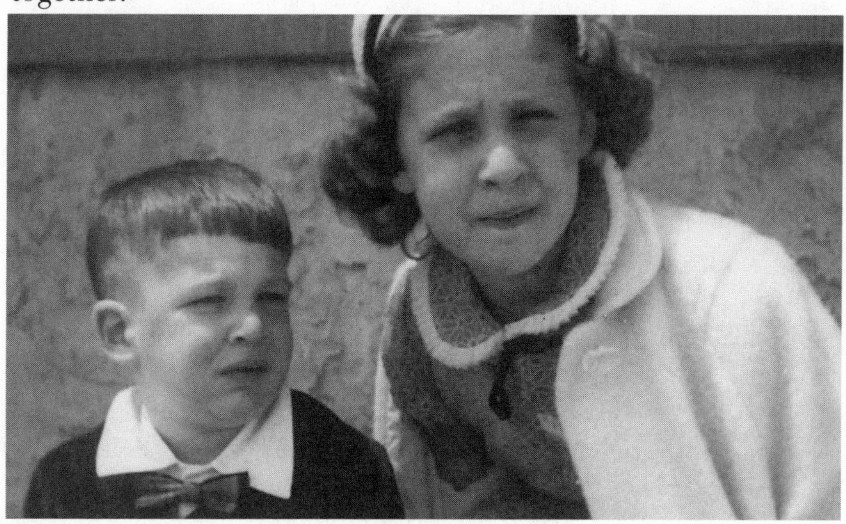

My mother was no King Solomon. That was a shitty solution. A ten-year-old girl and a six-year-old boy don't watch the same shows. Hell, the first thing I did when I had kids was put a TV in each of their rooms. I did that before I got medical insurance. Life's too short. I don't need to teach my kids to watch TV together. Shit, to this day I can't even watch TV with my wife. I want it quiet and I don't want to be hassled during my special shows. *Beverly Hills, 90210* is meant to be viewed alone. In fact, it gives me an opportunity to pretend I'm one of the 90210 gang.

So my mother laid down the law. She said I could have control of the TV for one day and then my sister would have control of the TV for the next day. Every other day I would have to watch love movies instead of Yogi Bear. That was the deal. Okay, sounded fair. So I went downstairs to watch Yogi the next morning, and it was my sisters day, but I wanted to watch my bear cartoons. I begged my sister.

"Please let me watch my fucking bear cartoons," I cried.

"No," my selfish sister said, "it's my day."

So I whined some more and finally she said, "Okay, you can watch your RETARDED cartoon today if you let me watch whatever I want for a year."

Now, I was six years old and I was not the swift negotiator I am today. So I agreed. I had no idea what a year was. Of course I gave my tricky sister a year of TV so I could watch Yogi that day, because I thought a year was like two days. I was six years old!

Six months went by. I got fed up with the arrangement and I blew my stack. I hadn't seen Yogi in ages. I ran up to my mother crying and whining and I told her that my sister tricked me. I explained the whole situation to her. I defended myself like a professional attorney. I was a regular F. U. Bailey.

"Ma," I whined. "I'm only six . I didn't know what a year was. She tricked me." You know what my mother said to me? My mother said, "Howard, you made a deal and you can't go back on your word. You have to watch whatever your sister wants."

My mother must have been **SMOKING HEROIN** because she made as much sense as Courtney Love backstage at the MTV Awards. If she'd been thinking clearly, she would have hauled my sister's ass upstairs and told her that fooling a six-year-old was a dirty, rotten trick. It was dishonest for my sister to take advantage of a baby. But my mother made a dumb-ass decision. Just like that. There was no court of appeals. No arbitration. Boom. A dopey, illogical decision with no recourse. By the time I got to see Yogi again I was too old to enjoy him. This is what I call getting a good ass fucking by a wiseguy. ***My sister and my mother fucked me in the ass.***

So, what's my point? I don't know. I knew I had a point; I just don't remember it. I'll go eat something and see if I remember my point.

Okay, I'm back. I just ate diet pizza. My wife bought a vegetable pizza with no cheese and whole wheat dough. Fucking yuppie pizza. No cheese, just tomato sauce and a bunch of vegetables. It tasted good, damnit! If it tastes good, it must be bad for you. Now I'm all freaked out that I ate something FATTENING. I'm obsessing on how I shouldn't have eaten it. Fuck it. So I'll be fat. **It's not like I have to look good for anybody. I'm married.**

Anyway, halfway through this New Age pizza I remembered my point. The point is I'm still getting fucked in the ass, but this time it's by five guys I don't even know. I can't even tell you their names or what they look like. I'M GETTING GANG **RAPED BY FIVE OLD MEN** and their dicks are going in dry and ***my bunghole is bleeding***. I'm getting the worst ass fucking in history. It's happening in front of the world and no one will help me.

Everyone knows about my stupid rape. In fact, they report about it on TV and in the newspaper. I'M TALKING ABOUT THESE SHITHEADS ON THE FCC. Five of the worst human beings Satan has ever created. Five pricks who insist on ***ending my livelihood*** because . . . because, I have no idea why. Maybe it's because they can't stand the fact that their jobs are boring, dull, and meaningless. These guys were probably the dweebs who dreamt of stardom way back in college radio but failed. By fining me, they'd see their names in print, a last shot at doing something that would get them noticed. They are bureaucrats plain and simple and you can't beat them when they target you. You can whine to millions of people, you can hire fifty fucking lawyers, and you can suck off every politician in the country, but these pricks will win. Government workers don't make a lot of money. They don't get a lot of recognition. **BUT WHAT THEY GET IS POWER. AND ONCE THEY HAVE IT IN FOR YOU THEY WILL SUCK YOU DRY OF ANY AMBITION OR INNOVATION YOU HAVE. THEY DON'T CARE ABOUT YOU. THEY DON'T CARE ABOUT THE CONSTITUTION. THEY WILL FUCK YOU. OVER AND OVER AGAIN. MOTHERFUCKER COCKSUCKERS!! I WANT TO BLOW UP MY COMPUTER I'M SO DAMN PISSED!A;LKJDJ;TEUETOIFOKNJ;'IUR;—— I'm throwing a tantrum.**

YOU WORK SIX MONTHS A YEAR FOR UNCLE SAM

Look, we have a government that is out of control. You know it's true. We are working six months out of the year for Uncle Sam—six months! Half our paycheck out the window and we don't even know what they're doing with the money. And don't ask what they're doing with the money or they'll put you under surveillance. Why do you think people are scared of the government? What do you make of that Randy Weaver case? This dude Randy Weaver is a small-time guy. ***Just a regular dopey guy*** who is real antisocial and decides to move his family to some remote place and live on a mountain. He goes around town screaming about the Jews 'cause he's a white supremacist, but it's not like he's the head of the Ku Klux Klan or anything. He's just running around screaming about everyone. **Hey, what's wrong with screaming about the Jews?** I get paid a lot of money for that.

The feds get wind of it and they run an undercover operation on him for years and then, when the guy is almost broke, they persuade him to sell them two sawed-off shotguns. They beg him and he finally breaks down and agrees. Now that he's sold two guns they go up to his mountain and kill his ninety-pound asthmatic only son, the family dog, and his wife, while she's holding a little baby in her arms.

That's called Government Out of Control. It was all unnecessary. Who gave a shit about a **harmless loudmouth** like Randy Weaver? A bunch of nutty bureaucrats, that's who.

But when the government has it in for you, you can ***kiss your ass goodbye***. Don't expect any help because, buddy, they will get you. Randy Weaver, at least, is getting a congressional investigation. ME, I CAN'T GET SHIT. I WANT A FUCKING CONGRESSIONAL INVESTIGATION. WHY WON'T ANYBODY TAKE ME SERIOUSLY? OH, OOOHHHHH!,FAD'AJKDFSA;'ADF;LK JASDF;JK —another fucking tantrum.

HOW THE FCC FUCKED ME

The FCC went after me, boy, and I fought back and they fucked me worse. How did they fuck me? Okay. Okay. Here you go. Try to follow this: Nobody seems to understand any of this, and I'm gonna spell it out so even a retard could follow it.

1. They fine Infinity, the company I work for, because I said "LESBIANS FILLED WITH LUST" on the air. WHEN A GUY PLAYED THE PIANO WITH HIS PENIS, they fined Infinity some more.
2. Infinity refuses to pay these ridiculous fines. They say to the FCC: "We want to go to court."

3. Instead of taking Infinity to court, the FCC decides to fuck with the company behind the scenes.
4. THIS IS TOTALLY UNCONSTITUTIONAL. Legally, the company did nothing wrong, but every time my company tries to buy radio stations, the FCC LOSES the paperwork. Every time a bunch of minorities challenges the station's license, the FCC pays attention to the minorities. Infinity ends up paying off the minorities—**AND WE'RE TALKING MILLIONS OF DOLLARS.**

How's that, motherfucker? See any constitutional problems with this? The company did *nothing legally wrong* and the government went after them. Am I any fucking different than Randy Weaver getting harassed? Where is my congressional investigation? Isn't that Government Out of Control? There isn't an American around who doesn't think the government was out of control at Waco and, boom, there's a congressional investigation. *Why the hell is everyone sitting back and letting me get fucked over?* I represent the whole damn freedom-of-speech issue. I have a right to say "vagina." Don't you think I should be allowed to say "vagina"? If I can't say "vagina," soon *you* won't be able to say it. ***Don't give up the right to say "vagina."***

I want to say "penis." Oprah, Phil, and fucking Ricki Lake say "penis." *I have rights, don't I?*

Ahhhh, what's the use?

Are you still reading this or did you skip over to the dirty parts, **you rat Jap bastard?** I don't think you are following the severity of all this, so I'm going to give you a pop quiz to see if you know anything.

THE INDECENCY QUIZ

Here's a test about my stupid problems with the FCC. Answer the questions properly and you can move ahead in this story. Flunk and you have to come down to the station and let me paint your genitals green.

1. HOW MANY TIMES WAS I FINED BY THE FCC?
(a) 3
(b) 7
(c) 43
(d) 0

ANSWER: (d) 0. I was never fined by the FCC. The company I work for, Infinity Broadcasting, was fined. PAY ATTENTION!

2. WHAT WAS I DISCUSSING WITH ROBIN WHEN THE FCC DECIDED TO ARBITRARILY FINE ME A HALF-MILLION DOLLARS?
(a) Putting ice cubes up my ass
(b) Blowing air in my wife's vagina during pregnancy to kill her
(c) The relative merits of shaving vs. waxing pubic hair

ANSWER: (c) I had a conversation with Robin about the relative merits of shaving vs. waxing pubic hair. Boom. That's it. A half-million dollars because I like my wife's pussy shaved. Can you imagine? Tell me how that's indecent. By the way, **waxing is bullshit.** Yeah, it looks great for a day but then you have to wait for the stubble to get long enough before she can wax again. I don't want to get laid by anyone with a five o'clock shadow, whether it's ON THE FACE OR BETWEEN THE LEGS. Shaving is quick and clean.

By the way, I have my wife shave right down to her asshole. And why not? That's the way they do it in Playboy and Penthouse.

3. WHY DID THE FCC FINE ME FOR TALKING ABOUT PEE WEE HERMAN?
(a) Because they are fucking uptight, anal retentive dipshits

(b) Because they have nothing better to do

(c) They are all big nerds who identify with Pee Wee

(d) all of the above

ANSWER: (d) All of the above.

4. WHAT DID I SAY ABOUT PEE WEE WHEN HE GOT BUSTED FOR WACKING OFF IN A THEATER THAT CAUSED THE FCC TO FINE INFINITY AGAIN?

(a) I suggested that he be sentenced to community service, rubbing the gunk off the back of the seats.

(b) I suggested they punish Pee Wee by Krazy Gluing his scrotum to the floor and then, after lighting the room on fire, give him a knife. Then watch him cut his own balls off.

(c) I suggested they change the name of his show to Pee Wee's Play-with-Yourself House.

ANSWER: (a) I merely suggested that I thought Pee Wee wacking away at a porno movie was disgusting. I'm sure the Christian Coalition would agree with that. What the hell is so indecent about that? What if you're sitting in front of this guy and he squishes you with his love jizz? I can't stand going to the movies anymore. Everybody thinks they are at home watching television and they can talk and SNEEZE and FART through the whole damn picture.

Now, here's a guy jerking off behind you. His fucking mess hits you in the head–then what do you do? Sit there and take it? What do you do? That fucking insensitive motherfucker should go home and jerk off.

Sure, it was a porno movie, but I don't care what kind of theater it is, you have to behave yourself. Where the fuck is your decency? When I used to go to porno theaters I would memorize every detail of the movie and then go home and hide in my bedroom and jerk off. That's the only way to do it. This guy's rich enough to buy a VCR. Hell, he's rich enough to buy sixty VCRs and can certainly jerk off in the privacy of his own home. Sick bastard.

5. WHICH STATEMENTS GOT INFINITY ADDITIONAL FINES?

(a) I was talking to my wife and I told her, "You know what I do when you're not in bed with me? I put a can of tuna next to me so I won't know you're gone."

(b) I asked my general manager if he ever used a VIBRATOR ON HIS WIFE AND SON.

(c) I had a gay man come on the air and shove a drum stick up my ass to see if I could play the drum solo from "Wipeout" with my sphincter.

(d) All of the above

ANSWER: A and B are both correct and C is never correct. I got fined $1.7 million because I talked about a vibrator and sleeping with a can of fish.

6. WHO THE FUCK IS THIS SO-CALLED OFFENSIVE TYPE OF CONVERSATION GOING TO HURT?

(a) Everybody

(b) Nobody

(c) Somebody

ANSWER: (b) Nobody. Even five-year-olds know about vaginas and penises and they make doody jokes all day long.

7. WHO COMPLAINED TO THE FCC ABOUT ME?

(a) A guy in Vegas

(b) A woman in Michigan

(c) An old lady from Jersey

(d) All three

ANSWER: (d) All three. Well, that's a lot of people, huh? Out of millions, THESE THREE get to speak for an entire community. The Michigan lady doesn't even get our show. We're not on in Michigan.

8. WHY WON'T I MENTION THESE THREE PEOPLE'S NAMES IN THIS BOOK?

(a) Because the only time they have any excitement is when jackasses like me pay attention to them

(b) Because if you continue to give these people attention, they will be encouraged and start to believe they are actually celebrities

(c) Because most of them are trying to make money off this

(d) All of the above

ANSWER: (d) All of the above. One of them keeps trying to get a radio program to talk about me, and another one of these superstars started a foundation to raise money. A MORALITY FOUNDATION or some such BULLSHIT. She isn't just going after me. I think her latest complaint was about the television program Sea Quest because it showed the naked buttocks of an alien. She was convinced that this was a plot by the perverts in Hollywood to introduce nudity on television by using naked aliens. Then, she thinks, when we become desensitized to that, they'll substitute real, live, naked human beings. Way to go, FCC.

Pay attention to people like that and you are being Government Out of Control. People who have so much free time that they can file transcripts about radio shows should examine their lives. They should all spend their time doing something important–like maybe helping the homeless if they care so much about humanity.

9. IF ANYBODY IS OFFENDED BY ANY OF THE MATERIAL ON MY SHOW WHAT SHOULD HE OR SHE DO?

(a) File a complaint with the FCC

(b) Call up one of my sponsors

(c) Simply turn the fucking radio off

ANSWER: (c) It's obvious what the answer is. It's obvious to me and you and to everyone but the five racketeers who sit on the FCC.

FINAL BONUS—TRUE OR FALSE

Which of the following statements was Infinity fined for? Add an additional point for each correct answer. Deduct one for each wrong answer.

1. T or F: When talking about the Menendez brothers getting molested at six years old by their father, I said, "Hell, I'm not for child molestation, but if I knew that anal sex was the punishment, I'd keep my room clean."

2. T or F: When talking about my relationship with my father, I said, "Hell, my father had sex with me a lot. My father always had me. It wasn't the greatest sex, but it wasn't that bad either. When my dad got a good groove going it was a real joy."

3. T or F: When Robin said, "Mr. Menendez molested the boys so they would be better tennis players," I said, "I tell you what, to avoid anal sex, I'd be the next Jimmy Connors."

Well, if you said true to all three statements, you are correct. I said all of those things and was hit with $1.7 million in fines. Pretty offensive stuff, huh? *Why not throw me in jail and let Charles Manson run free?*

You did well with those bonus questions? Try these additional FCC brainteasers. Answer true or false. Each one is worth one point. Which of the following excerpts was Infinity fined for?

1. T or F: During a show on breasts, Infinity was fined because I said: "BOOBS, ZONKERS, HEADLIGHTS, WATERMELONS, SWEATER PUPPIES, POINTERS, KNOCKERS, JUGS, TATAS—these are some of the words to describe women's breasts."

2. T or F: Infinity was fined because after talking to a female guest about her breasts I said, "If I were to ask you about your chest and I called them zonkers or bonkers or watermelons or boobs—how would you react?" And then my guest answered, "I would just say, 'Mmmmmm, well, why don't you feel them and see how much you like them?'"

3. T or F: When I was doing a show about a club for men with big penises, Infinity was fined when the guest said, "People qualify by sending in photos of themselves both limp and erect. While most of the men are endowed anywhere from five to seven inches, the men in my club are mostly endowed eight to ten inches. And speaking of measurements, there is a RAGING debate on how you measure an erection."

4. T or F: On a show about sexual addiction my employer was fined when a guest said, "Well, there was cruising and masturbating when driving by a schoolyard. Masturbating in a restaurant. Yes, in a restaurant. Sit down and have dinner and masturbate. Masturbating in public places wouldn't happen all the time, but certainly when life was very difficult to deal with that would be something that I'd turn to."

5. T or F: On a show about living out your sexual fantasy, Infinity was fined when I asked a caller, "Do you like the hog-tied position or suspension?" The caller answered, "Well, I'd like to run my tongue up and down, swirl it around, and then I'd like to get on my hands and knees for you."

6. T or F: On a show about bedroom activities, the following excerpts were spoken and Infinity was issued fines: "Almost everyone, married or single, masturbates. You ask a man, 'Do you masturbate?' and of course he'll say, 'No, no, no.' But you say, 'Well, how often are you masturbating now?' And he'll say, 'Oh, maybe once a week or whatever.'"

7. T or F: When a female guest was talking about condoms, Infinity was fined when she said: "The trick is initially just getting the condom over the *girth of the tip*. And then once it's over that, it just kind of—just kind of slides on. I can do it one-handed."

ANSWER: If you said true to any of these, you are in deep shit. I didn't say any of this stuff. *This shit is ten times more fucking graphic than the shit I do.* Geraldo did numbers 1, 2, 4, and 5. Sally Jessy Raphael did number 3. Phil Donahue clocks in with 6 and 7. **All these shows air *during the day, when children are home.***

AMOUNT OF FINES AGAINST THESE PROGRAMS:

Zero. Nothing. Zilch. Why? Probably because the FCC would get laughed out of Washington if they went after the big-shot television hosts. Hi, boys and girls, my name is Mr. Rogers. Can you say, "selective enforcement?" Can you say, "Let's go after Howard and no one else?" Can you say, "Let's fuck Howard Stern in the ass without lubrication?"

WELL, *LET'S SEE HOW YOU SCORED:*

0 or below

You are a **MORON** who cares little about your ***inalienable rights***.

1–2 right

Don't be too proud. You will most definitely be eligible for the lead in *Forrest Gump, The Sequel.* Gump finally gives up the shrimping business after declaring bankruptcy because Captain Dan has stolen everything but his socks. Forrest is now doing what every dimwit does—he gets a job as a general manager of a radio station.

2–5 right

Not too bad. You care a little bit about the right of free speech. You know just enough. You are a healthy individual who isn't completely out of it.

If you got more than five right you are a First Amendment buff. Feel bad about yourself because all this knowledge is **ABSOLUTELY WORTHLESS.** Even though you know about your rights it doesn't matter, you will still get fucked in the ass by the United States government.

FRIENDS IN HIGH PLACES

I knew all the answers. I figured I knew it all. I scored a hundred on the test. I figured I'd take these assholes on. You can't call *me* a pussy. I fought back. I did what any respectable American did: *I tried to buy influence.* I made friends with people in high places. That's what all these lawyers do. I figured I'd get me a few fancy buddies to take up my cause, and guess what? It didn't do **JACK SHIT.** I became close friends with United States Senator Alfonse D'Amato, Governor of New Jersey Christine Todd Whitman, and the great governor of New York, George Pataki. I didn't just become friends with these fine public servants—I became **asshole buddies**. I became so

close with Christie Todd that we talked about her breasts, she confessed to me that ***she had smoked pot and inhaled***, and she named a highway rest stop after me.

I'm so tight with George Pataki that on the day he was inaugurated, I sat right behind him. After the inauguration, I was the only one allowed back to the governor's mansion for a tour. I stood by him while he signed an important piece of legislation regulating road construction. He even named the bill the Howard Stern bill.

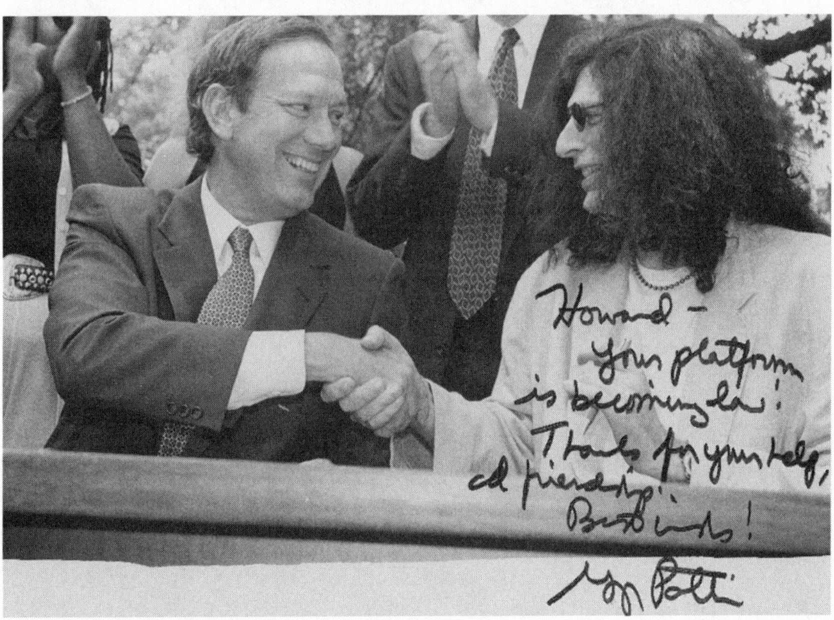

Am I impressing you? NO? Okay then, how's this: I'm so intimate with our great senator from New York Alfonse D'Amato that we regularly play cards together. How's that for muscle? But guess what? ***I still can't fucking beat the FCC.***

I've **BLOWN ENOUGH POLITICIANS** to get myself in the Hooker Hall of Fame and I still can't win.

When I first started getting fined by the FCC, I thought I was fucked. I figured that was it. They win. You can't fight City Hall. But then I realized that was a bullshit attitude. I looked at the guys on the FCC and realized that they weren't all faceless bureaucrats. I noticed that one guy actually seemed to enjoy fucking with me. He started giving out interviews and coming up with snappy soundbites every time I'd get fined. This commissioner was an eighty-one-year-old guy from Michigan who used to be a general manager for an easy-listening station, the kind your grandparents used to listen to.

It figured that a former general manager of a **shithole radio station** would be making my life miserable. But then I remembered that I had always won my battle with the other asshole general managers who had fucked with me over the course of my radio career. So I sat down and I developed a strategy to do battle.

THE SILENT, GOOFY MAJORITY

Like the great warrior Genghis Khan—Khan? That's Jewish, isn't it? A Jewish warrior? See, you can't believe stereotypes. Like Genghis Khan I analyzed the situation. The company I work for, Infinity Broadcasting . . . nice name, "Infinity," isn't it? They named it that because their FCC problems have lasted for an infinity. Infinity's lawyers were doing a great job picking apart these stupid fines in their legal responses, except the FCC refused to come into court and do battle with us. Dirty rat bastard cowards. I knew I couldn't rely on the media in my war, because the media basically hated my guts. The jealous bastards wouldn't say a word to support me when the FCC came down on me with all the fines.

Then it hit me. I realized that I *did* have power. I had the power of the people on my side—millions and millions of people who dug my radio show. We were a community: **THE SILENT, GOOFY MAJORITY**. If one or two nuts with a letterhead could impress some bureaucrats, think what the goofy voting bloc could do at the ballot box.

I decided I would harness my audience's power and create a voting bloc that could make the difference between victory and defeat in any election where my voice could be heard. For the most part, we were talking about a group of people who didn't normally vote but who could swing an election. I decided we would elect candidates who not only wouldn't mind being in the ***same room with an idiot like me,*** but who would also press our agenda in Washington. And we had a very simple agenda: **GET THE FUCKING FCC OFF MY BACK.** I decided right then and there that the King of All Media would become the Kingmaker of All Elections.

SENATOR AL

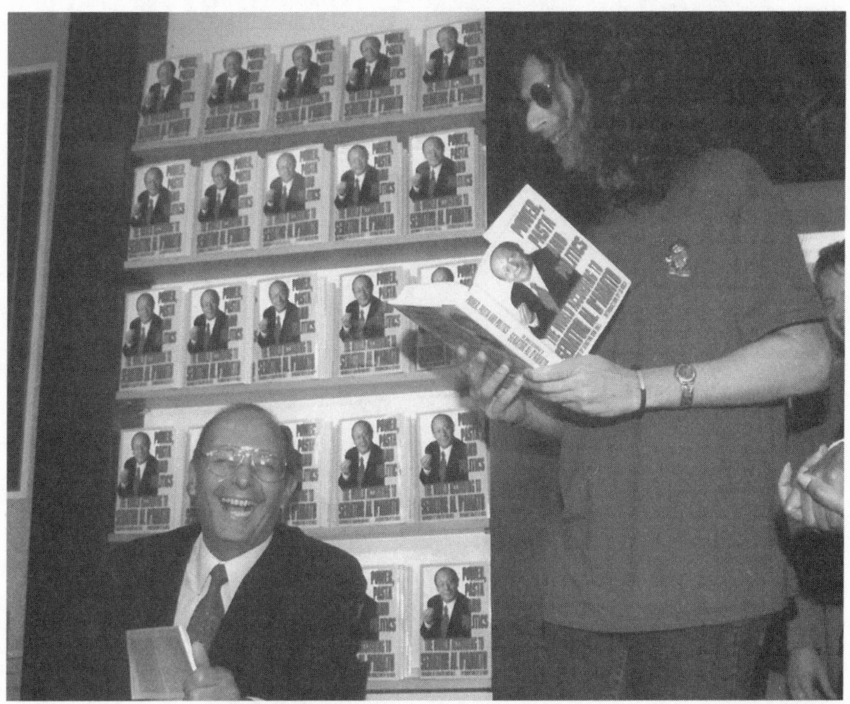

I had my first chance to flex my political power in the 1992 senatorial election in New York. Clinton was way ahead in the polls and he was expected to sweep the state. That would mean that Robert Abrams, the Democrat who was running for the U.S. Senate, would unseat the incumbent Republican, Senator Alfonse D'Amato.

I'm not really a Republican or Democrat, but I've always loved Senator Al—always. The guy fights for New York. He is fanatical about his job. He always brings home the bacon. For years I had said great things about him on the radio, but I'd never met the man—nor did I ever expect to become friendly with him. I was used to having **politicians avoid me**. I was friendly with a lawyer friend of his and we met. We immediately hit it off. He was no pompous jerk, he was a regular guy. He couldn't care less about image and I thought that was cool. We got friendly and he began calling me at home. That was so cool, to actually field a call from a United States senator. And he didn't have secretaries call. He'd call up and if I wasn't in, he'd leave wacky messages. He'd sing, he'd do Doctor Ruth impressions, he was just being a regular guy—**NO POMPOUS BULLSHIT**. None of this I'm-better-than-you-and-my-shit-doesn't-stink attitude.

I knew that Al would be a real friend of the show if he got re-elected. He was in the political fight of his life. So I got on the air and started hammering away on why everyone should vote for

him. I really went wild the last two days before the election. The senator was down in the polls, but I really pushed hard. I know that most people are like me—they don't really make up their mind who they're going to vote for until the day before the election. So I gave them reasons to vote for D'Amato: If they cared about the show, he'd help us. If they cared about New York, he'd help them too.

All my exhortations worked. Sure enough, D'Amato sneaked past Abrams even though Clinton won big. I didn't get any credit in the press, but it was obvious to political insiders that the GOOFY VOTING BLOC had made the difference.

I know the senator was appreciative. A few weeks after being re-elected, he pressed our agenda. He got up on the Senate floor and made a stirring speech defending me and my show against those jerks at the FCC. It was such an effective speech that the eighty-one-year-old FCC commissioner sent D'Amato a fifteen-page letter attacking me! You wouldn't believe what this skeeve wrote:

> *It would embarrass any responsible adult—let alone we* ***Catholic Italian-Americans****—to condone the egregious Stern broadcasts.*

This creep was supposed to be serving the American public and he's writing letters about how ***paisans*** should stick together. Senator Al was so infuriated that he immediately released the letter to the press and denounced it, once again blasting this commissioner for trying to impose his own views on the First Amendment.

I love Senator Al. He's since made many visits to my show, and he's continued to be a consistent supporter of me in my battles with the FCC. He recently published his autobiography and I was proud to read of his views about me:

I TAKE GREAT JOY IN BEFRIENDING AND DEFENDING HOWARD STERN, AN OUTRAGEOUS MAN AND A GREAT FAMILY MAN WHO HAS SUCH A GOOD TIME LAMPOONING THE PURITANS ON BOTH THE LEFT AND THE RIGHT AND WHO IS NOW A VICTIM OF A RIDICULOUS VENDETTA

BY THE FCC, ONE THAT HAS MADE THE GOVERNMENT A BIG BROTHER OF CENSORSHIP AND SOCIAL CONTROL.

GOVERNOR CHRISTINE TODD WHITMAN

Even though we had a United States senator as a friend, I felt it was important to increase our power base. So when Governor Florio of New Jersey was up for re-election, I decided to intervene. I offered to back the first candidate who called in. I knew "Governor Arrogance," Jim Florio, wouldn't stoop so low as to call me. But his Republican opponent, Christine Todd Whitman, **DID**.

Right away, I knew there was something special about this woman. Even though she was a total unknown and more than twenty points behind in the polls, I could discern that this woman had what it took not only to run the state house in New Jersey but also to go on to prominence on the national political scene. I heard her in several early debates, and I was blown away by her attitude and enthusiasm. I knew she would be a great governor.

I also knew that she had **one hot body** for a politician.

"By the way, may I say that I find you somewhat attractive?" I told her the first time she called in. "Seriously, you keep yourself in good shape. You're good looking, you've got our endorsement."

"I'LL TAKE IT ANY WAY I CAN GET IT," Christie said, thankful.

"And, at your inauguration, may I recommend **wearing a thong?**" I added.

We threw ourselves full force into the campaign. The gap between the two candidates began to narrow, but by the day before the election, the conventional wisdom and all the polls had Florio in a landslide. But I knew that the GOOFY VOTING BLOC had not been taken into account. That day, Christie called the show. I told her if we could give my audience one stupid reason to vote for her, she'd be a shoe-in. She suggested naming a tollbooth after me, but I held out. I had always wanted a rest stop named after me. How cool would that be? A tollbooth was a negative—you got to pay to go through it. But to have ***a place where people go to the bathroom and feel relieved***—that would be the ultimate.

Christie agreed to name a rest stop after me. Then I asked her about reports that she had tried pot once. Not only did she confirm that **SHE HAD INHALED** but she told us that she got so sick from the pot that she ran right to the bathroom AND THREW UP. This woman was great. Instead of being arrogant like that jerk Florio, she was acting like a **human being**.

Immediately, the Florio camp tried to smear her by making a big deal about her admitting to smoking pot on my show. But Christine went right on the offensive.

"This is a desperate tactic by a governor who knows he's gonna go down, because he isn't talking about the issues of importance to the people. He's been on Imus all week and Imus is number two in the ratings. Howard's number one, and he's endorsed me. And since I'm gonna win, one and one's stick together," she told the press.

Wow! It was nice to hear a political candidate who was actually proud to be associated with me. If Florio had been on top of his game he would have known that no one listens to Imus. Shit, EVEN IMUS LISTENS TO ME. If Florio opened a window and yelled to people on the street he'd reach a bigger audience.

I hit really hard for Christie the day of the election. I blasted Florio with the force of a hurricane. I spoke about politics and the reasons we needed Mrs. Whitman in a rational, down-to-earth way. But ***the rest stop, ooohhhh,*** the rest stop really turned my audience on. When I woke up the next morning, I got the amazing news: We had just elected our second public official—the new governor of the great state of New Jersey.

PATAKI FOR GOVERNOR

Even though it was obvious that my voters put Whitman over the top, the pundits still refused to recognize that I had become a kingmaker. I had my next chance to show my political clout in the New York state gubernatorial contest. When I was still running for governor myself, my good friend Senator Al called me and asked me to endorse his pick, George Pataki, if I should drop out of the race. When I finally did withdraw, D'Amato intensified his lobbying.

It was hard to say no to a United States senator, and I agreed to endorse Pataki. I explained to Senator Al that I would not endorse Pataki until a few days before the election. My audience didn't want a long political process on the show. **THEY WANT LESBIAN STORIES AND BLACK JEOPARDY.** I explained to the senator that people don't care about an election until two days before. The senator thought I was yanking his chain and just blowing him off. But I really felt the election would be decided in the final two days of the race, and there was no need to bore my audience. No matter how far Pataki was down in the polls, I knew that with some constant hammering from me, we'd put this guy over the top.

And believe me, that was no easy job. ***Nobody knew who the fuck this Pataki guy was.*** Meanwhile, even if they didn't particularly care for the long-incumbent Governor Mario Cuomo, at least they were comfortable with him. People don't like change. Even though Pataki was an unknown, I knew that we could make him known in one phone call.

About two weeks before the election, we started our push. I

needed a little more than two days. This was a tough sell. Pataki was an exceptional candidate but no one knew it. They were scared of the unknown. Pataki called in to seek my endorsement. He went through a litany of his positions on the issues and it turned out that he was a supporter of every one of my gubernatorial planks. His command of the issues and his no-nonsense approach to government were exceptional. I was all set to endorse him wholeheartedly when Robin reminded me that I had already endorsed the Libertarian candidate. Pataki was crestfallen.

"George, read between the lines. I am saying I have to endorse the Libertarian candidate—you understand? I don't even know his name. But I'm feeling very positive about you." I switched into Pig Latin. "I really will ote-vay for ou-yay. You understand?"

"I do understand," he said.

"So everything is on the Q-T here. Everyone ote-vay for Ataki-pay."

Then we began some serious negotiations on the air.

"You're against the FCC, right?" I asked.

"I think what they've been doing to you is wrong—absolutely," he affirmed.

I remembered that Governor Whitman had still not come through with the rest stop that was to be named after me and it was almost a year after the fact. I told Pataki how disappointed I was.

"Well, we'll have you up to the mansion," he promised.

I asked for my own office in the mansion. Pataki thought that was going a little too far. But he countered with a promise to let me stand behind him at his inauguration.

"How about if I hold the Bible?" I asked.

He stood firm at his offer. He'd have me up on the stage. That was enough for me. I gave him a full endorsement.

My endorsement came at just the opportune time. Pataki had been freefalling at the polls, based in part by an endorsement of Cuomo by Rudy Giuliani, the Republican mayor of New York. When we endorsed Pataki, some polls had him down by as many as twenty points. True to my word, I began to push Pataki hard the last stretch of the campaign.

His chances were boosted even more when his wife, Libby, called in a few days before the election. I had seen photos of this woman in the press and she was a babe. She looked a little like Susan Anton. "**LIBBY PATAKI'S CALLING IN.** That's George Pataki's wife, who is **A REAL PIECE OF ASS,**" I told my listeners. When she finally called, I dispensed with the small talk and got right to the heart of the matter.

"This is the first time we're getting to talk, but I gotta tell you something: You are some gorgeous woman. You have to be the ***sexiest political wife*** I've ever seen."

"A week ago I was introduced at a campaign stop as a Renaissance woman," she said, "and I stood up and said, 'I get called a lot of things on this campaign, and I'll answer to just about anything. But this morning I got called a piece of ass for about the **seventh time in a row,** so I'm kind of happy to be a Renaissance woman,'" she said.

Libby was great on the air. If the perception of her husband was that he was a little stiff, she was as LOOSE AS A GOOSE. My whole audience fell in love with her. They started to think that this just might be a fun couple to have in the governor's mansion.

Before I let Libby hang up, I began my own negotiations with her.

"If your husband wins and I'm there the day that he's sworn in, I can expect a kiss from you?" I asked.

"You can get a kiss, but you're not gonna hold the Bible," she shot back.

"On the lips?" I pressed.

"I don't know," she demurred.

"I believe I will," I said.

"You probably will," she agreed. "That's not to say I'll give you permission."

I painted a scenario for her.

"Imagine it's Inauguration Day. We're standing there up on the stage and your husband's being sworn in. All of a sudden, the cameras are watching, and Mrs. Pataki is being tackled onto the floor by me and she's fighting me off. Could you imagine the scene? All of a sudden, you see me and I'm kissing her, and then the kiss is lingering. And she starts to push me away. And somehow we trip and fall, and go crashing to the floor."

"It's a hell of a way to get press, Howard," Libby cracked.

A few days before the election, I began my full court press. I mocked Cuomo as a tired old man. I told everyone that just because they were born in New York didn't mean they had to vote Democratic. I went on to extol the virtue of change. Why should they fear George Pataki? New York State was such a bureaucracy that **A RETARDED MONKEY COULD RUN IT** for four years and we wouldn't know the difference. Besides, Pataki was a Yale graduate. He ran a business. He was the mayor of a thriving town. He had a nice family and a knockout wife. Plus, if we would deliver the votes, I might be able to get some sex off his good-looking running mate, Betsy McCaughey.

My constant hammering away had begun to show results. Pataki was coming back up in the polls. By now, he was just nine points back.

"We could be heroes," I told my audience. "We will singlehandedly be credited for winning this election for Pataki. *I say we put him in—and then we got a guy who owes us.* He's gotta give me an office."

I really nailed Cuomo hard the day of the election. Pataki called up and credited his comeback in the polls to our endorsement. That energized me even more. That whole morning, we pushed for Pataki. I pounded my audience with "Don't be afraid of change—Yale graduate—you've all wanted a death penalty and you finally got a guy who will give it to you." I was so drained that I went to bed early that night. I was a little nervous. I had put my ass on the line. All the polls said Cuomo would win and now I would have a real enemy in a high place—just what I needed.

I woke up to what would have been the unthinkable two weeks earlier: Pataki had come from behind and narrowly beat one of the most prominent Democrats in the country.

That morning, my show was a love-in. Everyone called in and congratulated each other on our wonderful win. Both Governor-to-be Pataki and his lovely wife, Libby, phoned in to personally thank both me and my audience. I had to gloat a little bit.

"It stuck in my craw that this Cuomo couldn't come on this show all these years," I said. ***"I'm some kinda dirtbag.*** Well, I taught you, you pussy ass! Now you're just a citizen, like everybody else."

FRITO-LAY PITCHMAN MARIO CUOMO

There was no denying that we were responsible for this stunning upset. When the returns were analyzed, it was clear that Pataki won because MEN BETWEEN THE AGES OF EIGHTEEN AND TWENTY-FIVE turned out in droves and—for the first time *ever*—voted Republican.

A few days later, the *New York Post* publicly acknowledged the goofy vote:

THERE WERE UNSUNG HEROES IN THE GEORGE PATAKI VICTORY WHO HAVEN'T BEEN GIVEN THEIR DUE, STARTING WITH HOWARD STERN . . . MANY POLITICAL INSIDERS, INCLUDING SEN. ALFONSE D'AMATO AND PATAKI HIMSELF, SAY HE WOULD NOT HAVE WON WITHOUT STERN'S HELP. THE KING OF ALL MEDIA IS DEVELOPING A REPUTATION AS A KINGMAKER . . . STERN IS SEEN AS HAVING A FAR BIGGER IMPACT THAN RUSH LIMBAUGH OR BOB GRANT, WHO ARE PREACHING TO THE CONVERTED—BECAUSE STERN'S LISTENERS CUT ACROSS THE POLITICAL SPECTRUM. AS ANOTHER OBSERVER PUT IT: "A LOT OF STERN'S LISTENERS FOLLOW HIM BLINDLY. THEY ARE UNINFORMED, HAVE NO OPINIONS OF THEIR OWN, AND VOTE ANY WAY HOWARD TELLS THEM TO."

I couldn't have written it better myself.

When it came time for the inauguration, Pataki showed that he was a man of his word. His office called and insisted that my wife and my parents attend the ceremony. Alison and I drove up in Ronnie's limo. Once we got to Albany, we were given a special state trooper escort. The same guys who made fun of me in high school were now looking after my ass. We were whisked to a green room behind the stage. Ten minutes before the actual swearing in, Gov-to-be Pataki and his entire family came into the room to greet us.

The ceremony itself was awesome. They put me in one of the most honored places on the stage. I joked with Justice Kaye, the

'FRIENDS OF GEORGE' GET BEST SEATS IN THE HOUSE

By FREDRIC DICKER
State Editor

ALBANY — You could tell how important you were by the seats you got at Gov. Pataki's giant inaugural.

FOGs — or Friends of George — got the best seats in the house yesterday.

Some non-FOGS barely made it into Knickerbocker Arena.

Mayor Giuliani, clearly no FOG, was placed three rows back on the stage and directly behind mega-FOG U.S. Sen. Alfonse D'Amato, who was in the front row.

That position assured that D'Amato would be seen by the assembled 12,000 — and the TV audience.

Giuliani and his wife, Donna Hanover, could hardly be seen at all — even with binoculars.

New York Post: Michael Norcia

SITTING PRETTY: *Former Gov. Carey (2nd from left) chats with Susan Bruno, daughter of the Senate majority leader Joe Bruno, while Chief Judge Judith Kaye cracks up shock-jock Howard Stern.*

Former Gov. Carey, a secret FOG, was seated almost directly behind the Pataki family and next to Chief Judge Judith Kaye — with a good view and easy access to the new governor.

Shock-jock Howard Stern, who endorsed Pataki, was given an excellent aisle seat close to the dignitaries.

Stern — the state's most controversial FOG — was in regular conversation with Kaye, who appeared downright thrilled to be bantering with the salacious celebrity.

But Stern appeared most animated during the swearing in of Lt. Gov. Elizabeth McCaughey.

Stern intensely eyed McCaughey, his mouth wide open at times.

Ex-Gov. Cuomo and his wife, Matilda, were given well-placed front-row seats, in spite of the at-times bitter gubernatorial campaign and the bad feelings that resulted.

It looked like Cuomo was being slighted when a woman "signing" Pataki's inaugural speech for the deaf stood directly in front of him — blocking his view and casting an obvious shadow on the defeated governor.

But Pataki spokeswoman Zenia Mucha said no slight was intended, and that t "signer" was in the wro position.

To avoid what real could have been an emba rassing seating arrang ment, Charles Gargan Pataki's key fund-rais and the newly named sta economic developme czar, was seated next Matilda Cuomo.

That made him a buff between the Cuomos ar D'Amato, Cuomo's mort political enemy and t man given the most cred for helping to elect Pataki

Other FOGs who got go stage seats included: t staff aides Michael Finn gan, Bradford Rac Mucha and James Nato Brooklyn Democratic A semblyman Dov Hikind, strong Pataki backer; sta GOP boss William Power and John Sweeney, t GOP's executive director.

Three of the state's bi gest non-FOGS — haple state Republican controll candidate Herb Londo former state GOP Chai man Patrick Barrett ar Westchester GOP Chai man Anthony Colavita never made it to the stage.

London and Colavita both of whom work against Pataki's nominati — weren't even at the ina gural ceremony, and Barr was relegated to a seat in t general audience.

woman who swore Pataki in, and former Governor Hugh Carey. One prominent politician after another came up to shake my hand. In fact, the only person who gave me the cold shoulder was old stonefaced Mario. He wouldn't even acknowledge my presence.

As soon as the ceremony was over, the governor and his wife invited us right over to the mansion. It was incredible. We were treated like royalty. I was thrilled because my father was in seventh heaven.

Never in his wildest dreams did he ever think ***his stupid son*** would be his ticket for a private visit to the governor's mansion.

Libby gave us a personal tour of the house. We saw the room where Mario used to hole up and write his great philosophical speeches, the room where he was so busy pondering and writing speeches that **HE FORGOT WE HAD A FIVE-BILLION-DOLLAR DEFICIT.** Skeevosa.

After the tour, we all had lunch. I was real thrilled to be treated this great, but it was a little weird. I kept thinking that Pataki's kids were sitting there waiting for me to **light my farts**—"Hey, lookit the blue flame!"—but I fooled them.

I behaved myself.

After all, I was now a respectable kingmaker.

THE GREAT REST STOP CONTROVERSY

Soon after Governor Pataki accorded me such a wonderful reception at his inauguration, we heard from the other

CELEBRATION of the ARTS... NEW JERSEY Style

governor we had elected. We got a surprise visit in the studio from Governor Whitman of New Jersey, who told us she was there to make good on her campaign promise to name a rest stop after me. I was, to say the least, moved. I had never really held her to her promise because I was thrilled that she was doing such a great job as governor. Within a year, **SHE HAD ALREADY DELIVERED ON HER CAMPAIGN PROMISE TO DRASTICALLY CUT TAXES.** That was enough for me.

But she was a noble woman. She whipped out a plaque that read HOWARD STERN REST STOP. ESTABLISHED 1995. Being a shrewd politician, she informed us that she didn't even use taxpayer's funds to purchase the plaque. So I was to take my place next to Clara Barton, Walt Whitman, James Fenimore Cooper, Woodrow Wilson, Thomas Edison, Alexander Hamilton, and Vince Lombardi, all great Americans who also had ***crappers named after them*** in New Jersey.

Our pride was somewhat punctured when we did a little research into the rest stop that the Governor had designated to bear my plaque. First of all, she picked the most OBSCURE one possible. It was just barely in New Jersey. If you passed wind there, they could smell it in Delaware. Then a listener who drove a truck called in and informed us that the proposed site was ***a mecca for homos who wanted to get quick blowjobs***. On the other hand, there were also a lot of hookers who worked the parking lot.

The governor had hardly left my studio when the backlash

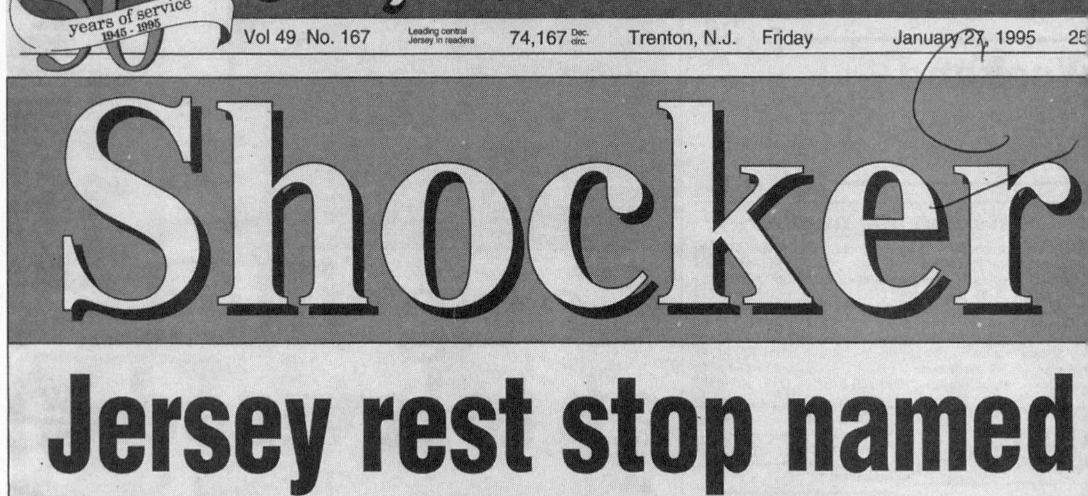

50 years of service 1945 - 1995

Vol 49 No. 167 Leading central Jersey in readers 74,167 Dec. circ. Trenton, N.J. Friday January 27, 1995

Shocker

Jersey rest stop named for (gasp!) Howard Stern

Christie has dedicated this rest stop on I-295 to shock jock Howard Stern to fulfill a campaign promise.

began. Right away, the New Jersey chapter of the National Organization of Women sent her an open letter denouncing her for naming a rest stop after me, a monster who "promulgates stereotypes that label women as **WHORES, LESBIANS, OR BITCHES.**" Hey, where was their open letter to O.J.? Why weren't these bitches worried about the fact that **women who do the same job as men earn half of what a man gets?**

Then the war veterans got into the action. It seemed the stretch of highway that my future rest stop was on was already dedicated to the veterans of World War II. Immediately, some local politicians began sending out press releases trying to grab a headline off my back. Instead of worrying about **CRIME OR POTHOLES**, they were driving over to the rest stop for photo ops.

PREDICTABLY, THE MEDIA HAD A FIELD DAY. YOU WOULD HAVE THOUGHT THAT GOVERNOR WHITMAN HAD PROPOSED ***CLIMBING UP THE STATUE OF LIBERTY AND PAINTING MY FACE ON IT.*** Jersey newspapers gave the controversy front page headlines. It was the lead story on the evening news. Thousands of letters to the editor were written.

But this wasn't frigging Bosnia—it was a governor showing a little bit of a sense of humor. Besides, patronage goes on all the time in politics. I wish I had a dime for every job that that lame-o Florio gave out to his friends. That, they don't worry about.

But I was horrified by the reaction. Governor Whitman had just finished the greatest week of her life. The state was running beautifully. She had delivered the

Republican response to the president's State of the Union address, and she'd garnered rave reviews. Already they were talking about her as a possible vice-presidential candidate—***and she was mine.*** It was like *The Omen*: I had taken this obscure candidate and she was now virtually heartbeats away from the highest political offices in the land. The last thing that I wanted was to fuck this up. I could envision all my influence going right down the drain **BECAUSE OF A STUPID TOILET.**

I called up Governor Whitman's people and told them they didn't have to go ahead with the rest stop, but they were already committed to it. It wouldn't look good to bow from pressure from

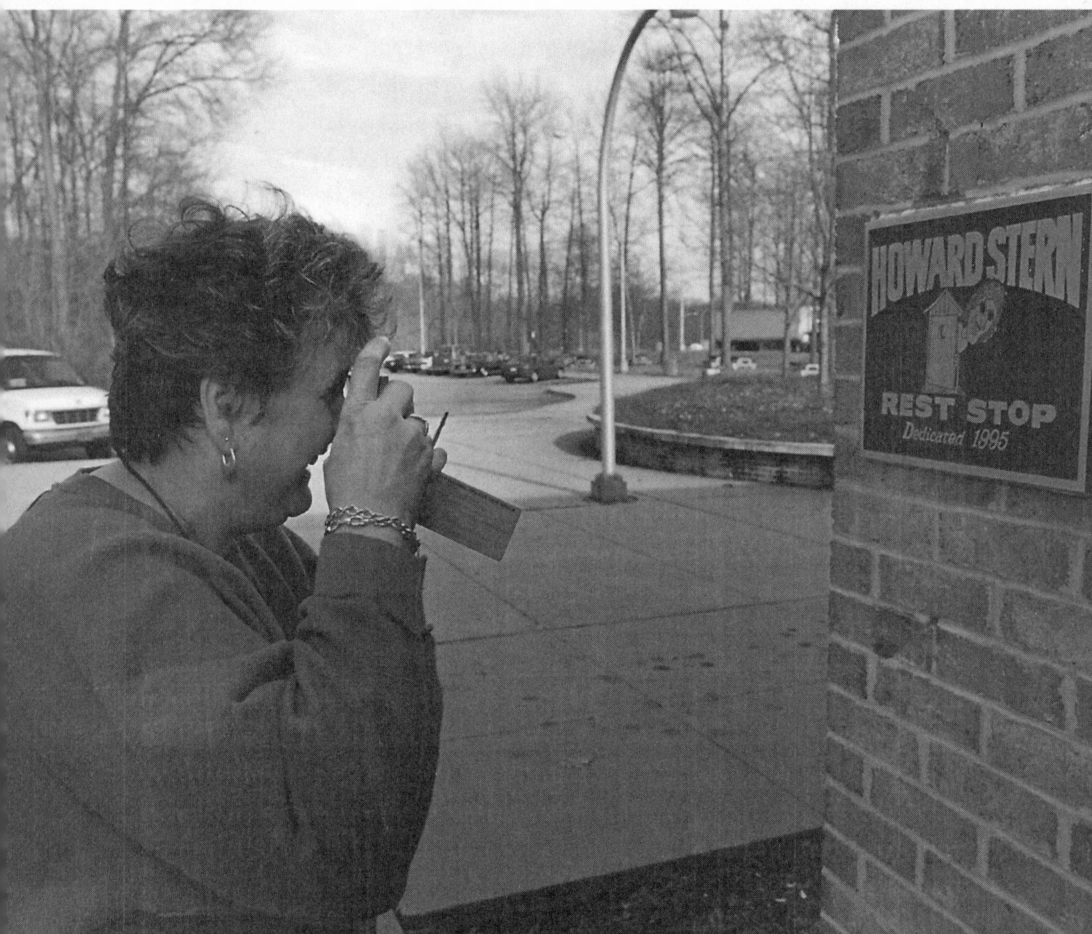

a bunch of **loser feminists** and partisan Democrats. So we decided to take my father's advice: We would just let the whole thing blow over.

Of course, I had to give up my vision of bringing a high school marching band and doing a four-hour show on the day the rest stop was to be dedicated. I had already commissioned a design for a life-sized statute of ***me with my ass cheeks cut out and an eternal flame shooting out of my anus.*** But it was not to be. Instead, a few months later, while both Governor Whitman and our show were on vacation, New Jersey officials quietly snuck the plaque onto the side of the rest stop—the side that faced the woods.

They didn't do a good job affixing it, either. They glued the frigging thing to the wall. Within a week, three twenty-something white males were seen speeding from the rest stop in possession of my plaque. Governor Whitman was thrilled. She immediately called the press and denied responsibility for the robbery since she was out of town at the time. She also said she would make **NO EFFORT TO REPLACE IT.**

A few days after the theft made headlines all over New Jersey, Jackie "Jokeman" Martling received an incredibly heavy package in the mail at K-Rock.

It was the plaque.

The three guys who stole it wanted us to have it. So now the plaque is sitting in a desk drawer in Gary's office—out of sight, out of mind. Meanwhile, Governor Whitman has escaped unscathed from the restroom scandal.

And I've got a friend who just might wind up sleeping in the same bed George Washington did.

THE NEXT PRESIDENT OF THE UNITED STATES

You may wonder how having a bunch of governors indebted to me for their victory was going to help me in my battle with the FCC. I'm no dummy. I knew that the president of the United States could pick up a phone and make one call and my FCC nightmare would go away forever. And that's exactly what I was trying to do with my endorsement of Governor Pataki.

When I got Pataki elected, I was really sending a message to President Clinton: ***Watch what I do.*** You might think that I'm a buffoon, but I am getting these people elected. People don't know that I had an opportunity to endorse Chuck Haytaian when he ran against Senator Lautenberg in the last New Jersey Senate election. Haytaian was **UP MY ASS EVERY DAY** for my support. Haytaian was a Republican and I purposely didn't endorse him. I didn't want any doubt that I had gotten Pataki elected. If Haytaian had won, Pataki's win would have just seemed like voter backlash against Democrats. But I wanted to show Clinton: ***I endorse you, you win. I hold back, you lose.***

Frankly, I don't know why Clinton hasn't done anything for me in the three years he's been in office. I supported him against Bush and got him millions of votes. He still thinks Imus helped him in New York. (Imus can't help himself and persuade anyone to listen, so how could he persuade voters?) Clinton has pissed me off by ignoring me. I don't care if he comes on the show. I wanted his fucking help with this bullshit FCC issue. I'm always attacking THAT FAT PIG RUSH LIMBAUGH and his right-wing cronies because they don't even accord any respect to the office of the presidency. They're busy attacking the shit out of Clinton, but they're such lackeys for the Republicans that they'll never open their mouths when Republicans fuck up.

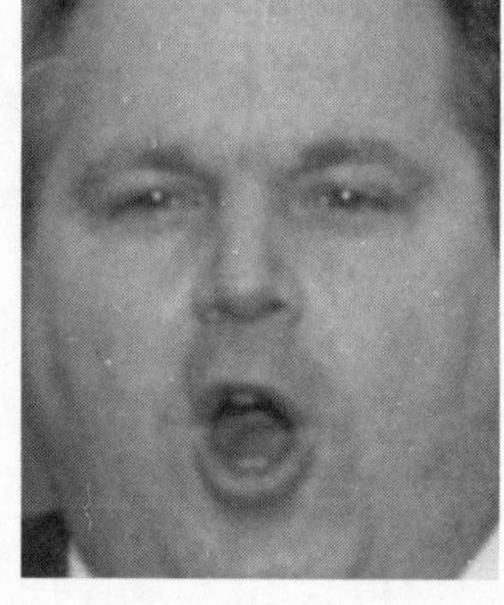

I even defended Chelsea Clinton when *Saturday Night Live*

trashed her in a skit. I got right on the air and said that just because she ain't the prom queen doesn't give people the right to blast her. Every day after those raps, I'd go back into the office and ask Gary if anybody from Clinton's office called. We didn't hear a peep.

It got so bad that I turned to his brother just to get a word to the president. Roger promised me that he could arrange a meeting, but this dude can barely get in the White House himself. Big help he is.

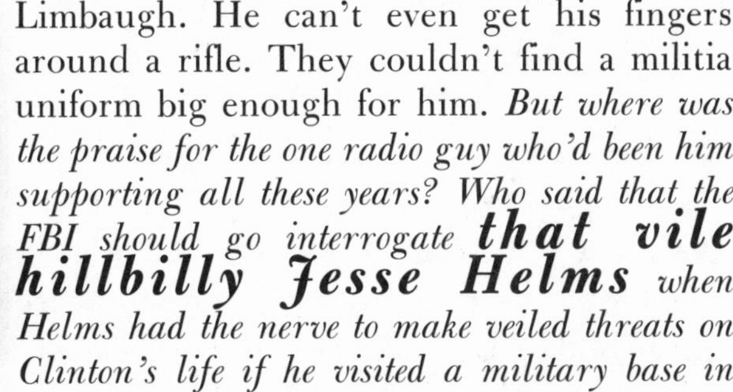

Then Clinton goes to the press after the Oklahoma bombing and condemns talk radio. Hey, stop worrying about that fatso Limbaugh. He can't even get his fingers around a rifle. They couldn't find a militia uniform big enough for him. *But where was the praise for the one radio guy who'd been him supporting all these years? Who said that the FBI should go interrogate* ***that vile hillbilly Jesse Helms*** *when Helms had the nerve to make veiled threats on Clinton's life if he visited a military base in North Carolina?* Me, that's who! Can you imagine—a United States senator cautioned the president to stay away from the military and nothing was done? I fuckin' blasted Jesse Helms: "**ARREST HIM!** If he knows about a military plot against the president, he should be investigated."

But instead of acknowledging me, Clinton was busy sucking up to the right wing by claiming that violence in the media is bad. That's futile. He can fucking get on a stage and **chop his own nuts off,** and the right wing still won't vote for him.

I like President Clinton. I thought he was doing a great job. He was working hard. I wasn't in agreement with him on every issue, but I wanted America to give him a chance. At least he was showing up for work and not vacationing every weekend in Kennebunkport and that fucking Camp David. I still think that place should be demolished because every damn president ends up snoozing away like a king up there. I felt Clinton was getting badmouthed from day one and he stood for some good things. ***Me and Clinton are the only two people on the planet who want to see gays in the military.*** But in reality, all I wanted him to do was to get the fucking FCC off my back. And he did nothing.

So I began making contingency plans. Of course, the pickings were slim on the Republican side of the fence. You got that front-runner, Robert Dull. He's my father's age. There's no way a seventy-three-year-old guy is going to get fired up to be president. He's ready for the links. Although it might be hard playing golf with that baby arm he's got there.

Then there's Newt. I like him. He actually has a few good ideas about trimming government waste—namely, eliminating the FCC. The only time he gets in trouble with me is when he tries to lecture on morality. Quite frankly, I don't believe he is really sincere about any of this family values shit but he needs to pander to the religious nuts. ***It sounds nutty to hear about family values from a guy who married his freaking high school math teacher and then went to her bedside and tried to get her to sign divorce papers when she was still coming off anesthesia after her third cancer operation.*** This Newt's another one who tells women not to have abortions. **Let me inject the sperm of a Cuban boat person into his tuchis and see if he doesn't go run for an abortion.**

But there's one Republican who actually makes sense: **SENATOR ARLEN SPECTER** of the great state of Pennsylvania has been a frequent guest in my studios the past few months. And we've actually bonded a bit. He's for a flat tax, which I like. He's a firm believer in the separation of church and state, which sets him apart from 98 percent of the other Republican presidential candidates.

And he's got one other great virtue: He chairs the Senate committee that appropriates the funding for the FCC.

Senator Specter was very interested in my FCC problems. He pulled me aside after his last visit and listened to me rap about them for five minutes. Then he went right to work and wrote two letters to the FCC demanding to know why they hadn't adjudicated all the fines yet. This is one caring public official. If Senator Specter manages to stay in the primaries until he gets into one of the markets I'm heard in, we'll make sure he wins.

MY MASTER PLAN

So there I was. The man with a plan. I had never planned anything for so long and so well. Victory would be mine. I had spent years developing contacts and friendships with the high and mighty. In my mind, the only thing left was to establish a relationship with the president of the United States. I now knew enough people to pull it off. I was so patient with this whole FCC thing. Instead of wandering around like a helpless victim, I was getting the balance of power on my side.

I was all set to be the ultimate kingmaker—the man who single-handedly elects a president of the United States.

But I was on vacation when I woke up to those awful headlines. HOWARD PAYS $1.7 MILLION.

Rock my world baby! Whoa! I was so close! I needed just a little more time. Christie was just inches away from being the next vice president and Bob Dole is D'Amato's man. **SHEEEET! SUCK MY DICK!** I was shocked that Infinity would buckle under to the extortion-like tactics of the FCC and pay the fines.

While I was plotting and planning my victory, the demons on the FCC weren't sitting idly by—they were continuing to screw with my employer, Infinity Broadcasting. If Infinity tried to buy a radio station and the FCC lost the paperwork, the delays would cost Infinity millions in penalties because the purchase price would go up after a certain amount of time. **A group of black people** from Washington got together to challenge

Infinity's radio station license and the FCC paid attention to them. The black group said I was racially insensitive—blackmail. Infinity had to shell out $2.75 million for "programs" that would aid minority businesses in the Washington area. The FCC usually ignores this type of stuff. Infinity had an excellent record as responsible broadcasters. The only reason the FCC was paying attention to minority challenges was to get Infinity to pay up. **Extortion.** It's a good thing I bring in a lot of ratings and money or else I would have been a goner.

The only broadcast publication to come to my defense was *Broadcasting* magazine. In an editorial they said that the FCC had resorted to extortion. And then they said:

"INFINITY HOPES THE PAY OFF WILL HELP 'NORMALIZE' ITS RELATIONSHIP WITH THE FCC. THE PAYOFF SHOULD BE MADE IN UNMARKED BILLS IN A PLAIN PAPER BAG PLACED IN A TRASH CAN OUTSIDE 1919 M STREET."

The editorial referred to the FCC as "godfather," as in the movie about the Mafia. These dudes on the FCC, like Mafiosi, were going to bring Infinity to their knees and get them to kiss their ring way before I could get them in court. By the way, thank you, *Broadcasting* magazine, for sticking up for me even though ***nobody gives a shit.*** It would have been nice if there was more screaming and yelling, but my fellow broadcasters have always been COWARDS.

After a long, hard struggle, Infinity finally gave in. Paying the fines was an understandable business decision. In the settlement, they didn't even call them fines. Both sides agreed that Infinity was making a "voluntary contribution" to the government coffers. ***Yeah, just like a guy in a suit makes a voluntary contribution to a mugger who's got a knife at his throat.***

The settlement was great for Infinity and the FCC. They both saved face. BUT WHAT ABOUT ME? What happened to *my* rights? Now everyone thinks that Infinity paid close to $2 million because I was guilty of being an indecent, obscene, foul-mouthed shock jock. But that's bullshit. I WAS JUST SINGLED OUT, held out as an example so a bunch of toothless bureaucrats could feel like they accomplished something.

Meanwhile, nothing's really changed. The shadowy figures who make up the FCC are said to be huddling together right now, drawing up new guidelines on "indecency."

Who knows what they'll object to me talking about next?

Who can guess what they don't want you to hear?

I'm not gonna take this lying down. I am a man who can elect senators and governors. *You can't push Stern around!*

First, I will call my close friend, the great Senator Arlen Specter. If he can hold hearings about the FBI **blowing Randy Weaver's wife's face off,** he can certainly convene a hearing into why the FCC is persecuting me.

I will not be satisfied until the FCC is completely dismantled, until every American has the God-given right to hear the word ***"vagina"*** *without fear of reprisal.*

It won't be easy fighting the thought police. But rest assured your hero will be fighting behind the scenes. Gaining influence. In fact my good friend, Governor Pataki, has been so spectacularly effective that people are already talking about him as a possible presidential candidate. Within a few short months since taking office he has taken a tough stand on New York's bloated budget, signed the death penalty, made good on his promise to have road construction done at night, and cleaned up organized crime from the Javits Convention Center. Not bad for a white man! Hey, maybe I lost the battle when Infinity paid out $1.7 million, but I might not lose the war.

Yeah, I got fucked in the ass by a bunch of wiseguys. There is nobody who will help me, no matter how right I am. Just like when my mom took away my beloved Yogi Bear, I have no one to turn to. But the pain is temporary. Like any rape victim, I just might get my revenge.

Wait a second, I have to go. There's a report on TV—they're talking about Christie Whitman for vice president.

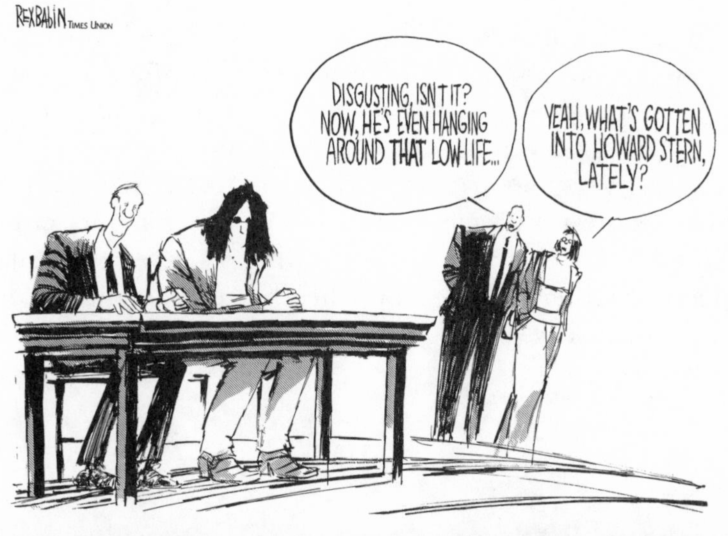

AFTERWORD

a listener analyzes the show

February 24, 1995

Dear Howard,

I have been a big fan of yours for years. I THINK THERE ARE SOME INTERESTING PARALLELS BETWEEN YOUR RELATIONSHIPS WITH THE PEOPLE ON YOUR RADIO SHOW, AND THE RELATIONSHIPS BETWEEN ADOLF HITLER AND THE MEMBERS OF HIS NAZI INNER CIRCLE. PLEASE ALLOW ME TO ELABORATE.

MR. STERN, YOU ARE THE ADOLF HITLER OF THE SHOW. Okay, maybe you haven't gassed anybody to death yet, but you do have absolute power regarding the content of your radio show. Those close to you will do almost anything to earn more airtime. EVERYONE BEGS FOR YOUR FAVOR, WHICH CAUSES IN-FIGHTING AND JEALOUSY AMONG YOUR SUBORDINATES. These subordinates are involved in constant power-playing to reshape and improve their status on the show.

PEOPLE SHAKE IN FEAR WHEN YOU ARE IN A FOUL MOOD BECAUSE THEY DO NOT WANT TO BEAR THE BRUNT OF ONE OF YOUR TEMPER TANTRUMS. Members of Hitler's inner circle loved to see their peers squirm when they were the subjects of Hitler's tirades, but they hated to be put on the spot themselves. The same can be said for your cast of cronies.

LIKE HITLER, YOU HAVE EXTREME INTOLERANCES FOR DISLOYALTY AND INEFFICIENCY. You expect your orders to be followed completely and without question. You expect your subordinates to show some energy and initiative. HITLER SEEMED TO GET BETTER RESULTS THAN YOU IN THIS AREA.

There are many people who praise you as their leader when they are in your presence, but behind your back they conspire against you. YOU HAVE THE POWER TO MAKE OR BREAK CAREERS, AND SOME WHO ARE CLOSE TO YOU RESENT YOU FOR THIS.

Hitler was vicious in his treatment of political enemies. You have proven to be no less vicious in your treatment of the enemies of the show. Your feuds with the likes of Bon Jovi and Andrew Dice Clay show that you know how to torture an opponent.

IF YOU ARE THE HITLER OF THE SHOW, RALPH CIRELLA IS EVA BRAUN. You may remember Eva wanted to marry Adolf for many years before they actually married. EVA WOULD FIND ANY EXCUSE, NO MATTER HOW LAME, TO SHOW UP WHEREVER THE FUEHRER HAPPENED TO BE. Eva wanted to spend each minute of each day at her Fuehrer's side.

Hitler was fond of Eva and he liked to spend some time with her, but she was much too demanding of his time. HITLER ORDERED HIS ASSISTANTS TO LIMIT EVA'S ACCESS TO HIM, BECAUSE HE FOUND EVA'S PRESENCE COULD OFTEN BE EMBARRASSING AND DISTRACTING. Hitler was aware that his image could be damaged by being seen too often in public with the insignificant Eva Braun. HOWEVER, EVA WAS RELENTLESS IN HER PURSUIT OF HITLER.

Many of Hitler's associates did not care for this woman who would take up so much of their leader's precious time. THE OTHER NAZIS WANTED EVA OUT OF THE PICTURE SO THEY COULD HAVE MORE OF HITLER'S ATTENTION. They were annoyed at Hitler's refusal to be rid of Eva. They could never understand their Fuehrer's bond with Eva Braun.

JACKIE MARTLING PLAYS THE ROLE OF HERMANN GOERING. He shares many of Goering's traits. Goering had a better sense of humor than most of the other top Nazis. He was fat, and he abused drugs and alcohol. HIS LOYALTY TO THE NAZI CAUSE ALWAYS TOOK A BACK SEAT TO HIS DESIRE TO BUILD A PERSONAL FORTUNE. He spent more energy acquiring European art treasures than he did on improving the Luftwaffe.

GOERING CONSIDERED HIMSELF THE ONLY WORTHY SUCCESSOR TO THE NAZI THRONE IN THE EVENT OF HITLER'S DEMISE. LIKE JACKIE, GOERING MAY HAVE WISHED FOR HIS FUEHRER'S PREMATURE DEMISE.

Goering was always at odds with other Nazi officials, and money usually was the reason for these conflicts. He considered himself the hero of the common German folk. Could Goering be history's most famous example of White Trash?

FRED NORRIS IS THE HEINRICH HIMMLER OF THE HOWARD STERN SHOW. Fred seems to share Himmler's love of secrecy and mystery. No one ever knew where Himmler would turn up, and no one knew when he would disappear. But everyone felt Himmler's sinister presence.

Much like Himmler, NO ONE KNOWS WHAT EVIL THOUGHTS ARE BREWING BEHIND THOSE CLEAR, COLD FRED NORRIS EYES. FRED COULD PROBABLY ORDER THE DEATHS OF MILLIONS WITHOUT BATTING AN EYE.

Can you be certain that Fred does not possess a secret army of brainwashed blackshirt warriors, sworn to obey his every command? When Fred disappears after the show each day, I think he is updating the secret files that he keeps on all of you.

Hitler was always concerned about the loyalty and the size of Himmler's SS. He did not want Himmler to become too powerful. I suggest that you keep a close eye on Fred. JACKIE GOERING MAY BE THE MOST OBVIOUS THREAT TO UNDERMINE YOUR POWER, BUT FRED HIMMLER MAY POSE A LARGER, WELL-DISGUISED THREAT.

BA BA BOOEY IS THE MARTIN BORMANN OF THE SHOW. The top Nazis felt that Bormann was not worthy of ANY power or prestige. They believed Bormann was a man of extremely limited ability who became powerful because of his willingness to be a complete lackey. BORMANN WAS NOTHING MORE THAN A COMMON SECRETARY-CLERK, BUT HIS CONTROL OVER PERSONAL ACCESS TO HITLER MADE BORMANN A POWERFUL MAN.

Anyone who wanted to see the Fuehrer had to go through Bormann. Hitler's mail was opened by Bormann. Bormann answered Hitler's phones. If you showed a lack of respect for Bormann, he would block your access to Hitler. BORMANN HAD TO WITHSTAND MANY OF HITLER'S ANGRY TIRADES, AS HE WAS A FAVORITE TARGET OF HITLER'S HOSTILE OUTBURSTS.

Bormann was universally despised by the Nazi inner circle because he was very aware of the power he commanded. BORMANN WAS NOT SHY ABOUT ABUSING THIS POWER. HE WOULD SASS AND BACKTALK TO VITAL AND TALENTED NAZIS AND GENERALS, AS IF HE WERE THE FUEHRER HIMSELF! Military leaders were insulted because they had to deal with scum like Bormann and because they had to treat him as an equal.

I WONDER IF HITLER EVER MADE BORMANN REPEAT AFTER HIM, LIKE YOU HAVE DONE WITH BA BA BOOEY. Like Bormann, Ba Ba Booey has earned no respect on his own. Any gestures of respect for Ba Ba Bormann are obviously efforts to earn access to Herr Stern.

ROBIN QUIVERS PLAYS THE PART OF BENITO MUSSOLINI PERFECTLY. Mussolini considered himself superior in talent and intellect to Hitler. Of course, he was mistaken.

MUSSOLINI WATCHED WITH JEALOUSY AS HITLER TOOK COMMAND OF THE EUROPEAN POLITICAL STAGE DURING THE 1930'S. Il Duce wanted desperately to become a major player in European and world politics. Due to lack of talent and resources, he could do little except sit on the sidelines and hope that someone would notice him.

JUST AS ROBIN AGREES WITH AND LAUGHS AT EACH WORD YOU SAY, MUSSOLINI WAS HITLER'S BOOT LICKING PUPPET. HIS FAVORITE WORDS WERE, "YES, MEIN FUEHRER!"

Mussolini showered Der Fuehrer with gifts and compliments whenever Hitler enjoyed a political or military success, but Mussolini would secretly complain to his own Fascist ministers that the arrogant Hitler would soon meet his match and suffer devastating defeats.

Mussolini did dare to start a few projects of his own, such as the invasions of Ethiopia, Albania, and Greece. IN MOST OF THESE INDEPENDENT VENTURES MUSSOLINI WAS IN OVER HIS HEAD, AND HE HAD TO SEEK HITLER'S HELP TO BAIL HIM OUT OF TROUBLE.

Mussolini was the last person in the world to realize that his rise to world prominence came upon the coattails of Adolf Hitler. MUSSOLINI WOULD HAVE BEEN A COMPLETE FAILURE IF HITLER WAS NOT AROUND TO HOLD HIS HAND. Hitler ignored Mussolini's many shortcomings and remained extremely loyal to the fallen Il Duce. HITLER WAS WILLING TO DO ANYTHING TO PRESERVE THE ILLUSION THAT MUSSOLINI WAS STILL A POWERFUL AND TALENTED MAN, ALTHOUGH NO ONE ELSE BELIEVED THIS TO BE TRUE.

Mussolini might have been better served if he could have recognized his limitations. HE COULD NOT ACCEPT THE FACT THAT HE WAS NOT A WORLD CLASS TALENT. HE WOULD HAVE BEST SERVED THE AXIS CAUSE BY ACCEPTING HIS ROLE AS HITLER'S POLITICAL MISTRESS AND BY FOLLOWING HITLER'S INSTRUCTIONS.

TOM CHIUSANO PLAYS THE PART OF COLONEL CLAUS VON STAUFFENBERG. On July 20, 1944, Von Stauffenberg planted a bomb in Hitler's headquarters in an attempt to assassinate the Fuehrer.

I GET THE IMPRESSION THAT TOM CHIUSANO IS CONSTANTLY ATTEMPTING TO SABOTAGE YOUR RADIO SHOW. He is a traitor and a spy.

He burdens you with outdated and failing equipment. Like Von Stauffenberg, Tom ensures that your telephone communications are primitive and unreliable. He drains you and distracts you with pointless meetings. He keeps you surrounded with people who lack intelligence and have more loyalty to himself than to you.

Tom almost always sidesteps your probing questions without giving any definitive answers. When he does give you answers, he finds scapegoats to explain away problems that fall under his responsibility. He always has an excuse!

You have caught Tom lying several times. You know that he cannot be trusted. It is obvious that Chiusano is a traitor to your cause. I believe that he is conspiring to get rid of you so he can put his beloved Greaseman in your morning spot. He might be working as a spy for Imus. Like Von Stauffenberg, Tom Chiusano would be anonymous if he did not act like a meddling fool.

I am a 34 year old married white male. I work as a claim authorizer for the government.

Thank you.
George Murphy

THE AUTHOR WOULD LIKE TO

THANK:

Alison, for always believing in me and being understanding, especially while I wrote this and missed the entire summer with you and the kids. Thanks for the quickies in the hot tub. I love you.

Ray and Ben Stern, for being good sports and giving me my sense of humor.

The absolute **brilliance** of Judith Regan. There are not enough words to describe how great a job you did with this book. You've always believed in me, and your encouragement and ideas set you apart from everyone else. And you're a great mother. Don't let anyone tell you any different.

Larry "Ratso" Sloman, I feel like we've been through a war together. Thanks, Rats, for putting in the endless hours and earning the title "Keeper of the Flame" of the Howard Stern Literary Juggernaut. You are a real ***friend*** and your ***professionalism*** and ***dedication*** are very much appreciated. You is a GENIUS.

Superagent Don Buchwald. Don is my adviser, my savior, my business partner—the SMARTEST guy I know. He took me out of the gutter of radio with the dream that I could cross over and sit on the throne as the King of All Media. I love this guy, and he loves me. Superagent Don Buchwald ... THE KING OF ALL MEDIA AGENTS.

A special thanks and appreciation to Laura Lackner, my trusted friend and assistant, who has worked endless hours coordinating this entire project. It takes lots of research to dig out the show tapes and pictures and to organize the whole mess. **I love you, Laura,** for all the help you give me.

Gary Dell'Abate, I couldn't have done this without you. Thank God for your memory and knowledge of the show. About ten billion times I picked up the phone and asked you for quick information, and you always had it. **You are the best.** And thanks to Cathy Tobin, who provided invaluable assistance to Gary during this project.

Ralph Cirella, way to go on set-designing the color insert and coming up with *great picture concepts.* If it weren't for you, we wouldn't have had the cover of this book. You are the King of All Stylists.

Jack Heller, you are so ***damn talented.*** Art direction second to none, and the cover design is spectacular. Good move finding Paul Aresu, our photographer.

Drew Friedman—B R I L L I A N T !

Richard Basch, my friend, agent, and legal brain with a steel-trap mind.

Ronnie Mund, thanks for being patient.

Jeff Schick, IBM's shining star. Thanks for all the hours of help. For all you do. This Bud's for you.

Chip Kidd, no one could have done a more ***clever*** and INTELLIGENT job of designing this book.

Nina Gaskin, **endless hours**, complete dedication, a true professional—thanks, Nina.

Mitchell Ivers, thanks for being there every step of the way and lending me your PATIENCE and WISDOM.

J. F. Lawton, thanks for being a good friend and giving life to Fartman.

Tom Morgan, your work is classic.

Barry Morgenstein, your work is always appreciated.

David Dalrymple of House of Fields, for providing the stunning clothing, and Persidia Field, Fabian Garcia, and Danna

Bradley at Patricia Fields, FOR MAKING US REALLY LOOK LIKE WOMEN.

Lonnie Hanover and the girls at Scores (Athena, Brittany, Jana, Paris, Cat, Justin, Brooke, Michele, Juliana, Lorraine, Harper, Xena, Nadine, Carla, JoLyn, Julie, Cheri, Heaven Lee, Stacey, Ashley, Kelly) ... thanks for helping with all the pictures and giving us all your free time.

And thanks also to:

Jonathan Abbruzzese
Jack Adler
Antoinette Anderson
Anne Aquilina and *The New York Post*
Derek Bandler
Dominic Barbara
Paula Barbieri
Jennifer Barretta
Amy Lynn Baxter
Daniel Berkowitz
Big Blackie
Carol Bravy
Shawn Burns
Joseph Cammarota
Al Canaletich
Dexter Carter
The Chez Company
Tom Chiusano
Richard Christensen
Lisa Ciolino
Eugene Corey
A. C. Cowlings
Cindy Crawford
Dan Cuddy
M. Dade and Elizabeth
Mike D'Altrui
Senator Alphonse D'Amato
Chris Damphouse
Terry DeMartini
Javier Diaz
C. Linda Dingler
Neil Drake
Ellen Dunn
Peter Dunn
E! Crew
Scott Einziger
Jennifer Euston
Joe Famaghetti, America's Lawyer
Berns family
Lisa Feuer
Dan Forman
Mark Friedman
Liane Fuji
Darren Gange
Mike Gange
Mark Garten
Jennifer Gates
Cody & Cassidy Gifford
Kathleen Grillo
Chauncé Hayden
Tom Helberg
Hellfire Club
Susan Hughes
IBM OS/2 Team

Lance Ito
Mel Karmazin
Daniel Kaye
Sandi Kirkman
Bill Knaub, Jr.
Jim Lackner, Jr.
Robert Lackner
Brian Laiacona
Ruth Lee
Spike Lee
Lori Leven
Kim Lewis
Keith Lodzinski
Lulac
Maurice "Chip" Maloney
Josh Mann
Nancy Margolis
Matthew Martin
Lee Masters
Matt Mayer
Joseph Montebello
Lady in the Moon
Suzanne Noli
James Nugent
O. J. Mask
Governor George Pataki
Mechel Pavlishin
Sandra Pedraza
Nancy Peske
Pink Pussy Cat Boutique
Pope John Paul III
Pope of Pot
Kevin Powell
Alan Prachar
Robin Radzinski
Jody Revenson
Burt Reynolds
Al Rosenberg
Jessica Rubin
Brian Sacks
Frank Scalia
Steve and Linda Schwab
Jillian Schwartz
Fran Shea
Wayne Siegel
Yakov Smirnoff
Dee Snider
Senator Arlen Specter
Josh Sussman
Debbie Tay
Tempest
Scott Terranella
The Trader
Keith Trimble
Donald Trump
Richard Virgilio
Ed Voskinarian
Glenn Waldman
Danny Watt
Christine Weathersbee
Dr. Lew Weinstein
Aaron Wertheim
Jerry White
Governor Christine Whitman
Linde Williston

PHOTOGRAPH AND ILLUSTRATION CREDITS

Drew Friedman: illustrations on pages 2, 22, 23, 42, 50, 51, 77, 102, 136, 240, 243, 311-314, 316 (with K. Bidus, © 1994, originally appeared in *The New Yorker*)

Paul Aresu: pages 8, 16, 18, 19, 20, 21, 24, 26, 27,, 29, 32, 33, 34, 35, 36, 37, 38, 41, 44, 45, 59,63, 64(upper) 69,71,73,75,79,81,83,89,, 99, 100, 101, 107 (left and right), 119 (all), 128, 129, 133, 135 (bottom right), 152 (center), 154, 156, 157, 231, 258

Paul Aresu with art direction by Jack Heller and Ralph Cirella: pages 55, 142, 164, 166, 178, 179, 181 (right), 187, 190, 193 (right), 194, 198 (lower), 207 (upper), 219 (lower), 220 (all), 221 (right) 222, 223 (all), 324, 374, 409, 444

Vivid Video: pages 10, from *Extreme Sex*; 153 (lower)

AP/Wide World Photos: pages 12, 30 (lower), 48 (left), 56 (left), 57 (all), 97, 144 (lower), 151 (upper), 232, 233, 234, 236, 245, 246 (left), 378, 381, 383, 387, 405, 418 (top), 422 (lower), 424 (top), 442 (right), 447, 462

Judith Regan Collection: page 14

Neal Peters Collection: pages 30 (upper); 430, © Hanna-Barbera

SYGMA: pages 52, © Sam Emerson; 145 (upper), © Ted Soqui; 145 (lower), © Eric Robert; 146 (upper), © Rick Maiman; 148, © John Van Hasselt; 150 (lower), © Ted Soqui; 151 (lower), © Frank Trapper; 246 (right), © Eddie Adams

UPI/Bettmann: pages 56 (right), 423 (lower), 437, 440, 442 (left, center), 456, 465 (top)

Fort Worth Star-Telegram: page 117, Etta Hulme

Camera 5: pages 121, Ken Regan; 424 (center right), Ken Regan

Barry Morgenstein: pages 127, 149, 150 (center), 198 (upper), 206, 215, 221 (left), 226, 227, 228, 358

Gary Dell'Abate: pages 134 (bottom right), 183, 418 (center)

Victor Greene Studio N.Y.C.: page 135 (top center), Kerry Rae

Globe Photos: page 144 (upper)

Charles William Bush: page 146 (lower)

Ron Moss: page 150 (upper)

Hustler magazine: pages 158; 275B (bottom), Dan Collins;

Jeff Darcy: page 163

Triton magazine: page 210

Michael St. Sauveur: page 214 (upper)

Jens Johnson: page 219 (upper)

USA Today: illustration on page 248, Mike Smith; 424 (center left)

Middlesex News, Massachusetts: page 275B (bottom), Dave Granlund

Gustave Doré: illustrations from Dante's *Inferno* on pages 250, 273, 309, 315

Bruce Bennett Studios: page 266 (lower), Warren S. Fishman

Orion Pictures Corporation: artwork on pages 269, 270

Susan Berkley: page 277

Larry French: page 293

Trenton Times: pages 297, Frank Jacobs III; 459, editorial cartoon by Ralph Schlegel

Big Shout magazine, Wilmington, Delaware: illustration on page 300, Steven R. Cobb

San Francisco Chronicle: page 301 (top), © Tom Meyer

Mainline Times: page 305

New York Post: page 318, Sean Delonas; 320, Sean Delonas; 352; 428; 457

Steve Kelley: page 321

Milwaukee Journal: page 323, © Gary Markstein

Doug Marlette: illustrations on pages 327 (upper), 328, 448

Jason Epstein: illustration on page 329

Gamma Liaison Network: page 332 (upper), © Michael Hirsch; 426, Jacques Chenet; 464, Dirck Halstead

John Driscoll: pages 332 (lower), 344, 346

Keith Thomson: illustration on page 333

Albany (N.Y.) *Times Union*: illustrations on pages 334, Rex Babin; 355 (upper), Rex Babin; 469, Rex Babin

Gannett Suburban Newspapers: pages 339 (lower), 353

Peter Bennett: page 345

Ralph Cirella: pages 347, 348

Tribune Media Services, Inc.: pages 350 (lower), mixed media; 396, © Dave Miller

Bettmann: pages 363, 384, 419 (lower), 466

Jack Heller: graphic design on pages 372, 373

Chris Stanley: page 376

Lester Glassner Collection: page 421

Reuters/Bettmann: pages 424 (lower), 450, 465 (bottom)

The Record: page 445 (top), © Jimmy Marguilies

The Trentonian: page 460

Garden Statements Cartoons: pages 461, Al Kratzer; 463, Al Kratzer

COLOR INSERT:

PHOTOGRAPHS BY PAUL ARESU
ART DIRECTION BY JACK HELLER AND RALPH CIRELLA